Fairness, Globalization,
and
Public Institutions

Fairness, Globalization, and Public Institutions

East Asia and Beyond

Jim Dator, Dick Pratt, and Yongseok Seo

University of Hawai'i Press
HONOLULU

Library of Congress Cataloging-in-Publication Data
Fairness, globalization, and public institutions : East Asia and beyond /
Jim Dator, Dick Pratt, and Yongseok Seo.
p.   cm.
Includes bibliographical references and index.
ISBN-13: 978-0-8248-2950-6 (hardcover : alk. paper)
ISBN-10: 0-8248-2950-6 (hardcover : alk. paper)
ISBN-13: 978-0-8248-3055-7 (pbk. : alk. paper)
ISBN-10: 0-8248-3055-5 (pbk. : alk. paper)
1. Globalization.   2. Public institutions.   3. Fairness.
4. Public institutions—East Asia.   5. East Asia—Politics and government.
6. East Asia—Foreign relations.   I. Dator, James Allen.
II. Pratt, Richard, 1941–
III. Seo, Yongseok, 1969–
JZ1318.F35 2006
337—dc22
2005027402

University of Hawai'i Press books are printed on acid-free
paper and meet the guidelines for permanence and durability
of the Council on Library Resources.

Designed by University of Hawai'i Press production staff

Printed by The Maple-Vail Book Manufacturing Group

Contents

Part 3. Responding to Globalization:
Public Institutions Present and Future

Part 4. Responding to Globalization in East Asia

Part 5. Conclusions

Acknowledgments

The conference upon which this book is based was funded by the Globalization Research Center, a consortium for research on globalization associated with the University of Hawai'i. Additional funding came from the State of Hawai'i Department of Business Economic Development and Tourism, whose mission includes the development of education and training. The conference was cosponsored by the World Academy of Art and Science, the Public Administration Program of the University of Hawai'i, and the Hawai'i Research Center for Futures Studies of the University of Hawai'i. The Center for Korean Studies of the University of Hawai'i generously made their facilities available for the conference. Professors Christopher Grandy of the Public Administration Program and Carolyn Stephenson of the Department of Political Science of the University of Hawai'i took careful notes during the sessions that greatly aided in capturing the basic themes discussed.

We offer very special thanks to James Rae, who helped greatly in shaping the volume into its present form, and to Brandon Palmer for his proofreading services. The authors also thank Sharon Togashi for extraordinary assistance during the final editing process.

PART 1
Introduction

CHAPTER 1

Introduction

JIM DATOR, DICK PRATT, AND YONGSEOK SEO

This book focuses on linkages among fairness, globalization, and public institutions that were discussed during and after an intensive, three-day international "dialogic" conference held in Honolulu, Hawai'i, in 2002. However, it is not a record of papers presented at the conference, since no papers were presented at all. Nor is it organized according to the format of the conference, since it is not possible to capture the essence of the highly interactive process in chronological form. This book is, however, fully informed and guided by the discussion of the three days of the conference and of a great many days of research, writing, and group discussion thereafter. Hence the "dialogue" continued long after the conference was over and the visitors had gone home. Indeed, we hope this volume will continue and expand the discussion worldwide, and we invite comments sent to the Web site of the conference.[1]

The book is divided into five sections that reflect the main ideas about the processes and effects of fairness in respect to globalization, responses to globalization, and what next to research and teach about fairness, globalization, and public institutions in East Asia and elsewhere. We purposely invited to the conference scholars and practitioners with differing experiences and viewpoints in order to exemplify varying notions about fairness and globalization itself and the wide range of available responses to its potentially beneficial as well as harmful impacts. We supplement many chapters with "Further Thoughts" written by conference participants in order to elaborate on significant points raised in the chapter or to gain an alternative perspective to a controversial subject.

Thus part 1 is an introductory consideration of each of the three major themes of the book, answering the question "What is fairness, globalization, and public institutions?" The three chapters explain and link the concepts and build a foundation upon which to explain how public institutions can and should promote fairness in an era of globalization. Jim Dator's first chapter reviews various philosophical and ethical ideas about the concept of fairness, especially raising

3

the new concern of responding fairly to future as well as to current generations. Further Thoughts by Sohail Inayatullah and Edgar Porter give substance to the adage "Think Globally, Act Locally," or question the universality of the idea of "fairness," suggesting it might be a Western cultural concept, while "harmony" might make more sense in the East Asian context. Dator's next brief chapter, "What Is Globalization?" presents historical as well as current examples that remind us that what we now call "globalization" is in fact not new, but merely a contemporary manifestation of an age-old process. Finally, Dick Pratt concludes the introductory part of the book by examining the concept of "public institutions" (stressing that the term implies more than formal governmental structures and actors alone) while discussing the role public institutions can, and should, play in the global context.

Part 2 offers theoretical, critical, and personal perspectives on competing notions of fairness and globalization in order to situate the debate in the contemporary environment. Christopher Grandy defends economic growth and trade by highlighting the benefits of globalization. James Rosenau follows with an innovative plan to achieve fairness in a world that is simultaneously fragmenting and integrating. Next, Ivana Milojevic challenges conventional views of fairness and globalization by employing a range of critical lenses, from feminist to environmentalist to social constructivist. Finally, Sohail Inayatullah's warm personal reflection on the experience of citizenship and globalization in his own life provides a human dimension to the more esoteric aspects of the debates.

Part 3 presents a rich variety of contemporary responses to globalization and discusses many innovative opportunities available to address the challenges of the future. Dick Pratt critiques the "New Public Management" (NPM) that swept governments worldwide during the 1990s and early years of the twenty-first century. However, Jim Dator once again reminds us, in the following chapter, that NPM is simply the latest in a long line of worldwide fads of governance and administration and speculates on what is coming next. Doug Allen's chapter is a poignant personal tale of the travails of a Canadian public servant who has labored on behalf of fairness for many years in various parts of the world. Ron Brown then shows how globalization is impacting national as well as international law and is tending toward a kind of global common law. Martin Khor considers fairness and globalization within an environmental context by focusing on the necessity of global governance for sustainable development. Fred Riggs, a longtime world expert in comparative public administration and practice, offers his thoughts about the futures of bureaucracy, democracy, and representation, while Jim Dator concludes part 3 with a long review of proposals for governance reform.

Part 4 provides brief case studies of various attempts of public institutions in East and Southeast Asia to respond fairly to globalization. Yongseok Seo and

Shunichi Takekawa first show that "responding to globalization" can be considered a leitmotif throughout the entire history of the region, and not something novel. Jingping Ding, Yong-duck Jung, Ryo Oshiba, Chanto Sisowath, and Le Van Anh (all participants at the Honolulu dialogic conference) discuss the contemporary situation in China, South Korea, Japan, Cambodia, and Vietnam, respectively. The way each approaches and displays the subject matter in their country is as illustrative of the challenge as is the material they specifically present in their individual chapters. Yongseok Seo and Sohail Inayatullah close part 4 by focusing on generational differences regarding culture and "Asian values" in East Asia.

Part 5 states our conclusions. Since a major purpose of the conference was to come up with education, training, and research projects dealing with fairness, globalization, and public institutions in East Asia, Chris Grandy and Dick Pratt provide a chapter that draws together the wide range of issues discussed and develops pedagogical and research projects that should become the next steps in our project. This is followed by a chapter that draws more general conclusions.

Conference That Inspired the Book

Our interest in the issues that link globalization, public institutions, and fairness first found expression in a "dialogic" conference held in January 2002 at the Center for Korean Studies at the University of Hawaiʻi.[2] (See Walt Anderson's Further Thoughts, "The Need for Global Dialogue," on page 11, for an expanded discussion.) The goal of the conference was to have a conversation among knowledgeable individuals that took place within three broad parameters. First, we felt that many of the concerns about globalization were directly related to notions about fairness. Second, we were certain that, in one way or another, public institutions (including governments, nongovernmental organizations [NGOs], and other organizations that emerge from civil society) will be significant in dealing with, or ignoring, fairness in relation to globalization. And third, we felt it would be valuable at this point in the evolution of globalization to address these links in relation to Asia, especially East Asia.

We agreed that a small group composed of both scholars and practitioners was needed to undertake this conversation. We also believed that while most participants should come from East Asia, other perspectives ought to be represented. While we looked for diversity in backgrounds, the ability to work in spoken English was a common requirement. In the end, we were pleased to have representatives from the People's Republic of China, the United States, South Korea, Cambodia, Japan, and Laos. Participants' backgrounds included employees of NGOs (such as the Asia Development Bank), two American academics, a Canadian practitioner, and a futurist from Yugoslavia living in Australia.

We did not want these carefully selected individuals to come and tell us, in a series of presentations, what they already knew. The objective instead was to have a multifaceted and intimate dialogue that explored complex issues, and thereby to have understandings emerge from interacting across the represented cultures and professional perspectives. To accomplish that, we set up a three-and-a-half-day "dialogic" process that seemed risky but turned out to work well. First we asked each participant to come with an example from his/her personal experience of something connecting the three conference themes of fairness, globalization, and public institutions. Second, we asked participants to write down their initial thoughts to the following twelve questions, around which twelve one-and-a-half-hour sessions were organized.

1. What kinds of societal, environmental, and intergenerational challenges to public institutions do you believe can be attributed to globalization?
2. How do you see public institutions presently responding to these challenges? That is, what are the specific practices that are wholly or in part responses to challenges presented by globalization?
3. How do you think globalization may be changing our ideas of what public institutions are?
4. How is globalization changing what is meant by fairness in society, or for future generations, or in relation to the environment?
5. What goals and specific practices should public institutions, as we understand them, adopt in your society in the immediate future to respond to globalization fairly, in relation to society, future generations, or the environment?
6. What obstacles do public institutions currently encounter that prevent them for doing what you believe is desirable?
7. What obstacles are public institutions likely to encounter in the future (more than five years) that may prevent them from doing what is desirable?
8. What are the existing developments and forces that, if encouraged or supported, can help to facilitate the desired responses of public institutions? Similarly, what new forces or factors need to be encouraged or supported in order to facilitate the desired responses of public institutions?
9. What educational, training, and research activities should be undertaken in order to overcome the obstacles, nourish the opportunities, and invent new processes that address fairness in relation to the societal, environmental, and intergenerational issues raised by globalization?
10. To what extent is this range of education, training, and research activities being done, or not done, in, or for, your society?
11. What are the educational, training, and research needs likely to be in the future (more than five years) that are different than today?

12. When the current or anticipated educational, training, and research activities are not being addressed, who should undertake these activities? Are those who should undertake this likely to be different in the future?

We asked each participant to initiate one of the twelve sessions by sharing his/her thoughts and then facilitate a discussion. The organizers talked to each of the facilitators in advance to be clear on the facilitation norms we wished to use and were available to provide assistance as needed (which was very little). Third, at the end of each session we asked a participant and/or an observer to sum up and interpret what he/she had just heard. Composed of faculty and graduate students from different programs and departments at the University of Hawai'i, Mānoa, the observers listened to the conversation. Some became commentators, and others are contributors to this volume. Finally, at the end of the last session, participants and observers were asked for final thoughts, and as the organizers we offered our own.

The results of this process were very positive. The conversations were intense, so much so that we all were exhausted by the end of the third day. Participation across the cultures, professions, ages, and genders was quite even and very open. Most felt fully involved, even though differences in English ability sometimes worked against this. The questions, which intentionally built on one another, created a logic, or at least continuity, in the conversation. Time restrictions on presentations reinforced the willingness to listen and engage one another. Substantively, what came out of the conference was rich. Shared concerns about the implications of globalization were evident, but also apparent were differences about what globalization means for the futures of these societies and their relationships with each other.

Even though questions about balancing the interests of future generations with those of present generations were asked of the delegates, most of the participants did not raise the issue during the discussion or subsequently. Those few who did, such as Sohail Inayatullah, have long been participants in the future generation debate sponsored by the Kyoto group (discussed later in the book).

One clear example of why the needs of future generations need to be fully addressed occurred during a spirited discussion of fairness and economic growth. Some people said that if China were to develop by the same processes and achieve the same standard of living as the West, then the impact on the environment would be catastrophic. "China cannot be allowed to 'develop' at the cost of global survivability," they said. "No, that is not fair," said others in response. "It is not fair to deny the Chinese (or anyone else) the right to achieve the same standard of living people in the West have. Chinese have every right to catch up with (and surpass) the West economically as soon as possible."

Although the impact on the environment was mentioned, no one took the opportunity to bring up the question of what is fair for future generations. Even though present generations in China might want to develop as soon as possible, what about future generations in China, never mind elsewhere? Are they likely to be happy with the current Chinese policy if that means (because of the severe toll on the environment) that they actually will live in even greater misery and poverty than present generations do now, which of course they may or may not?

The point is that the issue of fairness to future generations was not even brought up during the discussion or spontaneously anywhere else during the three days, showing, we believe, how utterly absent this ethical obligation (and structural requirement) is among even ethically oriented people concerned about globalization and fairness today. Some might be concerned about the environment, but few think to care about future generations.

As we will argue more fully later, we believe it is absolutely essential that all polities, especially those that are willing to experiment with notions of fairness in relation to globalization, should include discussions of how to be fair to future generations. The absence of this discourse and of looking for structures and processes of governance that enable present generations to fulfill the obligation is a huge and terrifying failure of all governance specialists and practitioners today.

Recently, we discussed this issue with some students. There were several that were very active in efforts to restore sovereignty, stolen by the United States in 1898, to the Hawaiian people. One activist noted that many young Hawaiians are busy tracing their genealogy back to see where their ancestors stood and what they did during the overthrow of the Hawaiian monarchy. Since they are now so opposed to the overthrow and so desirous of restoring Hawaiian sovereignty (perhaps even the monarchy), they expected to find that their ancestors bravely fought against the overthrow.

Sometimes they do find that. But sometimes they find that their ancestors were either silently, or actively, complicit in the overthrow. And they are ashamed of their ancestors and of themselves. So, the students suggested, why don't we develop and formalize an ethic that says that we should live now so that when future generations trace their genealogies back to us, they will be proud of us, pleased that at least we did our best, that we cared enough to try to live with the needs of future generations effectively in mind, even if we did do things that future generations in fact don't like?

Once upon a time, we all tried to live so that our dead ancestors would be proud of us. That is still good and noble. But now we also need to live so that our descendants, not yet born, and all future generations will cherish our memories and not curse us for the misery we have unnecessarily and selfishly visited upon them.

Defining the East Asian Region

A survey of how East Asian public institutions respond to the pressures of globalization with fairness might begin with recognition of the region's characteristics. In defining the East Asian region, as with any region, various characteristics might be considered, particularly traditional geographical classifications and degrees of "interdependence" and "integration" in the region. In general, East Asia could include the five countries of northeast Asia (China, Japan, Korea, Mongolia, Taiwan) and eleven Southeast Asian nations (ASEAN 11). However, we will focus only on the Confucian-led societies of East Asia, namely China, Korea, Japan, Vietnam, and Singapore. These conceptions of region still remain ambiguous and competing and are subject to change. East Asia is indeed a region of diversity; the countries in the region are all quite distinct politically, economically, linguistically, religiously, and ethnically from each other.

Along with these differences, the countries of East Asia also share characteristics such as common histories, cultural values, writing systems, and political attitudes with others throughout the region. Among other things, one of the most common conceptualizations of East Asia is probably Confucianism, which has spread and permeated all of East Asia throughout many centuries. Confucian values were greatly important as principles of social value, which are still deeply embedded in the societies of East Asia. Confucianism in particular has had a profound influence on political and administrative concepts of East Asia that have provided the necessary cosmological framework for the politics and institutions of this region. More significantly, "Confucian concepts have been reinterpreted and adapted when East Asian countries have faced pressures for renovation in development."[3]

The East Asian countries in our book are known as "Confucian countries" or "Confucian-based societies" where Confucian values such as faithfulness to authority, social harmony, conformity, sincerity, and dedication to collectivity are still considered important. As Dao Minh Chau states, "[M]ost institutions of the modern governments in Confucian countries have been borrowed from the West, but they do not work in the same way as those in their countries of origin. Rather, they have been modified according to the spirit of Confucianism."[4] In brief, the preexisting Confucian traits in administrative concepts are still embedded in East Asian public institutions, and they have enabled East Asia to be unique and stand out from other regions, particularly in relation to the West.

An additional reason we focus on East Asia is that we still remain confident that the region will be especially important over the twenty-first century. Scholars often say that East Asia is a region of dynamism, as East Asia has been playing a major role as an "engine of growth" for the world economy. In fact, no one has questioned the unprecedented economic development of the region since the end of World War II. This development started in Japan and was followed by the so-called Newly Industrializing Economies: Hong Kong, Singapore, South Korea, Taiwan, and most recently the People's Republic of China. In particular, many argue that the rise of China as an economic power will likely become a new engine of growth for the world economy as well as for the region.[5]

However, our reasons for focusing on East Asia are not due solely to the region's economic dynamism. The primary reason for our focus on East Asia lies in the region's tremendous human and intellectual resources. We believe that the manner in which the region "responds in fairness to globalization" will be important not only within the region, but also for all humanity. Indeed, East Asia has been a very dynamic region and has a long tradition that has provided abundant "human and intellectual resources" for world development in many respects, namely philosophies, writing systems, political thoughts and institutions, and scientific devices. As Gilbert Rozman has put it,

> East Asia is a great region of the past, having been in the forefront of world development for at least two thousand years, until the sixteenth, seventeenth, or even the eighteenth century, after which it suffered a relatively brief but deeply felt eclipse. Projecting recent patterns of achievement by countries in the region and by transplanted persons whose families have moved abroad, most observers now agree that East Asia promises to be a great region of the future.[6]

The East Asian intellectual resources that contributed to world development have been conspicuous "in the areas of humanities and social and political thoughts."[7] As Su-Hoon Lee observed, the inherent profusion of scholarly learning and Confucian traditions such as commitment to education and reverence for scholarship has enabled East Asian societies to develop their own solid intellectual tradition in social knowledge.[8]

As a resurgence of East Asian dynamism continues, we believe that the way this region "responds in fairness to globalization" will continue to be important for all of humanity. Although socialist systems have failed in practice, capitalist systems are still an incomplete and insufficient system for humanity since they lack fairness to future generations resulting from its destructiveness to the environment, its unequal distribution of wealth, and its rewarding of materialism at the expense of other values. We are also facing the problems of a modern society such as the debates over a lack of morality, the growth of greed and selfishness, and the termination of families and communities.[9] In this vein, we are confident that the resurgence of human and intellectual resources in East Asia (which once had a splendid tradition and made great contributions to humanity) will act as a new alternative to unrestricted global capitalism or provide a foundation in a post-globalization epoch by interacting with other great traditions in the world.

Finally, even though we focus on political institutions in East Asia, broadly defined, we also include discussions of the United States, Canada, and other parts of the world from time to time when their experiences seem especially relevant to our discussion.

FURTHER THOUGHTS

The Need for Global Dialogue

Walt Anderson

IF THERE IS to be a strong and lasting global civilization, it will come about not merely from wise leadership or high levels of public participation, but because many people have learned to practice the simple (yet somehow elusive) art of dialogue. Dialogue is not debate, negotiation, or decision making (all of which are necessary to politics and governance), but the deeper human interaction that precedes them and makes them possible, as people begin to understand the frames of reference of others and develop shared visions and common language. Dialogue is not just about policy, but also about morality, worldviews, and emotions.

The frames of reference that shape personal convictions about public issues are largely implicit, are rarely examined or deliberately revised, and play a large part in triggering emotional responses. In smaller and more homogenous societies, people's frames of reference may be quite similar and dialogue over differences relatively easy to achieve. This is certainly not the case in pluralistic, multicultural societies. Indeed, there are some indications that advanced industrial societies may be becoming less, rather than more, capable of serious, informed deliberation around major issues. Increasing mobility and access to communications make it easy for people to seek out and join subcultures of like-minded others rather than engage in dialogue with those who think differently. This makes it easy to demonize those who are on the other side of issues concerning such matters as globalization, free trade, environmental protection, and the ethics of biotechnology. We may be getting better at generating controversy and confrontation than at encouraging civil conversation aimed at achieving understanding and consensus.

James Rosenau has argued eloquently in various writings that more and more people all over the world are taking part in a "skill revolution" as they learn how to mobilize, form coalitions, use information/communications technologies, and influence public opinion. There is much evidence to support this, and it is one of the most hopeful developments of our time. But it is urgently necessary that the skill of engaging in dialogue across cultural, political, and worldview boundaries be a part of this revolution.

Notes

1. www.fairglobe.hawaii.edu.

2. The conference was originally scheduled for the week of September 20, 2001, but was postponed because of the September 11 attacks.

3. Dao Minh Chau, "Administrative Concepts in Confucianism and Their Influence on Development in Confucian Countries," *Asian Journal of Public Administration* 18.1 (June 1996): 46.

4. Ibid., 58.

5. The rise of China as an economic and political power has been paid much attention lately. The debate has centered on whether a rising China would be a threat or an opportunity both for the region and for the world. In any case, this controversial debate is proving that China is rapidly emerging as a world power and is obtaining its past reputation as the central country in the region.

6. Gilbert Rozman, ed., *The East Asian Region: Confucian Heritage and Its Modern Adaptation* (Princeton, N.J.: Princeton University Press, 1991), 6.

7. Su-Hoon Lee, "The Rise of East Asia and East Asian Social Science's Quest for Self-Identity," *Journal of World-Systems Research* 6.3 (Fall/Winter 2000): 768–783.

8. Ibid.

9. See Wei-ming Tu, ed., *Confucian Traditions in East Asian Modernity: Moral Education and Economic Culture in Japan and the Four Mini-Dragons* (Boston, Mass.: Harvard University Press, 1996).

CHAPTER 2

What Is Globalization?

Jim Dator

"Globalization" and its twin sister "anti-globalization" rank high among the favorite and most contested concepts of the moment. The words appear with many different meanings and in many different contexts in newspapers, magazines, television commentary, and political-economic discourse everywhere. "Globalization" is itself globalized.

For us here, globalization means not only the worldwide capitalist system called "neoliberalism," but also the full range of forces and factors that are sweeping across the globe totally unhindered, or barely hindered, by the boundaries and policies of the nation-state. Thus factors in globalization include jet planes, supertankers, and container ships; migratory labor; electronic and genetic communication technologies; anthropogenic global climate change; air, water, and ground pollution; new and revived diseases; religions; criminal and terrorist activities and their countervailing state-terrorist, police, and paramilitary forces; mass media; popular culture; and sports. Globalization also includes the spread of certain ideas, values, and practices, such as "democracy" and "human rights," and "best practices" in all of the factors listed above. All of these are also forces of globalization that challenge conventional theories and methods of governance, driving some people to ecstasy and others to despair about the future.

Globalization is not new. It is as old as humanity, indeed, older. Joseph Nye says,

> The oldest form of globalization is environmental: climate change has affected the ebb and flow of human populations for millions of years. Migration is a long-standing global phenomenon. The human species began to leave its place of origins, Africa, about 1.25 million years ago and reached the Americas sometime between 30,000 and 13,000 years ago. One of the most important [forms] of globalization is biological. The first smallpox epidemic is recorded in Egypt in 1350 B.C. It

13

reached China in 49 A.D., Europe after 700, the Americas in 1520, and
Australia in 1789. The plague or Black Death originated in Asia, but
spread [and] killed a quarter to a third of the population of Europe
between 1346 and 1352. When Europeans journeyed to the New World
in the fifteenth and sixteenth centuries they carried pathogens that destroyed up to 95 percent of the indigenous population.[1]

Historically, the speed and extent of globalization has increased with each change
in modes of transportation and of communication. The initial spread of humans
across the globe, whether "out of Africa" alone or by the coming together of independently evolved human communities, was no faster than a human could
walk or a raft could drift. Then, from the domestication/invention and diffusion
of the horse (and other beasts of burden) and the wheel, to oceangoing canoes, to
sailing ships, to steamships, to railroads and automobiles, to propeller and then
jet airplanes, the speed and ease of transportation has increased, and so the limitations of distance imposed by earlier technologies have decreased.

Similarly, the inventions of speech, writing, the printing press, the telegraph,
the telephone, radio, motion pictures, television, satellites, computer networks,
cell phones, and the World Wide Web each also increased the speed and scope of
global communication, minimizing limitations of the earlier technologies and
creating new social possibilities and problems.

But the fundamental processes underlying each of these technologies were
not new. With each new level of technology, it may have seemed new to those
experiencing it because of the transforming qualities of each change in mode
of transportation and communication. So many of the current concerns about
"globalization" are in fact very old when looked at historically, even though the
people actually experiencing them now (not having been around five hundred
or five thousand years ago) cannot be blamed for their feelings of fear or of ex-
hilaration. Please see Walt Anderson's Further Thoughts, "From the Local to the
Global," on page 17.

Later in this book we will look specifically at the way ideas of governance
spread globally before and during the modern age in order to remind ourselves
that the neoliberal ideas and policies in back of the New Public Management, for
example, are simply the most recent of a long line of globalized governance "best
practices" that might well be in the process of being superceded by new ideas
about the domestic "security state" and the New American Empire spawned by
fears of global terrorism.

Until September 11, 2001, and America's response after March 19, 2003,[2] it
was possible to imagine that there was something new about recent aspects of
globalization associated primarily with the collapse of communism as a serious alternative to global capitalism. For a short period of time, it appeared that

humanity had arrived at the "End of History"[3] where there was only one global economic ideology supported by one set of global political superpowers, facilitated by oligopolistically controlled global media all singing versions of the same global economic song.

The singing continues, but the song is now quite different from what it was only a few years earlier. Now, the United States seems bent on imposing its version of globalization on everyone whether they like it or not, while at the same time resisting many forms of globalization it once embraced, arguing that they thwart its narrowly defined national interests. In contrast, parts of Europe and Asia still hold high the flag of a more temperate form of economic globalization that the United States seems to reject.

This comment reminds us again that globalization is much, much more than a set of economic factors alone (more than the global flow of capital and goods) and more even than the transborder flow of labor, though that latter aspect of globalization is generally underappreciated. Globalization is also the flow of genes (of genetic information), the flow of popular culture and of new ideas, and the flow of environmental problems including diseases.

There is very little that is not touched by and part of the globalization process, including most of the anti-globalization forces who could not organize nearly as effectively against globalization were it not for all of the globalizing technologies and ideologies they use to fight it. This is the ultimate paradox: anti-globalization is a major part of globalization. "Terrorism" and state terrorism in response have made this even clearer.

Attitudes toward globalization thus are highly fickle. They are strongly influenced by current events. The year I was being recruited to join the University of Hawai'i (1968) was the first year that the number of people arriving by airplane was greater than the number arriving by ship. Everyone in Hawai'i then was accustomed to organizing their lives around boat days, when the great steamships arrived with new people and new goods and new information about the outside world. Our only direct and immediate contact then came via very expensive and cumbersome telephone connections and telegraph. Radio and TV were all local. Routine direct-satellite broadcast of live TV came a few years after I arrived. Then came direct-dial long-distance telephone. And then the fax.

I was the first civilian on the islands to use what came to be known as "e-mail" in the late 1970s. I had the good fortune to be invited to participate in an experiment conducted by Murray Turoff of the New Jersey Institute of Technology called EIES (Electronic Information Exchange System). Using a Texas Instruments workstation connected with an acoustic coupler as a phone modem to a computer in New Jersey and a printer (there was no electronic memory whatsoever) to "echo" the comments, I was able to participate in synchronous or asynchronous typed discussions with scholars spread across the globe.

As a consequence, I knew about developments well in advance of most of my colleagues in Hawai'i whose main source of information was printed material flown—and often floated—in well after the events. I thus participated in most aspects of the emergence of what is now the World Wide Web and learned very early on what a powerful, globalizing tool it could be. Without it, it would have been almost impossible for me to be as globally involved as I am while also living in Hawai'i, one of the most geographically remote spots on Earth.

Another important, but frequently overlooked, technology that facilitated my globalization was the credit card, which not only allowed me to spend money I did not have, and never would, but eventually to do so almost everywhere in the world.

I was not isolated at all. I was increasingly globalized and globally connected. My friends and neighbors were not simply those people physically around me, but increasingly spread all over the world. During the 1980s and 1990s, I became the secretary general and then the president of the World Futures Studies Federation. For two decades, because of advances in information and transportation technologies, I spent much more of my time, physically and emotionally, outside of Hawai'i and the rest of the United States than I spent in them.

So I now by no means feel myself to be primarily an American. I am an American by citizenship and by fundamental culture and language, to be sure. But I have spent far too much of my time deeply engaged in the lives of non-Americans to feel exclusive loyalty to any one country. I have, for better or worse, become profoundly globalized over my lifetime.

In the late 1980s and early 1990s, globalization was viewed as inevitable and highly desirable by many leaders in Asia. It was mainly a question of how soon it might come and how they might be among the first to take advantage of it. There were critics of course, but they were a distinct minority. Almost everyone was singing the neoliberal song with full voice and chorus. But then the Asian economic crisis occurred in 1997–1998, and there was a vast outpouring of criticisms of globalization throughout Asia. While, of course, many people continued to support globalization without restraint, many more began urging caution and reconsideration, suggesting that Asian communities might want to find a different, an "Asian," way.

The collapse of the fondest dreams of the so-called "dot-com" New Economy in 2000 led many more people (especially in North America) to reevaluate the desirability and inevitability (or at least the timing) of globalization. Shortly after assuming the presidency, George W. Bush began a series of actions that suggested his administration did not believe in "globalization" with quite the fervor one might expect of a Republican. He began by abrogating treaties, failing to sign international agreements, and enacting protectionist policies for domestic agricultural and industrial protection that seemed to fly in the face of the neoliberal version of globalization.

Then, with the events of September 11, 2001, the concerns of what was originally termed a "strange alliance" of a few labor unions, environmentalists, students, and America First! patriots in the United States (who first made major headlines at the anti-WTO [World Trade Organization] demonstrations in Seattle in 1997) suddenly lurched forward in the consciousness of most Americans. Foreigners of all stripes found it increasingly difficult to get into the United States even to attend scientific conferences. Foreigners were also imprisoned without arraignment or trial. American citizens were stripped of long-held fundamental rights. "Security" was said to take precedence over "trade," and intrusive inspections of imports began. French fries were renamed and Dom Perignon champagne poured down toilets.

Then, after a series of vain attempts to find and punish the apparent sponsors of 9/11, Osama bin Laden and Al-Qaida, the United States turned its vengeance on Iraq and, acting without significant global or even regional support, launched an unprovoked attack on a country that even the American president had to admit had nothing to do with the 9/11 events but would be punished anyway. So what is next? What events or trends might shape further views and actions for or against globalization by the time you read these words?

FURTHER THOUGHTS
From the Local to the Global
Walt Anderson

MANAGEMENT THEORISTS SAY that executives fall into one or another of three categories: some have an ability to survey the grand scheme of things. Others lack that kind of vision but are nevertheless proficient at understanding the nuts-and-bolts realities of how things work at the lowest levels of the organization. The best and most effective are those who have learned to "helicopter," integrating a vision of the big picture with practical application. Today it has become necessary (not only for executives, but also for ordinary people) to cultivate the third ability.

There was a time, not so long ago, when local knowledge and traditional skills (in such areas as agriculture, hunting, and crafts) were all that most people needed. The new discoveries of explorers, scientists, and inventors did little to alter the conditions or the tempo of everyday village, pastoral, or tribal life. That is no longer the case. Increasingly, all people everywhere are being drawn into an interconnected global civilization, impacted by technological changes and global forces (economic, political, cultural, biological) that can touch their lives in many ways: a farmer may find that global climate change requires him to change his practices. A woman in a tribal community may find that she has internationally recognized rights that give her the power to make decisions about her reproductive life.

People continue to be members of local communities, but they are also awakening (sometimes slowly, sometimes rapidly) to the reality of being members of larger systems and networks of many kinds and learning how important the things that happen in those larger systems may be to them. In this world of open systems, local knowledge is not enough, certainly not enough to recognize the full potentialities of human life, and sometimes not even enough for survival.

Notes

1. Robert O. Keohane and Joseph S. Nye, Jr., "Introduction," in *Governance in a Globalizing World*, ed. Joseph S. Nye and John D. Donahue (Washington, DC: Brookings Institution Press, 2000), 3.

2. On this date, the United States launched a "preemptive" war against Iraq.

3. Francis Fukuyama, *The End of History and the Last Man* (New York: Free Press, 1992).

CHAPTER 3
What Is Fairness?

JIM DATOR

"That's not fair!" We often hear young children say that to each other when they play. What do they mean? What is fairness or unfairness? Where do their notions of fairness come from? Is fairness universal, or entirely culture dependent? "Zurui na!" young Japanese children say. But are they objecting to the same kind of behavior an American child might object to when she calls her playmates "unfair"? And now, research on capuchin monkeys suggests that a sense of fairness is biologically based and not solely learned.[1] But still, even if the sense of fairness is innate, are the rules the same everywhere?

Imagine two children, one piece of cake, and one cutting knife. How can the cake be cut fairly? One frequently given answer[2] is to have one child cut the cake and the other choose the first piece. The presumption is that the cutter will do everything in her power to see that each piece of cake is exactly the same size so that the chooser will not have a clear choice between a bigger piece (which she will certainly take) or a smaller piece (which she will certainly leave). That seems fair, doesn't it?

But can we be sure that this would be the correct answer in all cultures and situations? In some cultures, the chooser feels obliged to take the smaller piece, leaving the larger for the cutter. In this situation, the chooser might feel that the cutter was being unfair by providing him/her with clearly a smaller piece of cake to choose so that he/she could show proper respect, or humility, or gratitude to, or love for the cutter by leaving the larger piece for the cutter to enjoy. In related Further Thoughts, both Ed Porter ("Globalization and Fairness," page 33) and Sohail Inayatullah ("Culture and Fairness: The Idea of Civilization Fairness," page 31) raise questions about the universality of fairness as a positive value, much less as a value with similar meanings, across cultures.

A curriculum on "fairness" thought suitable for young American school-children defines fairness as "treating people honestly and justly, respecting the rules of society and the rights of others." Related words are "equality, golden rule, impartiality, objectivity, respect, code, and law." A list of "Practical Applications" included "playing fairly and following the rules at recess and in gym class." "Being tolerant of people of all ages, occupations, races, religions and those who have disabilities." "Being willing to do, in our family, what is best for everyone." "Treating others the way you want to be treated." "Mediating disputes in the classroom." "Showing students that being fair just doesn't always mean absolute equal treatment for all in every circumstance."[3]

Fredrick Bendz says that "[o]ur sense of fairness comes from our conscience, which in turn has to do with our ability to imagine the feelings and thoughts of others, . . . called empathy or compassion. . . . What is fairness then? We all have desires and we want people to treat us according to those desires. We also know that people around us have similar desires and want to be treated accordingly. Fairness is closely related to fair play so it seems logical to conclude that a fair system is a system where everybody is treated in a similar way and where they have the option to fulfill their desires in any way they wish."[4]

Though arguments about fairness go back to the earliest philosophers, a name frequently associated with current ideas of fairness is that of the philosopher John Rawls. Discussions of fairness underlay his famous book, *A Theory of Justice*.[5] Rawls says that a "well-ordered" political society is "a fair system of cooperation over time from one generation to the next, where those engaged in cooperation are viewed as free and equal citizens and normal cooperating members of society over a complete life."[6]

> Immediately the question arises as to how the fair terms of cooperation are specified. For example: Are they specified by an authority distinct from the person's cooperation, say, by God's law? Or are these terms recognized by everyone as fair by reference to a moral order of values, say, by rational intuition, or by reference to what some have viewed as "natural law"? Or are they settled by an agreement reached by free and equal citizens engaged in cooperation, and made in view of what they regard as their reciprocal advantage, or good? Justice as fairness adopts a form of the last answer: the fair terms of social cooperation are to be given by an agreement entered into by those engaged in it.[7]

How can this be done fairly? Even if everyone tries to eliminate all personal biases, they cannot. Thus Rawls says each person has to work behind a "veil of ignorance." "In the original position, the parties are not allowed to know the social positions or the particular comprehensive doctrines of the persons they represent. They also do not know the persons' race and ethnic group, sex, or various native endowments such as strength and intelligence, all within the normal range. We express these limits on information figuratively by saying the parties are behind a 'veil of ignorance.' "[8]

"Since the content of the agreement concerns the principles of justice for the basic structure, the agreement in the original position specifies the fair terms of social cooperation between citizens regarded as such persons. Hence the name: justice as fairness."[9] Thus a "well-ordered political system as a fair system of co-operation over time from one generation to the next" is designed on the basis of two rules.

1. Each person has the same indefeasible claim to a fully adequate scheme of equal basic liberties, which scheme is compatible with the same scheme of liberties for all.
2. Social and economic inequalities are to satisfy two conditions: first, they are to be attached to offices and positions open to all under conditions of fair equality of opportunity; second, they are to be to the greater benefit of the least-advantaged members of society.[10]

Steven Suranovic, an economist who focuses on fairness in international trade, says,

> Fairness is a normative principle. It is a principle used to suggest outcomes or actions that ought to, or should, occur. To be fair is good, to be unfair is bad. To be fair is right, to be unfair is wrong. To be fair is just, to be unfair is unjust. To be fair is ethical, to be unfair is unethical. Actions and outcomes ought to be fair, they ought to be just, and they ought to be ethical. Unfair actions and outcomes should be opposed, they should be avoided, and they should be reversed or eliminated.[11]

Since there is a considerable amount of circularity and apparent wordplay in this explanation, Suranovic then goes on to give seven different ways in which "outcomes or actions" are judged to be fair or unfair.

1. *Distributional Fairness.* "To many people, the unequal distribution of income, wealth, and economic well-being is unfair. . . . Consequently, policies seen as increasing the disparities . . . are often judged to be unfair policies, while policies that reduce these inequalities are seen as fair. In the debate over globalization, there is widespread concern that freer trade and the expansion of multinational firms throughout the world is making the rich richer and the poor poorer. Globalization opponents often contrast the abysmally low wages of workers in less developed countries, and abject

poverty, especially in Africa, with the high levels of compensation paid to CEOs and sports stars for their endorsements. . . . With respect to this concern, fairness in trade, or fair globalization would correspond to a narrowing of the income gaps between countries and between peoples."

2. *Nondiscrimination Fairness.* "To be fair, equals should be treated equally. To be fair, the actions of businesses or the policies of governments should be non-discriminatory among equals. Thus businesses should not refuse to serve customers because of their race, gender, or religion. Nor should they refuse to hire employees for these same reasons. To do so would be discriminatory, unfair, and in most countries, illegal. . . . Opponents of globalization who are concerned about labor standards in less developed countries have argued that workers should be treated equally across countries."

3. *Golden-Rule Fairness.* "The Golden-Rule is a behavioral rule-of-thumb that has guided moral behavior for several millennia. Simply stated, it says, 'Do unto others as you would have them do unto you.' Actions that violate the golden-rule are typically viewed as being unjust, immoral or even sinful. . . . The golden-rule implies a 'do no harm' moral imperative. . . . It is very common to describe cheating in a game as unfair behavior. Cheating means that that person violated the accepted 'rules' of the game. . . . When a country violates [a treaty or international agreement it has signed] it is common for other countries . . . to charge the former with unfair behavior since it is cheating on its agreement." Another example is "when businesses engage in predatory dumping."

4. *Positive Reciprocity.* "Positive reciprocity occurs when an action that has a positive effect upon someone else is reciprocated with an action that has approximately equal positive effect upon another. If the reaction is not approximately equal in positive value, or if even worse, the reaction has a negative effect upon the first person, then the reaction will likely be judged unfair. . . . Positive reciprocity fairness implies that workers be compensated with wages that are approximately equal in value to the effort they put forth. . . . CEOs may receive compensation in millions of dollars sometimes even when the company is losing money and laying-off workers. Many consider this unjust or unfair."

5. *Negative Reciprocity.* "Negative reciprocity occurs when an action that has a negative effect upon someone else is reciprocated with an action that has approximately equal negative effect upon another. . . . Punishments [should be] proportional in size to the seriousness of the crime. . . . Retaliatory tariffs must be set equal in value to the value of the foreign export subsidy" to which it is responding.

6. *Privacy Fairness.* This is "a neutral application of the golden-rule": the right to be left alone to do things that do not harm others. "Similar logic has

been used to support abortion laws or drug legalization. . . . Sovereignty means the 'right' of a nation to determine its own laws and policies, especially those that primarily affect its own domestic residents. . . . Critics of globalization have sometimes argued that the WTO acts in a way that reduces the sovereignty of individual actions. . . . Similarly, concerns about a loss of sovereignty have been raised by LDC countries with regard to labor and environmental standards."

7. *Maximum Benefit Fairness.* "The final type of fairness is the one that, arguably, does not really belong as a fairness category. Indeed, in economics there are considerable discussions about the trade-off between equity (i.e., equality or fairness) and efficiency (i.e., maximum productiveness). Nevertheless a desire to maximize profits or benefits or well-being is certainly applied as a normative principle. . . . In the debate over globalization, maximum benefit fairness tends to be applied more frequently by economists and others who generally support movements toward freer trade and more open global markets. The focus of most welfare analysis in economics is to identify policies that will maximize economic efficiency. In essence this means maximize the net benefits that will accrue to a nation."[12]

Fairness in Economic Theory and Practice

Neoliberal, free-market economics assumes that all persons are rational actors who try to maximize their own advantages in economic transactions. Thus fairness is not a matter of particular concern in these economic theories. If everyone looks out for his/her own interests, the result will be as fair as possible. For the state to intervene to enforce "fairness" will result in irrationalities, and probably ultimately greater unfairness.

I have suggested above the extent to which this is supposed to be a factual statement of economic behavior and not merely a theoretical construct unrelated to actual economic behavior that might be false. In some cultures (and certainly for some people) selfishness, or self-centered behavior, is rare and disapproved, while altruism or group-centered behavior is more common and socially approved.

Recently there has been some impressive cross-cultural research to support this view. Joseph Henrich, Robert Boyd, and Samuel Bowles state,

Recent investigations have uncovered large, consistent deviations from the predictions of the textbook representation of *Homo Economicus*. One problem appears to lie in economists' canonical assumption that individuals are entirely self-interested: in addition to their own material payoffs, many experimental subjects appear to care about fairness and reciprocity, are willing to change the distribution of material outcomes at personal cost, and reward those who act in a cooperative manner while punishing those who do not even when these actions are costly to the individual. These deviations from what we will term the canonical model have important consequences for a wide range of economic phenomena, including the optimal design of institutions and contracts, the allocation of property rights, the conditions for successful collective action, the analysis of incomplete contracts, and the persistence of noncompetitive wage premia.

We undertook a large cross-cultural study of behavior in ultimatum, public good, and dictator games. Twelve experienced field researchers, working in twelve countries on four continents, recruited subjects from sixteen small-scale societies exhibiting a wide variety of economic and cultural conditions. Our sample consists of three foraging societies, six who practice slash-and-burn horticulture, four nomadic herding groups and three sedentary, small-scale agriculturalists.

We can summarize our results as follows. First, the canonical model is not supported in any society studied. Second, there is considerably more behavioral variability across groups than had been found in previous cross-cultural research and the canonical model fails in a wider variety of ways than in previous experiments. Third, group-level differences in economic organization and the degree of market integration explain a substantial portion of the behavioral variation across societies: the higher the degree of market integration and the higher the payoffs to cooperation, the greater the level of cooperation in experimental games. Fourth, individual-level economic and demographic variables do not explain behavior either within or across groups. Fifth, behavior in the experiments is generally consistent with economic patterns of everyday life in these societies.[13]

In short, whatever formal economic theory might say to the contrary, most people, in many very different cultures, believe that fairness matters, and try to behave fairly in their day-to-day economic transactions. This suggests that formal economic policies should reflect and not ignore these widespread human preferences.

Recent research using functional magnetic resonance imaging (fMRI) to scan the brains of players engaged in an "ultimatum game" appears to have located what is happening electrochemically in the brain when people share, cheat, or feel they are being treated fairly or being cheated. The research field is sometimes called "neuroeconomics" or "behavioral economics." It is redefining the rational assumptions of game theory, which is often used to model economic decision making.[14] When people participate in fair deals their levels of oxytocin rise and their cortex activates so that they feel a "warm glow" that the fMRI shows comes from "being trusted" or "receiving reciprocation."[15]

Fairness to the Environment

Fairness as it relates to the environment also takes many forms. I will discuss three. First, at the very base is the position that all living things have rights, and therefore when humans kill or injure other life forms, ethical considerations and procedures should be brought to bear. At one end of the spectrum are those who say that humans should not willingly kill any life form (including insects, microbes, or even trees and plants). At the opposite end are those who argue that only humans have rights that need to be protected or considered, so that humans may utilize all "lower" forms of life for their own advantage and pleasure. In between are people who take a vegetarian position—for example, believing that while it is permissible for humans to kill, consume, and otherwise utilize vegetables, it is not permissible to kill, consume, or use animals. Others might say that it is acceptable for humans to kill and consume plants as well as animals and otherwise to use animal and vegetable products, but that the killing of life should be done humanely or according to certain cultural or legal protocols. There are various other distinctions made along this continuum of what is fair in interactions between humans and nonhumans.

A second element of fairness in relation to the environment raises the question of using up or polluting current resources for the benefit of present generations but to the detriment of future generations. A third element focuses on the fact that in the process of economic growth, it is usually poor and otherwise marginalized people who live in environments degraded by those processes while rich and powerful people (and countries) typically enjoy the advantages of economic growth but seldom suffer directly or immediately from the environmental consequences of growth.

Fairness toward Future Generations

Who are "future generations"? Why should public institutions become responsive to the needs of future generations so that they can and will govern in fairness to future, as well as present, generations? How can public institutions fulfill that obligation?

Who are "future generations"?

Many people, when they hear the term "future generations," think only of their own children and grandchildren, or at least of their own biological descendants. This is an accurate, but restricted, meaning of the term. Being mindful of and helping provide for the needs of one's own direct descendants would appear to be relatively easy, one might say almost natural and instinctive. Yet even this apparently spontaneous obligation seems to be beyond the abilities of many parents. It is well known that many parents physically and psychologically abuse their children, max out credit cards, take out one-hundred-year mortgages, and run up other debts and obligations that will burden children for many years.

It is even more difficult for most humans to care sufficiently for the unborn whom they will never see and never know and who are not their own descendants. And yet that is precisely what the term "future generations" may need to signify: not only one's own biological descendants, not only others' children whom we can come to see and know, but all humans whom we will never know but whose lives we impact significantly by the way we live our own lives. Future generations thus are all people we will impact but who can never thank us for caring for them or bring us to task for failing to do so.

Ethics and Reciprocity

As we have seen in our discussion of "fairness" above, all ethics is fundamentally based on reciprocity, and that is the nub of the problem. Versions of the Golden Rule are found in almost all societies: "Do unto others as you would have them do unto you" (or, negatively, "Do not do to others what you do not want done to yourself"). In the small clans, tribes, and villages that characterized human settlements for tens of thousands of years until only recently, the Golden Rule made perfect sense. You should not insult or hit others since they could hit and insult you in return. This still makes sense.

But as humans became more mobile and able to live in larger and larger settlements packed with people who did not know one another personally and could not "get back at" others if they were injured or insulted (or praised and strengthened) by them, the Golden Rule became less and less sufficient as a moral guide. Indeed, as people from once-separate cultures came into closer proximity, "doing unto others what you want done to yourself" often became a cause of conflict itself! What is a tribute in one society might well be an insult in another. In our modern, congested, multicultural world, a better, new Golden Rule might be, "Do unto others as they wish you to do unto them." In this sense, then, ethics becomes "situational" (something to be negotiated between strangers or newcomers) rather than something absolute and obvious for people who live together from birth to death. And yet in spite of this change in the human condition, many ethical codes and formal laws derived from them remain absolute and based on the old Golden Rule.

Ethics and "Others"

This reciprocal basis of ethics is a huge problem today. We live in a world where people in the industrialized countries can and do influence the lives of people in less industrial regions (usually without intending to, or even being aware that they are), while the people in these regions cannot effectively show "advanced" peoples how they feel about it. It is very difficult for most humans to assume responsibility for how their lives unintentionally impact "Others" around the globe whom they do not know and may never meet. This ethical challenge is at the basis of much of the debate about local responses to globalization: while people favoring globalization may profit from it, it is not possible for most of the people who feel negatively impacted by globalization to "get back" at those who benefited.

Nothing has made this fundamental asymmetry of relations between Americans and Others clearer than the September 11, 2001, events and American reactions to them. Before September 11, most Americans were ignorant of the fact that many people outside of the United States were furious and frustrated at them for real or imagined abuses and deprivations that they blamed on America's economic and military policies. And among the few Americans who did know about it, most did not care because there was nothing the Others could do about their anger.

And then, suddenly, a handful of the previously invisible Others did "get back" at Americans in a very big way. They gained the full attention of Americans because they were able to inflict a tremendous killing force and destruction on major American icons of capitalism and militarism.

But as US focus on terrorists, Iraq, Iran, and North Korea makes very clear, America appears to be mainly concerned about responding to those Others who can "get back" at them. Americans still do not seem to feel a general ethical obligation toward those whose lives they negatively impact but who are too weak or diffused or distant to register telling blows in return.

Reciprocity and Future Generations

The situation in regard to future generations is even more grave since present generations now can and do impact the lives of future generations who are helpless to tell us what globalization means to them. There are (so far) no terrorists from the future successfully getting our attention.

And yet the futurist Faith Popcorn is quoted as saying, "[T]he present is the future getting back at us." That is to say, even we are currently living largely under the influence of and in reaction to what people did or did not do in regard to their future, our present. We might be either pleased or displeased with what our ancestors did or did not do that made their future what our present is. But we can neither thank them nor chastise them nor cause them to act differently on our behalf. We are forced to deal now with their actions then.

So also are our future generations hopelessly dependent on our concerns and actions on their behalf. Moreover, the ability of present generations to predetermine the quality of life of future generations has never been as great as it is now, though it will be greater still tomorrow. Because of impressive and rapid technological developments over recent decades (technologies with profound and long-lasting consequences) and because of vast and complex changes going on in the global environment caused by past and present human activities, present generations have substantially greater impact on the lives and well-being of future generations than ever before.

Thus we argue, along with others, that it is now necessary for humanity to understand that it has an ethical responsibility toward future generations because of the powerful yet asymmetrical relationship between present and future generations. Humanity also has the obligation to develop political, economic, and other social institutions as well as ethical systems that enable present generations to respond fairly to the needs of future generations.

A New Governance Concern

Thinking about the needs of future generations when acting in the present is relatively new. It has been said that some indigenous societies recognized an obligation to think seven generations into the future when making decisions. This may have been so, but it is also more likely that in traditional societies the past, present, and future were, for thousands of years, so much alike that if one followed the ways of the past, that was all one could, or needed, to do in order to be responsible to the future as well. This reasonably enough led to the belief that the best way to look forward is to look backward and to do now and forever whatever had been successfully done before.

This situation was generally found in stable agricultural, feudal, and other premodern societies where knowledge of the past was necessary and arguably sufficient for anticipating the challenges of the future. There was more dramatic social change, and hence uncertainty about the future, in premodern, agricultural societies than in traditional hunting and gathering communities. However, there was not enough change, or fast enough change, to require anything more than knowledge of the past and reason in the present in order to make the best decisions possible in anticipation of the uncertainties of the future.

Consider an American example: this was the general situation for the founding fathers when they created the US federal government in the 1780s and 1790s.

They designed a government through which a few knowledgeable, reasonable, privileged, and responsible men could gather together after the crop harvest to discuss and decide for the entire new nation the one or two novel and important matters that might arise every year or so. No special competence in or structure for governmental foresight was even imagined then. Living (as they did not know) at the end of the agricultural era when the industrial age was just faintly beginning to emerge, the founders created a cautious, slow, and restricted government to respond to the rhythms and experiences of an agricultural society now long since gone.

By the middle of the nineteenth century, the situation had changed dramatically. Industrialization was underway, and the new idea of (and direct experience with the fruits of) "progress" now provoked a profoundly different vision of the future. During the industrial era the future was expected to be significantly different from and better than the past or the present. Past, present, and future were no longer continuous and similar, but discontinuous and qualitatively dissimilar, with the future always being better than the present, just as the present was clearly so much better (for many people) than the past, as long as the industrial economy kept growing.

Many new social institutions, including agencies of governments unimagined by the founding fathers, had to be created and the older ones refocused in order to assure that society could and would move continuously forward toward a better tomorrow. However, creating new political structures proved to be challenging because a "strict construction" of the words of the written Constitution forbade such novelty. And yet the new economic and social situation demanded new political institutions as well as new policies.

This tension between the still, cold words of the written Constitution of the agricultural era and the hopes, desires, and fears of living flesh and blood in the industrial and now post-industrial era has been the basis of many political struggles in the United States. However, by the end of World War II, the "development paradigm" became dominant as the official image of America's future, and various ways were found to reinterpret the silent words in order to make it a "Living Constitution" that permitted policies and actions favoring development and progress as the sole official image of America's future.

Similar challenges were found in many other countries of the world as "development" became the official view of the future for all industrial and industrializing countries. Indeed, during the second half of the twentieth century, the vision of "development" was aggressively promoted and actively implemented worldwide by all of the various units of the United Nations and by the creation and actions of the World Bank, the International Monetary Fund, the World Trade Organization, and scores of similar agencies. The mass media (especially television and movies, fueled by advertising that created desires for ever-new and changing products and services) embedded the vision of development deeply into the hearts and minds of all people everywhere.

Eventually, no nation, government, corporation, or citizen anywhere in the world was expected to have any image of the future except "continued economic growth." And all were expected to be an actively contributing partner in the creation and operation of the globally expanding economic system.

Appeals to progress and growth were often made in terms of future generations. Every day, in every way, it was said, the world was getting better and better. By enabling continued economic growth through the global spread of modern institutions and values, the lives of all children would be better than, and different from, our own, just as the lives of their children would be even better than theirs, and so on forever.

Doing whatever was necessary to make development possible became the sole duty of all governments and their subsidiary agencies (such as schools, universities, the military, and the media) everywhere in the world. Whether "communist" or "capitalist," development was the goal. As long as a nation kept growing economically, it was automatically fulfilling its obligations to future generations, with no further thought about the matter necessary.

Competing Images of the Future

Nonetheless, very soon after World War II, other orientations toward the future emerged. Among the first was the idea of a "post-industrial society," a world in which automated technology, efficiency, and affluence would reach such heights that issues of economics and productivity would recede into the background. Of course, society would have to wrestle with how equitably and quickly to distribute the material abundance that would be produced without human labor, and what humans would do peacefully with all their leisure time.

Simultaneously, and in stark contrast, "the environmental movement" began to question whether Earth (and the diversity of human cultures) could survive continued economic growth. Many people became convinced that responding to environmental pollution, resource depletion, overpopulation, and global climate change was vastly more important than continuing to urge blind economic growth. Fretting over the problems of a world of abundance and leisure was ridiculous, this group concluded. Indeed, the unanticipated consequences of continued economic growth led many people to fear the future.

Shortly thereafter, more and more indigenous peoples began to question development since it involved the conscious destruction of their cultures and values as well as the theft, exploitation, and degradation of their native lands and waters. At first the voices of indigenous peoples were too weak and marginal to be heeded by leaders of nations anywhere. But ultimately they joined hands and voices worldwide, and with persons concerned about cultural and environmental preservation generally, they now reckon as a major factor in contemporary politics.

More recently, globalization and anti-globalization have emerged as competing images of the future, changing both the discussion about development and, as we have seen, "the environment." So, whatever view one might have of the future—be it bright or dark, prosperous or penurious—more and more people (though still only a tiny minority on the planet!) have become aware of their obligation to take the needs of future generations effectively into account when making present decisions. It is no longer clear to them that continued economic growth will automatically lead to a better world for future generations. And in addition to environmental concerns, many have come to wonder if continued technological innovations (both a producer and product of economic growth) such as genetic modification of plants and animals and runaway nanotechnologies might lead us blindly into a darker, rather than a brighter, future.

It is time, they say, for societies to look ahead and try to anticipate more rigorously the possible consequences of their decisions and actions. We should no longer drive into the future while staring into the rearview mirror. Dietrich Bonhoeffer said, "The ultimate test of a moral society is the world it leaves to its children." Or as the Kyoto Future Generations Group puts it, "Future generations: they are our conscience." Foresight is necessary.

FURTHER THOUGHTS
Culture and Fairness
The Idea of Civilization Fairness
Sohail Inayatullah

FAIRNESS IS OFTEN considered to be a universal, and yet it is not a constant across civilizations. For example, in the Islamic world, justice and fairness are in tension. Islamic civilization was born in the context of tribalism, focused on punishment and sameness (eye for an eye) and in violent opposition to forces bent on its destruction. Justice thus became central in terms of external politics. Internally, however, Muhammad's contribution was *adl,* or distributive justice, focused more on multiple levels of fairness (social, economic, political, and environmental). Thus Islamic civilization exhibits a tension between justice and fairness—between retributive justice and the fight against injustice, and distributional justice, focused on creating a caring society.

In current Australian politics, reconciliation is considered more important than justice per se. Aboriginal leaders ask for an apology from the current government so as to restore what is right. While partly based on regaining or retaining access to land essential to their perceived notions of justice, it is also a spiritual, emotional quest, about healing self and Other, aboriginal and "white fella."

In contrast, justice is far less foundational in the classical Indic episteme. Notions of understanding the self, transcending the self, and maintaining the self are more important. Lack of fairness, one might argue, has been the cost of the stability of the caste system. This grand eugenics experiment removes fairness from the mix since the classical texts have determined one's dharma (duty, mission) in life. At the same time, it is one's karma (consequences of previous actions) that defines one's current circumstances. The universe thus is essentially moral and fair. However, it is not surprising that those at the bottom are more likely to convert out of the vedantic structure since there is little intercaste mobility. Fairness within the system is high, but the entire system can be seen as stunningly unfair.

Thus civilizations construct the notion of fairness differently. In the Islamic world, because of its colonial history and because of the Sunni-Shia split, justice is far more important than fairness. In the aboriginal world, fairness comes through reconciliation, through the offender apologizing and community harmony being restored. In Indic civilization, fairness is less central because notions of dharma and karma reign supreme. In recent times, with institutionalized Hinduism (modeled after Islam and Christianity) in vogue, justice suddenly has become important for some Hindus, and thus there have been recent attempts to push back Muslim Indians in order to regain temples unfairly occupied.

What different civilizational notions of fairness point out is that fairness must be approached from, and at, different levels. If one takes the entire globe as a category, then different civilizations' notions of fairness might seem narrow. Civilizational differences experience prejudice within the world system. Certain broad notions of truth, nature, reality, and beauty have become the global norm. For the most part the global norms are not multicultural but are based on Western civilization. What this means is that Others see themselves through the eyes of the West. The results, as in the Islamic world, can be devastating. Conspiracy theories abound, individuals seethe with hate toward the West, or alternatively, as in the work of V. S. Naipaul, the Other acquiesces to the West and becomes but a pale (or brown) imitation.

Over time, either response destroys the backbone of the community as cultural vitality is lost. Seething with hate destroys cultural vitality since pathological forms of political and social practice emerge. Identity becomes a weapon used within and without. The losers in this tend to be those most vulnerable—take, for example, women in Islamic nations.

Civilizational fairness emerges once Western civilizational hegemony is named, understood, and challenged, especially in terms of its implications for society, nature, and gender. That done, a dialogue can emerge and spaces created for other civilizations.

Globalization, even as it leads to uneven development, has been one of the modes of increased multicultural hybrid music, food, and identity. As the non-West has clawed, through immigration, back to the West, this has created hybrid identities. These have the potential to create planetary notions of fairness. Hybrid identities and the softening of the past are necessary factors of global fairness, but not sufficient. For that, a new view of the future and a globalization far more sensitive to the quadruple bottom line than we have now is required.

Globalization and Fairness

Edgar Porter

CAN FAIRNESS BE understood in a global context? Does culture still matter when striving to define fairness in an era of global relationship, or have we become so global in our lives that culture evaporates and we see a clear sky of universal truths writ large? The answer, I think, is that universal truths are not to be found, and culture still matters. A lot.

The story is told of American philosopher Mortimer Adler attending an international conference on philosophy in Honolulu, eager to engage his Asian colleagues in a dialogue on the "great ideas" of justice and freedom. But all they wanted to talk about, he reported, was *harmony!* To the Asian philosophers the search for harmony was paramount, well ahead of justice and freedom. To Adler, it was just the opposite. How does one convince "the Other" of the absolute, universal importance of his or her view when each is tied to rich and diverse cultures built on distinct core ideals? One does not, even in these heady days of globalization.

Does this mean that globalization has no impact on our ability to address the "big" questions such as fairness, justice, and harmony? No, it means that addressing them in order to agree on a common definition is fruitless. Globalization does not guide us to universal truth, or even universal agreement. Globalization does, however, thrust up moral dialogue in an exploring, intimate, cross-cultural environment never imagined before. Therefore, diverse cultures sitting down to discuss globalization and fairness can agree on fairness as a universal "concept." What globalization cannot do is lead to an agreement on what constitutes fair behavior.

How in this globalizing age do we guide the discussion of ideas and values toward an even more positive and constructive exchange? We might start by organizing the next conference. It will be called "Globalization and Harmony."

Notes

1. S. Milius, "Unfair Trade: Monkeys Demand Equitable Exchanges," *Science News* 164.12 (September 20, 2003): 181.

2. Duen Hsi Yen, www.noogenesis.com/malama/fairness.html.

3. www.calvertnet.k12.md.us/instruct/justfair.shtml.

4. Fredrik Bendz, www.update.uu.se/~fbendz/philo/fairness.htm.

5. John Rawls, *A Theory of Justice* (Cambridge, Mass.: Harvard University Press, 1971). More recently, a collection of his essays has been published. See John Rawls, *Justice as Fairness: A Restatement* (Cambridge, Mass.: Harvard University Press, 2001). In addition to focusing more directly and exclusively on fairness, this newer book contains numerous "corrections" that Rawls made in response to some of the criticisms of his earlier book.

6. Rawls, *Justice as Fairness*, 4.

7. Ibid., 14f.

8. Ibid., 15.

9. Ibid., 16.

10. Ibid., 42f.

11. Steven Suranovic, "International Trade Fairness," http://internationalecon.com/fairtrade/index.html.

12. Ibid.

13. Joseph Henrich, Robert Boyd, and Samuel Bowles, "In Search of *Homo Economicus:* Behavioral Experiments in 15 Small-scale Societies," *American Economic Review* 91 (May 2001): 73–78.

14. Colin Camerer, "Strategizing in the Brain," *Science* 300, (June 13, 2003): 1674f, commenting on the research paper by Sanfey et al., www.sciencemag.org/cgi/ content/ short/300/5626/1755>.

15. Ibid., 1674.

CHAPTER 4

What Are Public Institutions?

Dick Pratt

Public institutions throughout the world are changing, often in dramatic ways. These changes are not only because of globalization, but globalization is an important factor. At the same time, public institutions are a response to globalization, reflecting efforts to cope with new economic, social, cultural, and political forces and events. Because of this dual role as object of change and agent of change, the relationship between public institutions and globalization inevitably is significant and complex.

This chapter defines what is meant by "public institutions" and then explores differing views of their purposes and effectiveness. It concludes with an analysis of the differences between public and private power, suggesting the desirability of a continued, and probably increased, role for public institutions in a globalizing world.

Globalization is not a new phenomenon, but we are witnessing a period of its more rapid development, what some have referred to as "turbo globalization." Contemporary globalization's reshaping of public institutions internationally is a distinctive feature of its current acceleration. This reshaping is occurring at the same time that these institutions also must play a meaningful role in determining the winners and losers from globalization and must directly address issues of fairness—that is, to see that globalization has broad public benefits.

What Are Public Institutions?

"Public institutions" refer first to government at all levels and in all dimensions. They therefore include local, regional (i.e., provinces and states), and national governments, as well as the compact conventions and other arrangements that are made between governments. Within governments, this includes the legislative, executive/administrative, and adjudicative components. The legislative and judicial branches have experienced some globalization-related reform, but the most attention by far has been focused on the administrative apparatus. (This is examined through an analysis of the New Public Management and related issues in chap. 9.)

Nongovernmental organizations (NGOs and the not-for-profit sector within nations, and international organizations [IOs] internationally) are part of public institutions. The number of IOs and NGOs has increased enormously in recent years throughout much of the world. Joseph Stiglitz and others have underscored the enormous influence some of these organizations, such as the International Monetary Fund (IMF), have on behalf of certain conceptions of globalization.[1] There is also the civic sector of voluntary associations and citizens groups. The civic sector has come into prominence as an important form of public institution in the last decade. It has gained media visibility through protests against globalization but established a broader foundation in association with efforts to increase social capital and broaden democratic options. Globalization is helping to create a new phenomenon: a global civic sector whose members are linked by instantaneous communication and shared public concerns.

More ambiguous as public institutions are those parts of the private-for-profit sector that are involved in "the public's business" through contractual agreements or as hybrid organizations. With the rise of privatization and sustained efforts internationally by the private sector for more of the work traditionally done by governments, there now are many more organizations that are ambiguously public. These for-profit businesses provide public services but are contractually overseen by one or more government agency. What Lester Salamon has labeled "indirect government" has raised a number of issues. The once "terrifying authority" of government is replaced by dispersed and ambiguous authority. With the separation of the authorization of action by government agencies from the undertaking of that action by other actors, accountability is complicated.[2]

Shifting National Orientations toward Public Institutions

In *The Commanding Heights: The Battle for the World Economy,* Daniel Yergin provides what can be thought of as an intellectual history of the shift from public institutions—meaning here primarily government—toward private institutions. Yergin describes the evaporation, in country after country, of an early twentieth-century consensus about the necessary role of government in monitoring economic activity and distributing its benefits. That consensus, referred to as statism, Keynesianism, or the mixed economy, was replaced in the 1970s and 1980s by another that favors market-based solutions.

The old consensus was attacked for its perceived inability to solve specific problems that arose in the post–World War II period. These problems included high inflation rates, national debt originating in expanding public-sector social programs, and restrictions on the ability of individuals to select the products or services they preferred.

These dissatisfactions were both economic and political and focused on the opportunity costs of government activities as well as their threat to individual liberty. A new school of economic thinking, located at the University of Chicago in the United States and later referred to as the Chicago School, spearheaded the argument that government is an unacceptable drag on the efficient creation of wealth. Economists like Milton Friedman argued to policy makers everywhere that the resources allocated to public institutions should be used in places that would be societally more beneficial. Politically, public agencies were described as monopolies, but monopolies backed by terrifying state authority. The danger was seen to occur when this exclusiveness and authority was coupled with normal public agency characteristics of goal confusion, low public or business participation, and little internal criticism. These critics pointed out how this combination of factors led to highly undesirable interventions in social, political, and economic life. For these soon-to-be mainstream economists, the threat of private monopolies was much less serious than that posed by a public monopoly.

Their new consensus emphasized a smaller scope of government activity, policies seeking low inflation over those seeking full employment, the promotion of savings for investment, low government deficits, education and training that supported entrepreneurial activity, and more international trade. The political figures that came to embody these views to varying degrees (Ronald Reagan in the United States, Margaret Thatcher in Great Britain, Carlos Menem in Argentina, Tadeusz Mazowiechi in Poland, Lee Kwan Yew in Singapore, and Kim Dae-jung in South Korea) favored policies to control inflation, spoke against the planning role of government, argued for the benefits of entrepreneurial activity as the best way to create a healthy society, and were more willing to open their borders to international trade. Their shared views reflected a swing away from belief in public-sector institutions as embodiments of shared values toward prioritizing consumer sovereignty and the publicly beneficial power of autonomous markets.

Globalization and the Roles of Public Institutions

If we raise our view beyond changes in domestic orientations to public institutions, we can see that the global movement for their transformation focuses on three things: size, form, and purpose.

Size refers to efforts in many places to reduce the resources put into public institutions, particularly the administrative agencies of government. Size also includes, in addition to the question of how big governments should be, whether, or when, it is more important to emphasize their improvement or their reduction.

As we will see later, despite calls to reduce government's role everywhere, whether reduction or improvement is appropriate depends upon specific circumstances.

Attention to the *form* of public institutions recognizes the contemporary movement away from seeing them exclusively or primarily as government and focuses instead on the types of integration that are occurring across different kinds of public institutions. One type of integration is horizontal. Here diverse parts of government, different governments, or government together with other sectors such as NGOs, businesses, and the civic sector look for informal and formal ways to focus on the same societal issue. For example, an environmental problem may be tackled jointly by the provincial Departments of Environment and of Health, a municipal Office of Community Relations, an NGO, a citizens group, and a collection of private service providers.

Another form of integration is vertical. Here the connection is up and down, institutionally speaking. It might begin with an international organization and run "down" through the national, regional, and local governments. To use the same example, an international body might adopt a standard, such as for trade, that changes national policy and is then communicated downward in terms of programs and budgetary shifts.

The third issue raised by the global transformation of public institutions is about *purpose*. The purposes of public institutions are critical because if we do not know what they are supposed to do, then we cannot answer the first two questions—that is, what size and what form they should take. At the same time, in the real world it is difficult to attain agreement on what those purposes are.

The purposes of public institutions are disputed and can be understood in a number of ways. As a broad overview, however, these purposes can be understood using three broad, and sometimes overlapping, categories: conserving, facilitating economic activities, and moral valuing.

Conserving refers to activities that emphasize the maintenance of order and security from internal and external threats. Police forces, private security companies, prisons, large parts of the legal system, border patrol, and the military are all performing functions primarily associated with conserving. Since September 11, 2001, much more has been invested in the conserving function of public institutions worldwide, but especially in the industrial societies. As is observed in chapter 10, some even see this event as marking a re-embrace of public institutions.

A second broad category of public institution purpose is the facilitating of economic activities. *Economic facilitation* focuses on the public institution's role in the generation of wealth. This role has taken a wide variety of forms historically, including state ownership of firms, management of economic relations, tariffs, tax policies, and regulatory interventions. In more recent times, with the collapse of the Soviet Union, the economic facilitation role in many more places has come to emphasize activities that support a private market within a loose or dense regulatory framework.

The third category of institutional purpose is *moral valuing*, which refers to the values that public institutions attempt to incorporate, legitimate, and make authoritative. In a society that is dominated by business culture, the values will be primarily those that support the success of private-sector firms. In other societies they may reflect the values of particular groups or the consensus (i.e., public) values held by most people. The public education system, citizen education, social welfare policies, discretionary budget priorities, the inspirational rhetoric of leaders, and court decisions all reflect the moral valuing role of public institutions.

One of the shared concerns mobilizing people against globalization is that the values that animate traditional, or at least evolving local, cultures will be lost to a much more homogeneous consumer culture, and public institutions, national and international, will reflect mostly the social priorities of large corporations. From this perspective, concerns about public institutions and fairness in a globalizing world (the question of who will benefit from globalization and what role public institutions play in determining that) is closely connected to their moral valuing role.

The important questions about public institutions do not invite either/or responses, but, instead, an understanding of what is being emphasized at a particular time and in particular circumstances. As noted above, after 9/11 there is more of an emphasis on the conserving purpose, but in many parts of the world, where religious traditions are strong or resurgent, moral valuing is heightened. It is also clear that countries feel pressure to emphasize the economic facilitation role because of globalization.

Public Institutions in a Globalizing World

This chapter began with reference to Yergin's *Commanding Heights* and its review of the shift from public institutions to private institutions. It is noteworthy that while the entire book appears to be sympathetic to the rise of the market and private decision making within nation-states, in the end even Yergin finds an important place for government when considering a globalizing world. In a chapter titled "The Age of Globalization: The Battle for the World Economy," he moves back toward an essential role for it. He argues that a world that contains both nation-states and intense global-level interrelations "leaves governments with a daunting challenge: to figure out ways to reduce their intervention in some cases, and to retool and refocus in others, while preserving the public trust. . . . What this means is that for all the erosion of boundaries and fundamental technological change governments still matter enormously, as does political leadership."[3]

In the book's final chapter, "The Balance of Confidence: The New Rules of the Game," Yergin asks whether the current shift from state toward market is likely to be permanent, a transformation rather than a phase in a cycle.[4] His answer to that question is that it will depend on the results of five tests. One of these tests, which he terms "Delivering the Goods," refers to what is produced in "measurable economic goods: growth, higher standards of living, better-quality services and jobs."[5] The other tests focus on fairness, the future of the environment, how demographic shifts are handled, and the ability of people to maintain meaningful cultural identities.[6]

While he embraces a role for government, Yergin's views on globalization and public institutions are unduly narrow. For him, public institutions are only the government, and NGOs, IOs, and civil society are ignored. Concerns about fairness are addressed secondarily in comparison to an overriding focus on economic performance and wealth making.

In *Globalization and Its Discontents*, Joseph Stiglitz, the winner of the 2001 Noble Prize in economics and a former vice president of the World Bank, goes much further than Yergin in making the case for the essential role of public institutions in addressing fairness in a globalizing world.[7] At one level Stiglitz's book is an expression of discontent with international financial organizations, particularly the policies of the International Monetary Fund. He argues that the IMF has been ineffective and often destructive in its responses to problems associated with economic globalization. It is has been ineffective, he believes, because its focus is narrow and its policies are rigidly focused on controlling inflation and stabilizing currency exchanges. He sees these policies as a reflection of a deeply held "market fundamentalism" or "Washington Consensus," an outlook the emergence of which is traced by Yergin in *Commanding Heights*.

For Stiglitz, the fundamentalism that has over taken the IMF is a reflection of the fact that the IMF serves the worldview and the interests of financial institutions, especially American. He argues that the IMF, formed by Keynes, has changed its purpose from fiscal policies that would create demand and support full employment to policies that protect lenders. At the time the IMF was formed, markets were not seen as self-correcting, a view that followed the worldwide depression of the 1930s. Now markets are seen as natural and, to a much greater extent, self-adjusting.

From this perspective, what is referred to in domestic politics as "agency takeover" has taken place in an IO. The current directors of the IMF have moved away from Keynesian assumptions about the limitations of markets (encapsulated in the concept of market failure) and adopted policies that assume the market is best left alone. For Stiglitz, "We have an obvious problem: a public institution created to address certain failures in the market, but currently run by economists who have both a high level of confidence in markets and little confidence in public institutions."[8]

Stiglitz's concerns about globalization and public institutions go beyond his criticism of the IMF to broader issues. Globalization is here to stay, and the amount of good or harm it does can be positively affected by human actions, but not by the "economic fundamentalists," who he argues are not even in touch with economic research. He refers to their policies as "trickle-down plus."[9]

Stiglitz places much more emphasis than Yergin on alternatives that are appropriate to each country's setting, not ideologically prescribed policies that emphasize low inflation, lower taxes, liberalization, and privatization for all circumstances. We are not, however, pursuing those alternatives because "[s]implistic free market ideology [has] provided the cover behind which the real business of the 'new' mandate could be transacted."[10]

Public institutions and international governments are, for Stiglitz, at the center of the potentially positive human actions, and their role in shaping globalization toward fairness will be crucial. He states, "Globalization can be reshaped, and when it is, when it is properly, fairly run, with all countries having a voice in policies affecting them, there is a possibility that it will help create a new global economy in which growth is not only more sustainable and less volatile, but the fruits of this growth are more equitably shared."[11]

Private versus Public Power

There is much to commend in Stiglitz's thinking about the complexities of globalization and public institutions. His point that the economic fundamentalists put too much faith in the market and too little in public institutions is well taken. At the same time, there is another dimension to the role of public institutions that he skims over but is nonetheless essential in understanding their significance.

In "Private Order under Dysfunctional Public Order," John McMillan and Christopher Woodruff describe how private institutions create the conditions for commercial transactions to occur in developing economies where the public systems are viewed as ineffective or unreliable.[12] In a response to their work, Ellen Katz, though agreeing with much of their analysis, argues that they have misunderstood and understated the importance of public institutions. Their exchange is used here to develop a framework for public institutions globally in the light of the analysis in the previous sections of their perceived shortcomings and shifting purposes in a globalizing world.

McMillan and Woodruff contend that in developing societies private institutions can be effective as substitutes for public order in establishing the rules and norms needed to facilitate efficient economic activity. They also note that there are important downsides to this, what has been termed "darkside public ordering." These darksides include practices of control, exclusion, collusion, and criminality that, among other things, inhibit vibrant private relations and generate significant negative externalities. McMillan and Woodruff and others observe that these darkside practices are to be expected. Without these state-imposed penalties, the short-term benefits outweigh, from the individual actor's perspective, any societal or longer-term losses. For McMillan and Woodruff, the reality of darkside practices, which take hold when there are no public institutions capable of creating an environment in which darkside activities are no longer rational, are the justification for public institutions.

Katz expands this point and argues that the work of public institutions goes beyond creating the conditions that reduce the private-order inefficiencies that McMillan and Woodruff describe. One reason for this is that the promulgation of norms and rules by public institutions may, in concert with private institutions, create a more optimum environment for economic activities or, at a minimum, keep the private order from "becoming sluggish," such as through the creation of monopolies or oligopolies. Of more significance, there are important justifications for public institutions not connected to economic efficiency. In Katz's words, "[E]ven where private order may be efficient, and flexibly so, it may run counter to fundamental principles that a society, upon proper reflection, decides should not be subject to the calculus of efficiency."[13]

What are those fundamental principles that public institutions must stand for and that mean private order cannot be substituted for public order? These are the rules and norms created and implemented by institutions that are truly "public." They are public because they are developed and implemented through deliberation, inclusion, and transparency. Katz points out that in fact it is their freedom from the constraints of inclusion and transparency that "yields much of private order's effectiveness and productivity."[14] Public rules by their very nature are, in economic terms, inefficient, forcing compliance with procedural norms, including public processes in which all affected parties are able to participate.

Katz also acknowledges, as any observer of "public" institutions must, that their reality falls short of our aspirations for their performance. Among other things, public agencies can be captured by factions to advance their private economic or other interests. She argues, however, that public-order decision making is worth its cost in inefficiency and that "that aspiration and a commitment to strive toward achieving it distinguish the public from the private realm and provide a basis to prefer the former over the latter."[15] This is because public institutions and the processes associated with them are able to do two things not possible by even effective private-regarding rule making. The first is to confer broad-based legitimacy upon both public and private policies. "Democratic public-order institutions are needed to confer public legitimacy on well-functioning private-order norms. . . . [Their] deliberation certifies the fairness and public acceptance of the private system and thereby confers public legitimacy that the private-order system would otherwise lack."[16]

The second thing public institutions do involves the act of participation itself. The value here is independent of specific outcomes and is found in the ways participation works to discover and act on what is held in common, build community, and create positive identities. The participation that must underlie truly public institutions embodies a conception of the common good, as opposed to purely private preference, and a conception of individuals as effective, independent, and interdependent actors. Katz underscores this point by observing that citizen participation "should not be understood as simply another sort of market."[17]

The Future of Public Institutions

Where does this leave us? We have looked at three different interpretations of public institutions that are quite different in their orientations. Yergin thinks they will continue to play a role in relation to globalization, but his primary interest is the move away from government and toward autonomous markets. Stiglitz is interested in international organizations and government and is concerned that both are being taken over by an economic fundamentalism that is too private regarding. He advocates a set of policies in which public institutions more directly address fairness and the distribution of economic success. Both Yergin and Stiglitz concentrate heavily on government and public institutions in relation to economic globalization. Katz's point of departure is the broader issue of private versus public rules, and she makes the case for public institutions using noneconomic criteria.

The boundaries between public and private are not fixed. They shift over time within societies, and in the future they very likely will shift for international institutions. In the United States these shifts have been cyclical, swinging from reliance on the virtues of the private sector and distaste for government to trust in government and skepticism about the private sector.[18]

We are undeniably in an era of boundary shift toward the private sector. As we will see in chapter 9, even historically more stable boundaries of "public" administration are being shifted through movements such as the New Public Management. Globalization presents new questions and raises new issues with respect to where the boundary should be drawn, now and in the future.

It is realistic to suggest that where these boundaries are drawn will differ from place to place and time to time and that there will be ongoing experimentation that takes into account institutional histories, resources, political culture, and current political-economic circumstances. This is reflected in Katz's point that "the design of public institutions in developing economies should be seen as a distinct project from the design (or redesign) of such institutions in developed ones."[19]

Without ignoring these complexities, it is my contention that if globalization is to be public regarding, then public institutions, those that are truly public in the sense developed by Katz, must participate in determining how globalization's diverse benefits and costs are distributed. This is even more the case if we are to incorporate into our ideas of fairness the concerns of not only the members of current societies, but also the impact on the environment and on the interests of future generations.

Whatever the experimentation, there must be a balance between the facilitation of economic activity and other social and political priorities that are not focused on the creation of wealth. As Katz points out, it is the private sector's freedom from many of the rules that constrains public organizations and that "yields much of private order's effectiveness and productivity."[20] At the same time, the legitimacy of the market depends on publicly created rules that prohibit and encourage certain kinds of behavior. The argument, often heard in the current shift toward private institutions, that "the market" should be "left alone" ignores the complexities of each market's creation, the ongoing dance of principles and interests that shape its rules, and the legitimacy of nonmarket-related public values.

Public institutions are far from perfect. They reflect the complexities of the societies of which they are a part while at the same time are expected to be "above" those complexities. Their reform internationally is often appropriate, sometimes absolutely necessary. Reform, however, must be grounded in a continuous process to make more public regarding the balance of conserving, economic facilitation, and moral-valuing functions. Our focus on fairness, globalization, and public institutions is intended to underscore that their moral-valuing purposes can be ignored only at great peril to both public *and* private institutions.

Notes

1. Joseph Stiglitz, *Globalization and Its Discontents* (New York: W. W. Norton, 2002).

2. See Lester Salamon, ed., *The Tools of Government: A Guide to the New Governance* (Oxford: Oxford University Press, 2002), for an analysis of the issues associated with the rise of "indirect government."

3. Colin Camerer, "Strategizing in the Brain," *Science* 300 (June 13, 2003): 396–397.

4. Ibid., 408.

5. Ibid.

6. Ibid., 410–415.

7. Stiglitz, *Globalization and Its Discontents*.

8. Ibid., 196.

9. Ibid., 80.

10. Ibid., 88.

11. Ibid., 22.

12. John McMillan and Christopher Woodruff, "Private Order under Dysfunctional Public Order, *Michigan Law Review* 96 (2000): 2421.

13. Ellen Katz, "Private Order and Public Institutions, Comments on McMillan and Woodruff's 'Private Order Under Dysfunctional Public Order,' " *Michigan Law Review* 98 (2002): 2488.

14. Ibid., 2491.

15. Ibid., 2493.

16. Ibid.

17. Ibid.

18. Theo A. J. Toonen et al., *Civil Service Systems in Comparative Perspectives* (Bloomington: Indiana University Press, 1996), 191.

19. Katz, "Private Order and Public Institutions," 2487.

20. Ibid., 2491.

PART 2

Globalization and Fairness
The Debate

This section introduces and discusses some of the various contentions about fairness and globalization. Four very different stories are told from four very different perspectives. The first is written by Christopher Grandy, an economist in the Public Administration Program at the University of Hawai'i who considers the prospects for fairness to be generally good, if economic processes are allowed to operate as they should. After discussing the fact that economic globalization limits the ability—and more important, the desirability—of nation-states (and their units) to protect certain interests of citizens and the environment, Grandy carefully, clearly, and sympathetically lays out the dominant view of economists who support economic globalization. He concludes that "[f]airness equals equity *and* efficiency." He also maintains that a robust body of literature supporting that conclusion has been in existence since the 1970s and 1980s, though he admits that "it is fair (no pun intended) to say that it has had little direct influence on public policy."

In contrast, James Rosenau, an American political scientist who has for many years thought long and hard about fairness and globalization, argues that the issues can best be understood by a new word—"fragmegration"—that expresses in a single term their simultaneously integrated and fragmented nature. Rosenau attributes fragmegration largely to microelectronic technologies, the worldwide "skills revolution," the rise of citizen organizations and networks, increased population mobility, the dynamic tension between state-centric politics, and the multicentric world of NGOs and transnational entities of many kinds. This fragmegration is associated with the concomitant weakening of traditional sources of power and authority; all are strongly influenced by and influencing the globalized economy and the globalization of all national economies. Rosenau concludes that prolonged fragmegration suggests that fairness for most people will be hard to obtain.

Ivana Milojevic finds little good in global economic integration as currently envisioned and manifested. While there are various anti-global positions, she says that there are basically two positive visions of a global society. One, Globotech, is dominant and is put forward largely by white, academic males situated in developed countries. The vision is presented as inevitable and basically unproblematic. While some people might suffer in the short term, in the long run the Globotech future will be good for everyone. The other positive vision of a globalized world, Ecarmony, comes primarily from women and others on the margins of contemporary society. It is viewed as naive, fanciful, and unrealistic. But of the two, it is only Ecarmony that is sustainable, Milojevic believes.

Finally, Sohail Inayatullah presents a humorous and bittersweet personal story of what passports, visas, national boundaries, and citizenship mean to him. During his life, he has lived in many parts of the world, but his brown skin and ominous-appearing name often make boundary crossing quite an adventure. He is riding the wave of a swelling future.

CHAPTER 5

Through a Glass, Darkly

An Economic View of Fairness, Globalization, and States

CHRISTOPHER GRANDY

This chapter takes up terms central to the focus of the conference—fairness, equality, globalization—from a distinctly economic perspective. As an economist working closely with non-economist social scientists, I feel the occasional barb of the economist caricature: exclusively focused on efficiency; seeing the web of social relations as a self-propelled, optimizing mechanism; the comments of whom are counterintuitive, callous, and (most distressing of all) wholly beside the point. One purpose of this chapter is to challenge some of those characterizations.

The first of the following three sections describes a serious attempt by economic theorists to define "fairness" in a way that makes the term susceptible to rigorous economic (including mathematical) analysis. These ideas yielded some fascinating results that, while having little influence on public policy, challenge a view of economists as apologists for the status quo. The second section moves to a discussion of inequality, an idea related to, but not antonymous with, fairness. Here the economist's penchant for counterintuitive argument comes forward in exploring the social virtues of inequality. The chapter's final section then makes the argument that just as ideas of fairness and equality are important to individuals, the relative merits of globalization must be decided ultimately by its impact on individuals. In particular, concerns about the impact of globalization on political entities (states) are relevant only in the context of the welfare of their constituents.

From Efficiency to Fairness

Economists often seem obsessed with efficiency. At a minimum, they certainly have more to say about economic efficiency than about equity or fairness. Perhaps efficiency issues are more tractable than fairness issues, or perhaps developing ideas on the efficient allocation of society's resources requires more effort—and hence more resources.

Yet issues of equity and fairness regularly come to the mainstream economist's attention. For example, economists often point to a trade-off between efficiency and equity. The trade-off might arise with respect to policies that promote greater equality of wealth or income but that weaken individual incentives to produce. In addition, economists have contributed to a variety of measurements of inequality including the Gini coefficient, the coefficient of variation, and entropy. Economists also contribute to debates and empirical work on the inequality of income or wealth at a moment in time, over an individual's life cycle, and intergenerationally.

Still, prospectively, we rarely, and reluctantly, make policy proposals with respect to equity or fairness. Many of us feel that we have no particular comparative advantage when discussing such issues.

Yet since the late 1960s a strand of economic research on equity and fairness developed that is consistent with standard economic theory. Moreover, in the spirit of much economic reasoning, this research has policy implications. The following discussion reviews the basic notion of economic efficiency and its associated ethical problems. This provides a background to the description of an innovative treatment of equity and fairness from an economic perspective.

Efficiency

The economist's notion of efficiency is named for the Italian theorist Vilfredo Pareto. In some ways, the concept of Pareto efficiency (or Pareto optimality) skirts issues of equity and fairness by focusing on situations in which a change implies that no one is harmed while at least one person is made better off. Thus relative to existing conditions, such changes are arguably socially acceptable.

However, a Pareto-efficient allocation of society's resources is one in which it is *not* possible to reallocate resources to improve the well being of at least one person *without* harming at least one other person. The idea is that if, conversely, we could change the current allocation of society's resources so as to make at least one person better off *without* making someone else worse off, then the current allocation of resources cannot be efficient: we could do better by effecting the proposed reallocation.

Note the focus of this definition of efficiency on individual welfare. Economists employ the concept of a *utility function* to characterize an individual's welfare. And they define this function over virtually everything relevant to the individual: all goods and services, all states of nature, all time periods. Also note that the definition of efficiency is not (in this context) a statement about how well inputs (such as land, capital, labor, and technology) can be combined to produce outputs (cars, haircuts, computers, and music). In fact—critically—the notion of efficiency is defined with respect to whatever each individual cares about.

From a policy perspective, an important problem with Pareto efficiency is that it insufficiently narrows the set of desirable resource allocations. That is, one may agree that a "good" allocation of society's resources should be Pareto efficient (if not, then by definition we could reallocate resources to improve the welfare of at least one person without hurting anyone else—a proposal difficult to oppose). But the set of Pareto-optimal allocations is usually quite large. How to choose among them?

Moreover, Pareto-efficient allocations can include very skewed distributions of resources. For example, one can imagine a society in which a single individual controls virtually all resources and the remainder of society lives in abject poverty. Nevertheless, this allocation of resources could be Pareto efficient in the sense that moving to a more equitable allocation would harm the wealthy individual—and thereby violate the condition for what is called a "Pareto-improving" reallocation. Thus Pareto efficiency gives only limited insight into "desirable" ways of allocating society's resources.

It is worth noting the relationship between this definition of efficiency and the workings of competitive markets. They are captured in two prominent theorems in the field of "welfare economics." First, an equilibrium allocation in competitive markets for all relevant resources is Pareto optimal. Second, almost any Pareto-optimal allocation of resources can be achieved using competitive markets and an appropriately chosen initial allocation of resources. Both propositions are "theorems" in the sense that given certain assumptions, they can be proven mathematically.[1]

This is the essence of the economist's infatuation with competitive market forces. Put another way, competition will lead to an allocation of resources such that all "win-win" (indeed, "all win-no lose") exchanges have been exhausted. While this is no mean trick, the normative problems with Pareto efficiency mentioned above suggest that people may care about more than exhausting mutually beneficial possibilities.

Envy

In 1967, Duncan Foley published his Yale doctoral dissertation, which contained an interesting refinement of resource allocation characterizations.[2] Foley defined the term "envy" to refer to a situation in which an individual preferred someone else's allocation of resources to his own. In this characterization, individuals use their own preferences to consider the allocations of other people. Thus the question becomes, Would I rather have your set of goods and services than the set that I, in fact, have? If yes, then I envy you.

A Pareto-optimal allocation of resources can easily exhibit envy. The example above illustrates that if one individual enjoys most of society's resources while the remainder of the community has almost nothing, then presumably at least some of the destitute envy the wealthy individual. On the other hand, the wealthy individual probably does not envy anyone.

Equity

The concept of envy leads immediately to the question of whether there exist allocations of society's resources that are envy free—that is, allocations in which no individual prefers the set of goods and services of another to the set he or she currently enjoys. Such allocations, if they exist, have been called "equitable." A moment's thought will suggest that there is at least one such allocation—the distribution of resources such that everyone has an equal division of the available resources. Since everyone has the same allocation, there is no envy.

Note that an equitable allocation need not be efficient (Pareto optimal). One can imagine that tastes differ sufficiently so that one person would prefer more of good A and less of good B, while another person would prefer the reverse. Thus the equal-division allocation of resources may well be inefficient in the sense that a different—"unequal"—allocation of resources could make some people better off without reducing the welfare of anyone. In other words, relative to an equal division of resources, there may be many opportunities for "win-win" (Pareto improving) exchanges. This is one example of the trade-off between equity and efficiency mentioned in the introduction.

Fairness—equity *and* efficiency

Combining the concepts, an allocation that is *both* equitable (in the sense of being envy free) and efficient (in the sense of Pareto optimality) has been called "fair."

Interesting, though specialized, analytical results stem from these ideas. One of the most intriguing is an extension of the relationship between competition and efficiency mentioned above. Recall that the first fundamental theorem of welfare economics says that under specified conditions competition will lead to a Pareto-efficient allocation of resources. It turns out that if an economy starts from the equal-division allocation of resources—which we know is equitable (envy free)—then competitive forces will lead to a fair allocation—an allocation that is both efficient (Pareto optimal) and equitable.

The ideas described here, and their implications, developed in the economic literature of the 1970s and 1980s.[3] While the strand of literature continues, it is fair (no pun intended) to say that it has had little direct influence on public policy. Yet it is also the case that the strand treats the concepts of equity and fairness with a conceptual rigor for which economics has shown itself useful. Perhaps at some point this work will contribute to making economics a bit less dismal.

The Virtues of Inequality

The discussion above focused on specific definitions of equality and fairness. This section reverts to more standard usage of those terms. At this point these familiar understandings seem more relevant to public policy.

Those troubled by globalization often point to increases in income and wealth inequality. But they usually leave the reasons unstated. Perhaps the reasons are obvious. Certainly, as discussed in this volume (and above), issues of equality and fairness are related. Of more urgency, perhaps we fear that people will respond violently to inequality. Yet this need not happen. People could also respond to inequality in socially positive ways. Distinguishing among the environments in which inequality exists may prove decisive in determining whether we should worry about it.

Inequality concerns us when people are likely to respond negatively. At a mild level, feelings of unfairness and resentment in the face of inequality can lead to socially disruptive behavior. Productivity may suffer as people act from apathy, anger, or retaliation. Managers see this every day in work situations involving disgruntled employees who feel they have been treated unfairly or inequitably—that is, who perceive that they face unjust inequality. At the extreme, income or wealth inequality can lead to revolution, as in France, Russia, or Cuba. Revolution can liberate, but it is destructive, and one would hope to find policies that address the underlying issues without such cataclysms.

When pushed, objections to inequality often refer to situations in which individuals feel trapped: they cannot do anything about their relative position. Such circumstances seem unfair. Henry George conceived of his land tax as a response to rising wealth inequality that appeared structural—a part of the social framework against which individuals felt powerless. The perception that you can do nothing to improve your position in life, that your life's opportunities were fixed at birth, creates anger, frustration, and desperation—emotions that can undermine society.

Yet where individuals can respond positively, inequality may lead to socially valuable behavior. Inequality often motivates people to act productively. Seeing someone with something you want can lead to a return to school, a search for a better job, or the start of a new business venture. In these cases inequality induces action that confers social benefits. Moreover, where positive action seems a plausible response to inequality, our measures of inequality may mislead us. Individuals at the bottom of the scale at one point in time may appear at a higher level at the next measurement date.

This observation carries policy implications. Public policy could address inequality by lowering the cost of positive responses relative to the cost of responding negatively. Examples might include making continuing education accessible, facilitating the search for employment, or easing entrepreneurial activity. In such an environment, these avenues of response may make more sense—and therefore become more common—than clubbing a wealthy capitalist or manning the barricades.

Even in cases where unequal wealth or income seems the result of luck, rather than merit, inequality may not be socially objectionable. Lotteries perceived as "fair" in the sense of open access and equal probabilities of winning do not cause people to take up arms. It is "natural lotteries" buttressed by undue influence in political and economic spheres that make people see red. Thus, again, the circumstances surrounding inequality are crucial.

In itself inequality is not objectionable. What matters is the context within which the world is unequal. This has everything to do with social structure, institutions, and public policy. It has everything to do with making sure that positive responses to inequality are more effective than negative responses. Perhaps we can make a virtue of necessity: the poor(er) may be always with us, but if the possibility of a better life is perceived as real, then differences in relative positions can prove healthy rather than destructive.

Globalization and States

At a number of points during the conference from which this book is derived, participants expressed concern about globalization's effects on the survival of states. These concerns beg the question of why we should care. If globalization works to the net benefit of people, should we be concerned if it also happens to undermine state authority? We might feel concern if globalization undermines state authority that helps individuals. The real issue seems to be whether individuals benefit more from the protective functions of the state or from the liberating features of globalization. I suspect this is an empirical issue to be resolved differently in different contexts.

Thomas Friedman's "golden straitjacket" describes one version of the dilemma that globalization poses to states.[4] In his view globalization requires countries to forego certain policies over which they previously enjoyed discretion so that their legal and economic environments become compatible with the needs of global trade. For example, nations that adopt high protective tariffs would find themselves giving up the benefits of trade, improving technology, and falling costs that come from other countries. Similarly, the economies of nations that protect traditional cultural practices, establish high labor standards, or protect valued environmental areas could be undermined by the competitive pressure from foreign firms not faced with those constraints. In other words, globalization presents countries with a trade-off between policy discretion and the promise of higher (by some measures) standards of living.

State Purpose

Individuals form groups and institutions—including governments—to achieve goals. Thus society might wish to ban child or prison labor even though it is in the interests of employers to oppose such bans. Or governments can help achieve the commonly shared goal of preserving valuable natural resources by adopting strict environmental controls.

Global competition can undermine these efforts. The ban on child or prison labor will threaten domestic industries in the face of products imported from other nations lacking such bans. Similarly, the products of countries that have not adopted similar controls may undercut strict environmental regulations.

Yet in the real world these issues often get resolved through the adoption of standards across countries. No one any longer views slavery as an ethical form of economic activity, and it is universally illegal (though not necessarily stamped out). Despite private incentives to ignore external costs, issues like global warming, eradication of species, and excessive harvesting of the Amazon rain forest succeed in reaching the international agenda.

The real issue is that globalization makes it more difficult for a country to adopt standards out of step with others. Some worry about a "race to the bottom" in standards. Yet this often does *not* happen. For example, the United States (sometimes a leader in establishing high standards) has faced criticism for its resistance to the Kyoto Protocol and its opposition to the International Criminal Court—two attempts to adopt international standards and procedures. The Kyoto Protocol has recently been adopted and the International Criminal Court is still very much alive.

States Can Hurt People

Unfortunately, some states seem primarily interested in promoting the welfare of only their "most influential" citizens. Examples include the prosperity of the Suharto family in Indonesia, protection of the *chaebols* in Korea, and so on. More generally, tariffs or quotas on trade, restrictive labor regulations, business entry requirements, discriminatory taxes, and so on, protect some local producers but harm larger groups of entrepreneurs and consumers. In these cases the state authority favors the few at the expense of the many. Richard Katz has argued that Japan's economic development between 1960 and 1990 involved favoring specific industries such as steel, automobiles, and agriculture at the expense of higher prices and lower standards of living for the Japanese people than might have been possible under alternative policies.[5]

Presuming the economic purpose of government is to help the general population achieve high standards of living, such cases of favoritism suggest the state has failed in this arena. It is hard to understand why we would want to protect such states from being opened and made more responsive to the majority of their people. Globalization forces may have that effect.

Globalization Can Hurt People

Of course, globalization can also trample individuals. Many call for international labor standards to address the negative fallout of globalization. As voiced by organized labor in developed countries, such demands may be self-serving. But few would argue with calls that something be done to prevent actual slavery in workplaces. The drive to lower costs and to increase profits through transnational activity can allow the unscrupulous to act in universally condemnable ways.

The process of globalization treats different people in different ways—creating losers as well as winners. Those already familiar with international trade and relatively free economic exchange will likely benefit. In contrast, low-productivity workers, those entrenched in their jobs, or people highly resistant to change will likely suffer from the effects of global competition. They simply are unable, or even unwilling, to adapt.

While people generally prefer the status quo, often the most effective responses to change take place at the individual level. Because individual situations and skills differ, it may be better for individuals to find ways to respond and adapt to global pressures. But change is uncomfortable. It requires thought and effort. It often requires bearing some personal costs. From a policy perspective, an important mitigation of globalization's negative effects may lie in making change easier and more comfortable for people.

But what about the victims of globalization who cannot change? A state that adopts policies to protect such people may find its work undermined as globalization breaks down social protections. Fortunately, responding to economic change is not unique to globalization, and we have plenty of experience with it. Standard economic prescriptions recognize better and worse ways to help people who have trouble adapting to changing environments. Positive responses can involve transfer programs mixed with education and training. Change is ubiquitous, however, and it may be necessary to accept that some people's living standards will fall if they fail to respond and adapt. Putting floors under such living standards, perhaps mixed with incentives to adapt, should play an important part in the public response to globalization.

Globalization's Promise

Yet for all those harmed, globalization can also expand the well-being of individuals. Globalization expands economic opportunities and improves people's standards of living by lowering the costs and raising the quality of goods and services. That most international trade takes place among developed nations suggests the force of this lesson. Moreover, the forces of globalization may work to ameliorate the problems created by states that fail in their function of advancing the welfare of their citizens. Political developments in Korea and China over the last two decades and in Taiwan and Indonesia in the last several years suggest that increasing transnational interactions (both economic and non-economic) work toward the improvement of people's lives in those countries. Global economic forces may induce self-interested public officials to treat their citizens better with an eye to gaining some of the economic benefits of the globalization process.

This discussion suggests that the ultimate goal of globalization and states is to advance the welfare of individual people. Concerns about states and globalization are ultimately concerns about their effects on people's well-being. Individuals do have interests in collaborating with one another to achieve shared goals. Pooling resources to provide for national defense is an age-old example. But not all goals or desires are shared. The potential benefits of globalization include rising income and wealth, improved standards of living, increased knowledge, and so on. The concern about globalization undermining the independence of countries is relevant only as it applies to individual welfare.

The state is not an end in itself. Nations, provinces, cities, and wards are all formal groupings of individuals presumably motivated by promoting their interests. If alternative means of promoting individual interests come along, then it may make sense to abandon a previously useful institution. For example, a variety of economic and political forces reduced the power of and the demand for guilds of skilled labor. While some might regret the passing of guilds, on balance their demise seems the result of having outlived their usefulness. The welfare of individuals—both workers and consumers—was better met in other ways.

States or Globalization?

Where there is a conflict between globalization and the independence of states, the real issue is where the net benefits for individuals lie. In some cases, independent national authority may be most effective in advancing individual welfare—as in monitoring unacceptable working conditions or in protecting people from financial fraud. In other cases, the forces of globalization may offer such large increases in standards of living that state-protective trade barriers or restrictions on foreign business activity should fall. The concern that globalization will undermine states really makes sense only as a shorthand for concern that the benefits to individuals of a well-functioning state may be sacrificed for the benefits to individuals of globalization—and that the net balance is negative. In this guise, the proposition comes down to an empirical issue, likely to be answered differently in different situations. The state, like the globalization phenomenon, can work for either good or ill with respect to people's welfare. See Dick Pratt's Further Thoughts, "The Contested Terrain of Outsourcing," below.

Conclusion

This chapter has ranged rather widely. But that seems consistent with this volume's themes. Economists sometimes feel like the (barely) tolerated party guest at such meetings. Some of us see our role as telling rude truths; others may see us as merely rude. Yet as I hope these discussions on fairness, equality, globalization, and the role of states suggests, the sometimes bizarre economic perspective on the world can offer thought-provoking insights. Perhaps that is why a few of us keep getting in the door.

FURTHER THOUGHTS
The Contested Terrain of Outsourcing
Dick Pratt

"OUTSOURCING" is the word used to refer to the process by which a product or service once done within a firm is done somewhere else. Until fairly recently a word unknown to most Americans, it has become an everyday part of our language.

Outsourcing first gained visibility in the United States as a domestic process in which a large producer would elect to use smaller, highly specialized firms to produce things it would be less cost effective to handle internally. The automobile industry provides a good model of this. The major producers obtained critical parts of their cars from firms with which they subcontracted.

In more recent times outsourcing moved from firms within a nation to firms in other countries. The motivation was of course cost savings, and the primary sources of these savings were cheaper wages, fewer health and safety rules, and lax environmental laws. Global outsourcing has turned what began as a trickle of unskilled work into a torrent. That torrent now carries much more than unskilled jobs from one place to another. India currently is the beneficiary of professional work that requires masters' and doctoral degrees. Americans who had felt they or their children would obtain secure, high-paying jobs if they achieved higher education now are uncertain. This uncertainty has done as much as anything to force Americans to think differently about globalization's effects.

Today the largest recipient of outsourcing from the United States is China. Consumers in the United States have come to expect that many of the products they buy from well-known American firms will carry a note informing them that although the product was created in the United States, it was produced in China. Despite being commonplace, it still can be a surprise, as when the small American flags that appeared everywhere to show national unity after 9/11 were found to be "Made in China."

In addition to being a torrent, outsourcing also has the quality of a set of dominoes. As the current recipients of outsourcing become prosperous, they also become more expensive relative to other places. In a globalized world, they fall as desirable production sites. In China today, for example, production is moving from the now more costly urban areas to the cheaper cities and towns in the interior. There is no reason to expect it won't later move to other countries.

Each fall of the domino, from internal outsourcing to cross-national outsourcing, from one global location to another that has become relatively less expensive, raises a basic concern in the places left behind. The concern is about the net effect, and it is this: will enough jobs be created to make up for those that are lost?

Most mainstream economists argue that this process reflects the market flexibility that is necessary to use resources efficiently and thereby to create the greatest aggregate wealth. They argue that in the long run there will be a net gain. Real people, of course, are confined to living their lives in the short run. The social and political, if not economic, question therefore is whether this domino process will create, in a short-enough run, sufficient jobs.

The public institution equivalent of private-sector outsourcing is most commonly referred to as privatization. Privatization means that a service once performed by a government agency is now delegated to a private firm. Trash collection, public transportation, and prisons are all examples in the American context. Some government agencies send their services to other jurisdictions, such as one state sending prisoners to another where there is more capacity.

The exporting of public-sector jobs abroad is a noteworthy recent development. Food stamps is an example. A state agency contracts with a private company to provide services to food-stamp clients, and that firm subcontracts with a foreign firm in order to reduce costs and increase profits. This practice raises some interesting issues for taxpayers and their elected representatives. On the one hand, costs are reduced, which might help to contain or reduce taxes. On the other hand, jobs funded directly by taxpayers are going abroad.

Privatization has been a contested process in most places because of three issues: the loss of government jobs that have better pay and benefit packages, questions about the areas where private firms in fact cannot be more cost efficient, and the likelihood that private companies will ignore due process or access and equity values and policies that are built into public organizations.

A new term has appeared to cover what once was referred to only as "privatization." Public Private Partnerships (PPPs) points to the complex relationships that have developed around certain kinds of services. A government agency (or agencies) still authorizes and funds the service, but it is provided through a network of private-for-profit and private-nonprofit entities. This might be the case, for example, in the area of drug prevention and treatment.

PPP networks raise a number of challenging, and interesting, issues. Are the relationships so complicated as to be more inflexible than the bureaucratic apparatus they replace? What new skills do public servants need to learn? What will be the political dynamics of the networks? How is public accountability maintained? Can the public purposes that created the network be maintained over time?

Notes

1. As a brief introduction, see Allan M. Feldman, "Welfare Economics," in *The New Palgrave, A Dictionary of Economics,* ed. John Eatwell, Murray Milgate, and Peter Newman (New York: The Stockton Press, 1987).

2. For a brief description and review of the early literature, see Hal R. Varian, "Fairness," in *The New Palgrave, A Dictionary of Economics,* ed. Eatwell, Milgate, and Newman.

3. The ideas reviewed here developed in at least two independent strands. Confusingly, different terminology for similar ideas has persisted. William J. Baumol developed these ideas in a book-length treatment, providing applications to policy issues. Baumol's preface amusingly recounts his "invention" of the "superfairness" theory, only to quickly discover the emerging literature in the area. See William J. Baumol, *Superfairness* (Cambridge, Mass.: MIT Press, 1986).

4. Thomas L. Friedman, *The Lexus and the Olive Tree* (New York: Anchor Books, 2000), 105.

5. Richard Katz, *Japan, The System That Soured: The Rise and Fall of the Japanese Economic Miracle* (Armonk, N.Y.: M. E. Sharpe, 1998), 102–106.

CHAPTER 6
Fairness and Globalization

JAMES ROSENAU

Order and fragmentation have always been integral features of world affairs, but due to technological developments that have shrunk time and distance, today they are considerably more interactive than ever before. The tempo of global life within and among countries has accelerated to the point where it is plausible to assert that each increment of order gives rise to an increment of fragmentation, and vice versa. So as to stress and capture the extent of this interaction, I have long argued that its centrality to the course of events justifies a special label, one that highlights the ways in which the tensions between order and fragmentation are inextricably linked to each other. My label for this linkage is "fragmegration," a term that derives in part from fragmentation and in part from integration and that has the virtue, despite its grating and contrived nature, of capturing in a single word these contrary tendencies and thus serving as a reminder of how closely they are interwoven. Indeed, I would argue that the best way to grasp global life today is to view it through fragmegrative lenses, to treat every circumstance and every process as an instance of fragmegrative dynamics.[1]

To appreciate the underpinnings of globalization, therefore, it is important to recognize that both order and fragmentation are loaded with values, that one person's order is another's disorder and that what is fragmentation for some is coherence for others. Both order and fragmentation, in other words, can be desirable or undesirable, depending on the value perspective through which they are assessed. Put more specifically, order can suggest group or societal arrangements that enhance fairness, allowing diverse groups to prosper and participate freely in how issues are handled; or it can connote a deadly stagnation and tyrannical hierarchy that denies justice and sustains unfairness for those encompassed by the issues. Likewise, fragmentation can highlight the breakdown of coherence and the onset of chaos; or it can point to a pluralism that affords opportunities for various groups to pursue their goals. Table 6.1 depicts four different societal conditions and political forms that may prevail when the value dimensions of

Table 6.1 Desirable and Undesirable Order and Fragmentation

	ORDER	FRAGMENTATION
Desirable	Centralized Democracy	Decentralized Pluralism
Undesirable	Tyranny	Chaos

order and fragmentation are taken into consideration. Viewed from the perspective of fairness, two of these conditions, centralized democracy and decentralized pluralism, have the potential of expanding the degree to which globalizing dynamics promote fairness for people, while the other two, tyranny and chaos, are likely to foster a wide range of inequities that deprive many of their material and spiritual needs.

It follows that while our inquiries into the equities and inequities inherent in globalization must in good part be founded on empirical assessments, they are equally rooted in our temperaments, our inclinations toward optimistic or pessimistic conceptions of the human condition. It is a mistake, I think, to resort to our professional training and treat questions about fairness as simply a matter of gathering data and sifting them for evidence. Inevitably our assessments are rooted in coherent values schemes or uncoordinated impressions as well as in systematic data and cogent analysis. In an intensely fragmegrative era, empirical materials cannot alone yield an adequate understanding of where globalization is taking humankind. Perforce we must engage in nuanced inquiry even as we acknowledge our underlying impulses and intuitive feelings. We must also recognize that all the sources from which globalizing processes spring can lead both to greater fairness and greater injustice.

Major Sources of Fragmegration

Implicit in the foregoing is a strategy of inquiry for assessing how fairness and justice may be affected as the fragmegrative epoch unfolds and becomes increasingly institutionalized. The strategy calls for clarity on the prime sources of fragmegration in the present era and an analysis of how these sources might be operative through micro-macro processes. Table 6.2 seeks to summarize these two analytic steps by listing in the rows eight major sources that underlie fragmegration throughout the world, while the columns encompass the micro, macro, micro-macro, and macro-macro levels of aggregation.[2] The entries in the cells of table 6.2 are crude and untested hypotheses intended to suggest how each source might shape attitudes or actions at each level. Inferentially they also point to ways in which fairness or unfairness may be affected at each level of aggregation.

Table 6.2 Eight Sources of Globalization at Four Levels of Aggregation

LEVELS OF AGGREGATION

SOURCES OF GLOBALIZATION	MICRO	MACRO	MICRO-MACRO	MACRO-MACRO
Microelectronic Technologies	Enable like-minded people to be in touch with each other anywhere in the world	Render collectivities more open, connected, and vulnerable; empower them to mobilize support	Constrain governments by enabling opposition groups to mobilize more effectively	Accelerate diplomatic processes; facilitate electronic surveillance and intelligence work
Skill Revolution	Expands people's horizons on a global scale; sensitizes them to the relevance of distant events; facilitates a reversion to local concerns	Enlarges the capacity of governmental agencies to think "out of the box," seize opportunities, and analyze challenges	Constrains policy making through increased capacity of individuals to know when, where, and how to engage in collective action	Multiplies quantity and enhances quality of links among stages; solidifies their alliances and enmities
Organizational Explosion	Facilitates multiple identities, subgroupism, and affiliation with transnational networks	Increases capacity of opposition groups to form and press for altered policies; divides publics from their elites	Contributes to the pluralism and dispersion of authority; heightens the probability of authority crises	Renders the global stage ever more transnational and dense with nongovernmental actors
Mobility Upheaval	Stimulates imaginations and provides more extensive contacts with foreign cultures; heightens salience of the outsider	Enlarges the size and relevance of *subcultures*, diasporas, and ethnic conflicts as people seek new opportunities abroad	Increases movement across borders that lessens capacity of governments to control national boundaries	Heightens need for international cooperation to control the flow of drugs, money, immigrants, and terrorists

Table 6.2 *continued*

LEVELS OF AGGREGATION

SOURCES OF GLOBALIZATION	MICRO	MACRO	MICRO-MACRO	MACRO-MACRO
Bifurcation of Global Structures	Adds to role conflicts, divides loyalties, and foments tensions among individuals; orients people toward local spheres of authority	Facilitates formation of new spheres of authority and consolidation of existing spheres in the multicentric world	Empowers transnational advocacy groups and special interests to pursue influence through diverse channels	Generates institutional arrangements for cooperation on major global issues such as trade, human rights, the environment, etc.
Weakening of Territoriality, States, and Sovereignty	Undermines traditions and national loyalties; increases distrust of governments and other institutions	Adds to the porosity of national boundaries and the difficulty of framing national policies	Lessens confidence in governments; renders nationwide consensuses difficult to achieve and maintain	Increases need for interstate cooperation on global issues; lessens control over cascading events
Authority Crises	Redirect loyalties; encourage individuals to replace traditional criteria of legitimacy with performance criteria	Weaken ability of both governments and other organizations to frame and implement policies	Facilitate the capacity of publics to press and/or paralyze their governments, the WTO, and other organizations	Enlarge the competence of some IGOs and NGOs; encourage diplomatic wariness in negotiations
Globalization of National Economies	Swells ranks of consumers; promotes uniform tastes; heightens concerns for jobs; widens gap between winners and losers	Complicates tasks of state governments vis-à-vis markets; promotes business alliances	Increases efforts to protect local cultures and industries; facilitates vigor of protest movements; polarizes communities	Intensifies trade and investment conflicts; generates incentives for building global financial institutions

Microelectronic technologies

While it is important to avoid deterministic interpretations of the surge of information technologies, they are surely central to the emergent epoch. They serve to undermine time and distance, thereby rendering developments that enhance or set back fairness anywhere as potentially integral features of life everywhere else in the world.

The data are stunning that depict the ways in which a variety of communications technologies (from the fax machine to the fiber optic cable, from the cellular phone to the orbiting satellite, from television to the Internet) continue to shrink the world and reduce the relevance of geographic boundaries. Today there are more than one billion telephones in active use throughout the world, and the number is just as great for mobile phones, of which there were less than a million in 1985.[3] In 1964 there was one TV set for every twenty persons, whereas in 1999 there was one for every four. More than two hundred functioning satellites orbit Earth, each capable of carrying tens of thousands of calls and numerous TV signals at once. The number of Internet hosts, or networked computers, grew more than sixfold between 1995 and 1999.[4] Stated even more dramatically, the number of computers linked to the Internet grew from two hundred in 1981 to more than fifty million in 1999.[5] More than 1.4 billion e-mail messages are estimated to cross national boundaries every day.[6] It is presumed that the Internet is growing by one million Web pages a day.[7] At the end of 2001 the number of persons online throughout the world was 505 million, of which roughly 43 percent used English, 32 percent used a European language, and 25 percent used an Asian language; by 2003 the number of persons online had grown to 793 million.[8] A historical perspective provides an even more impressive picture of the Internet's ubiquitous growth: it took the telephone forty years to reach its first ten million customers, the fax machine roughly twenty years, personal computers about ten years, and e-mail little more than one year.[9]

Quite possibly, moreover, these dynamics are poised for another step-level leap forward with the advent of new computer technologies, which include the prospect of a computer chip ten billion (repeat, ten billion) times faster than those available today.[10] Future generations might look back to the early twenty-first century and the widening scope of the Internet as the historical starting point for a new phase of modern globalization. As indicated by the hypotheses in the cells of table 6.2, it is not difficult to extrapolate from these data the conclusion that increasingly people have close encounters with foreign cultures through global networks.[11]

The skill revolution

Taken together, the several dimensions of the skill revolution are pivotal to all the other sources of fragmegrative dynamics noted below. The data descriptive of enlarged skills are hardly voluminous and many are anecdotal, but those that have been systematically collected all point in the same direction:[12] the skill revolution enables people to trace more readily the course of distant events back into their own homes, to know more precisely what they favor and oppose as situations unfold, to imagine more fully other cultures, to appreciate more explicitly the possibility that the identity and bases of their citizenship may be changing, to know more clearly the ways in which they may be treated unfairly, and to engage more effectively in collective action. Of course, the working knowledge of people has expanded at different rates, depending on the salience of their life experiences as well as the varying sources, amounts, and types of information and education they receive. To posit a worldwide skill revolution is not to say that everywhere people are becoming equally skillful, but it is a safe wager that the complexities of ever-greater numbers of urban communities are giving people a robust and ever-growing working knowledge of how the world works in the twenty-first century.

Citizen organizations

Hardly less so than the population explosion, recent years have witnessed a veritable explosion in the number of voluntary associations that have crowded onto the global stage. In all parts of the world and at every level of community, people (ordinary folk as well as elites and activists) are coming together to concert their efforts on behalf of shared needs and goals. (See James Rosenau's Further Thoughts, "Election Monitoring in Paraguay: A Personal Story of Globalization and Public Institutions," on page 72.) Exact statistics on the extent of this pattern do not exist (largely because so much of it occurs at local levels and goes unreported), but few would argue with the proposition that the pace at which new associations are formed and old ones enlarged is enormous, so much so that to call it an explosion is almost to understate the scale of growth.[13] It has been calculated, for example, that registered nonprofit organizations in the Philippines grew from 18,000 to 58,000 between 1989 and 1996; in Slovakia the figure went from a handful in the 1980s to more than 10,000 in 1999.[14] By one estimate, "there are now two million [nongovernmental organizations] in America alone. . . . In Russia, where almost none existed before the fall of the Soviet Union, there are at least 65,000. Dozens are created daily; in Kenya alone, some 240 NGOs are now created every year."[15]

The importance of networks can hardly be overstated.

The rise of network forms of organization (particularly "all channel networks," in which every node can communicate with every other node) is one of the single most important effects of the information revolution for all realms: political, economic, social, and military. It means that power is migrating to small, nonstate actors who can organize into sprawling networks more readily than can traditionally hierarchical nation-state actors. It means that conflicts will increasingly be waged by "networks," rather than by "hierarchies." It means that whoever masters the network form stands to gain major advantages in the new epoch.[16]

In sum, the proliferation of organizational networks contributes to bridging the gap between people at the micro level and their collectivities at the macro level. It offers a vast array of routes through which individuals can move into the political arena. It also serves to sustain the dynamics of de-territorialization and the spread of the skill revolution. If hierarchically structured states still dominated the course of events and were thereby able to contain and control the vibrant spread of horizontal networks, it is doubtful whether a new epoch would be emerging. For better or worse (and given the vitality of the drug trade and crime syndicates, sometimes it is for the worse) the ever-greater salience of organizational networks is serving to restructure the underpinnings of world affairs.

The mobility upheaval

The vastness of the mobility upheaval can be readily depicted. The movement of people has been so extensive that around 5 percent of the people alive today are estimated to be living in a country other than the one where they were born.[17] Indeed, every day one-half-million airline passengers cross national boundaries.[18] In 1997 a total of 220.7 million people (a 4.6 percent increase over the previous year) went abroad by airplane.[19] Even more stunning, it is estimated that by 2020, every year 1.56 billion tourists will be moving around the world, a figure more than double the roughly 668 million foreign tourists in 2000.[20]

Perhaps also indicative of the mobility upheaval is the pattern whereby "personal international calls have burgeoned, fed by immigrants talking to relatives or friends. The number of calls from the US to other countries in 1997 was 21 times that in 1980."[21] In 1965, on a worldwide basis, 75 million people were migrants from another country, whereas the figure for 1999 was 125 million.[22]

Despite the positive benefits that follow from people being exposed to greater economic opportunities, new cultural premises, and alternative lifestyles as they move around the world, the mobility upheaval can also foster negative consequences. The vast movement of people from the developing into the developed world has generated a backlash against "strangers" (i.e., migrants) and thereby precipitated a rise in immigration issues and a surge of unfair macro policies, not to mention right-wing politicians, to salience on political agendas in a number of countries. In short, while the distinction between the global and the local has been further obscured by the mobility upheaval, in some communities it has become increasingly salient.

The bifurcation of global structures

As the density of the global stage has increased with the proliferation of organizations, the structures of world politics have undergone a profound and pronounced bifurcation in which a multicentric macro world comprising a variety of nongovernmental, transnational, and subnational actors (from the multinational corporation to the ethnic groups, from the NGO to the social movement, from the advocacy network to the humanitarian organization, from the drug cartel to the terrorist group, from the local government to the regional association, and so on across a vast range of collective endeavors) has evolved to cooperate, compete, or otherwise interact with the state-centric world.[23] States may still be central to the course of events, but their international system is no longer as predominant as it once was. Now there are two worlds of world politics, a bifurcation that has heightened the relevance and intensity of fragmegrative dynamics.[24] These two worlds are still working out their respective domains as the emergent epoch unfolds. While in some instances the actors in the two worlds go their separate ways, most of the time they interact even as the boundaries separating them are maintained. Their interactions turned violent in Seattle in late 1999 and subsequent meetings of international financial institutions, but prior to that, starting in 1992 in Rio de Janeiro, they interacted peacefully. In effect, the bifurcation of global structures has become institutionalized and, as a result, contributes to the weakening of states (noted below) by creating spaces for the formation or consolidation of collectivities in the multicentric world and, thus, for the activation of individuals who have not previously had an outlet for their global or local orientations.

The weakening of territoriality, states, and sovereignty

Although some analysts insist states are as viable and competent as ever,[25] many (myself included) contend that they are in decline. For all its continuing authority and legitimacy, key dimensions of the power of modern states have undergone considerable diminution. In many states, for example, the assertions of monopoly over the use of force has been undermined by the emergence of private security forces that operate alongside, if they do not supercede, official police and military organizations. Put more generally, the ability of states to cope with the dynamics of change has lessened as the complexities and contradictions of fragmegration have become more pervasive. In the words of one analyst, "As wealth and power are increasingly generated by private transactions that take place across the borders of states rather than within them, it has become harder to sustain the image of states as the preeminent actors at the global level."[26]

In other words, while state institutions still have a modicum of authority and are not about to disappear from the global stage, their state-centric world is, as already noted, in continuous competition with collectivities in the multicentric world, an indication of the degree to which their capacity to exercise their authority has lessened. States cannot prevent ideas from moving across their borders. Many cannot control the flow of money, jobs, and production facilities in and out of their country. With few exceptions, they have only minimal control over the flow of people and negligible control over the flow of drugs or the drift of polluted air and water. At best they have difficulty controlling the flow of terrorists across their boundaries. In short, the obstacles to containing or redirecting transnational flows are considerable, and often states lack the will to exercise the full range of controls available to them.

To be sure, the United States' preemptive attack on Iraq following 9/11 demonstrated that its military power is unparalleled, but the subsequent insurgency against US forces made clear the extensive limitations on force as an instrument of state power. Just as the intensive nationalism and flag-waving diminished as memories of the 9/11 terrorist attacks faded, so did the appreciation grow that the superpowerdom of the United States is easily exaggerated. Yes, the United States successfully flexed its muscles by making it more difficult for foreigners to enter the country, but this lessened permeability of its borders hardly negates the presumption that the capabilities of the country have diminished.

Closely related to the weakened capabilities of states is a decline in their sovereignty, their ability to claim the final word at home or speak exclusively for the country abroad and, if necessary, to use force in support of their actions at home or abroad that is widely considered legitimate. Indeed, in some ways sovereignty claims have long been a major source of state capabilities. Strictly speaking, sovereignty is a legal fiction and not a capability, but as a legal fiction it accords legitimacy to states and is thus a source of their capacities.[27] Historically sovereignty was conceived in dichotomous terms—either states do or do not meet certain formal requirements such as having a specified territory and a functioning government. Although most states have not been able to exercise full sovereignty at all times, the myth of states as sovereign has long remained intact. But in the emergent epoch the new uncertainties and contradictions over where, when, and how states can exercise their sovereign rights under particular circumstances are posing serious challenges to this myth.

In all probability the erosion of sovereignty is also lessening the readiness of people to view their states as the object of their highest loyalty.[28] In the absence of threatening enemies, people in many parts of the world experience lessened concern about the preeminence of their state as their expanded skills and ties to a proliferating array of organizations enable them to evolve new commitments or otherwise reorganize their hierarchy of loyalties. In addition, national loyalties have been further undermined by the mobility upheaval that has spawned multicultural societies. Put differently, with the distinction between domestic and foreign affairs increasingly confounded, the sovereignty of states can seem increasingly peripheral.

Stated more generally, the long-term and worldwide process whereby authority is undergoing relocation in response to the skill revolution, the organizational explosion, and the mobility upheaval has hastened the decline and decentralization of national governments. In some instances this trend has resulted in vacuums of authority filled by criminal organizations or by uncertainties as to where the rule-making power lies, but more often than not local, provincial, or private authorities move into the vacuums and sustain the processes of governance.[29]

Authority crises

With people increasingly skillful, with states weakened, and with other types of organizations proliferating, governments everywhere are undergoing authority crises in which traditional conceptions of legitimacy are being replaced by performance criteria of legitimacy, thus fostering bureaucratic disarray, executive-legislative stalemate, and decisional paralysis that, in turn, enhances the readiness of individuals to employ their newly acquired skills on behalf of their perceived self-interests. Indeed, there is hardly a national government today that is not caught up in one or another form of crisis that severely restricts its capacity to frame innovative policies and move toward its goals. To view most states as deep in crisis, in other words, is not to have in mind only street riots and the violence that can accompany them; it is also to refer to cross-cutting conflicts that paralyze policy-making processes and result in stasis, in the avoidance of decisions that would at least address the challenges posed by a fragmegrative world undergoing vast and continuous changes.

Nor are these crises confined just to governments and states. The fragmenting tendencies are also operative within other institutions and organizations. Political parties are in disrepute in many parts of the world, with the long-standing dominant parties of Mexico and Japan having undergone major setbacks in recent years. Some churches have also experienced rifts that lessen their authority, and so, even more conspicuously, have the Mafia. Likewise, increasingly shareholders are challenging the decisions of corporate boards and, in a few cases, bringing about resignations and changes in their memberships. Given fragmegrative dynamics, it follows that some authority crises have enlarged the jurisdiction of intergovernmental organizations (IGOs) and NGOs, while others have contracted the range of national jurisdictions and extended that of local institutions.

The globalization of national economies

In contrast to the tendencies toward decentralization and subgroupism, the dynamics at work in the realm of economics are powerful sources of centralizing tendencies. A few states may be able to exercise their power to disrupt or divert these tendencies on occasion, but for the most part economic globalization in the last few decades has resulted in financiers, entrepreneurs, workers, and consumers now being deeply enmeshed in transnational networks that have superseded the traditional political jurisdictions of national scope. Such a transformation has served to loosen the ties of producers to their states and workers to their firms, to expand the horizons within which citizens ponder their self-interests, and to contribute to the proliferation of organizations that can operate on a global scale to protect and advance the economic interests of their members. The rapid growth and maturation of the multicentric world can in good part be traced to the extraordinary dynamism and expansion of the global economy. No less important, the global economy has also accentuated the identity of most people as consumers and, in so doing, possibly weakened their sense of affiliation with national communities.

Clearly, then, economic globalization is a key dynamic of fragmegration. Since it is virtually impossible for any national or local economy to be self-contained and independent of global economic processes, the lives of people everywhere are affected in one way or another by these processes. This intrusion may vary from community to community or from occupation to occupation, but no community and few occupations are immune to the global forces of supply and demand. Of course, the vulnerabilities of workers, business executives, and politicians to economic developments abroad are not new and have been observed in earlier centuries. In the past, however, neither the scale nor the pace of foreign economic consequences was nearly as great as is the case now that national economies are increasingly absorbed into the vast global market.

Conclusion

In sum, despite the value and empirical obstacles that inhibit cogent analysis, it seems clear that the prospects for fairness throughout the world are shaped by a number of powerful dynamics. No single set of reforms can reduce the injustices at work and increase the prevalence of fairness. Rather, it appears inescapable that bringing about movement toward greater fairness will require efforts at all levels of aggregation and in a vast number of institutions and issue areas. Stated even more pessimistically, the long-term future may consist of islands of desirable order and fragmentation surrounded by oceans of undesirable tyranny and chaos, with neither capable of encroaching on the other, a prolonged stalemate that is unlikely to yield to efforts to improve greatly the extent of fairness throughout the world.

FURTHER THOUGHTS

Election Monitoring in Paraguay

A Personal Story of Globalization and Public Institutions

James Rosenau

ASIDE FROM many relevant experiences in my teaching career of some five decades, I have had one encounter that lasted ten minutes but that nevertheless reflects the convergence of globalization, public institutions, and fairness. Indeed, it proved to be a classic instance of my long-held contention that the boundary between international and domestic affairs has become even more porous!

The encounter occurred at 5:20 p.m. on May 9, 1993, in Asuncion, Paraguay. I was a member of a team led by former president Jimmy Carter to monitor the first open election in Paraguay's history. We arrived a few days before the election and were immediately photographed for the purpose of giving us identification badges that certified we were official International Election Monitors.

On the day of the election, May 9, the members of the team were split up and given a variety of monitoring tasks around the country. My unit's assignments were in Asuncion and included being present at a school at 5:00 p.m. to observe the opening of the balloting boxes and the counting of the ballots. But our driver got lost, and we did not get to the school until 5:20 p.m. The gate to the school had been closed and was under the guard of a large soldier with a gun dangling from his hip. With some trepidation I approached the gate and waved the ID badge hanging from my shirt pocket at the guard. He squinted at the card and then swung the gate open, at which point I crossed the boundary between international and domestic jurisdictions and entered the school.

It was an experience that has always lingered and was reinforced by the thought that here was globalization at its best in the sense that it compelled an authoritarian regime to accept external election monitors. Moreover, the monitoring process was administered by a public institution, namely the Organization of American States (OAS), as well as the Carter Center and numerous other transnational NGOs. No less important, it was an expression of fairness in the sense that it involved people who had never previously voted in an open election. They patiently stood in the very hot sun for hours to vote. It was obviously an important moment for them even though the polling places were not air conditioned. But the hot sun was hardly a negative dimension of this exhilarating and beneficial experience. It was not even a trade-off: no one has said that fairness has to occur under tolerable weather condition.

Notes

1. For an elaboration of the concept of fragmegration, see James N. Rosenau, *Along the Domestic-Foreign Frontier: Exploring Governance in a Turbulent World* (Cambridge: Cambridge University Press, 1997), chap. 6.

2. Both the contents of table 6.2 and parts of the ensuing discussion of the eight sources of fragmegration are adapted from James N. Rosenau, *Distant Proximities: Dynamics beyond Globalization* (Princeton, N.J.: Princeton University Press, 2003), chap. 3.

3. Jan Aart Scholte, *Globalization: A Critical Introduction* (New York: St. Martin's Press, 2000), 75.

4. These data are from the National Geographic Society, *Millennium in Maps: Cultures* (Washington, DC, June 1999).

5. Scholte, *Globalization,* 75.

6. Office of the Press Secretary, "Remarks by President Clinton at University of Chicago Convocation Ceremonies," available from www.whitehouse.gov/WH/New/html/19990612.html (June 12, 1999), 2.

7. Ibid., 1.

8. Available from www.glreach.com/globstats/index.php3.

9. *The New Yorker,* December 6, 1999, 96.

10. John Markoff, "Tiniest Circuits Hold Prospect of Explosive Computer Speeds," *New York Times,* July 16, 1999, A1. See also Kenneth Chang, "I.B.M. Creates A Tiny Circuit Out of Carbon," *New York Times,* August 27, 2001, 1.

11. To be sure, the benefits of the information revolution have been enjoyed by only a small proportion of the world's population, thus resulting in a huge gap between those who are rich and poor with respect to their access to information. However, there are reasons to anticipate that the gap will slowly narrow with the passage of time. New technologies will enable poorer countries to leapfrog some of the communications stages experienced by more advanced societies. To cite but one example, in 1999 China had nine million Internet addresses, and in 2000 the figure had grown roughly to twenty million. See William Jefferson Clinton, "China's Opportunities, And Ours," *New York Times,* September 24, 2000, section 4, 15.

12. See, e.g., Ulric Neisser, ed., *The Rising Curve: Long-Term Gains in IQ and Related Measures* (Washington, DC: American Psychological Association, 1998); James R. Flynn, "Searching for Justice: The Discovery of IQ Gains Over Time," *American Psychologist* 54 (January 1999): 5–20; William T. Dickens and James R. Flynn, "Heritability Estimates versus Large Environmental Effects: The IQ Paradox Resolved," *Psychological Review* 108.2 (2001): 346–369; and James N. Rosenau and W. Michael Fagen, "Increasingly Skillful Citizens: A New Dynamism in World Politics?" *International Studies Quarterly* 41 (December 1997): 655–686.

13. For a counter-argument with data interpreted as tracing a decline in organizational life in the United States, see Robert D. Putnam, *Bowling Alone: The Collapse and Revival of American Community* (New York: Simon & Schuster, 2000).

14. David Bornstein, "A Force Now in the World, Citizens Flex Social Muscle," *New York Times,* July 10, 1999, B7.

15. "Sins of the Secular Missionaries," *The Economist,* January 29, 2000, 25–28.

16. John Arquilla and David Ronfeldt, "A New Epoch—and Spectrum—of Conflict," in *In Athena's Camp: Preparing for Conflict in the Information Age,* ed. J. Arquilla and D. Ronfeldt (Santa Monica, Calif.: RAND, 1997), 5.

17. Shashi Tharoor, "The Future of Civil Conflict," *World Policy Journal* 16 (Spring 1999): 7.

18. Office of the Press Secretary, "Remarks by President Clinton," 2.

19. National Geographic Society, *Millennium in Maps.*

20. "Boom in World Tourism Called Threat to Culture and Ecology," *International Herald Tribune,* July 12, 2000, 2.

21. National Geographic Society, *Millennium in Maps.*

22. "Now You Can Have 5,999,999,999 Friends," *New York Times,* September 19, 1999, section 4, 4.

23. Given the diversity and multiplicity of collectivities in the multicentric world, it would be logical to describe the emergent structure as an n-furcation rather than a bifurcation (with the "n" representing any number). However, I continue to use the bifurcation label in order not to unduly downplay the importance of the state-centric world.

24. For an extended discussion of the bifurcation of global structures, see James N. Rosenau, *Turbulence in World Politics: A Theory of Change and Continuity* (Princeton, N.J.: Princeton University Press, 1990), chap. 10.

25. See, e.g., G. John Ikenberry, "The Myth of Post-Cold War Chaos," *Foreign Affairs* 75 (May/June 1996): 79–91.

26. Peter Evans, "The Eclipse of the State? Reflections on Stateness in an Era of Globalization," *World Politics* 50.1 (1997): 65.

27. An extensive elaboration of this perspective can be found in Stephen D. Krasner, *Sovereignty: Organized Hypocrisy* (Princeton, N.J.: Princeton University Press, 1999).

28. Discussions of this assessment can be found in Joshua Cohen, *For Love of Country: Debating the Limits of Patriotism* (Boston: Beacon Press, 1996); and Samuel P. Huntington, *Who Are We? The Challenges of America's National Identity* (New York: Simon & Schuster, 2004).

29. These processes of proliferating spheres of authority are probed at length in Rosenau, *Distant Proximities,* chap. 13.

CHAPTER 7

A Critique of Globalization
Not Just a White Man's World

IVANA MILOJEVIC

I believe that the globalization debate is a gendered discussion about directions for the future rather then merely being an objective and impartial description of "how things are." This is because globalization has been promoted with a particular future vision in mind. It has been assumed that certain actions in the present are necessary in order to adjust to an already given (globalized) future. This given future has been described in terms of economic and technological determinism; it is an image of an economically developed global society in which everybody benefits, eventually.

However, in the meantime it is commonly understood that a globalized future is following a particular trajectory: mostly in terms of the future becoming (even) more competitive, challenging, and basically insecure. In this future world there is little space for alternative ways of living and doing things, given the victory of economic globalization. Not only is globalization understood and described mostly in terms of this economic dimension, but the discourse on globalization also presents capitalism as an irresistible force. Implicit in this future is that globalization continues to be influenced mostly from "above," by multinationals and states. Also, the world is populated by the global consumer within a social order that is profit oriented, focused on "wants" and the instant satisfaction of needs. To fulfill these wants there are ever-increasing material products and material choices.

With all the discussion about the need to acknowledge human, social, and cultural differences, there is no assumption that indigenous, other nonwestern, or women's ways of knowing and perspectives are recognized within this global future. Rather, a certain kind of intellectual development remains paramount, and only certain so-called "rational" aspects of knowledge are valued. As argued by Scholte, "Most knowledge that has circulated in global spaces to date has continued to exhibit the core rationalist attributes of secularism, anthropocentrism, scientism and instrumentalism. To this extent, contemporary globalization has tended to spread and strengthen the position of modern rationality."[1]

This version of the future (the globalized world) has now become hegemonic, representing "the truth" about the future. It is rarely questioned; rather, it is used as a guiding image of inevitable trends that inform policies and actions in organizations and institutions across the board.

Another reason I argue that the debate on globalization is also a discussion about the direction of the future is because while the processes of globalization have a very long history, the "globalization hypothesis" is more recent. Most important, the globalization hypothesis has become distinctively different during the last few decades, coinciding with a period in western history that can be characterized by a void of visions of socioeconomic futures. As narratives on progress and development were weakened by postmodern, postcolonial, and feminist discourses, the space opened and the need arose for another guiding image of the future to appear. As the "Left" proclaimed the end of utopia, refusing to develop another master narrative, this new guiding image of the future (of a globalized world understood in a particular way) developed from within a neoliberal perspective. This can perhaps help explain why globalization is "not normally linked to" multiculturalism, or issues of global social sustainability[2]—or, indeed, given all the discussion about a global "knowledge economy" or a global "learning society," why globalization is not normally linked to demands for *increased* funds for education.

While globalization processes themselves open up spaces for the assertion of a multitude of perspectives and positions, the globalization hypothesis and the previously described hegemonic/guiding image of a globalized world remain firmly locked within western and patriarchal intellectual history. The image of a globalized future as it is understood today has not emerged out of intercivilizational dialogues or from multiple temporal frameworks. Rather, it is associated with the expansionist drives of hegemonic powers that have imposed their own approach to time (globalized, linearly compressed) and the vision of the future to geographically, culturally, developmentally, and temporally different societies.

Geography of Globalization Hypothesis

Of course, as postmodernists remind us, every reality has an author.[3] The same is true of futures visions. The current globalization hypothesis has not emerged from an epistemologically and politically neutral place. Rather, it has a history and geography.[4] While debates abound about the history and the nature of globalization (mostly meaning discussions about various globalization processes), the globalization hypothesis can be more easily located both geographically and historically. Geographically, the globalization hypothesis originated in western societies, the vast majority of its theorists being American or western European male academics. That is, globalization has been predominately theorized from the western spatial location as well as from the perspective of male embodiment. This means that, so far, globalization has itself "been analyzed from a very un-global perspective."[5] The absence of gender and nonwestern perspectives in the theories of globalization often means an inappropriate universalization of particular experiences. For example, globalization understood as the "shrinking of time and space" is possible only if one has access to financial, political, and technological resources that make some old boundaries disappear.

At the same time, mostly because of the environmental and social effects that result from economic "developmental" policies, a large number of the world's women are forced to spend more time and cover larger territory (looking for food, fuel, or jobs) in order to satisfy basic household needs. It could be argued, then, that at least for these groups of people space has not shrunk but become more vast. Similarly, while there is a focus on the "unification" of our world in western theories of globalization, conflicts in the developing world violently diversify people (nationalize, reify ethnicity, religion, and tribe). As well, the "global networked society" is theorized in the world where access to the information superhighway is still a privilege denied to many. In a similar fashion, the "global post-scarcity" society is seen to be emerging while each year millions of people die of hunger and poverty-related illnesses.

History of Globalization Hypothesis

While globalization is seen as a new phase of development in the west, many disadvantaged social groups may, in fact, experience it as a continuation (and further enhancement at the global level) of processes such as colonization, imperialism, and patriarchy. One's own positioning and worldview, therefore, determine how globalization is experienced and seen. It also partly determines whether "globalization" itself would be seen as an issue.

Historically, the globalization hypothesis has coincided with the coming of the Christian millennium, emerging in the 1980s and increasing in influence during the last decade of the twentieth century. It has helped name more concretely the vaguely described "New World Order." It has also helped replace more problematic terms such as "monopoly capital" or "world capitalism," conveniently neutralizing anti-capitalist rhetoric. The globalized future has therefore not come to represent the victory of "the Right" in the historical ideological battle with "the Left." More conveniently, it has come to represent a whole new system with a whole new set of rules that can potentially benefit all humanity. While, arguably, this may be the case, this globalized future can clearly be identified as a new phase within western and patriarchal understanding of time and social change. As Cvetkovich and Kellner write,

> In many mainstream social theories, the discourse of the global is bound up with ideological discourses of modernization and modernity, and from Saint-Simon and Marx through Habermas and Parsons, globalization and moderniza-tion are interpreted in terms of progress, novelty and innovation, and a generally beneficial negation of the old, the traditional, and the obsolete. In this discourse of modernization, the global is presented as a progressive modernizing force; the local stands for backwardness, superstition, underdevelopment, and the oppres-siveness of tradition.[6]

The "Global Age" has therefore come to represent a new, emerging order, in line with similar theorizing that puts an emphasis on slightly different phenomena (e.g., "postindustrial," "postmodern," "information," or "knowledge society"). As previously discussed, this periodization arises from within the western timeline and a particular western understanding of time, progress, and development.

Globalized Utopia, Dystopia, and Eutopia

Various utopian, eutopian, and dystopian narratives underline many of the de-bates and discussions on globalization.[7] This further illustrates my point that the discourse on globalization is in essence a debate on the trajectory of the fu-ture. According to the utopian and eutopian versions, globalization will lead to an "irreversible shift of power away from the developed countries to the rest of the world . . . delivering billions of people from poverty, creating opportunities for choice and personal development, and reinforcing democracy all round the world."[8] In sum, the liberal market economy, by its very nature being global, is also "the summit of human endeavour."[9]

Other expected positive developments that are mentioned most often include the shift toward the understanding of human differences within a unified view of humanity; increased ecological consciousness; higher cultural interchange; more consumer and employment choices; and the opening up of the possibilities in travel, communication, and business.

The dystopian version, on the other hand, most commonly mentions the widening gap between the rich and poor globally and within nation states; fur-ther environmental degradation; and the continuation of cultural colonization. These and other perceived negative effects of globalization are nicely summa-rized in the following paragraph.

Among these [negative effects of globalization] are the obliteration of local cultures, the demise of nation-states, the erosion of cultural identity and tradition, the loss of sense of place and home, the technologizing of everyday life and concomitant compression of space and time and loss of "authentic" communications, a global sameness of desired and consumption patterns, and a dramatic blowout of social inequalities and unequal capital accumulations.[10]

Of course, because the processes of globalization are "deeply asymmetric,"[11] "dialectical,"[12] and "disjunctive,"[13] it is impossible to determine whether consequences of globalization are mostly good or bad. There is even disagreement on whether the prevailing discourse on globalization is "rather optimistic"[14] or mostly about "unmediated negative effects."[15] In addition, the same trends and visions are to be seen in both a positive and negative light, depending on one's own positioning, embodiment, and/or worldview. However, the above-mentioned utopian, eutopian, and dystopian narratives are, in general, presented as universally agreed upon. This, too, is a part of "globalization," the development of what is assumed to be a universally shared globalization discourse.

Moving Away from the Nation-State as the Default Unit of Analysis

Another universally shared discourse, connected to and preceding the globalization hypothesis, is that of the nation-state. And while the globalization hypothesis asserts that globalization is, in general, weakening the power and relevance of the nation-state (or alternatively creating the need to respond with reactive policies toward strengthening national boundaries), the nation-state remains a core unit of analysis that is used to "describe reality." Of course, the nation-state is only one important level within a much broader system. As Henderson says in *Beyond Globalization,* other levels include the global ("human societies beyond the borders of nations and their planetary ecosystem effects"), the international, the corporate, the provincial and local, civil society, and the family individual.[16]

Thus if we are to move to a world that is significantly better than the old "world order," then our units of analysis may need to change as well. The nation-state as the default unit of analysis made some sense before the introduction of such players as nongovernmental organizations (NGOs) and the environment. Many studies have shown that the nation-state is simultaneously "too big and too small" to coordinate effective responses that address urgent social problems and issues.[17] The sovereignty of nation-states needs to be balanced by subnational and supranational entities by both local communities and the world as a whole.

If we do this we might be able to reconcile diverse elements within the anti-globalization movement expressed by right-wing parties on the one hand and environmentalists on the other. In the case of the latter, the environmental crisis can be addressed successfully only if we step away from "nation-state sovereignty" as the dominant worldview. From an ecological perspective, as opposed to the current anthropocentric and statist one, the sovereignty of Earth not only precedes but also supersedes all human sovereignties.[18] This is but one example of why the nation-state cannot remain the default unit of analysis and consequently the main player when addressing numerous global problems and imbalances. See Sohail Inayatullah's Further Thoughts, "The Triple Bottom Line, Plus One: Economic Prosperity, Environmental Sustainability, and Social Justice for Future and Present Generations," on page 84.

Globalization scenarios: Globotech versus Ecarmony

While commenting on the meanings of "globalization" above, I suggested that globalization can be seen as a contest between two contrasting images of the future. These two scenarios can perhaps best be termed as Globotech, representing a hegemonic futures vision, and Ecarmony, representing the main emerging alternative. Of course, these two scenarios represent two "ideal models" or two main tendencies and political choices for the future and are, ultimately, deducted from the multifaceted reality with all its complexities, "hybridities," and "heterogeneities." The main characteristics of a Globotech scenario are as follows:

1. "Business as usual" continues.
2. The world is populated by the global consumer.
3. Social order is profit oriented, focused on "wants" and the instant satisfaction of needs and with ever-increasing material choices.
4. Free flow of capital is not accompanied by the free flow of people.
5. Welfare policies are implemented mostly to ward off political upheavals.
6. Poverty remains higher among women, racial and ethnic minorities, and other marginalized social groups.
7. The positive impacts of new technologies include flexibility of work, increase in communication across the world, increased human longevity, wiping out of certain genetically inherited diseases, and higher security in some areas (though provided by global monitoring and surveillance).
8. There is an increased interaction between humans, machines, and artificial intelligence.
9. The main growth industry is space exploration and excavation.
10. In general, global society is arranged hierarchically; the exploitation of the underprivileged is not direct but structural.
11. Globotech societies continue to admire individualism, competition, success, breaking the boundaries of the physical world, appearance, youth, abundance, and excess.

12. Multiculturalism is tokenistic (to satisfy demands for inclusion) and pragmatic (to stimulate penetration of foreign markets).
13. Gender and family relationships are slightly changed; the nuclear family is still seen as the most desirable family form because it is best at fostering individualism. But among the wealthy, parenting and other social functions that the family used to satisfy are increasingly being outsourced.
14. Among the elites and the wealthy, population is controlled in terms of "quality" (search for perfection), while among poor populations it is controlled in terms of "quantity."
15. Ethical issues are discussed mostly within organized religions, but these discussions are rarely followed in the "real world," where "anything goes." Science and technology are given the privilege of being amoral and are still considered objective and value-free human endeavors.

As I previously argued, states and multinationals mostly pushed this scenario from above, and it remains firmly rooted in patriarchy. At the same time, various social groups, including numerous women's movements, push globalization in a different direction, toward the Ecarmony model. The main characteristics of this model are as follows:

1. It requires global (cultural, epistemic) transformation.
2. The push comes from social movements in western post-scarcity societies and is mobilized around issues of purpose, identity, higher goals, and meanings. Another push comes from the "majority world" as well, but here it is facilitated out of necessity.
3. The eutopian "one world" is imagined as a guiding principle for human unity. The desire for belonging to one unified world is facilitated by huge demographic changes.
4. Ecarmony attempts to develop expansive multiculturalism, based on the need to learn so that persons or groups can prosper, as well as on the desire to push the boundaries of the known.
5. Economic development is seen as important but defined in broader terms. Indicators of economic progress are connected with long-term indicators of continuation/sustainability and horizontal indicators of stress/indicators for quality of life.
6. The main values in Ecarmony are justice, equity, fairness, peace, inner and outer transformation, security, long-term view. While the main principle leading societies was previously that of expansion, in Ecarmony conservation and sustainability are the new norm.
7. Education is given priority because of the view that without awareness of social and natural processes, interpersonal and group relationships, as well

as the psychological and physiological processes within the self, humanity cannot prosper. Vast resources are invested in conflict prevention and resolution, as peace is seen as the prerequisite for progress.

8. The main organizational principle is a network, which is facilitated with the development of new information and communication technologies.

9. The main weakness is potentially too much focus on the distribution of wealth, which can then jeopardize the creation of wealth that is to be distributed. Also, inner development and transformation and focus on emotional and spiritual aspects do not always sit well with issues such as efficiency, punctuality, completion of (if perceived to be boring and irrelevant) mundane tasks, and so on.

The drivers for both scenarios are currently present, both in the form of the push toward the future (demographics, environmental issues, new information and communication technologies) as well as in the form of the pull toward the future (desired image/vision). However, proponents of the Globotech scenario are better equipped in finances, time, and energy resources. In addition, this scenario is also better supported by historical social structures such as capitalism and patriarchy. However, visions from within numerous women's and feminist movements, expressed in both feminine ontologies and epistemologies (visions, ideas, theories) as well as in feminine political activities, clearly prefer the other model.

The negative effects of the current economic globalization on women

There are many women who do and will continue to benefit from changes attributed to globalization. Demands for women's rights might be secured at home by appealing successfully to global standards, for example. However, most studies that focus on gender and globalization show that women in both Second- and Third-World societies provide, and are expected to provide, services that buffer the negative aspects of economic restructuring caused by the extension of global capitalism.[19] These studies also show that benefits that may result from national economic restructuring, such as more job opportunities and higher consumer choices, are usually reserved for younger and educated professional women. On the other hand, it is the most vulnerable women who suffer from existing inequalities and insecurities that are intensified by globalization.

Even when individual women do benefit from economic globalization, this happens in an environment that is increasingly hierarchical, unequal, and insecure. This is contradictory to certain visions developed from within feminist or other women's movements[20] or from visions developed by certain women futurists[21] as well, from implicitly and explicitly desired visions/alternative worlds that exist in feminist utopian and science fiction.[22]

Of course, globalization has many faces and is composed of many various processes. In addition to globalization governed from "above" predominately influenced by multinationals and states, there are also global forces that challenge this dominant futures vision and actively create alternatives. Here lies the potential for development of different visions and forms of globalization.

Currently there are two main scenarios for the future of globalization: one is a hegemonic vision of a competitive global society; the other is an alternative vision of a cooperative global society. Not surprisingly, perhaps because of certain individual and social capacities,[23] women play much more prominent roles in the development of alternative visions of a globalized world.

Unfortunately, the future has already been colonized with ideas and images that stem from the Globotech scenario, that is, being naturalized as "the truth" about the future. The Ecarmony model, on the other hand, is seen as optional, possibly naive and utopian (defined as unrealistic and unfeasible). As a group, women may be gaining ground through some spaces that are being opened by globalization (e.g., the increase in the influence of NGOs).

However, this process is still a long haul ahead. For the global world to be more "women friendly," much more is required, nothing short of global transformation toward societies focused on life maintenance rather than life destruction. While globalization is currently understood and governed in terms of a neo-Darwinian paradigm (e.g., survival of the fittest, competition, expansion), globalization can also be understood and governed in terms of a Gaian paradigm (e.g., creation of a more socially, economically, and ecologically sustainable global society). Certainly, this latter vision would be closer to feminine "ways of knowing and politics of doing."

Of course, reality is always more complex than what can be expressed, summarized, and categorized within even the wide range of scenarios, let alone only two. Still, despite all the claims and desires to the contrary (e.g., by postmodernists), our era is characterized by the emergence of two main meta-narratives or, alternatively, two main utopian visions that currently inform and express globalization discourse. Interestingly, both stem from western European history as two basic narratives about the relationship between "men" and "nature."[24] One is the several-centuries-old myth of "The Land of Cockaygne," the land of milk and honey, the "golden age" where nature provides abundant resources and the magic bowl of porridge never empties. This is the land of unlimited consumption, limitless choices, and ever-increasing growth and progress.

In European history, the Land of Cockaygne was especially popular during the Middle Ages amongst lower classes who sought to relieve the drudgery of their everyday lives "through the pure satisfaction of sensual pleasure."[25] The current version, of course, is consumer-based global capitalism where new wealth and products are constantly being created, both through technological and economic innovations as well as through the colonization of nature, lands, peoples, and space.

Another myth is that of Arcadia, where nature is bountiful but humans do not indulge themselves beyond their needs.[26] It is the idea and the image about the harmony between humanity and nature, rather than the image of domination and control of nature by humanity, to produce society and civilization. Arcadia originated in ancient Greece and was revived by Renaissance humanists who were "seeking to restrain the selfish tendencies of the rich and powerful classes."[27] Its modern versions are today's ecological, New Age, and anti-globalization movements.

Perhaps, as we move toward a "truly global society," we may witness the emergence of different futures visions and meta-narratives, those based on different epistemologies and different civilizational and cultural frameworks. And it will be then, perhaps, that real spaces for imagining alternative futures, including those based on feminist/feminine epistemologies, will also emerge.

Further Thoughts

The Triple Bottom Line, Plus One

Economic Prosperity, Environmental Sustainability, and Social Justice for Future and Present Generations

Sohail Inayatullah

WHILE MANY BELIEVE that globalization must be totally transformed (seeking a post-capitalist vision of the future), others work for achieving fairness within the system. Among those imagining within-system change is the Triple Bottom Line movement. The term comes from a book by John Elkington, *Cannibals with Forks*. The "three bottom lines" of socially committed enterprises are economic prosperity, environmental quality, and social justice.

This is a vision of an alternative value system that can be counted in a world where counting matters (and where things that are not counted do not count!). Nations, states, and local communities can measure the second and third bottom lines just as they do the first. Royal Dutch Shell buys advertising space to say that its strategies are based on the triple bottom line of people, planet, and profits, while the United Nations calls for policies and practices that focus on people, planet, and prosperity.

Profits/prosperity have always been the first bottom line, and capitalism will insist that it be so. But can people and the planet be brought into the equation? "People" refers to notions of fairness and social justice. For companies at one level, this means that minorities should be hired. Is there gendered and multicultural representation at all levels of the workforce? But once the boardroom has more women and people of color, then the issue becomes not just representation by number (which can be counted), but fair representation of different ways of knowing. Are the ways diverse cultures see and live in the world represented in policy and practice? Are holidays and cultural fairs only those of the majority culture, or are those of other communities fairly celebrated? While this may appear only a social justice issue, corporations are beginning to see that this leads to prosperity as well. Multiculturalism is good for the first bottom line.

Taking care of the planet may be good for business, too, if more and more shoppers and investors begin to purchase with their values. Corporations that are seen not to be "Green" will be punished, slowly but surely. And over time if more business operations become transparent and individuals have fuller information on products, consumer decisions may favor those companies that help the planet.

Alan Weinberg, an Australian futurist, has begun writing about the "Quadruple Bottom Line." This fourth bottom line is the future, or better, future generations. While environment and sustainability often are assumed to include concern for the future, Weinberg shows that the future needs to be a separate category. And this, too, can be measured to some extent. How will current financial, zoning, consumption, and production decisions impact future generations? The future cannot be left out of our most serious business and policy equations. It must be part of our ethics and practices, of how we live in communities and, indeed, on the planet.

The Quadruple Bottom Line provides a vehicle to test if organizations, businesses, and nations are moving toward a future that is sustainable, multicultural (including gender partnership), prosperous, and respectful of the needs and desires of future generations.

Notes

1. Jan Aart Scholte, *Globalization: A Critical Introduction* (New York: St. Martin's Press, 2000), 185.

2. S. Davies and N. Guppy, "Globalization and Educational Reforms in Anglo-American Democracies," *Comparative Education Review* 41.4 (1997): 440.

3. E.g., D. Haraway, *Simians, Cyborgs, and Women: The Reinvention of Nature* (New York : Routledge, 1991).

4. R. Edwards and R. Usher, *Globalisation and Pedagogy: Space, Place and Identity* (London: Routledge, 2000), 15.

5. Doreen Massey, *Space, Place and Gender* (Minneapolis: University of Minnesota Press, 1994), 166.

6. Ibid., 13–14.

7. Strictly speaking, "utopia" means "no place" and should be used only to describe "perfect" societies, impossible to achieve, standing in challenging contrast to the reality of all existing societies. "Eutopia" (meaning "good place") should thus be used to describe "the best possible real world"—not perfect, but the best imaginable and achievable. What is "utopian" and what is "eutopian" is obviously very debatable! "Dystopia" is a "bad place" (the frightening futures shown, e.g., in many movies and works of science fiction, warning us of the dark side of humanity's schemes and dreams, and especially technology).

8. Peter Martin, "The Moral Case for Globalization," In *The Globalization Reader,* ed. F. Lechner and J. Boli (Malsden, Mass.: Blackwell Publishers, 2000), 12–14.

9. Ibid.

10. Carmen Luke, *Globalization and Women in Academia: North/West South/East* (Mahwah, N.J.: Lawrence Erlbaum Associates, 2001).

11. M. Castells, *The Rise of the Network Society: The Information Age, Economy, Society, and Culture,* vol. 1. (Malden, Mass.: Blackwell Publishers, 1996).

12. A. Cvetkovich and D. Kellner, *Articulating the Global and the Local* (Boulder, Co.: Westview Press, 1997), 2.

13. Arjun Appadurai, *Modernity at Large: Cultural Dimensions of Globalization* (Minneapolis: University of Minnesota Press, 1996).

14. N. Stromquist and K. Monkman. *Education: Integration and Contestation Across Cultures* (Lanham, Md.: Rowman & Littlefield Publishers, Inc., 2000), 19.

15. Luke, *Globalization and Women in Academia,* 48.

16. Hazel Henderson, *Beyond Globalization: Shaping a Sustainable Global Economy* (West Hartford, Conn.: Kumarian Press, 1999), 23.

17. S. Burchill and A. Linklater, *Theories of International Relations* (New York: St. Martin's Press, 1996).

18. Patricia Mische, "Ecological Security and the Need to Reconceptualize Sovereignty," *Alternatives* 14 (1989): 389–427.

19. E.g., H. Afshar and S. Barrientoes, eds., *Women, Globalization and Fragmentation in the Developing World* (London: Macmillan, 1999); N. S. Heyzer, S. Kapoor, and J. Sandler, eds., *A Commitment to the World's Women* (New York: UNIFEM, 1995); United Nations, *1999 World Survey on the Role of Women in Development: Globalization, Gender and Work* (New York: United Nations, 1999); and UNIFEM, *Progress of the World's Women 2000* (New York: United Nations Development Fund for Women, 2000).

20. E.g., M. J. Ryan, ed., *The Fabric of the Future: Women Visionaries of Today Illuminate the Path to Tomorrow* (Berkeley, Calif.: Conari Press, 1998); D. A. F. Jones, *Women of Spirit* (Sudbury, Mass.: Visions of a Better World Foundation, 1995); and G. Sen and C. Grown, *Development, Crises, and Alternative Visions: Third World Women's Perspectives* (New York: Monthly Review Press, 1997).

21. E.g., E. Boulding, "Women's Visions of the Future," in *Visions of Desirable Societies,* ed. E. Masini (Oxford: Pergamon Press, 1983), 9–24; R. Eisler, *The Chalice and*

the Blade: Our History, Our Futures (San Francisco: Harper & Row, 1987); Barbara Marx Hubbard, *Conscious Evolution: Awakening the Power of Our Social Potential* (Novato, Calif.: New World Library, 1998); and E. Sahtouris, *EarthDance: Living Systems in Evolution* (San Jose, Calif.: iUniverse.com, Inc., 2000).

22. F. Bartkowski, *Feminist Utopias* (Lincoln: University of Nebraska Press, 1989); D. Holbert, *Feminist Fabulation: Challenging the Boundaries of Fact and Fiction. The Manoa Journal of Fried and Half Fried Ideas* (Honolulu: Hawai'i Research Center for Futures Studies, 1994); and Lucy Sargisson, *Contemporary Feminist Utopianism* (London: Routledge, 1996).

23. As argued by Eleonora Masini in *Visions of Desirable Societies; Women as Builders of Alternative Futures* (Trier, Germany: Centre for European Studies, Trier University, 1993); and "A Vision of Futures Studies," *Futures* 34 (2002): 249–261.

24. D. W. Hollis, *The ABC-CLIO World History Companion to Utopian Movements* (Santa Barbara, Calif.: ABC-CLIO, 1998).

25. Ibid.,14.

26. Ibid.

27. Ibid.

CHAPTER 8

Why I Hate Passports and Visas

A Personal Story of Globalization and Fairness

SOHAIL INAYATULLAH

"Soda," she said. "Is anyone called 'Soda' here?" she said a bit louder. I looked around at the handful of us in the immigration room in Honolulu, Hawai'i. No one looked like they could be called "Soda" but myself. In any case I knew she was yelling out my name, as I was used to its numerous pronunciations. Finally, I stood up and said, "Do you mean Sohail Inayatullah?" She smiled and nodded.

We walked over to her office. I expected the examiner to be an intimidating, tall, white, Texan male whose nose could ferret out illegal aliens; instead, she was a heavily tanned local Hawaiian/Japanese woman. As the interview began, I swore to tell the truth, all the time pondering on the nature of truth and identity. But that my hands were raised and not concealed—a weapon, perhaps—she believed me and I believed myself as well. I just hoped she would not ask me if I believed in the overthrow of the American government. Fortunately, the citizenship questions she asked were about the three branches of government, the Bill of Rights, and the Constitution. I answered them correctly, even giving her the Latin term for the law of the land, *Lex Legis*.

I had studied the hundred questions passed out by the Kalihi-Palama immigration center over and over. In those many times photocopied pages there were questions like "What is the color of the flag? Who said 'give me liberty or give me death'? Who helped the settlers when they came to the new land?" I had wanted her to ask the question, "What were the benefits for gaining citizenship?" In the crib notes, the answer was the very honest "to get a Federal job, to bring my relatives over to the US," but I was looking forward to saying, "To vote."

By voting I could finally participate in representative government. I could make the difference between democracy and despotism, between freedom and tyranny; I could save the United States from another four years of . . .

Born in Pakistan, I had never had the chance to vote largely because we were always out of the country, and when I had lived there, I was too young to vote. In any case, there was usually a dictatorship running the show. I remember once in

Hawai'i on election day a man walked by me, smiling, and told me how good it felt to vote. The power of participation in his face overflowed. I should have said nothing, but I told him that I did not vote. He walked away dejected, perhaps feeling that the republic had lost its legitimacy now that one of its citizens had not voted. I should have told him that I was not a citizen. But I guessed that he would know anyway by my color or look.

It was this look that the examiner asked me about next. She asked me what type of skin complexion I had. "Brown," I had written on the citizenship form.

"No. The only categories we have are fair, medium, and dark."

"Well, I am not dark and I am not fair."

She wanted to argue that I was dark. My being medium made her color problematic, since she was not fair and she was clearly not as dark as me. We both fought for the middle spot, with her finally relenting.

Next we could not find the category for my profession. Immigration had not heard of political scientists, planners, or policy analysts. I did not try to have her look up "futurist," the profession I am most often identified as having. She asked me if she should look under "biology" or "physics." I thought of the new approaches of quantum politics and biopolitics but asked her to try "social scientist." She found it, and after a few signatures (which had to be legible instead of scribbles, which I normally used to represent myself) the exam was over. I walked out to the corridor among the other Asians and Europeans.

This exam had been easier than the earlier one for permanent residency. Then my attorney had argued that I was a world expert in forecasting for court bureaucracies. The US Immigration and Naturalization Service believed him, forgetting to ask why anyone would want to forecast in state judiciaries. Earlier a doctor had cleared me of all types of venereal diseases, and I promised that I would not get any political diseases (communism or homosexuality).

But at least at the green-card hearing there was no questioning of my name. I did not mind the "Soda" incident, but before I signed the final paper the examiner asked me if I wanted to change my name. I took it personally. For years my name had been a source of trouble. I still remember the time in Manila when the immigration officer surveyed my passport and my body and finally asked me if I was any relation to the Ayatollah (Khomeni). I nervously laughed and said he was my uncle. The officer smiled and then suggested appropriate bathhouses for me to enjoy during my stay in the Philippines.

I made the same joke to the INS examiner and then commented that I was glad that my first name was Sohail, from the Arabic Al-Suhail, the southern night star, and not Saddam. She did not laugh. She asked me one more time if I wanted to change my name. "Sodaullah did not sound right," I thought. "How about Saddam Ayatollah," I said. She cringed in her seat. I tried to save the day by softly telling her that Inayatullah meant "the beneficence of God."

In the questionnaire prior to being granted an interview, one is allowed to omit agreeing to military service if one believes in a Supreme Being who deems such actions inappropriate. But this cannot be a political, sociological, philosophical, or personal moral code. That is, it must be one of the recognized religions. God as guru, as a tree, or as the eternal Zen nothingness of *mu* would not qualify. God must be objective *but* based on belief. Like voting.

I wonder if my Pakistani-born Muslim cousin, Aslam, knew of this when he became a US citizen. After Queens College, he joined the navy. Unfortunately, his first assignment was in the Middle East shooting at other Muslims. Was he American or Muslim first? His career in the navy did not last long.

In any case, the examiner was not impressed with my humor.

True, citizenship means changing one's identity and becoming Americanized. But I did not want to be called Sam like my friend Saleem. I merely wanted to make it easier to travel, to enjoy the fruits of *Pax Americana* (after all, I had been diligently paying American taxes for many years). A Pakistani passport invited all sorts of intrusions. In the summer of 1990, when I traveled to Yugoslavia, where I was to lecture at a conference on "Third World Visions of the Future," the immigration officer, suspecting I desired to use Yugoslavia to enter Italy and join Europe 1992 (as the emerging European Union was then called), questioned me extensively as to my intentions. Finally he was convinced I had a job somewhere and let me in. In Hawai'i, when I worked for the justice system in the 1980s, I was frequently tested by customs officers to see if I really did work for the Hawai'i courts or if I was actually using the judiciary as a front for an international heroin-smuggling operation. Indeed, once the FBI stalked me, thinking I was part of an operation selling passports/drugs to and from Indonesians. They later apologized.

Even entering Pakistan I was once pulled to the side, as the officer did not believe I was Pakistani. He believed that I was an Afghani or Soviet spy. "Where and how did you get the Pakistan passport?" I did not say I forged it so that I could enter Pakistan's dynamic and high-paying job market.

Years later, when I desired to travel to Yugoslavia to visit my pregnant wife while we waited for a job in Australia, the Serbian authorities denied me a visa. They argued I was a quasi-intellectual using marriage as a ruse so as to write negative portrayals of the Federal Republic of Yugoslavia. That we had traveled through Macedonia in the previous year made my getting a visa nearly impossible. I tried to tell the officer that the Macedonian guards had served me delicious chocolate cake at the border (why cannot he be that kind?) and that we were merely tourists on our way to Athens, but he suspected otherwise. Fortunately, my wife, Ivana, phoned from Yugoslavia and managed to take a few minutes of the officer's valuable time (earlier they claimed they were too busy—obviously from the deluge of tourists desiring visas to visit the Balkans) and convince him that I was no Pakistani or Bosnian or American spy.

But India for Pakistanis is far worse than Yugoslavia or America. Constant threats, suspicion, and visits by the secret police are common. I well remember the chilling words spoken by a Central Intelligence man: "We know you are here, Dr. Inayatullah, and we would like to speak to you." It is this coercive power that makes traveling difficult. It is this utter sense of powerlessness that makes me afraid every time I land. I fear I might be arrested for being different. I have no legal rights, and the power of the visa officer is arbitrary. And then there is that computer at every entry point in the world. What are they looking up? Is there a master file for every infraction we have committed against God, the nation-state, or the global interstate system?

That is my crime and guilt. I do not believe in the nation-state. When applying for a Pakistan identity card many years ago (I know who I am; why do they need to know?) I had to proclaim that Muhammad was the last prophet of civilization and that a sect of Islam, the Ahmedis, excommunicated from the faith by then prime minister Zulfikar Bhutto, was no longer Muslim. Believing in the plurality of tradition, I was in doubt of the legitimacy of excommunication as a religious practice, but to travel in Pakistan I needed the card. I signed. Somehow, my agreement gave legitimacy to the state. The social contract was sealed, the boundaries of Islam clarified, the polity strengthened, and again I could travel.

States control movement. They control my movement. Perhaps for my own good. Perhaps so the poor will not inundate richer economically developed areas. Perhaps because all foreigners are in fact potential terrorists, borders must be watched carefully, just as in medieval times when entrance into the city was regulated by passes. But in those days, the area outside the city was free. Today, we have no free areas. In exchange for our loss of freedom, however, we are promised protection (unlike the medieval era, when bands of men attacked the weak). But our protection is short-lived, for when another state threatens our collective security, then fight we must. In exchange for the right of citizenship is the duty of war. When placed within statist categories, boundaries and ownership of territory must be clarified, meaning we must all live in war, patriotism, self-aggrandizement, and expansion.

To avoid the draft, the war plans of any nation, we want our young son, Saim Dusan (born in Australia, our current home), to have as many passports as possible. The Americans have given him one, but only after he raised his right hand and swore allegiance to the Constitution. Pakistan and Yugoslavia as well have offered citizenship. The Yugoslavian passport will take a while, as their Parliament cannot decide what the passport cover will look like, as the number of states that will join or leave remains uncertain. But Australia has refused. More than refusing him a passport, the Australians placed numerous conditions on his possible return to the country after we were to leave on a family vacation to Pakistan. Without a reentry visa, he would be deported on arrival. After numerous forms, including many that required him to state his occupation ("baby," I never tired of writing), he was required to have a health examination. When I told the health department that he was born here and regularly went to Australia's finest doctors and nurses, their faces remained unyielding. In the exam, the doctor (an immigrant from India) checked to see if he had a heart. I told him that he smiles at everyone. He then asked if we could remove his diaper. The doctor desired to check to see if he had two testicles. Fortunately Saim did, and even more fortuitously, he managed to "pooh," thus leaving a gift to the Australian immigration system. But they preferred the eighty-eight dollars I had to give them so they could ensure that he could breathe and excrete. When our daughter, Mariyam Lena, was born in Australia, we went through the same process. This time, the immigration doctor—from Hong Kong—just checked her heartbeat; she assumed everything else was fine. Mariyam, in turn, left no gift.

But Australia is famous for its colonial immigration system. After having waited six months for my academic visa, I was granted a mining visa. I said that while certainly deconstruction was part of the job, mining might be difficult, but I would do my best. Only after numerous pleas from the university did they manage to switch my visa category. But few wars are fought in Australia, and thus we are saddened that Saim will not get an Australian passport.

Our problem is that we exist in many spaces; our son is a mixture of Punjabi, Serbian, Russian, and Slovenian. My wife only recently discovered she was a Serb, always believing she was a Yugoslav. She was equally stunned to find out that she was now the Other, that obtaining visas to OECD (Organization for Economic Cooperation and Development) nations is nearly impossible, and that when gained, she must go through the line for those from the former colonies: Africa and Asia.

I hope my son's journeys outside national boundaries will be less difficult than my trespassing of boundaries. Growing up both in Peshawar, Pakistan, and Bloomington, Indiana, was confusing. Before we left for the United States, when I thought about that country I mostly imagined snow. I had heard it was cold. Cold, indeed. We were not allowed to stay in the classroom during the break. We had to go out and walk around. It was at MaCalla Primary School that I learned the national anthem and "America the Beautiful." I never liked having to stand up and sing, even though the words were lovely.

After many years of traveling with my parents—my father is one of the lucky ones of the modern era, as he traveled with a UN "Laissez Passe" passport—we returned to Pakistan, where once again I had to swear allegiance and sing a national anthem I did not believe in. We stood in perfect lines, oblivious that our school was an old British private school called St. Mary's. These memories became more concrete when at a Pakistan Day ceremony in Hawai'i we all had to stand up and sing. I dreaded that my organizer friend Lubna would ask all the Pakistanis to stand up and walk to the stage. I do not know if I would have had made it there. Luckily, only the official Pakistanis who were already at the front of the room sang. I could slink back and think about my identity.

Another Pakistani friend, Asma, knows this and always introduces me with, "This is Sohail; he is Pakistani, I think, sort of. . . ." I would prefer she skipped the "sort of" introduction and either stayed away from the nation identification theme or said that I am Pakistani. I think it is because she is really saying, "He looks like us, but he is not really one of us. But he is not one of you either." However, she does not then give me official cultureless status either; rather, I am left to stand in the middle of some large landscape of cultures, colors, and nations when a middle may no longer exist.

The Pakistan Day ceremony made me realize that I disliked all anthems and that it was fear of reprisal that kept me in line. At baseball games and other expressions of patriotic strength the temptation to stay seated is strong, but the fear of being attacked by bona fide Americans is even stronger. Recently, I have justified my standing by saying that I am being culturally sensitive. Wouldn't I want all of them to stand at the flag of the planet Earth whenever that day comes about?

At the final US citizen swearing-in ceremony, we were each given flags as we entered the courthouse. The US Immigration attorney warned all of us potential voters that we had to recite an oath of allegiance. She would be watching our lips and listening to our voices. If we did not renounce all fidelity and allegiance to any "foreign prince, potentate, state or sovereignty," our application would be denied. Along with the others, I said the holy words.

Afterward, the judge gave us a citizenship speech in which he focused on the right to religion and the right of free speech. He commented that we could believe in any god, even no god. Atheism and the Zen *mu*, or nothingness, were allowed. We could also say anything we wanted. He then told us to welcome the new citizens around us, thus sealing the social contract and cementing civil society.

I looked around at the room full of immigrants and was touched by the many colors. But the diversity was quickly replaced by uniformity as we all turned toward the flag and recited the mantra that would make freedom so. And even though we had all earlier said that we were ready to bear arms, few in the room looked prepared—many were elderly men and women—and others were here because of processes created by global economic currency structures, for in the United States we could triple our economic level. A rupee is not a dollar.

After the pledge, the bailiff called out our names to get our "naturalization" forms. She mispronounced mine, and there was laughter as the new citizens knew that their names would be mispronounced next. Along with my naturalization certificate, I was given a letter from the president and a book on citizenship. George H. W. Bush does care about immigrants. I quickly went to the passport office and applied for a passport.

My friend Tom of the US State Department, with whom I went to high school in Malaysia, was initially disturbed by my desire to gain citizenship so that I could travel more easily to India and Europe as well as to other places where a Pakistani passport is tantamount to an indictment. He lectured me on my civic duty (but I work with numerous volunteer agencies, I responded—I do contribute), on voting (but does Congress represent our interests?), and democratic government (don't all legislators get reelected anyway?). But what left him most perturbed, I believe, was my violation of the nation-state. My values were not patriotism but ease of travel. I was not ready to submit to the melting pot. I had no intention of ceasing to write pieces critical of US (or any national) policy, domestic and international. It is not that I am robbed of meaning, decency, and faith; it is just that I no longer believe in the modern world system, I would argue with Tom. Finally, he gave up and we went back to discussing the problems Malaysia faces in forging a unified identity with its many ethnic, religious, and temporal divisions (postmodern, modern, and traditional).

But still I violate sovereignty. Capital can violate it; labor cannot. And if labor travels, it must submit itself to the new rules of employment. To live in the United States and criticize its values even as one enjoys them is a bit too much. Much too much. But Tom wants to do the same. He is sensitive to other cultures, bright, and wants to be an ambassador, preferably to Pakistan or Malaysia. But he wants to remain in his Washington position of privilege even while he enjoys the cultures of the Third World. He violates identity, but the interstate system allows these *official* excursions.

But I should not fault Tom. We want humans to have allegiances. We do not want humans to become like capital, going to the highest bidder. After I told my Indian friend Manomita Rao that I was applying for citizenship (my euphemism is that I am switching passports), she "jokingly" said I was a traitor. She and I have applied for a green card, the right to work but to retain identity, while I have gone a bit too far by changing official identity as well.

Getting to changing my citizenship has been a long-term process. The fear is that there will be a loss of Third World identification—an identification with the oppressed. But all intellectuals like to believe that they are merging their minds with the poor and the marginalized even as they lead privileged lives. Moreover, we forget that nationality and citizenship are practices, not eternal, a priori structures, however concrete they seem.

But it is not just my Indian friend who felt I had gone too far. I called the Pakistan embassy to find out visa requirements for US citizens. I told him that

I was switching passports and asked if dual citizenship was possible. He paused. "Why are you so afraid of a Pakistani passport?" he asked. I, feeling guilty, could only respond that I had lived in Hawai'i most of my life and thus could no longer be counted on as an official Pakistani.

Fortunately, Pakistan now allows dual citizenship, and thus when I fly in and out of Pakistan, I can show either passport. In a recent departure, I asked which passport I should show when leaving Pakistan. The Pakistani immigration official smiled and said, "It does not matter; either one is fine." Coming from a colonial outpost where nationalism is revered but where Pakistan's place in the world division of labor is quite clear, he understood. His message was, "whatever is most convenient to you—passports are commodities." While this airport official was quite relaxed, government officials in the Ministry of Interior remain in Raj days. It took us five days of sitting in offices to gain a four-day visa extension for my wife and our children. After endless questions and long waits in line, she received the visa. It took so long because bureaucrats with salaries low and egos large have little power but to make others wait. With bribery more and more problematic in the ministry, the only joy is to make others wait (and, of course, to offer tea while they wait).

But while having dual nationality in Pakistan is no longer seen as loss of self, in an earlier conversation with an American friend, who is a South Asianist, I did not tell her that I was changing citizenship for fear that she would interpret my actions as selling out. Rather, I said that I was switching passports for technical reasons. Escaping the nation is easier written than done. Visas to Mars, anyone?

But I do understand the charges of treason. In a Pan Am hijacking in Karachi many years back, an Indian who was on his way back home had just switched to American citizenship. After the plane was hijacked, he told the hijackers that as he was now a US citizen, he should not be harmed. While this might have been appropriate in the United States or in an embassy where sovereignty extends through borders, in front of hijackers, outside the city walls of sovereignty, it was a mistake. They shot him.

I hope my movements and attempts to move in and out of sovereign spaces of identity do not lead to the same fate. And if they do, I am not sure who will claim me. Will you?

Responding to Globalization
Public Institutions Present and Future

Part 3 focuses on the various ways in which public institutions have or have not responded to globalization in terms of fairness. Dick Pratt opens with an extensive review of the latest movement in governance and public administration—the New Public Management (NPM). He begins by quoting an author who says that NPM may be as profound a revolution in governance and administration as was the movement described and provoked by Max Weber a century earlier. NPM is largely a critique of the salient aspects of the Weberian system. Pratt explains the various perspectives and proposals of NPM, the basic argument being that bureaucracies are too rigid and rule bound and thus wholly unsuitable for the dynamic, flexible, creative world we live in now—or would live in if our bureaucracies were more dynamic, flexible, and creative as well.

Pratt is critical of the claims of NPM. He argues for a greater diversity of approaches and the need for models of public institution reform and renewal that take local context, including resources and political culture, into account.

Jim Dator extends Pratt's opening comments by tracing the history of administrative reforms in the United States. He concludes that American history can be understood as endless calls for administrative reform while bureaucracies waxed and waned in concert with the growth and militarization of the industrial state. But at the same time, the burgeoning corporate sector required and requested the enforcement of basic rules of the economic game by public administrators. While focusing on the US experience, Dator also insists that these governmental reforms (beginning with the very idea of "constitutionalism" itself) were in fact global movements—every bit as global and driven by special interests as

NPM is now. From this perspective, NPM is just the latest in a long line of calls for reform in the interest of certain groups over others.

Doug Allen then pulls the discourse down from the lofty heights of history and theory and tells the story from the point of view of a practitioner—a person who has been active in administration and administrative reform in Canada as well as in diverse parts of the world, including Ethiopia, Hawai'i, Japan, Malaysia, and South Africa. Allen observes that "a major challenge is the need for each public institution to stay relevant to those it serves while operating globally in an increasingly connected world."

After briefly outlining his experiences, Allen concludes that among the major problems are the inability to be certain what policy—in the vast organization called "government"—is to be followed, the inadequacy of the resources provided to governments to do the job the public expects, the rise of private short-run interests that are overwhelming public long-run interests, and indeed the difficulty of having a consistent and effective long-range view with policies based on it.

The apparent emergence of a global common law is described by Ron Brown of the University of Hawai'i's William S. Richardson School of Law. As Brown notes, one of the most interesting things about this development is that it is entirely driven by both local and national judiciaries attempting to incorporate "best practices" that they learn about from other judiciaries. It is not something imposed on them by their own legislatures, nor the result of reformers attempting to build a system of world law from the top down. It is, rather, (in the words of Fred Riggs) "glocalization" at its potential best—learning from others anywhere in the world and adapting it to local conditions.

Martin Khor, director of the Third World Network in Penang, Malaysia, was invited to attend the Honolulu conference upon which this volume is based primarily to assure that the question of fairness to the environment from a Third-World perspective would get a proper hearing and discussion. He unfortunately was not able to attend, but he did submit a chapter dealing with the issue that is included here.

Khor notes that the world is locked in an uneven competition between two worldviews—the globalization paradigm and the sustainable development paradigm—"with globalization without doubt running away as the winner, and moreover a winner whose speed, direction, and effects seem to be uncontrollable [resulting] in a crisis of sustainable development" that he clearly outlines. There is thus an urgent need for appropriate and democratic global governance to deal with the uneven competition, Khor maintains, an issue that Yoshiko Kojo, of the University of Tokyo, also discusses in her Further Thoughts, "Globalization and International Economic Institutions."

Khor calls for a reform of the global economic system, including the WTO, so that it operates more to the benefit of the South, especially in the area of agriculture and intellectual property rights, primarily concerning the issue of who owns the genetic information of native plants in Third-World areas. Sohail Inayatullah elaborates on this issue in his Further Thoughts on "Food Politics."

Khor ends his analysis with a discussion of the need for technology assessment and the judicious use of the precautionary principle, especially in the area of genetic engineering, a matter that Walt Anderson also discusses in his Further Thoughts on "Biotechnology and Fairness."

Fred Riggs, professor emeritus of the Department of Political Science of the University of Hawai'i, is a longtime contributor to the theory and practice of public administration at various places around the world. In chapter 14, Riggs focuses on an issue often overlooked—the representativeness of bureaucracies as a measure of their ability to administer fairly. Representation is typically linked only to legislatures or perhaps executives, but Riggs points out that unless the bureaucracy is seen somehow as broadly representative of the people it serves, it may fail to act—or be seen as acting—fairly.

Riggs adds that discussions of representation also tend to focus on individuals, but in some cultures group representation may be more important. In others, the exclusion of women and children or other marginalized groups (or even diaspora) might be significant. Riggs is also exceptional in discussing the need to represent future generations, and the emerging possibility of electronic virtual representation.

Part 3 concludes with a longer chapter by Jim Dator that argues for fundamental rethinking about "governance" in place of piecemeal attempts at reform. After a quick review of the evolution of governance systems, Dator shows that "structure matters" and that many current problems are a consequence of our continued reliance on once novel and creative structures that now are obsolete and (in the case of the "presidentialist" system) pathological.

After reviewing a few current attempts at governance redesign (primarily proposals for governmental foresight on the one hand and the creation of the European Union on the other) and the currently popular concept of "civil society," Dator looks at governance redesign from a more fundamental philosophical and epistemological perspective, concluding that "quantum" theories should replace the old "Newtonian" ideas that form the basis for all current governmental structures. He ends by noting that work done by Ted Becker, Christa Slaton, and others incorporating quantum politics into "Teledemocracy" might well become the model for the next governance design paradigm. Walt Anderson also contributes Further Thoughts on ideas of "Global Governance."

CHAPTER 9

New Public Management, Globalization, and Public Administration Reform

DICK PRATT

In "Globalization and Public Administration Reform," Elaine Ciulla Kamarck concluded that there can be no doubt that for several reasons the end of the twentieth century has seen a revolution in public administration that is every bit as profound as that which occurred at the turn of the nineteenth century, when Weberian bureaucratic principles began to influence many governments around the world. How real, and how extensive, this revolution in government is remains to be seen.[1]

This chapter looks at pressures for reform of the administrative apparatus of public institutions. There is an international movement for administrative reform, which in turn is associated with globalization. One of its manifestations, referred to as the New Public Management (NPM), is a loose package of prescriptions that have been promoted by influential international organizations and have found their way to many different countries. Yet as Kamarck's statement also suggests, the direction, extent, and impact of these global prescriptions remain unclear.

The chapter proceeds by first reviewing the problems of administrative agencies that reforms attempt to address. It then examines NPM as an agent of globalization and a response to it. The closing sections summarize concerns that have been raised about NPM and propose that a true "public" reform must be driven by a diversity of approaches to change that are explicitly public regarding.

Traditional Problems with Public Bureaucracies

Kamarck's article summarizes her survey of the 123 largest countries (i.e., those with a population greater than 3.4 million), inquiring about reforms that addressed "the actual operations of the state or the traditional ground of public administration."[2] She concludes, "These countries have different histories and different electoral systems; they are at different stages of development and yet, to a surprising degree, they are employing a set of reform concepts and strategies that are remarkably similar. Many of these concepts come from a reform movement known as 'new public management.'"[3]

Before turning to the reforms that fall under NPM, it is useful to remind ourselves of what they purport to be a reaction to. In doing this there is the risk, of course, of making generalizations that fail to take into account critical differences in historical, institutional, and political experience. For example, Richard Stillman notes significant disparities between American and Continental European public administration. The American style is more pragmatic, grassroots, and experimental, whereas the Continental one is more fixed, top-down, and legalistic.[4] Stillman makes the interesting observation that these differences account for why administrators in the United States came to be called "public" administrators, while those in Europe were named "state" administrators.

Other descriptions would be necessary to capture the distinctive features of administration in Asian societies, which may share more features with Continental Europe than the United States. Some scholars refer to Asian administrative forms as Confucian, highlighting their emphasis on expertise, practicality, hierarchy, and tradition. Even this, of course, does not apply equally well, or in some cases at all, to every Asian society and ignores places were colonization and authoritarianism had an important impact.

These regional and national differences notwithstanding, the bureaucratic model summarized so well by Max Weber has been powerful and widespread in both public and private organizations. It has been a familiar presence in most, if not all, systems of public administration, appearing in hugely different cultural, economic, and political contexts.

Given its pervasiveness, it is possible to identify concerns that have for decades preoccupied scholars and frustrated practitioners. These are summarized in the following list.

1. Roles are overspecialized; most people have no sense of an overall process to which their work contributes.
2. Rules are too often confused with policies, and as a consequence rule keepers become too powerful; employees spend too much time getting around rules, which is inefficient, undermines accountability, and creates confusion about the real goals.
3. Structures are rigid and unadaptive; administrative organizations are anti-experimental and attempt to mold the environment, including citizens, to their needs; there is low efficiency even when efficiency is emphasized.
4. There are no direct incentives, financial or otherwise, that reward good work and punish bad work.

5. Middle-management supervision is ineffective, and there is too little control by individuals of their own work.
6. Participation by employees, when it occurs, is primarily symbolic; the people who know things through their direct experience do not decide things.
7. Criticism is discouraged; employees who point out problems become the problem.
8. The wrong kind of person is successful; submissiveness, endurance, and blind loyalty are valued over risk taking, honesty, and innovation.
9. Cooperation is difficult; specialization, turf issues, and communication protocols are disincentives to collaborative work within, or between, organizations.
10. Preoccupation with internal order and coded language (jargon) excludes "outsiders" such as citizens or clients.

Some observers do not agree that these are problems, or at least problems of such consequence that they outweigh the costs associated with fixing them. Good examples are found in respected scholars who argue that, at least in the American setting, public organizations are effective in doing their work (Goodsell), more innovative than commonly believed (Blau), and can be fixed only by undermining the larger political fabric of which they are a part (Wilson).[5] Whatever differences exist, we can agree that public organizations have been an object of concern and episodic reform for decades and that this inclination to reform has accelerated recently and is now global in scope.

New Public Management as Agent and Response

The manifestation of reform that is most associated with globalization is called the New Public Management. NPM is the global successor to what in the United States was labeled "Reinventing Government" and in Britain "Next Steps."[6] NPM is, on the one hand, only the best known of many recent efforts to improve administrative effectiveness. On the other hand, it is also something new. Theo Toonen observes,

> A difference with previous administrative reform episodes has been that globalization has accelerated the speed of the circulation and dissemination of ideas for administrative reform. The OECD, World Bank, UN and several international consulting firms have become global players that advocated "public sector management reform," thus contributing to a substantial "epistemic presence" of NPM.[7]

NPM is both a manifestation of globalization and a strategy for dealing with it. In its role as *global agent* it has been heavily promoted, and given legitimacy, by international organizations such as the International Monetary Fund. Their prescriptions have been powerful because of the resources they control. As a *response* to globalization, NPM is a means by which national governments attempt to reorganize their public institutions to meet the challenges and opportunities of globalization.

NPM emphasizes business practices, market incentives, and competition as the appropriate tools for obtaining greater efficiency and greater flexibility in public bureaucracies that commonly have the problems described earlier. Efficiency is key because governments everywhere are experiencing budget shrinkage and because resources given to public-sector organizations are seen as opportunity costs for economic development. Flexibility is critical in adapting to an economic and political environment that is changing rapidly, often as a result of globalization.

Within the framing of NPM decentralization is advocated as a way of increasing flexibility and legitimacy. The term "governance" replaces the historic focus on government because more actors are involved in doing what was once the responsibility of government. Government is now seen to have a "steering" function over a "rowing" function—that is, government provides fewer and fewer direct services, but instead sets the policy directions that are implemented outside of it by a variety of quasi-public, semiprivate, and private-sector organizations. Everyone involved with governance, including government agencies, is encouraged to see citizens as customers and to be motivated and disciplined by the market relationship that the term connotes.

The spirit of NPM is captured in a list of "Approaches, Tools, and Competences" created by David Osbourne and Peter Plastrik. Their list contains ninety-two entries. Not all of these are business, market, and/or competition based, but many are. A sampling is as follows:

sales of public assets
community-based funding
competitive customer choice
customer-service agreements
enterprise funds
managed competition
mass organizational deregulation
performance budgets
performance management
vouchers and reimbursement systems

Concerns about the New Public Management

A number of questions have been raised about the NPM regime. First, while its orientation is not exclusively economic or what is commonly called neoliberal, it is heavily so. The emphasis on privatization and contractual relations, measurable performance outcomes, and customer (vs. citizen) service has sounded alarms among scholars and practitioners internationally. Some of the ensuing debate revolves around the implications for accountability and the continued public status of "public" institutions. Here the question is this: will public organizations increasingly serve private interests?

A second question about NPM is its effect on our conceptions of citizen responsibility. It is useful to view citizens as having three kinds of relationships with public organizations. NPM focuses heavily on the *customer* role, in which citizens come with expectations that the services they desire are delivered expeditiously. This is a reasonable expectation, but it ignores the other roles that come with being a citizen. The second of these is that of *subject*. Here the person must do things in response to the exercise of public authority, even if they prefer not to. This includes obeying the police, paying taxes or tax penalties, accepting regulations, and so forth. While this relationship can be handled efficiently, it is also a different kind of a relationship than a customer has in a private-sector transaction. The third citizen role is that of *partner*. The ability of public agencies to carry out their work is heavily dependent upon community policing. If community members do not work with the police in a partnership, there is going to be little success in reducing neighborhood crime. The question here, then, is this: are we in danger of replacing the idea of a collaborating citizen with that of a demanding customer?

The next question about NPM concerns its powerful status. That status comes from its previously noted endorsement by influential international organizations, international scientific and professional groups, and some nations. Dorte Salskov-Iverson and her coauthors comment that

> [t]he history of the discourse of NPM shows a development from scattered ideas and pluralistic rhetoric to a more focused, normative discourse about the necessity of change and the *correct way* to create better public services, favoring managerial technologies over more traditional bureaucratic measures. By shaping the claims and declarations of prestigious organizations such as the OECD and the World Bank, NPM discourse [is produced] globally, with a specific view to local application in all places and at all levels.[8]

Although in the early life of NPM its advocates emphasized the importance of taking into account different cultures, political structures, and local traditions, that has since changed. NPM became so powerful that Salskov-Iverson et al. described it as a top-down "hegemonic process" that gives the appearance of only one way for public institutions to adapt to globalization. They referred to this sense of a "One Right Way" as the "naturalization of change."[9] Despite these claims that NPM is the indisputable "natural" way, what happens in practice varies. When NPM principles are implemented in specific settings, they are reshaped by the real worlds that people live in. The question here, then, is this: will NPM freeze out alternatives that are more contextually appropriate?

The final concern raised about NPM is about the values it will bring to, or take out of, public institutions. While it can be overstated, it is a fair generalization that private-sector organizations are mobilized by the values of efficiency and effectiveness and that public organizations are mobilized by equality and inclusion.[10] It is, in part, the historic commitment to equality and inclusion that has meant public organizations are less efficient. On the other side, it is the option that private-sector organizations have to give these values a lower priority that has allowed those organizations to be more efficient. The question here is this: will the adoption of NPM principles mean that the public-service values of equality and inclusion become less and less important in what public organizations do?

Administrative Reform in Response to Globalization

In 2001 the *International Journal of Administrative Sciences* published an article by Nick Manning, a senior public-sector management specialist for the World Bank. Titled "The Legacy of the New Public Management in Developing Countries," the article summarized Manning's conclusions about the impact of NPM. He observed the high expectations of its advocates that NPM would produce an effective reform agenda for improving public sector institutions worldwide.[11] Rather than seeing effective reform, Manning thought that "[i]n looking at whether it worked, we are forced to draw some conclusions from an eerie silence from the evaluators. It seems probable that the direct contribution of NPM to public sector responsiveness or efficiency outside of the OECD has been slight at best, and it has probably been positively harmful in some settings."[12]

Manning observed that in many developing countries the NPM label was applied to changes being undertaken, but nothing of any significance resulted. In other cases the prescriptions were indeed implemented but were inappropriate in the setting and had the effect of making things worse.

This poor record did not lead Manning to conclude that NPM brought no gains. Instead, the failure of NPM to deliver on its claims has "highlighted that the underlying development task is that of creating meaningful public expectations and public sector disciplines."[13] His reference to "meaningful public expectations" reflects his view that perhaps the best hope for creating responsive public institutions in the most difficult environments is the development of public attentiveness combined with initiatives that matter to the general public, to NGOs and the media, and to other stakeholders.[14]

For Manning the bottom line is that although NPM did not come near to meeting its expectations, the failures and the debate over what they mean have created some new possibilities.

> In summary, if the excessive claims of NPM did little damage in the long run, this was more by luck than by judgment. One lesson from the NPM adventure is fundamental: there are no silver bullets. However, the relative failure of NPM has opened up some interesting, albeit untested, possibilities. We will certainly be fortunate if it turns out that its lack of success has inspired some much-needed fresh thinking.[15]

Lois Recasino Wise pursued a different issue in relation to the global dominance of NPM-related discourse. She observed that today, "[p]ublic management reforms often are portrayed as part of a global wave of change, and all organizational change is interpreted within a single reform paradigm that is rooted in economics and market-based principles."[16] Noting that opposition to NPM commonly is associated with concerns that it departs from traditional principles of democracy, she observed that historically reform has been made up of competing and recurring agendas that reflect different values. She assumed, therefore, that "alternative forces of reform do not disappear, but rather remain influential even when discourse is focused on other agents of change."[17]

To test this Wise utilized the concept of "competing drivers of change" to examine whether or not different sources of administrative reform, based on different values, may continue to be influential, despite being less visible. Her work looked for different "drivers of administrative reform during the same period in which NPM-style reforms became dominant."[18]

Wise named competing motivations for reform "The Demand for Greater Social Equity," "The Demand for Democratization and Empowerment," and "The Humanization of Public Service."[19] The Social Equity driver is animated by a focus on fair treatment. Laws, policies, and practices that prohibit employment discrimination and promote fair treatment in public organizations reflect this driver. So do policies to promote tolerance, level differences between social groups, and use the public sector to model and promote standards of fair treatment in society. The Democratization and Empowerment driver focuses on increasing participation and democratic accountability. This driver is seen in efforts to advance access to public-service leadership to more social groups, in the promotion of participative decision-making styles over top-down systems, in the active engagement of citizens in bureaucratic decisions, and in initiatives to redress the distribution of power in society. The third driver, Humanization of Public Service, prioritizes the human side of public-administration systems and the quality of working life for public employees. It is embodied in initiatives that emphasize employee development, work schedules that balance job and family needs, childcare options, and eldercare services.

To test for the presence of these drivers during the period of NPM's hegemony, Wise looked for evidence of language, policies, and programs that reflected the continued influence of these drivers in three countries: Sweden, Norway, and the United States.

Her analysis concluded that in fact these "competing drivers" for administrative reform remain influential despite not being dominant. The case studies "lend support to the argument that multiple factors determine the way reform waves affect different countries."[20] Within the limits of her study and the restrictions on generalizing from these particular national settings, Wise recommends that other researchers explore "the extent to which other drivers of reform have served as change agents of contemporary public management reform. We cannot assume that similar patterns for the three drivers studied here would be observed in other countries or at different levels of government."[21] The direction of change in administrative systems is unlikely to be the product of any one approach. "Normative influences are reflected in a stream of activities that occur within the same time period in different civil service systems. This comparative analysis provides insights into the potential capacity for change in different reform remedies in different national contexts."[22]

What can we conclude from this about the reform of administrative systems in an era that (1) produces global reform ideologies and (2) requires that these public systems respond effectively to the opportunities and challenges of globalization? In *The Future of Governing,* B. Guy Peters summarizes approaches that have been taken internationally to improve systems of public administration. He does this by arguing that there are four broad, sometimes overlapping, approaches to reform: the market model, the participatory state, deregulated government, and flexible government.[23]

The market model rests on the priority given to the values of high efficiency and low costs, objections to public monopolies, and the desirability of infusing business culture into public organizations. These elements place it nearest to what makes up NPM. Market-model advocates propose creating smaller, more manageable units, new incentive systems, internal and external competition, and true costing, including opportunity costs as well as incurred costs. This model implies that the *public interest* is found in low costs to taxpayers, good performance by public agencies, and responsiveness to consumers.

The participatory-state model is based in concerns about the current under-utilization of public employees; the belief that knowledge, power, and shared purpose matter in motivating employees; and the premise that direct citizen participation in agency activities is desirable. Advocates of this model propose less hierarchical organizations; more employee participation, such as might be found in total quality management programs; and more regular citizen participation in the life of public organizations. The *public interest* rests in the full utilization of public employees, open government and maximum inclusion of social interests in what government does, and building the value of citizenship.

Deregulated government is based on the importance of liberating public organizations from the tyranny of rules that have built up over time, as well as the need for public employees to take more risks. This approach to reform emphasizes reducing the power of central control agencies and the number of rules they generate regulating personnel, purchasing, and budgeting; putting more resources into auditing and evaluating what agencies actually do; and building a strong public-service ethic. The *public interest* implied by these reforms is found in reaching a better balance between the need for control and the need for action, recognizing that an active government is as important as complete accountability, and accepting that some errors are an acceptable price for energy released on behalf of public purposes.

Peters' fourth reform model, flexible government, focuses on the desirability of the public sector responding more quickly by using nontraditional structures and processes. These new approaches can include a combination of having more control over the labor force through new personnel policies, greater use of networks of private or nonprofit providers, and the utilization of information technologies to create "virtual organizations" that appear and disappear according to what issue is being addressed. The *public interest* implied by the flexible model of reform is found in cost savings and in getting rid of fossilized agencies that are unable to adapt their efforts to address contemporary issues.

Peters concludes on the basis of his analysis that there are, and should be, a variety of approaches to the reform of public institutions, reflecting their different purposes and varied settings. The crucial point is that responses to reform-related challenges raised by globalization are a matter of judgment and balance informed by context.

This point was illustrated in an experience of mine. Recently ten public officials from Guangdong, China, participated in a graduate seminar that focused on the reform of public organizations. We reviewed the different models of reform summarized by Peters and then discussed the pros and cons of each. The Chinese officials initially were intrigued by the idea of deregulating government agencies since they, too, suffer the frustrating inflexibilities of rule-encrusted organizations. After some discussion, however, they came to argue strongly that deregulation of their administrative apparati presented a threat to democratic prospects in their society. Their concern was that reducing the rules that controlled what public officials do would create an environment for new "cults of personality" and the establishment of administrative fiefdoms. From their perspective, deregulation may make sense for Americans, given their political history and current stage of political and organizational development, but it is not appropriate for the Chinese.

What, then, determines the framework for reform? One important factor is the current capacities of public institutions. Capacity refers to such things as resources, technical systems, a public-service ethic, and education and training. Where there are no mechanisms for effectively enforcing policies, or where public organizations are unresponsive, unaccountable, and/or inequitable, careful judgments will have to be made about where organizational reforms should take place to achieve long-term public purposes, how much the private sector can be utilized, economic viability, and institutional legitimacy.

What Peters refers to as "reform fatigue"—a history of experiments with total quality management, reengineering, or similarly heralded change strategies—will need to be factored into any decision to initiate a new series of reforms.[24] In some cases the strength of even the traditional model of public bureaucracy—the model to which NPM is a reaction—in providing predictability to citizens and the private sector may outweigh the desirability of greater flexibility.

Cultural values, specifically political culture, are another important factor affecting what public administration reform will look like. Political culture refers to shared views of such things as the appropriate role of government in social and economic life; the role of parties, elites, and interest groups in the political process; and the desirability of public participation. Political cultures form in specific locations in response to externally generated events such as wars or business cycles; local conditions such as social crises, climate, or resources; and, most important, the ongoing merging, overlaying, and conflicts of ethnic groups and ethnic-group values.

According to Daniel Elazar, for example, American public institutions tend to reflect an individualistic political culture that deemphasizes community and minimizes the role of public institutions in favor of personal relationships and private concerns.[25] Individualistic political culture favors private parties negotiating their own social needs and economic interests in a market-like setting.

This perspective on public life and public institutions competes with two others. The first is a moralistic political culture that emphasizes the nurturing of common values and the development of viable communities. This is, for example, a dominant strand in Japanese political life. Moralistic political culture rejects the unrestrained pursuit of private interests and is wary of the effects on community of an unregulated commercial marketplace. Here public institutions are valued insofar as they are able to balance commercial activities against broad public benefit. The second competing perspective is a traditionalistic political culture that favors arrangements that protect base values, continuity, and stability while rejecting both the pursuit of private interests and high levels of community involvement. Thailand provides a good example of this political culture.

The point is not that these particular political cultures will be found everywhere, although it would be surprising if elements of them were not in competition in many locations, partly as a result of globalization. Rather, the point is that, as this volume illustrates about East Asia, there are significant differences in the constellation of values and beliefs out of which public institutions must respond to globalization. The real challenge is to negotiate a path between dependence on traditionally rigid and ineffective public bureaucracies and reformed public organizations that are action oriented but inappropriate for their particular circumstances, and not public regarding.

Conclusion

As a symbol of a global reform agenda, the New Public Management is in part a product of globalization and a proposal to deal with globalization. This review argues that NPM is only one of a number of ways to frame the complex process of public institution reform. Sensitivity to this perspective is especially important if the administrative aspects of public institutions are to play a meaningful role in promoting the public-regarding outcomes of globalization.

Notes

1. Elaine Ciulla Kamarck, "Globalization and Public Administration Reform," in *Governance in a Globalizing World*, ed. John D. Donahue and Joseph Nye, Jr. (Washington, DC: Brookings Institution Press, 2000), 251.

2. Ibid., 230.

3. Ibid., 229.

4. Richard Stillman, "American vs. European Public Administration: Does Public Administration Make the Modern State, or Does the State Make Public Administration," *Public Administration Review* 57.4 (July/August 1997): 332–338.

5. Charles Goodsell, *In Defense of Bureaucracy*, 2d ed. (Chatham, N.J.: Chatham House Publishers, 1985); Peter Blau, *The Dynamics of Bureaucracy* (Chicago: University of Chicago Press, 1963); James Q. Wilson, *Bureaucracy* (New York: Free Press, 1989).

6. C.f. David Osbourne and Peter Plastrik, *Banishing Bureaucracy* (New York: Penguin Books, 1998).

7. Theo A. J. Toonen, et al., *Civil Service Systems in Comparative Perspectives* (Bloomington: Indiana University Press, 1996), 184.

8. Dorte Salskov-Iverson, Hans Hansen, and Sven Bislev, "Governmentality, Globalization, and Local Practice: Transformation of a Hegemonic Discourse," *Alternatives: Social Transformation and Humane Governance* 25.2 (April–June 2000): 38, as found in EBSCOhost.html. Italics added.

9. Ibid., 20.

10. On these points, see, e.g., Demetrios Argyriades, "Values for Public Service: Lessons Learned from Recent Trends and the Millennium Summit," *International Review of Administrative Sciences* 69.4 (December 2003): 521–533.

11. Nick Manning, "The Legacy of the New Public Management in Developing Countries," *International Review of Administrative Sciences* 67.2 (2001): 297.

12. Ibid., 298.

13. Ibid.

14. Ibid., 306.

15. Ibid., 308.

16. Lois R. Wise, "Public Management Reform: Competing Drivers of Change," *Public Administration Review* 62.5 (September/October 2002): 556–567.

17. Ibid., 556.

18. Ibid.

19. Ibid., 557–558.

20. Ibid., 563.

21. Ibid., 564.

22. Ibid.

23. B. Guy Peters, *Governing*, 2d ed. (Lawrence: University of Kansas Press, 2001).

24. Ibid., 168.

25. Daniel J. Elazar, *American Federalism: A View from the States*, 3d ed. (New York: Harper and Row, 1984).

CHAPTER 10

Administrative Reform in the United States

From Laissez-Faire to Empire

JIM DATOR

The United States was the first "new" nation,[1] the first nation to be specifically "constituted" by "the people" purposely coming together, throwing away a dysfunctional political design, and rationally inventing and creating a new one. The American example inspired a worldwide revolution in political design that has never been equaled, even though, as we will discuss later, creative new political designs are more sorely needed now than they were in 1787. But when this basic constitutional design was conceived and laid out in the late eighteenth century, America (though a "new nation") was not yet a "modern" nation. America was founded in the latter days of the premodern, agricultural era. And so, though the constitutional impulse, cosmology, and structure was new, the initial duties of the officers of the new nation were not much different from the duties of the officers of any of the old nations. When called upon to flesh out the bare bones of the Constitution, the first US Congress in 1790 created only three "departments" (ministries) for the first president. What the three were (and what they were not) is tremendously revealing of how little government (any government, old or new) was expected to do at that time.

The first three departments created by Congress were War, State, and Treasury. At the same time, Congress created the Office of the Attorney General (the Justice Department itself was not created as a cabinet position until a hundred years later, in 1870) and the Postmaster General.[2] The first four are about as generic governance functions as one can imagine: "War" (not renamed the more politically correct "Defense" Department until after World War II) in order to enable the United States to fight other nations (the monopoly on and use of organized violence being the definitional hallmark of a "sovereign state," then as well as now); "State" (Foreign Affairs) so that the United States could engage in diplomatic relations with other sovereign states and further its interests politically when it would not fight; and "Treasury" so that the finances of the nation could be managed (though there was not yet a national bank). An "Attorney General" was necessary as the lawyer of the nation who would defend the United States in courts of law, especially important given the loose federal nature of the union.

These are all very fundamental governance functions. But a Postmaster General? Why in the world would the founding fathers need a Postmaster General? Why should the federal government be responsible for the delivery of mail? That does not sound like a "generic" function of governance equal to War, State, Treasury, and the office of the Attorney General, especially considering all the other governmental departments that exist now, but not then. The answer in part has to do with the importance the founding fathers gave to their own experiences during the colonial period with the various "Committees of Correspondence." These had enabled them, often illegally and with considerable effort and danger, to communicate among themselves and to plan and foment their successful revolution for independence against England. Thus even the Articles of Confederation, the first attempt to create a kind of unified nation from among the several colonies after their independence, made the delivery of mail a duty of Congress and not of the individual states. Thus it was not a surprise that the US Constitution later specifically called for the creation by the federal government of "post offices and post roads" so as to enable the tiny, far-flung, and isolated communities of the vast, new nation to knit themselves together into a more perfect union.[3]

The first presidents led comparatively quiet lives. Their staffs were small and composed mainly of relatives, friends, and people to whom they owed some political favor. The staffs of the various departments also were miniscule and filled with political hangers-on who may or may not have been able to do competently whatever work was to be done. But there was not much work to do, and competence was seldom needed.

Frederick Mosher refers to the period from 1789 to 1829 as "Government by Gentlemen." During that time, presidents operated with what Mosher terms "surprisingly little guidance" from the Constitution in building the foundation of public service. There is consensus among historians that George Washington established a positive precedent in emphasizing competence and fitness of character, rather than personal ties or nepotism. It is important to note, however, that the pool of persons from which Washington chose his appointments was small, homogeneous, and elite.[4]

This soon changed. "Jefferson articulated the first argument for patronage in the system when he contended that a limited number of offices ought to be divided between the parties and that party service was a valid criterion for appointment to public service."[5] But President Andrew Jackson went even further in creating the "spoils system." In his first presidential address, Jackson argued that "there was no need to confine offices to the highly educated few, for the 'duties of all public officers are, or at least admit of being made so plain and simple that men of intelligence may readily qualify themselves for their performance.'"[6]

Thus when an old president left office and a new president came in, the personnel appointed by the old president left and the relatives and cronies of the new president came in to take their places. "Public service" was seen initially as a duty that the elite should perform for a while and as a temporary reward for political loyalty. It was not viewed as a vocation, much less a profession for which one should be trained and to which one should devote his entire career.

And as far as involvement in foreign affairs was concerned, Washington allegedly once remarked, "We have not heard from our Ambassador in Paris, Thomas Jefferson, for some time now. We should send him a letter." No urgency. The communication over, and back, would take months.[7]

Overall, the spoils system was dominant from 1845 to 1865.[8] From Jackson's time for many years onward, the powers and duties of American presidents were weak and few. They concerned themselves mainly with removing officeholders and appointing new ones. As McDonald says, "The nineteenth century presidents continued to be little more than chief clerks of personnel."[9] "Paul Van Riper notes that federal employment grew from three thousand in 1800 to six thousand in 1816. By 1831 the number had reached twenty thousand."[10] By 1870 the number of government functionaries had grown to more than fifty thousand.[11]

Relyea notes,

> As the federal government embarked upon the first year of the 20th century, the US consisted of 45 states and [four] territories. Congress counted 86 Senators (four vacancies) and 389 Representatives (two vacancies). The Senate conducted its business with 55 standing and eight select committees; the House of Representatives performed its functions with 58 standing and four select committees. . . . Eight departments were represented in the Cabinet, and these, together with 10 other principal entities, . . . constituted the major units of the executive branch. The American public, numbering over 76 million people, were being served by some 231,000 executive branch civilian employees, 5,690 legislative branch employees and 2,730 judicial branch employees of the federal government.[12]

It is informative to chart American history by observing which new departments, after the first five, were created by Congress and in which order they emerged. It clearly tells the story of America's transformation from an agricultural society to an industrial society to a post-industrial society.

1. 1849: Interior (Initially mainly concerned with Indian affairs and the redistribution of their stolen land.)
2. 1862: Agriculture (Farming was the primary occupation of most Americans, but the nation was already well on the way to industrialization, including the industrialization of agriculture, by 1862.)

3. 1870: Justice (Industrial society required the "rule of law" for its own "orderly" development.)
4. 1913: Commerce
5. 1913: Labor (Note the long interval between the creation of the Department of Agriculture and the creation of the Departments of Commerce and Labor. US departments always lagged well behind changes in society. Note also that the two were created together, balancing off the new interests of business and labor.)
6. 1953: Health, Education, and Welfare (Created twenty years after the New Deal!)
7. 1965: Housing and Urban Development (Most Americans now live in urban and not rural areas.)
8. 1966: Transportation
9. 1977: Energy (Created after the two "oil crises" of the 1970s.)
10. 1980: Health and Human Services
11. 1980: Education (These two were split from the Health, Education, and Welfare of 1953.)
12. 1988: Veterans Affairs (This had been a large "office" for years. Making it a department illustrates the central role of the military in America.)[13]
13. 2002: Homeland Security (Representing a fundamental change in America's view of itself and its world.)

This list masks the fact that, from the late nineteenth century to the second third of the twentieth century, as part of global administrative reform movements discussed below, most of the new administrative offices of the US federal government were created not as cabinet "departments" but rather as "independent" regulatory commissions. The powers of these commissions are extensive, perhaps even greater than those of the departments, since the commissions are in fact substantially "independent" of political control.

American Political History as Continual Administrative Reform

One way to read American political history can be as a never-ending series of attempts to find the right way to administer governance. There have been six major waves of administrative formation and reformation in the United States, with many surges and eddies between and among the waves. The major episodes (with a hint as to what might come next) are as follows:

1. 1789–1829: "Government by Gentlemen": serving for short periods of time as their civic duty.
2. 1830–1883: "Government by the Common Man": holding government

office for short periods of time as a reward for political service; the "spoils system."

3. 1883–1932: The "Progressive Era" of rational, scientific, professional, non-political, predictable (i.e., "bureaucratic" as a good word) globalized governance.

4. 1932–1978: "We're from the Government. And We're Here to Help You." And they were, and they did. New Deal through the Great Society; the heyday of the welfare state in the United States. "We're all Keynesians now," said Richard Nixon.

5. 1979–2001: Government as your enemy: Reaganomics, Reinventing Government, and the New Public Management.

6. September 11, 2001: Government by men and women in uniform; a new meaning of public "service." Security is now more important than rights. The military and paramilitary part of government is good and growing. When will this wave end? What will the next wave be?

The following documents those waves and eddies:

> Calls for reform of the system, emanating from a variety of sources, were being heard throughout the [earliest] period. Partly the calls were rooted in sheer disgust at the incompetence of government. . . . But there was in some quarters also a sense of moral outrage at the decadence of public life. . . . In 1838 the collector of the port of New York, Samuel Swartwout, had absconded with $1,235,705.69, a sum that . . . would have been equivalent to about $160 billion in 1992.[14]

Clearly, those were heroic times! But it took more than mere grand larceny to really get reform going. Military incompetence did the trick. In the initial stages of the US Civil War (1860–1865), many of the higher officers had attained their rank through the spoils system, and not as a consequence of their proven abilities. Thus "Congress created the Joint Select Committee on Retrenchment, one of whose tasks was to consider the use of examinations for entry to federal employment. The committee's report was issued in 1868; it was a ringing condemnation of spoils. The alternative report proposed was modeled on the British civil service system. Elements of the systems in China, Prussia, and France were also discussed,"[15] hence showing that the first formal governmental reform efforts in the United States were informed by examples in other parts of the world, yet another sign that notions of "good governance" have been globalized for a long time.

In 1883, Congress passed the Pendleton Act, which created the Civil Service Commission, requiring competitive examinations in order to qualify for certain jobs in the federal government. "By 1928 almost 80% of the positions below policy-making levels were covered."[16]

The first so-called "independent regulatory agency," the Interstate Commerce Commission, was created in 1887 to regulate railroads. From that point on, such regulatory agencies grew apace. By 1990 there were thirty-two "major" and twenty-three "minor" independent agencies. "Contrary to a widely held misconception, regulation of economic activity . . . had been the norm in America almost from the outset, . . . but [initially] such regulation was at the level of state and local government. . . . And, contrary to another widely held perception, the [first agency] was ardently sought by most interstate railroad operators as a means of escaping the clutches of ignorant and avaricious state legislators."[17]

Congress authorized President William Howard Taft "to study the bureaucracy to find ways of reducing expenditures." As Taft told Congress, the real problem was that "the United States is the only great Nation whose Government is operated without a budget." President Woodrow Wilson "laid the foundation for a managerial presidency of the kind Taft's commission had contemplated."[18]

"In December [1932, President Herbert] Hoover sent to Congress orders for changes in fifty-eight governmental activities." In 1936, President Franklin Roosevelt "appointed a committee on administrative management chaired by Louis Brownlow," which "complied by drawing a blueprint for reorganization that would place all federal agencies . . . under the direct and exclusive command of the president."[19]

The offices and scope of the US federal government vastly expanded during World War II. "As soon as Congress convened in January 1947, it passed an act establishing a Commission on Organization of the Executive Branch of the Government. . . . The intention was to undo the economic and social programs that had been introduced by Roosevelt's New Deal and Truman's nascent Fair Deal. . . . The reports of the Hoover Commission, released to Congress during the first few months of 1949, made 277 specific proposals for shifting agencies and consolidating them to create 'a clear line of command from the top to the bottom, and a return line of responsibility and accountability from the bottom to the top.' More than half of the proposals, among them the most important ones, were enacted into law or effected by executive orders."[20]

"Then, after the ill-starred Kennedy dream of Camelot, came two presidents whose design for the presidency knew no limits, and between them they reduced the prestige and power of the institution to a nadir it had not known since the days of Ulysses Grant."[21] They were Lyndon Johnson and Richard Nixon. They were followed by two weak and generally discredited presidents, Gerald Ford and Jimmy Carter.

"Carter was successful in obtaining passage of comprehensive civil service reform, the first since the Pendleton Act had created the merit system in 1883. The Civil Service Reform Act of 1978 was intended to make the civil service, particularly at the top levels of management, more flexible, more responsive, and more productive. . . . Ten years after the reform, however, the director of the

Office of Personnel Management, one of the new agencies created by Carter's reform, declared that the civil service system remained burdened by thousands of pages of rules and regulations and did not work."[22]

The history of administrative reform takes a substantially different turn from that point on, however. The president whose name is most closely associated with substantially changing the abilities of the US federal government and the attitude of the American people toward its government is Ronald Reagan. Armed with what then-rival Republican Party presidential candidate George H. W. Bush called "Voodoo Economics" (the "supply side" economic theory and practices of Arthur Laffer),[23] Reagan succeeded in transforming the US government from the number-one creditor nation in the world (the country to whom most of the world was in financial debt) to the number-one debtor nation (owing more to the rest of the world than did any other country). This is still a major feature of the US government, made even more prominent by the presidential son of George H. W. Bush, George W. Bush.[24]

But it would be wrong to assume this transposition was a mistake. To the contrary, it was one of the intentions of Reagan's policies. As McDonald says, Reagan's "aim regarding the administrative machinery of the federal government was not to manage it efficiently and economically but to minimize its functions and return as many of them as possible to the states or to private enterprise."[25] It was the aim of Reaganomics, in short, to destroy most of the existing US federal government and to restore it, if possible, to its original size and functions of 1790.

While Reagan was not entirely successful in this, he did set the federal government on a trajectory of downsizing and privatizing of its nonmilitary functions that is still in place. While the overall personnel and budgets of US government have continued to grow, and recently very spectacularly, this growth is overwhelmingly in military or paramilitary areas and in servicing the national debt. The ability of the government to function in other areas has been substantially reduced as taxes and personnel have been reduced and (with the exception of a brief bit of fiscal nonsense at the end of President Bill Clinton's administration)[26] the national debt increased.

Nonetheless, the American voters continue to favor lower taxes and smaller governments, so "President Clinton declared government to be 'broke and broken' and advocated a complete 'reinvention' of government."[27] He asked Vice President Albert Gore to take the lead in this, and considerable time and effort was spent on "reinventing government." But the civil service system apparently is still not fixed.

When George W. Bush was chosen president by the US Supreme Court in 2001, government downsizing and reform were very much on his mind. The primary weapon he used for this was cutting a variety of taxes for the rich, thus transforming the impressive budget surplus he inherited from Clinton into a massive and growing deficit in each succeeding year of his reign.

But it is hard to argue that the federal government downsized as a consequence. In fact, it grew as Bush created a new federal agency, the Department of Homeland Security, and then attacked, conquered, and occupied Iraq at great expense and for an indefinite duration. So, as with the Reagan era, the civilian parts of the US federal government under Bush continued to shrink while the military, paramilitary, and debt-servicing parts continued to swell.

Dick Pratt showed in the previous chapter that "the New Public Management" movement continues to advocate even more stringent reforms, as though for the very first time. Yet it is clear that demands to reform the administration of American government are not new. They have been a continuing feature of American history. What can explain that? What have been the major causes for these almost endless calls for reform? The answer to that is as contentious as the calls for reform themselves, but the following seem to be among the major factors: the experience of the American frontier; the emergence of industrialization, rationalization, routinization, and legalization, and of progressive ideologies; and the evolution of an America as a permanent war economy.

The American Frontier Experience

One reason governmental reform is a continuing theme may have to do with America's early history. People came (or were sent or brought) to what appeared to them to be a vast and empty North American continent. Many of the early pioneers were victims of political or religious persecution elsewhere and wanted nothing more than to be left alone to live, work, and worship in their own way. Some held religious convictions based upon the belief that God spoke directly to them and not through any intermediary of priests or pastors. If they heard God tell them to do something their pastor or other members of their congregation disagreed with, then it was their God-given right, and duty, to move out, move on, and found their own congregation of like-minded believers somewhere else.

The frontier was always there, enabling them—indeed, calling them—to drop whatever obligations they found stifling and go and create a new life somewhere else, free of government restrictions or government aid. America was seen as a nation of independent cowboys who loved only themselves, their horses, and their freedom. "Give me liberty, or give me death!" "That government is best which governs least!" "God and my rights!" "Don't tread on me!" Until 9/11, these were the dominant American mottoes. Of course, they were based entirely on myths.

While there have been some cowboys and some episodes of rugged pioneers, almost all American families (even those of the cowboys and pioneers) have been supported by government (often military) policies from the very beginning.

Stephanie Coontz tells the true story very well.

The myth of family self-reliance is so compelling that our actual national and personal histories often buckle under its emotional weight. . . . Few families in American history have been able to rely solely on their own resources. Instead, they have depended on the legislative, judicial, and social-support structures set up by governing authorities, whether those authorities were the clan elders of native American societies, the church courts and city officials of colonial America, or the judicial and legislative bodies established by the Constitution.

Pioneer families could never have moved west without government-funded military mobilizations against the original Indian and Mexican inhabitants or state-sponsored economic investments in transportation systems. In addition, the Homestead Act of 1862 allowed settlers to buy 160 acres for $10—far below the government's cost of acquiring the land. . . . In the twentieth century, a new form of public assistance became crucial to Western families: construction of dams and other federally subsidized irrigation projects. During the 1930s, for example, government electrification projects brought pumps, refrigeration, and household technology to millions of families.

The suburban family of the 1950s is another oft-cited example of familial self-reliance. According to legend, after World War II a new, family-oriented generation settled down, saved their pennies, worked hard, and found well-paying jobs that allowed them to purchase homes in the suburbs. In fact, however, the 1950s suburban family was far more dependent on government assistance than any so-called underclass family today. Federal GI benefit payments, available to 40% of the male population between the ages of twenty and twenty-four, permitted a whole generation of men to expand their education and improve their job prospects without forgoing marriage and children. The National Defense Education Act retooled science education in America, subsidizing both American industry and the education of individual scientists. Government-funded research developed the aluminum clapboards, prefabricated walls and ceilings, and plywood paneling that comprised the technological basis of the postwar housing revolution. Government spending was also largely responsible for the new highways, sewer systems, utility services, and traffic-control programs that opened up suburbs.

In addition, suburban home ownership depended on an unprecedented expansion of federal regulation and financing. Before the war, banks often required a 50 percent down payment on homes and normally issued mortgages for five to ten years. In the postwar period, however, the Federal Housing Authority, supplemented by the GI Bill, put the federal government in the business of insuring and regulating private loans for single-home constructions. FHA policy required down payments of only 5 to 10 percent of the purchase price and guaranteed mortgages of up to thirty years at interest rates of just 2 to 3 percent. The

Veterans Administration required a mere dollar down from veterans. Almost half the housing in suburbia in the 1950s depended on such federal programs.

Historically, the debate over government policies towards families has never been over whether to intervene but how: to rescue or to warehouse, to prevent or to punish; to moralize about values or mobilize resources for education and job creation. Today's debate, lacking such historical perspective, caricatures the real issues.[28]

So it is not the case that most Americans have been on their own and done things on their own without governmental help or regulation. But such has been the American myth, and strongly held, until the events of September 11, 2001, sent them once again back to the comforting arms of their militarized homeland with its well-defended borders, internal security, and police.

However, it is the case that the size and scope of the US national government has grown over the years from what it was in 1790. So why might that be? Probably the most compelling force was the globalizing influence of a new wave of technology, and of the software and orgware that went with it, that raced out of England and swept across the face of the planet over the nineteenth and twentieth centuries, changing everything in its path: industrialization.

Industrialization, Rationalization, Routinization, and Legalization

With industrialization, different attitudes and behaviors became possible, easy, and popular. Work was needed less and less on the farm and more and more in the cities, in factories where processes became increasingly routinized, rationalized, legalized, and scientific. Schools were needed to train workers for these routine jobs, and universities were needed to do the science that would enable them to invent new routines as well as new technologies. By the end of the nineteenth century it had become easier to communicate (via telegraph) and to move (via train or steamship) around the nation and across the globe.

The federal government was thus expected to change in order to keep up with the rapidly changing and diversifying demands of the globalizing, rationalized, legalized scientific economy and society. McDonald says,

> The civil service reformers gained ever-widening popular support as the nineteenth century wore on, for the disruptions attending the technological and industrial revolutions, together with massive urbanization and immigration, left millions of Americans feeling that they lived in a strange new world in which they had lost control over their lives. On the positive side, the new technology included such devices as the typewriter and adding machine, which appeared

to bring "scientific" administration within reach, and the emergence of gigantic corporations seemed to provide models of scientific management and also to necessitate scientific federal regulation. . . .

Similar forces were at work throughout the industrializing world, and American reformers were in communication with like-minded people in England, France, Germany and New Zealand. . . . A host of social scientists emerging from the newly instituted graduate schools formed part of an international network of champions of change. Their prescriptions varied in detail, but in essence what they sought was to remove power from professional politicians and legislative bodies, concentrate it in the executive branch, and place it in the hands of experts.[29]

"Bureaucracy" was thus the "New Public Management" movement of the nineteenth century (it was the solution to the dreaded "spoils system"), and Weber was its major theoretician. Weber developed an ideal-type bureaucracy that has the following characteristics.

Hierarchy
Impersonality
Written rules of conduct
Promotion based on achievement
Specialized division of labor
Efficiency

Lewis Coser states of Weber that

[b]ureaucratic coordination of activities, he argued, is the distinctive mark of the modern era. Bureaucracies are organized according to rational principles. Offices are ranked in a hierarchical order and their operations are characterized by impersonal rules. Incumbents are governed by methodical allocation of areas of jurisdiction and delimited spheres of duty. Appointments are made according to specialized qualifications rather than ascriptive criteria. This bureaucratic coordination of the actions of large numbers of people has become the dominant structural feature of modern forms of organization.

Yet Weber also noted the dysfunctions of bureaucracy. Its major advantage, the calculability of results, also makes it unwieldy and even stultifying in dealing with individual cases. Thus modern rationalized and bureaucratized systems of law have become incapable of dealing with individual particularities, to which earlier types of justice were well suited. The "modern judge," Weber stated in writing on the legal system of Continental Europe, "is a vending machine into which the pleadings are inserted together with the fee and which then disgorges the judgment together with the reasons mechanically derived from the Code."[30]

This statement by Weber, more than any other, captures the essence of what is desired from a bureaucrat. It is this feature of automaticity and predictability (a "government of laws and not of men") that is the most admirable and desired feature of bureaucracy and its most detested as well.

> [The calculability of decision-making] and with it its appropriateness for capitalism . . . [is] the more fully realized the more bureaucracy "depersonalizes" itself, i.e., the more completely it succeeds in achieving the exclusion of love, hatred, and every purely personal, especially irrational and incalculable, feeling from the execution of official tasks. In the place of the old-type ruler who is moved by sympathy, favor, grace, and gratitude, modern culture requires for its sustaining external apparatus the emotionally detached, and hence rigorously "professional" expert.[31]

Progressive Ideologies and Attractions

Another factor in the growth of governmental size and services in the United States during the latter half of the nineteenth century and the first half of the twentieth was the spread across the globe of something else that had been invented in Europe: socialism and communism.

The United States, of course, never had a significant socialist or communist movement, compared to Europe (and elsewhere), but the appeal (or threat) of communism led many Americans to embrace ideas and practices that borrowed from communist/socialist theory and practice or were intended to co-opt those theories (and their followers) by partially embracing them. The high water mark of this "liberal" expansion of governmental activities in the United States was the New Deal during the period of the Great Depression.

If the United States had not adopted the "progressive" rhetoric and policies of the New Deal, it is highly likely that there would have been substantially more violence and bloody conflict, with significantly larger numbers of Americans embracing communism than there were. The New Deal successfully blunted the appeal of more radical actions.

Permanent War Economy

But the New Deal did not end the Depression. That must be attributed to World War II, which saw massive powers sucked toward the center in Washington.

But this was not new. This was also a continuing American experience. As a consequence, in addition to the global spread of industrial ideas and practices themselves, war itself played a major role in the expansion of the US federal government, especially from the Civil War onward. Of course, mass warfare itself is a by-product of industrialism, but war eventually became an independent variable in the expansion of governance. The US government expanded and centralized its powers with each war, and while there would be some relaxation and decentralization afterward, the federal government always ended up with more power after each war than it had had beforehand. This was especially the consequence of World War II.[32]

In part this is because the war never really ended. Since World War II, America has simply moved from one war to another, with periods of wartime concentration being briefly interrupted with short interludes of "peace" and decentralization before war and centralization came again—the Korean War, the Vietnam War, the Gulf War, and now the never-ending "war on terror," with the Cold War being the underlying motif until the 1990s. America was a permanent war economy (and hence polity) from 1941 until the fall of the Berlin Wall and the collapse of the Soviet Union.[33]

There was a ten-year interlude of comparative "peace" during the 1990s when nonmilitary economic forces and theories became more prominent. But military forces and theories were neither weakened nor abandoned. Military spending remained a substantial factor in the American economy and bureaucracy throughout the 1990s, even during the height of the high tech, dot-com "New Economy" era.

The overall size of the US federal bureaucracy has continued to grow, rather than shrink, in spite of the fact that the budgets for most civilian agencies have been reduced and many personnel fired or not replaced after retirement. But the size and expense of government grew overall during the period of Reaganomics and with its Bush successors because the size of the military and paramilitary branches of government grew so rapidly in budgets and personnel, a trend now greatly exacerbated by the war on terrorism and the creation of the Department of Homeland Security.

So What?

But why are we spending so much time telling an entirely American story in what is supposed to be a volume focusing on globalization, public institutions, and fairness in East Asia?

It is first of all because of America's role as the "first new nation" that greatly influenced new nations. And it is mainly to show that fashions and fads in governance have always been subject to global pressures. "Constitutionalism," "democracy," "bureaucracy," and all the rest have been "glocal" phenomena—local adaptations to global forces. As with all aspects of globalization, contemporary attempts to create a New Public Management are not really new in purpose or in global sweep. They are merely the latest in a long line of global attempts to reform governance and especially to reduce the costs and personnel of the administration of government.

That is to say, America's story is by no means unique. That is the point of our telling it. The US story is just one variation of a global stimulus and local response (as well as one of many local stimuli provoking global responses).

Each of the European countries went through the same transformation from having, until the eighteenth century, decentralized, "irrational," "ad hoc" governance by titled and/or landed elites on a largely agricultural economic base to creating a centralized, rationalized, bureaucratic governance system with elites chosen by "merit" or "democratic election" responding to the rapid emergence of the global industrial systems during the nineteenth and twentieth centuries. While each nation did its own unique things, the underlying impulse and the resulting fundamental structures are remarkably similar.

And the story is not only European and American. It had its counterparts everywhere in the world, including China, Korea, Japan, Vietnam, and Cambodia, as we show elsewhere in this book. However, much of the non-European world (Africa, Asia, South and Central America) during this period was under colonial rule by Western nations. Thus none of them was free to develop a modern state its own way or for its own sovereign purposes. Rather, they were modernized and rationalized only to the extent this served their colonial masters. This resulted in enormous distortions from which most of these colonized nations, once freed, have not yet recovered. Most of the "underdevelopment" of the South today is a direct consequence of the "de-development" policies and practices of the North during the nineteenth and early twentieth centuries, exacerbated perhaps by the neocolonial, neoliberal global policies of the late twentieth century.

In short, all modern governments of the so-called "developed" nations, including those in East Asia featured in this book, have gone through remarkably similar transformations from what they were in agricultural times through industrialization and now to post-industrialization. Though there are important differences between them (primarily in terms of the relationship of the educational system to the merit system of the bureaucracy, and when bureaucracies are open for recruitment),[34] the fact is that they all followed similar paths from governmental administration by an elite and/or by political hacks who may or may not be competent to a period of Weberian bureaucracy by meritorious professionals, and now to pressures toward downsizing, entrepreneurial behavior, and privatization. These were global responses to global pressures then, just as they are now.

Fairness, Globalization, and the New American Empire

But what are the futures of fairness, globalization, and public institutions in light of the "New American Empire?" There is clear evidence, since September 11, 2001, and especially since March 19, 2003, the day the United States attacked Iraq, that the United States is determined to see that the world is ruled primarily in its interest and that the countries and the peoples of the rest of the world will either become part of that empire or enemies of it. Writing in the authoritative journal *Foreign Affairs,* John Ikenberry puts it the following way.

> In the shadows of the Bush administration's war on terrorism, sweeping new ideas are circulating about U.S. grand strategy and the restructuring of today's unipolar world. They call for American unilateral and preemptive, even preventive, use of force, facilitated if possible by coalitions of the willing, but ultimately unconstrained by the rules and norms of the international community. At the extreme, these notions form a neoimperial vision in which the United States arrogates to itself the global role of setting standards, determining threats, using force, and meting out justice. It is a vision in which sovereignty becomes more absolute for America even as it becomes more conditional for countries that challenge Washington's standards of internal and external behavior. It is a vision made necessary (at least in the eyes of its advocates) by the new and apocalyptic character of contemporary terrorist threats and by America's unprecedented global dominance. These radical strategic ideas and impulses could transform today's world order in a way that the end of the Cold War, strangely enough, did not.[35]

Somewhat later, Leon Fuerth, writing in the *Washington Post,* observed that "[t]he word 'empire' has been used fairly often as a metaphor to convey the global scope of American interests and of American military, economic and political influence. After the conquest of Iraq, however, it can be fairly argued that we shall have created not a figure of speech but a concrete reality."[36] Indeed, "empire" has become a term of pride (and by no means a pejorative) for some observers. Dinesh D'Souza wrote "[i]n praise of American empire," stating, "America has become an empire, a fact that Americans are reluctant to admit and that critics of the United States regard with great alarm," while concluding, after a survey of America's imperial actions and intentions, "If this be the workings of empire, let us have more of it."[37]

To the extent these actions and policies become a long-term feature of American policy (or made impossible because of the structural limitations of the US economy), this fact will have profound implications for the meaning of "fairness, globalization, and public institutions" in East Asia and everywhere else. Bruce Nussbaum, writing in *Business Week,* is not the only one to observe that "[c]hief executives are beginning to worry that globalization may not be compatible with a foreign policy of unilateral preemption. Can capital, trade, and labor flow smoothly when the world's only superpower maintains such a confusing and threatening stance? U.S. corporations may soon find it more difficult to function in a multilateral economic arena when their overseas business partners and governments perceive America to be acting outside the bounds of international law and institutions."[38]

Nonetheless, the intentions of the Bush administration are clear, and they are not the result of some irrational, knee-jerk reactions to 9/11. Rather, they are the realization of plans initiated by people in think tanks outside of government during the 1990s who were able to bring their plans to fruition though a combination of their own visionary foresight, strategic positioning, and good luck. In many ways, the administration's current actions are an example of futures studies successfully undertaken and implemented.

The visionary foresight can be seen most brilliantly in the "Statement of Principles" of a group called "The Project for the New American Century," promulgated on June 3, 1997. The statement opens,

> American foreign and defense policy is adrift. Conservatives have criticized the incoherent policies of the Clinton Administration. They have also resisted isolationist impulses from within their own ranks. But conservatives have not confidently advanced a strategic vision of America's role in the world. They have not set forth guiding principles for American foreign policy. They have allowed differences over tactics to obscure potential agreement on strategic objectives. And they have not fought for a defense budget that would maintain American security and advance American interests in the new century. We aim to change this. We aim to make the case and rally support for American global leadership.[39]

The "Statement of Principles" then concludes,

- we need to increase defense spending significantly if we are to carry out our global responsibilities today and modernize our armed forces for the future;
- we need to strengthen our ties to democratic allies and to challenge regimes hostile to our interests and values;
- we need to promote the cause of political and economic freedom abroad;
- we need to accept responsibility for America's unique role in preserving and extending an international order friendly to our security, our pros-

perity, and our principles. Such a Reaganite policy of military strength and moral clarity may not be fashionable today. But it is necessary if the United States is to build on the successes of this past century and to ensure our security and our greatness in the next.[40]

The statement was signed by Elliott Abrams, Gary Bauer, William J. Bennett, Jeb Bush, Dick Cheney, Eliot A. Cohen, Midge Decter, Paula Dobriansky, Steve Forbes, Aaron Friedberg, Francis Fukuyama, Frank Gaffney, Fred C. Ikle, Donald Kagan, Zalmay Khalilzad, I. Lewis Libby, Norman Podhoretz, Dan Quayle, Peter W. Rodman, Stephen P. Rosen, Henry S. Rowen, Donald Rumsfeld, Vin Weber, George Weigel, and Paul Wolfowitz.

When the US Supreme Court declared George W. Bush the president of the United States and Richard Cheney vice president, and when Cheney then became the head of the transition team responsible for choosing the major figures in the Bush administration, many of these same people found themselves in positions of governmental power that enabled them to move even closer to the opportunity to turn their principles into reality. In order to move beyond the principles, in September 2000 the group published *Rebuilding America's Defenses: Strategy, Forces and Resources for a New Century.*[41] The "Key Findings" of the report are as follows:

Establish four core missions for U.S. military forces:
- defend the American homeland;
- fight and decisively win multiple, simultaneous major theater wars;
- perform the "constabulary" duties associated with shaping the security environment in critical regions;
- transform U.S. forces to exploit the "revolution in military affairs."

To carry out these core missions, we need to provide sufficient force and budgetary allocations. In particular, the United States must

MAINTAIN NUCLEAR STRATEGIC SUPERIORITY, basing the U.S. nuclear deterrent upon a global, nuclear net assessment that weighs the full range of current and emerging threats, not merely the U.S.-Russia balance.

RESTORE THE PERSONNEL STRENGTH of today's force to roughly the levels anticipated in the "Base Force" outlined by the Bush Administration, an increase in active-duty strength from 1.4 million to 1.6 million.

REPOSITION U.S. FORCES to respond to 21st century strategic realities by shifting permanently-based forces to Southeast Europe and Southeast Asia, and by changing naval deployment patterns to reflect growing U.S. strategic concerns in East Asia.

MODERNIZE CURRENT U.S. FORCES SELECTIVELY, proceeding with the F-22 program while increasing purchases of lift, electronic support and other aircraft; expanding submarine and surface combatant fleets; purchasing Comanche helicopters and medium-weight ground vehicles for the Army, and the V-22 Osprey "tilt-rotor" aircraft for the Marine Corps.

CANCEL "ROADBLOCK" PROGRAMS such as the Joint Strike Fighter, CVX aircraft carrier, and Crusader howitzer system that would absorb exorbitant amounts of Pentagon funding while providing limited improvements to current capabilities. Savings from these canceled programs should be used to spur the process of military transformation.

DEVELOP AND DEPLOY GLOBAL MISSILE DEFENSES to defend the American homeland and American allies, and to provide a secure basis for U.S. power projection around the world.

CONTROL THE NEW "INTERNATIONAL COMMONS" OF SPACE AND "CYBERSPACE," and pave the way for the creation of a new military service—U.S. Space Forces—with the mission of space control.

EXPLOIT THE "REVOLUTION IN MILITARY AFFAIRS" to insure the long-term superiority of U.S. conventional forces. Establish a two-stage transformation process which

- maximizes the value of current weapons systems through the application of advanced technologies, and,
- produces more profound improvements in military capabilities, encourages competition between single services and joint-service experimentation efforts.

INCREASE DEFENSE SPENDING gradually to a minimum level of 3.5 to 3.8 percent of gross domestic product, adding $15 billion to $20 billion to total defense spending annually.[42]

Still, even with the policy and people now in place, the authors admitted they were not likely to be able to make the kinds of sweeping change they envisioned without a major stroke of luck. As they put it, "Further, the process of transformation, even if it brings revolutionary change, is likely to be a long one, absent some catastrophic and catalyzing event, like a new Pearl Harbor."[43]

And then, strangely enough, the incidents of September 11, 2001, occurred, and the world changed for America. Citizens' rights, long considered almost sacred in their inviolability, were swept away by a compliant Congress in the so-called "USA PATRIOT ACT" of 2001;[44] Bush articulated his doctrine of the right of preemptive war;[45] and on March 19, 2003, the United States attacked Iraq, and America changed for the world.

On the basis of various official statements by Bush and others, John Ikenberry concludes that America's "new grand strategy" has seven elements.

1. "[A] fundamental commitment to maintaining a unipolar world in which the United States has no peer competitor."
2. "[T]errorist groups cannot be appeased or deterred . . . so they must be eliminated."
3. "The use of force . . . will therefore need to be preemptive and perhaps even preventive—taking on potential threats before they can present a major problem."
4. "[T]he new grand strategy reaffirms the importance of the territorial nation-state. . . . On the other hand, sovereignty has been made newly conditional: governments that fail to act like respectable, law-abiding states will lose their sovereignty," with the Bush administration "leaving to itself the authority to determine when sovereign rights have been forfeited, and doing so on an anticipatory basis."
5. "[A] general depreciation of international rules, treaties, and security partnerships" that are "just annoying distractions."
6. "The United States will need to play a direct and unconstrained role in responding to threats. . . . A decade of US defense spending and modernization has left allies of the United States far behind." As a consequence, in the words of Rumsfeld, "The mission must determine the coalition; the coalition must not determine the mission."
7. "[T]he new grand strategy attaches little value to international stability. . . . [I]nstability might be the necessary price for dislodging a danger and evil regime."[46]

It is by no means clear that the United States has the will or even the ability to sustain this strategy over a long period of time. It requires the United States not only to conquer, but also to rebuild destroyed communities. America did this after World War II, and that example is sometimes used to suggest that it will do so again. But the two situations are quite different. First of all, in many ways it can be said that the United States was the only true "victor" among the major powers after World War II. While the rest of the industrialized world was devastated by bombing, killing, and looting, America was totally unscathed. It emerged from the war with its industrial base intact and spending power, pent up since the Great Depression and the rationing during the war, bursting at the seams. Also, the period after the war (and before the Cold War) was the high point of American global liberalism. It should not be forgotten that even the Republican candidate, Wendell Willkie, ran against then President Franklin D. Roosevelt in 1940 on the platform of (and wrote a book titled) "One World,"[47] a world in which the United States was a major partner, but not a hegemon. During the immediate postwar period, this kind of liberal globalism was exemplified in the economic and political policies the United States followed not only in creating the United Nations, but also especially in assisting the rebuilding of both Germany and Japan, two tremendous success stories (indeed, the constitutions of the two countries, and especially of Japan, may be the best examples of old-fashioned constitution writing in modern times).[48]

But the present American economy is "mature" rather than "robust," to say the least, and the political economy is overwhelmingly oriented toward enriching the rich while beggaring all forms of public activities not directly related to military and paramilitary force and/or directly in support of the rich themselves.[49] Whatever can be said for the policies otherwise, this is definitely not a good time for the United States to embark unilaterally and preemptively on global military destructive and nation-building activities. The burden these policies place on the poor and middle classes in America now will be exceeded only by the extreme burden (psychological as well as fiscal) placed on future generations to pay for them.

Nonetheless, the policies and actions of the first Bush administration were endorsed by a significant majority of the American voters in the national election of November 2004. Not only did George W. Bush win a clear majority of both the popular votes and the Electoral College votes this time, but Republicans made significant gains in both Houses of Congress. Thus issues of fairness, globalization, and public institutions in East Asia must be rephrased within the uncertain shadow of America's expanding imperial future. Most of the discussions of globalization during the 1990s have greatly diminished utility unless the United States can once again become a partner instead of a bully, and there is no sign of that occurring any time soon.

Notes

1. Seymour Martin Lipset, *The First New Nation: The United States in Historical and Comparative Perspective* (New York: Basic Books, 1963).

2. Sidney M. Milkis and Michael Nelson, *The American Presidency: Origins and Development, 1776-1998,* 3d ed (Washington, DC: Congressional Quarterly Press, 1999), 71.

3. For a history of the US Post Office, see www.usps.com/history/hisl.htm.

4. Patricia W. Ingraham, *The Foundation of Merit: Public Service in American Democracy* (Baltimore, Md.: Johns Hopkins University Press, 1995), 17.

5. Ibid., 18.

6. Forrest McDonald, *The American Presidency: An Intellectual History* (Lawrence: University of Kansas Press, 1994), 316.

7. Marshall McLuhan and Quintin Fiore, *The Medium is the Massage: An Inventory of Effects,* reprint (Corte Madera, Calif.: Gingko Press, 2001).

8. Ingraham, *The Foundation of Merit,* 21.

9. McDonald, *The American Presidency*, 320.

10. Ingraham, *The Foundation of Merit*, 18.

11. McDonald, *The American Presidency*, 315.

12. Harold C. Relyea, *Government at the Dawn of the 21st Century* (Huntington, N.Y.: Novinka Books, 2001), 2.

13. Michael Nelson, ed., *Guide to the Presidency*, vol. 2, 2d ed. (Washington, D.C.: Congressional Quarterly Press, 1995), 1157; and Bert Rockman, "Administering the Summit in the United States," in *Administering the Summit: Administration of the Core Executive in Developed Countries*, ed. Guy Peters et al. (New York: St. Martin's Press, 2000), 250.

14. McDonald, *The American Presidency*, 322f.

15. Ingraham, *The Foundation of Merit*, 22f.

16. McDonald, *The American Presidency*, 325f.

17. Ibid., 326f.

18. Ibid., 330f.

19. Ibid., 332f.

20. Ibid., 335.

21. Ibid., 336.

22. Ingraham, *The Foundation of Merit*, xvii.

23. Victor A. Canto et al., *Foundations of Supply-Side Economics: Theory and Evidence* (New York: Academic Press, 1983).

24. Eamonn Fingleton, "The Other Deficit," *The Atlantic Monthly*, April 2002, 32f; and Richard Stevenson, "Weakening Dollar Mirrors Economy," *Honolulu Star-Bulletin*, June 21, 2002, C5.

25. McDonald, *The American Presidency*, 342.

26. Clinton made a big show of paying $1 billion of a $6 trillion debt. *Honolulu Advertiser*, March 10, 2000, A2.

27. Ingraham, *The Foundation of Merit*, xvii.

28. Stephanie Coontz, *The Way We Never Were: American Families and the Nostalgia Trap* (New York: Basic Books, 1992), as adapted in *Harper's Magazine*, October 1992, 13–16.

29. McDonald, *The American Presidency*, 324.

30. Lewis A. Coser, *Masters of Sociological Thought: Ideas in Historical and Social Context*, 2d ed. (New York: Harcourt Brace Jovanovich, 1977), 230.

31. Ibid., 232.

32. Edward Corwin, *The President: Office and Powers, 1789–1984* (New York: New York University Press, 1984).

33. Seymour Melman, *The Permanent War Economy: American Capitalism in Decline* (New York: Simon & Schuster, 1985).

34. Bernard S. Silberman, *Cages of Reason: The Rise of the Rational State in France, Japan, the United States, and Great Britain* (Chicago: University of Chicago Press, 1993).

35. John Ikenberry, "America's Imperial Ambition," *Foreign Affairs* 81, no. 5 (September/October 2002): 44.

36. Leon Fuerth, "An Air of Empire," *Washington Post*, March 20, 2003, A29.

37. Dinesh D'Souza, "In Praise of American Empire," *The Christian Science Monitor,* April 26, 2002, available at www.csmonitor.com/2002/0426/p11s01-coop.html. Similarly, see Victor Davis Hanson, "A Funny Sort of Empire: Are Americans Really So Imperial?" *National Review,* November 27, 2002, available at www.nationalreview.com/hanson/hanson112702.asp; and Robert Kaplan, "Supremacy by Stealth: Ten Rules for Managing the World," *The Atlantic Monthly* 292, no. 1 (July/August 2002), 65–83.

38. Bruce Nussbaum, "Beyond the War: How Bush is Destroying Globalization," *Business Week,* March 24, 2003, 32.

39. Available at www.newamericancentury.org/statementofprinciples.htm.

40. Ibid.

41. Thomas Donnelly et al., *Rebuilding America's Defenses: Strategy, Forces and Resources for a New Century* (Washington, DC: The Project for the New American Century, 2000). Available at www.newamericancentury.org/RebuildingAmericasDefenses.pdf.

42. Ibid., 11f.

43. Ibid., 62.

44. "Uniting and Strengthening America by Providing Appropriate Tools Required to Intercept and Obstruct Terrorism Act," 107th Cong., 1st sess., HR 3162 (Oct. 25, 2001), "An Act to Deter and Punish Terrorist Acts in the United States and Around the World, to Enhance Law Enforcement Investigatory Tools, and for Other Purposes." Available at www.eff.org/Privacy/Surveillance/Terrorism_militias/20011025_hr3162_usa_patriot_bill.html. See also Charles Doyle, "The USA PATRIOT Act," Library of Congress, Congressional Research Service, Order Code RS 21203 (April 18, 2002), available at www.fas.org/irp/crs/RS21203.pdf.

45. The fullest exposition was given by the president in a speech at West Point on June 1, 2002. It became official as a formal document signed by Bush, "The National Security Strategy of the United States of America," September 17, 2002, available at www.whitehouse.gov/nsc/nss.pdf.

46. Ibid., 4–6.

47. Wendell L. Willkie, *One World* (New York: Pocket Books, 1943).

48. Lawrence W. Beer and John M. Maki, *From Imperial Myth to Democracy: Japan's Two Constitutions, 1889–2002* (Boulder: University Press of Colorado, 2002).

49. Kevin Phillips, *Wealth and Democracy: A Political History of the American Rich* (New York: Broadway Books, 2002); Kevin Phillips, *The Politics of Rich and Poor: Wealth and the American Electorate in the Reagan Aftermath* (New York: HarperPerennial, 1991).

CHAPTER 11

Public Institutions in an Era of Globalization

The Need to Keep Pace

Doug Allen

Globalization and Public Institutions

Over the last thirty-five years, the forces of globalization have intensified. Information and financial capital move at unprecedented levels and velocity. Trade arrangements now encompass multiple jurisdictions. Corporations and nonprofit societies operate across national boundaries offering products and services to many but are subject to rules, regulations, and business codes that are often less than transparent. People often live, work, and play in more than one jurisdiction. This interconnectedness has enormous implications for everyone, but particularly those individuals working in public institutions.

In this environment a major challenge is the need for each public institution to stay relevant to those it serves while operating globally in an increasingly connected world. This challenge is more complicated than it may first appear.

This chapter outlines the public administration and public-policy journey I have been on since first entering the halls of the Canadian Department of Finance. It is greatly influenced by the forces of globalization. It covers twenty-five years of direct public service, ten at the national level and fifteen at the provincial level. It also covers eight years as a management consultant specializing in the rigors of public-policy formulation and implementation in Canada and abroad, the latter including lengthy assignments in Japan, Malaysia, Hawai'i, Ethiopia, South Africa, and most recently Qatar.

It is my experience over the last three decades that the forces of globalization have complicated public-policy formulation and administration in three ways. Governance, that is, the manner in which a public institution conducts its affairs, is now generally more complex. Seldom is a public institution accountable to only one body. Today, the accountability on important issues is local, provincial, national, and increasingly international. Second, strategic planning for public institutions must be ever concerned with cross-jurisdictional implications and impacts. There is little point in solving a major public-policy issue in one jurisdiction by simply passing it on to another. Finally, private interests are both powerful and pervasive as well as increasingly difficult to define in relation to the public interest.

A good example to amplify the globalization forces noted above is climate change. Consider the challenge facing the public official in the city of Vancouver who is defining a climate change agenda for the city council to consider. The public official must think internationally but provide a series of actions that warrant local response. Performance targets and measurements cannot be confined to a single jurisdiction; the issue is a global one, and progress must be made and measured accordingly. Moreover, there are many private interests involved. These private issues are quite capable of influencing the public agenda, the challenge being to ensure that such influence is positive and consistent with the public interest. This chapter offers some observations on the ability of public institutions to be both fair and relevant in a world of increasing globalization.

My Experience with Public Institutions

In 1971, I joined the Canadian Department of Finance as an officer in the Capital Markets Division. For a recent MBA graduate with an undergraduate degree in political science, there could be no higher calling. The Department of Finance was at the center of fiscal federalism in Canada,[1] with a broad mandate in taxation policy, economic policy, and capital market development and regulation. Its dominant policy role in the federation was unquestioned. I entered the department with both optimism and determination, confident that a modern and well-run public institution can make a significant difference in the quality of life of the citizens being served.

I planned to stay one year in the Department of Finance; I stayed eight. I found public-policy formulation to be both interesting and important. I also learned some early lessons, as follows:

1. A clear articulation of the policy objective is essential.
2. There is no substitute for good analysis.
3. Policy makers, to be effective, need choices with clear analysis of the strengths and weaknesses of each.

At that time, I began learning how best to formulate real policy choices and to draw upon different perspectives to analyze and identify the real strengths and weaknesses of each. I also began understanding interest groups and their role in public-policy formulation.

I knew little, however, about the role of public consultation and the media and their influence on policy formation and implementation. Moreover, I was not particularly well informed on the direct or indirect impacts of policy on the average citizen. This was a major shortcoming of mine, one that got redressed only when I got more experience in the actual implementation of policy.

In 1981 I moved from the national government in Canada to the British Columbia provincial government in Canada. I spent the next fifteen years in various public administration positions, learning considerably more about the role of public consultation and the media and how best to assess policy implications for citizens. My initial grounding was in the Ministry of Finance, spending much of my time on the provincial budgeting process.[2] I also led the provincial debt-management program for two years. In 1986 I took a special assignment with the Canadian Imperial Bank of Commerce in Tokyo, Japan, working in the Japanese financial market.[3]

On return to British Columbia in 1987, I worked in economic development positions for the provincial government and then for the next six years led five different provincial ministries as diverse as economic development and health.[4] During that period I also took a one-year educational ieave at the University of Hawai'i to obtain a graduate certificate in public administration, an endeavor that included a five-week practicum working out of the office of the deputy prime minister of Malaysia.[5] In 1996 I left public service to establish a management consulting business, specializing in the energy industry, public-policy issues in British Columbia, and the Canadian international agenda in Africa, notably Ethiopia and South Africa.[6] I am still a management consultant today.[7] It is this background and experience that informs my observations and comments on public institutions and the challenges they are facing at a time of rapid globalization.

Governance: Who Is in Charge?

A clear distinction between policy and operational accountability is central to the workings of a parliamentary democracy. The elected body must be accountable for policy while the related public institutions support the work that goes on to choose the appropriate policy and then implement it. If the elected body is not accountable for policy, who is? More important, how are the policy makers held accountable other than through the electoral process? At the same time, the elected body must be supported by professional public administrators, with expertise and experience in the policy area from both formation and implementation perspectives.

In virtually all of my work experiences, this governance[8] structure has been an issue. It is this lack of clarity on governance that causes considerable strain within public institutions, while at the same time frustrating the policy makers in the Cabinet. Once the governance issue is properly understood, the ability of public institutions to perform is greatly enhanced. I spent much of my public-service career working with politicians, staff members of the organization, and stakeholders explaining the separation of responsibility between the elected body and public institutions that support it. In addition, I found the general public to be somewhat confused on the basic governance framework for public institutions.

This confusion on governance can best be explained through two examples. In 1999 and again in 2000 I went to Eastern Cape Province in South Africa to help the Ministry of Finance and Provincial Expenditure with its strategic plan. I went as a management consultant, spending seven weeks there during the first trip and three during the latter trip. South Africa has embarked on a large program of governmental renewal across the country, and Eastern Cape, being one of the poorer provinces in South Africa, has some significant challenges in this regard. I worked on several organizational issues in the Department of Finance and Provincial Expenditure, one of them being the internal-to-government approval process for the implementation of budgetary expenditures that had been formally appropriated by the legislature.

One of the first issues I faced was that pertaining to the role of the Member of the Executive Council (MEC)[9] and the Permanent Secretary,[10] or head of the department. Once expenditures had been approved by the legislature, who had responsibility for implementing the decisions? My position was clear: it is an organizational responsibility and as such falls to the Permanent Secretary to establish principles and criteria for assessment and then ensure that assessment is carried out appropriately, subject of course to any conditions that the legislature may have imposed in the first place. The then current practice in Eastern Cape seemed less than clear. Both the MEC and the Permanent Secretary seemed to be giving final instructions. There were principles and criteria in play, but they were not readily understood. Not surprisingly, the approval process had become chaotic.

Once principles for budgetary approval were clearly established and documented, the process improved.[11] It improved further when key participants were brought in to refine the process. The overall process took a major step forward when the MEC and the Permanent Secretary understood their roles better. Had these improvements not taken place, the decision-making process of the department would have remained chaotic. More important, the ability of the department to act fairly would have remained in question.

Planning Strategically for the Future

Public institutions have the same need to plan strategically for the future as do private corporations. Their ability to do so, however, is constrained by two critical factors.

The elected body or Cabinet, in the case of parliamentary democracies, seldom looks beyond a four- or five-year horizon, the maximum time to the next election. Near the end of a political mandate, the time frame becomes even shorter. This factor alone makes it extremely difficult for the public institution to carry out long-term planning effectively, supported by a clear vision of where it is going and a highly developed strategic plan to get there. As a result, the public institution is often operating in a short-term context that may well be out of step with longer-term influences and trends that are directly related to the public institution's mandate. This potential discontinuity puts the public institution at risk, most particularly in the institution's ability to stay relevant to the needs of the people being served.

The second constraint pertains to resources. Contrary to conventional wisdom, many public institutions are very poorly resourced. They often have too few of the right people to deliver on the mandate. Further, it is extremely difficult to attract high-quality, long-term thinkers to an institution that is preoccupied with today and often does not compete well with the private sector in providing financial compensation. Moreover, the forces of globalization simply make it more difficult to compete in attracting and retaining talent.

In 1994 I had the opportunity to review the strategic plans of many of the public institutions in Malaysia.[12] This was at a time when Malaysia was making good progress, both economically and culturally. In virtually all cases, Malaysian public institutions were doing long-term strategic planning. In many ways, the focus on strategic planning appeared a good deal more advanced than I had witnessed in other jurisdictions.

These strategic plans, however, were relatively short term in nature and focused mainly on inputs, as opposed to outputs and, especially, outcomes. Accountabilities were also somewhat unclear. The reasons were quite simple, as follows:

1. There were few rewards for focusing on the longer term, as the current political mandate of the government was the main determinant of activity within public institutions.

2. Accountability often runs counter to human nature; being held accountable carries potential risks and, in the public sector, few rewards.

3. Developing clear objectives in the form of outcomes is no easy task, particularly when it comes to social policy. Moreover, few of the senior mem-

bers of the Malaysian bureaucracy were well trained in strategic planning, particularly with the difficult aspects of how best to measure outcomes and in so doing hold the appropriate officials accountable.[13]

Dealing with Private Interests

One of the most significant challenges facing public institutions at a time of increasing globalization is the growing strength and complexity of private interests as well as the very nature and accountability of the private entities involved.

In the 1970s, at least in my job with the Canadian federal Department of Finance, private interests were readily understandable in most instances.[14] These interests were often expressed by Canadian financial institutions subject to Canadian law. When these private interests differed from the broader public interest, it was often clear why and therefore relatively easy for policy makers to assess if meeting the private interest put forward was also consistent with meeting the broader public interest. Moreover, there was the opportunity to discuss the private interest in the context of the broader public interest in Canada, since private institutions often had a reasonable grasp of the public interest involved.

Thirty years later, private interests and how they relate to the public interest are far more difficult to assess. Private interests are now put forward by highly sophisticated advocates. These private interests are often expressed as public interests, and in many cases the public interest being served transcends more than one national border.

The advocates of private interests often take the form of multinational enterprises with limited affiliation to Canada. At the same time, these advocates often have substantial resources to communicate their private interests in the broader public arena and in the process work hard to convince the public that private and public interests, if not the same, are certainly compatible.

In many jurisdictions, private interests now play a more active role in actual policy formulation. For example, it is not uncommon for a business association to work closely with a public institution on how best to develop a certain policy regulation. The challenge for the public institution, and the elected body ultimately accountable, is to ensure that the new regulation meets the public interest.

The growing complexity of private interests was made evident to me in 1996 when I was asked, along with another Canadian consultant, to build a Financial Administration Act for the national government in Ethiopia.[15] It was not until we were well in to the assignment in Addis Ababa that I realized the extent of the challenge. Not only were the International Monetary Fund and the World Bank insisting that Ethiopia impose greater financial rigor within the federal administration, but it was also becoming imperative within the country that cash and in-kind contributions be readily identified and employed for public purposes in a fair and transparent manner. The new financial legislation facilitated this by defining public money quite broadly and then establishing a number of responsibilities and accountabilities for managing it. Without such rigor, it was increasingly clear to me that such resources could easily be used for private purposes that were quite inconsistent with those of the public.

Improving the Performance of Public Institutions

The three public institution issues of governance, strategic planning, and private interests are interrelated. They are also central to public institution success and if managed properly can contribute significantly to better organizational outcomes that are both relevant to public needs and fair. Paradoxically, increased globalization has made the tasks at hand exceedingly more complex to deal with while, at the same time, providing new tools and approaches and access to better talent to do so.

Governance principles

Based on my experience within ministries or departments of government and within separate agencies of government, for that matter, governance in an era of globalization can be greatly enhanced with a number of specific actions taken by public institutions.[16]

1. Develop a forum and process to debate and agree on the basic principles of governance (ensure the key representative of the elected body to whom the public institution reports is directly involved) and use third parties to foster debate and thinking on what constitutes good governance.
2. Focus on the distinction between policy and operations.
3. Develop a team to define and manage governance; in the case of an agency of government, ensure that the board of directors has an ongoing committee specifically charged with such responsibility.
4. Use global best practices; good material on governance is available from many sources around the world.
5. Utilize global resources; good information and experts on governance are readily available.
6. Engage the staff, including front-line workers, in determining what governance issues are causing problems and how they might get resolved.
7. Document the governance philosophy and principles in play and make them widely known.

8.   Use third-party assessment that is independent of the public institution itself; many universities have experienced faculty and researchers who can play a direct role in this regard.

Strategic planning

Strategic planning is an ongoing pursuit of modern corporations. The same should be true for public institutions. The main problem is the near-term mandate of the elected body to whom public institutions report. Not much can or should be done about the mandate. Nonetheless, much can be done to improve the strategic planning capability and related outcomes of public institutions.

1.   Give a formal written obligation to develop and update the strategic plan on an ongoing basis; providing for this commitment in legislation is a good approach.
2.   Impose a sunset clause[17] of no more than ten years on the life of agencies; this alone will force a debate on the relevance of the public institution and will facilitate change in the mandate when required.
3.   Get the vision right even if it takes longer than expected.
4.   Use best practices; good examples are available from many parts of the world.
5.   Engage front-line workers in the strategic planning process; they are closest to those being served and therefore have special insight into how to deliver outcomes better.
6.   Spend considerable time on how best to define outcomes, being very creative in defining how best to measure outcomes.
7.   Link individual performance to outcomes, using as many incentives as possible.
8.   Engage extraordinary thinkers, futurists, and visionaries.

Public versus private interests

One of the main challenges in the public sector is utilizing the private sector while ensuring that the public interest, not private, takes precedence. This is much harder to do today than it was thirty years ago. Private interests abound and are often multinational in nature. Moreover, the public being served does not always distinguish clearly between public and private interests. Suggestions for dealing more effectively with private interests include the following.

1.   Define and document the public interest when undertaking public policy formulation; this definition will be highly instructive for policy makers and implementers alike.

2. Consider the forces of globalization to better understand the manifestation of the private interests involved.
3. Ensure that the policy objective and the public interest being served are widely understood, both inside and outside the public institution involved.
4. Bring private entities into policy formulation but demand that they define their interests clearly and in relationship to the public interest in question.[18]
5. Test policy outcomes against public interests. This is difficult and seldom done, but it will assist in the development of better public policy.

Conclusion

In a world of rapid change, coupled with unparalleled connections and information, public institutions almost everywhere are under stress, striving daily to remain relevant and fair. Better management of governance, strategic planning, and private interests, if done wisely and consistently using some of the benefits of increasing globalization, can make a significant difference in the public interest being met and the welfare of those individuals being served.

Notes

1. Canada is a federation and a parliamentary democracy with both the national and provincial governments having significant constitutional authority.

2. Strong financial management is essential to good government. That is why the public finance organization (often called the Department or Ministry of Finance) plays such a key role in the workings of parliamentary democracies.

3. Public institutions in Japan play important roles. Again, the importance of (and tremendous respect given to) the Ministry of Finance in Japan was evident to most who worked in the Japanese financial system when I was there seventeen years ago. Given seventeen years of very modest real growth in Japan since 1987, however, it would be instructive to assess the current stature of the Ministry of Finance and the transformation, if any, that it has undergone during this period.

4. In Canada, the head of the ministry or department is called the deputy minister, and the incumbent is a professional public servant who is not elected.

5. The Hawai'i program was at the School of Public Administration at the University of Hawai'i. The practicum took place in Kuala Lumpur and included reviews of the strategic planning capability of the key institutions and organizations in the Malaysian government.

6. Both African assignments were funded by the Canadian International Development Agency.

7. I am a partner in Sage Group Management Consultants in Victoria, British Columbia.

8. "Governance is the process by which stakeholders articulate their interests, their

input is absorbed, decisions are taken and decision-makers are held accountable" (taken from the Canadian Institute on Governance).

9. In South Africa, a minister in the provincial Cabinet is called a Member of the Executive Council (MEC).

10. The Permanent Secretary is the head of the department and is called the deputy minister in Canada.

11. Better process is only part of the solution. A good part of the credit in this instance goes to Andilla Magalela, the officer in charge of the approval function. Good people with the right motivation are essential to the success of all institutions, be they public or private.

12. This assignment was part of my graduate program at the School of Public Administration at the University of Hawai'i.

13. The word "accountable" means "required or expected to justify actions or decisions."

14. Much of my work in the Department of Finance pertained to changes to the federal Bank Act. In the latter part of the decade, most of that work dealt with the development of policy options for allowing foreign banks to do business in Canada.

15. The assignment ultimately resulted in the passage of a federal financial law in the national Parliament.

16. In British Columbia, some of the Crown agencies have been quite adept at getting governance right.

17. Sunset clauses are seldom employed but send a powerful message to all parties involved. This is the most important item to act on and applies to the institution itself, not just the strategic plan.

18. Private entities are not always comfortable defining the public interest. When forced to do so, however, their ability to contribute to good outcomes for the public generally goes up, not down.

CHAPTER 12

Globalization and the Law

Emerging "Global Common Law"

Ron Brown

Global Challenges to Public Institutions and Emerging Local Legal Responses

Law inevitably embraces the dynamic changes and accommodations of public institutions caused by the flowing influences of globalization. Stripping terminology to its essentials, "globalization," "public institutions," and "fairness" still invite lively discussion as to their meaning, and each variation brings with it different legal implications, whether under foreign, international, local, or "global common law." Gaining insight on desired future choices for public institutions in the East Asia region may be assisted by some familiarity with the law as it relates to issues of globalization. This chapter examines the legal aspects of the individual and multiple impacts of globalization and the responses of national and global institutions, which often come in the form of legal regulations and consequent legal interpretations. Also discussed is how at times global influences bring legal changes—as if there were a "global common law"—both creating legal obligations and, at other times, restricting these local legal changes.

Global Influences and Fashioning Local Legal Responses

Though international trade, investment, travel, and cultural exchanges have been ongoing for centuries, in recent times cross-border contacts, dependency, and impacts increasingly occur without choice and with greater intensity. While globalization itself is a neutral term, it quickly acquires connotations in the areas of health, safety, welfare, economics, and politics. The impacts and ripple effects of such phenomena as failing financial markets, SARS, anti-terrorism, music, or the Internet reverberate across the globe, regardless of borders, and local public institutions must grapple with finding appropriate responses.

A question can arise as to what is a "local" response. While many govern-

145

ment institutions are clearly identifiable, in recent years hybrid variations of government-related organizations have proliferated and are to some degree distinguishable from the "state." Moving still farther from that center core are intergovernmental organizations (IGOs), nongovernmental organizations (NGOs), and domestic and international organizations (United Nations [UN], World Bank Organization [WBO], and interest-group associations). In current times, private entities also undertake some functions historically reserved for governments, ranging from environmental protection to cross-border communications regulation.

The actions or responses undertaken by these various legal entities have clearly different legal legitimacies and priorities. Sorting out appropriate jurisdictional terrain and the reach and limits of state sovereignty is an ongoing task of public institutions, whether or not it is they who respond to the initial or the residual impacts of globalization.

Laws often incorporate "fairness" into the regulations. It is a term embraced by lawyers and politicians, as it says "everything but nothing"; it is a slippery concept, relative to changing situations and perspectives. In cold form, it can be described as an appropriate form of balance, in search of the dynamic, yet proper, standard to serve as the fulcrum of competing interests. Even current clarity gives way to shifting perspectives, as illustrated by the legality of slavery in the US changing under constitutional interpretation from property interests to a human rights issue under equality standards. Fairness in the future global environment likely will evolve through similar metamorphoses, as the views of Third World and industrialized states mix. It is likely that the law will help in sorting out what is "fair" and in deciding whose standards are appropriate.

One can easily find illustrations and categories of how societies are touched by "globalization," which is certainly more than "commercialization" and "internationalization." It is the phenomenon associated with the oncoming irrelevancy of state borders and the increasing impotence of single-state solutions in dealing with a growing and limitless number of issues involving aspects of health, safety, welfare, finances, economics, politics, education, and so forth, as illustrated below.

Social Policy

Increasingly, issues arise locally that cannot be resolved locally either because they raise a global concern—for example, SARS—or because the local issue is incapable of resolution except by international or global solutions—for example, cross-border pollution. Such issues require local social-policy responses, but perhaps more important, they may necessitate global legal responses.

Health

Pollution grows, flows, and blows cross-border, particularly in the East Asian region, as economic development interests have driven decisions on whether to erect "barriers" of environmental protection laws.

The global impacts of pollution on the health of citizens are well documented, and its effects on a particular society vary. Pollution caused by neighboring countries causes local public institutions to seek legal recourse to stop the pollution—locally by environmental laws and internationally by treaty, by finding compensable liability, by various cooperative measures, or possibly by a military show of force.

Diseases such as SARS do not stop at the border for a visa. The impact of this health threat caused China to reassess the state of its health-care institutions and abilities and its reporting mechanisms, a true reform of public institutions brought by global threat. Most important, it brought about a governmental reassessment of its place in a global community and a decision to be cooperative with the World Health Organization (WHO) and to be more transparent in that undertaking. It also brought about a spate of new legislation designed to curb the spread of the disease.

Safety

Criminal activities at times seem to cross borders with impunity, with criminals ducking back into "safe harbors" out of simple reach by the security forces in the border left behind. Likewise, global labor, including illegal aliens, flows from certain areas in the East Asian region to destinations in industrialized countries.

The effect of this lawlessness has caused government security institutions to join forces cross-border in informal and formal arrangements ranging from reciprocal practices to full-blown treaties, working together to stem criminal activities. For example, FBI agents are working in China in cooperation with government officials, yet there is still no formal extradition treaty.

Finance

Financial impacts of shifting world markets are self-evident, having caused considerable hardship in more than one country. Typically, regional and internationally coordinated responses, rather than a single state response, are required to undo the effects caused by, for example, the recent Asian financial crisis. Sometimes, solutions compel sovereign states to accede to mandates of international organizations, such as the International Monetary Fund (IMF), resulting in significant reforms in public institutions and regulatory legislation in areas such as banking and securities practices.

Economic

East Asian government policies for economic development all have embraced foreign direct investment and trade. Looking at Japan, South Korea, and China, the resulting effects are society changing. The economies developed, legal regulation dramatically increased to cope with the developing needs of increasingly sophisticated commercial transactions, and the average citizen's standard of living rose. Foreign expertise, currency, and culture were also introduced and to some extent absorbed, though with "local characteristics."

A side effect of the above has included claims of the "McDonaldization" of local cultures and a "race to the bottom" as foreign investors competitively seek low-wage countries for their investment. This has brought about nonbinding International Labor Organization (ILO) global labor standards. Likewise, there are foreign competitive interests in lower standards of protection for the environment, health, and safety (at least in the early years of investment) whose protections are often subordinated to decisions favoring economic growth and development.

Education

The effects of economic development and momentum toward world community integration created great needs not only for cheap labor jobs, but also increasingly for more sophisticated, skilled, technical, and professional jobs. Schools for each of these areas of education developed, some with foreign flavor (including joint degrees), and increasing numbers of college students chose overseas educational training.

Societal/cultural mores

Impacted by foreign investment, products, and culture, none had more impact than the phenomenon of communication bombardment of foreign ways of doing things—delivered in the home by television and more and more by the digital transmission of the Internet and e-mail. This phenomenon affects society by creating instant communication by NGOs, by citizens, and by government, all of which present East Asian governments and public institutions with their own set of legal challenges, ranging from Falun Gong to e-business.

Political

Global impacts on East Asian governments and their public institutions are easily chronicled in that they often caused the development of new or reformed institutions in order to deal with the changes in status quo—for example, foreign direct investment, banking reforms, transportation needs, communication development and control, safety, health, and crime.

Some of these reforms were responsive to perceived needs and some were "directive," brought about by the "carrot-and-stick" requirements of foreign or international funding sources (e.g., IMF, World Bank) that carried with them agreed-upon objectives. Other reforms undertaken were more independently deemed necessary and in the national interest, such as changes to conform to World Trade Organization (WTO) membership. Issues of national sovereignty persist in these areas in a search for limits of "outside interference" with national interests. However, as discussed above, many of the local changes are locally initiated responses to global influences, rather than outside "mandates."

Globalization of the Law

Developments in the globalization of the law are increasingly observable. These include reform of public institutions that are grounded in legislation and regulations, as opposed to mere policy directives, and patterns of "global common law," clustering around international standards, albeit with "local characteristics" and standards of assessment.

While one could glibly conclude that sovereign governments merely respond to the bidding of global influences, it is far more accurate to acknowledge that national decisions reflect many interests and needs, including domestic and global influences and patterns. Ad hoc responses of governments in the East Asian region are myriad. As stated, public institutions must grow with their country's developments, whether it be with stock markets or intellectual property protection. Typically, new laws and policies (and sometimes new institutions) are promulgated to deal with developing situations, whether they be financial crises, banking reforms, health crises (such as SARS), health and information reforms, communication needs, or limits and regulation of Internet use.

International organizations like the WHO and WTO have widespread effects on creating comparable and compatible responses by governments on agenda items of global concern with local impacts. A clear illustration occurred in 2003 with SARS in East Asia and how governments dealt with it and with the WHO, illustrating the power of global influences on local public institutions, at least regarding certain issues. China was initially prepared to "go it alone," protect its national interests, and deal with SARS in its own way. It quickly became apparent that global cooperation and some integration with "outside" bodies were required to meaningfully deal with the health threat. Public institutions were rapidly transformed and plugged into WHO standards and personnel. China's penchant for nondisclosure was replaced by transparency of its public institutions and practices in dealing with SARS. Government policies and new legislation were quickly put into place to curb the threat.

Joining the WTO is another example illustrating the generation of domestic reforms pursuant to global influences—a case in point, China. Laws, public institutions, and past practices were all locally reformed in order to meet the mandatory standards of the global organization. Interestingly, by joining the WTO, members submit to a "mini supreme court" to resolve international trade disputes. Such resolutions have required states to change protective laws to keep the nation in compliance with WTO requirements. Thus global responses are made to be compatible with global requirements.

Another approach in the global influence and legalization process is exemplified by several US laws that seek to regulate citizens, businesses, and employment opportunities in overseas locations. The Foreign Corrupt Practices Act follows businesspeople, limiting their conduct, and the Civil Rights Act limits employment discrimination on foreign soil under circumscribed situations. This long-arm, extraterritorial approach of the US government also attempts global influence on the human-rights practices of foreign countries under the Foreign Trade Act by limiting loans and other guarantees to US citizens, depending on the state of human rights and labor conditions in the foreign country. This attempted influence takes place at the political level, though at times it can spill over into practical agreements, such as when the practices of US companies in China precipitated an agreement between the American and Chinese governments to ban the export of prison-labor-made goods into the United States. It also is seen by Asian countries' adoption of UN covenants on civil, political, economic, social, and cultural rights.

Another method of global influence, alluded to earlier, is the carrot-and-stick approach of certain funding entities, such as the World Bank or IMF, that requires agreement to bring about reforms in order to receive financial assistance in those projects. While it certainly is a joint project, with domestic needs being met, one can hardly miss the global influence and the local response. Churning up after the waves of global influences and challenges and responses to crises (e.g., SARS), funded projects (e.g., WBO), foreign influences (foreign direct investment), and domestic economic needs, there is observable progress in the establishment of public legal institutions and processes. Legislation, prosecution, and administrative and judicial enforcement have all taken a turn for the better. While debate continues, as expected, on whether the East Asian countries have a "rule of law," a reliably functioning judiciary, or consistent nonpolitical prosecution, it can be clearly seen that legal institutions are dynamically responding to global influences and local needs.

"Global Common Law" Precipitating Local Legal Changes

The concept of "global common law" could be discussed in the context of "customary" international law, yet there is in the idea of global common law likely to be a more meaningful international enforcement mechanism than is often used in international law. In a sense, one can look comparatively at East Asian legal developments and find patterns of response by local as well as supranational public legal institutions to international standards and events that, with some literary license, allow one to observe a developing "common law" collection of responses. These responses ultimately could lead to emerging consensus or clarity on legal and policy issues that could be the basis for further uniform global standards or local legislation. The challenge to public institutions, as always, is to determine which global approaches to incorporate into local responses, as well as which global common-law decisions restrict those choices.

> [T]he model of the unitary, independent sovereign state, acting as the complete repository of law and order, becomes increasingly inadequate as an explanation of emergent global regulation, especially because of activities that, by their nature, cannot be confined to the territorial borders of the nation-state. These activities require an understanding of cross-jurisdictional regulation such as when states try to affect regulation unilaterally through extraterritorial exercises of regulatory power, bilaterally though agreements with other states, or collectively through regional and multilateral organisations. Equally, the development of informal regulatory networks of professionals and other experts seeking solutions to cross-border problems must be taken into account.[1]

The newly emerging "global common law" is as of yet piecemeal and area specific—for example, commercial law and human rights. Its development is observable and can be described as analogous to US labor law's "federal common law" illustrated in the 1957 US Supreme Court case, *Textile Workers Union v. Lincoln Mills of Alabama*. In that case the federal court was called upon to fashion its own law by interpreting the national standard embodied in a federal statute. In creating this new common law, it was to draw upon other federal interpretations and upon state laws and interpretations, but it was not to base its decision on local state laws. Rather, it was within the court's discretion to use local rationales but make its decision independent of local regulations and base its interpretation on the federal mandate and on broader federal interests. Likewise, in "global common law," whether it be created under the broad international/supranational/transnational standard of a UN covenant, a WTO mandate, or a European Union (EU) decision, "subordinate" national interests and their sovereign interpretations often give way in certain areas to the broader global interests, where decisions form a pattern to be respected in future cases. This can be explained in various ways, including the fact that whereas earlier "internationalization" stressed cross-border economic and legal activities, the new "globalization" often includes cross-border and multiple states' economic integration. This can be accomplished by governments or multinational enterprises (MNEs) or multinational organizations (intergovernmental or nongovernmental). It is apparent that it is easier to obtain multinational or global consensus and consent on commercial interests rather than on political or cultural areas, which is reflected, as stated above, in a piecemeal global common law, and with the addition of new legal institutions to oversee the new global order. However, global codes of agreement on trade issues often result in corollary global codes of agreements in related areas such as finance and banking. Therefore, even though the law is piecemeal, the strands connecting transnational interests are often sufficient to create a binding, yet porous, web of global common law.

Sources of Global Common Law

Common-law decisions presuppose that there are in existence standards to interpret and/or at least a fertile field of common values within which a decision can be fashioned around the bonds and aims of common interests. The need for global common law arises in the commercial area from the practical needs for certainty and predictability and the usual needs for enforcement of dispute resolutions. Thus the law provides substantive guidance as well as a process within which cross-border activities are facilitated.

Sources of legal obligation and their legal oversight institutions, which bind governments and/or private parties or organizations, arise from international law (public and private), "supranational" law (e.g., the EU), and intergovernmental and nongovernmental organizations such as the WTO, ILO, and WHO. Of course these legal standards, obligations, and/or guidelines also may arise globally, regionally, or locally across two borders. What they have in common is that by consent or by economic or social reality (as described below), sovereign decisions are affected or transcended by a "beyond-national-decision interpretation" of an obligation. This results in "global common law"—for example, under the WTO, which may either create or restrict local legal decision-making authority, not only for the nation member under the global institution's dispute-resolving mechanism, but also for the other members who will be guided by that outcome in ordering their own affairs. That is because they know that they, too, could have their decisions brought in that venue.

As national interests are increasingly "delocalized" and "regulated" by global standards and obligations, a new level of legal concern comes to the forefront and has

> generated fears that unaccountable private economic power possessed by MNEs, along with similarly unaccountable public power exercised by undemocratic IGOs and by informal international policy-making networks, will serve to de-

feat the democratic process in nation-states themselves. The fear is that national constitutional orders, created to deal with issues of legitimacy and accountability at the historical stage of national economic and social integration, will be bypassed at the international level. This process may also have been enhanced by the recent trends towards privatisation of state functions, market liberalisation and deregulation that are characteristic of the New Economy state. In response, there is now a growing interest in the question of how to make these three groups of entities more accountable.[2]

For example, US concerns over the authority of the World Criminal Court and the extent to which it might interfere with national sovereignty and existing legal order is the explanation given by the United States for not joining. The many legal nuances and issues that arise from global common law are illustrated in the case of the EU, with its multilevel system of authority, interfacing with law from the international level, the EU-international level, the EU level, and the national level. Each level has its own standards and processes for dealing with the legal issues, and each creates its own level of "common law." While these legal developments are in a regional setting, they reflect the genre of legal issues involved in the developing global common law.

"Global Common Law" Restricting Local Legal Changes

In a long line of decisions in the United States, federal courts have protected the integrity of the federal government in managing the nation's foreign relations vis-à-vis states' attempts to affect it by striking down state legislation that placed risks to the United States' performance of its international obligations. A recent illustration of this was found in 2000 in *National Trade Council v. Natsios,* where the US Supreme Court struck down a Massachusetts law restricting state purchases from companies doing business in Burma (Myanmar). The law had provoked protests from other countries that subsequently challenged the measure in the WTO as being inconsistent with the US government's international obligations under the WTO Agreement on Government Procurement. Thus one can see the interplay among state, national, and global law wherein the national law preempted the state law, due to the national law's requirement to follow the global law. This type of "precedent" is thereafter used as a type of global common law not only by the United States, but also by other countries.

In several recent cases under the WTO, US laws and regulations have been found to violate that organization's global obligations. One such case was the U.S. tuna dispute involving a controversy about international trade agreements and their effect on domestic environmental legislation. Trade agreements restrict specialized domestic legislation that can act as a disguised tariff, preventing or taxing the importation of foreign goods. In this case US legislation banned imports of tuna where the country had not practiced dolphin-safe tuna fishing. The decision found the United States in violation. A similar finding of violation occurred in 2003, when the WTO's Dispute Panel ruled that US steel tariffs violated the international trade agreements.

The WTO does not invalidate national legislation. Instead, after a series of procedures permitting member retaliation, it provides that follow-up legal issues of how to deal with the offending national legislation be left for the sovereign judgment of the violating nation.

Another field falling under global common law is human rights. An interesting case developed in Tasmania where, due to international pressures from an international organization—the UN Human Rights Commission (UNHRC), under the International Covenant on Civil and Political Rights (ICCPR)—the Tasmanian state government repealed laws that outlawed homosexual acts between consenting adults. In that case, an NGO filed before the UNHRC claiming that Tasmanian law violated Australia's obligations under the ICCPR to respect privacy and equality rights. Interestingly, as a state, Tasmania had no standing before the UNHRC, an international organization, and only the national government of Australia was a respondent.

Interesting corollary legal issues involve the potential precedential value of global common-law decisions by global legal institutions. Common-law countries with a common-law legal tradition, such as the United Kingdom and the United States, are experienced with the practice of *stare decisis,* whereby once a decision is rendered it is a binding precedent in future similar situations. By contrast, a larger number of countries fall under the civil law legal tradition that historically does not follow that practice of *stare decisis.* Therefore, the "legal reflexes" of countries may vary on how to deal with certain of the global common-law decisions.

Future Directions: Universal "Global Common Law" or Legal Pluralism?

Global common law, while certainly very significant in its influence and impact on local decision making by public institutions, is still only piecemeal and limited to certain areas, such as commercial and human rights. While these areas may develop the common-law patterns of decisions toward universal standards of global law (or "customs" of international law), other large areas of a nation's political and cultural identity may or may not succumb to global pressures. Diversity and legal pluralism will continue within nations, and any growth toward universality will come not just from the legal compulsion and influence of global common law, but also from social, economic, and cultural global influences or by consent to global norms, based on self-interest. Global common law may well be the beacon that lays out a practical pathway on which to proceed.

Notes

1. Peter Muchlinski, "Globalisation and Legal Research," *The International Lawyer* 37 (2003): 230.

2. Ibid.

CHAPTER 13

Global Governance and the Environment

MARTIN KHOR

It has been more than a decade since the Rio Summit of 1992. At the time it was hailed as an achievement for placing the environment crisis at the top of the international agenda and for linking environment with development in a new paradigm of sustainable development. There was a hope that the "Spirit of Rio" would carry the paradigm forward into practical programs and policies that would deal with both the environment and development crises in a new North-South partnership.

Today it must be admitted that the process after Rio has largely failed to fulfill the promise and hopes of Rio. The Rio Plus Five Summit, United Nations General Assembly Special Session to review the United Nations Conference on the Environment and Development (UNCED), concluded in June 1997 without a political statement because the divide between North and South countries was too wide to bridge. The world's environment had continued to deteriorate. For example, forests continue to disappear or be degraded at a rate of fourteen million hectares a year; greenhouse gases are still increasingly pumped in the atmosphere, but the United States has pulled out of the Kyoto Protocol and the present targets for emission reductions are clearly inadequate; and there is a looming crisis of water shortages around the world.

The reason is not to be found in the paradigm. Rather, the paradigm was not given the chance of being tested in implementation. Instead, the sustainable development paradigm came under competition from a rival, the paradigm of globalization. This rival had indeed already been gathering strength even before the UNCED process. But UNCED for a time gave globalization good competition, and UNCED was even given support by the Copenhagen Social Development Summit of 1995.

However, the globalization paradigm was given a great boost by the Marakkesh Agreement of 1994 that established the World Trade Organization (WTO). Globalization found a new institutional house with its many rooms in the

WTO's several agreements. Moreover, the WTO's dispute-settlement system, based on retaliation and sanctions, gave it a strong enforcement capability. The WTO agreements rivaled the chapters of Agenda 21 and the Rio Declaration. The UNCED did not have a compliance system or a strong agency for following up its agreements. As the 1990s drew on and the WTO agreements became more and more operational, the globalization paradigm far outstripped the sustainable development paradigm. Marakkesh 1994 overrode and undermined Rio 1992.

The competition between the two paradigms—with globalization undoubtedly running away as the winner and moreover a winner whose speed, direction, and effects seem to be uncontrollable—has resulted in a crisis of sustainable development, or rather a number of crises.

The environment crisis has not been checked. It is getting worse, including in the area of biodiversity loss, water depletion and scarcity, climate change, and deforestation. The effects are going to be devastating. The crisis of development has worsened. The plight of less developed countries (LDCs) continues, whilst many of the more successful emerging economies also fell into crisis and several development options have been diminishing in scope or possibility.

The conceptual, policy, and political link between environment and development that had apparently been made inextricable by the UNCED process seems to have broken all too easily, and "development" as a principle or right seems to be disappearing in the Northern establishment. Even on the narrower arena of environment, there is a backlash from commerce-backed forces, which has resulted in a weakening of multilateral partnership (as witness a small group of countries almost succeeding in scuttling the Biosafety Protocol and the United States rejecting the Kyoto Protocol).

In short, in the years after the Rio Summit, the environment has dropped many notches down the global and national agendas, while "development" is also fast vanishing as a principle and an agenda item in the countries of the North and thus in the international agenda. The process of globalization has gained so much force that it has undermined and is undermining the sustainable-development agenda. Commerce and the perceived need to remain competitive in a globalizing market and to cater to the demands of companies and the rich have become the top priority of governments in the North and some in the South. Correspondingly, partnership for environment and development concerns has been downgraded.

The most glaring weakness at Rio was the failure to include the regulation of business, financial institutions, and transnational corporations (TNCs) in Agenda 21 as well as other important decisions. These institutions are responsible for generating much of the pollution and resource extraction in the world, as well as greatly contributing to the generation of unsustainable consumption patterns and a consumer culture. UNCED, the Commission on Sustainable Development, the UN system as a whole, and individual governments have collectively failed to create international mechanisms to monitor and regulate these companies. Instead their power and outreach have spread much more, and this has been facilitated by the implementation of the WTO's rules.

However, while sustainable development is at low ebb, there are also signs of its revival as a paradigm. The limitations and failures of globalization have caused a major public backlash that may eventually result in some policy changes. Pro-sustainability forces within governments in developing countries are becoming more aware of their right or responsibility to try to rectify the present problems, including changing some of the rules in the WTO. The World Summit on Sustainable Development (2002) provides a good opportunity to refocus attention of the establishment and the public not only on the problems, but also on the need to shift paradigms.

Given the unequal economic effects of the present process of globalization and its adverse social and environmental costs, there is a need for fundamental reforms of policy and practice at both the international and national levels. The following are suggestions for changes to enable conditions for sustainable development.

Need for Appropriate and Democratic Global Governance

In order to have a favorable international environment for sustainable development, it is vital for the democratization of international relations and institutions so that the South can have an active role in decision making whilst civil society can also have its concerns taken into account. The role of the UN should be strengthened while the International Monetary Fund (IMF), World Bank, and WTO should be made more accountable to the public and to the poor. Democratization in global governance structures is a prerequisite to reforms in content of policies, which can then result in more equitable sharing of benefits and costs.

The major global economic actors are the TNCs, the international banks, the World Bank, IMF, and the WTO. The operations of the corporations and financial institutions should be made much more accountable to the public, and indeed to the governments. The decision-making processes in the Bretton Woods institutions and the WTO are mainly controlled by the industrialized countries. The procedural and legal aspects of decision making should be democratized so that developing countries can have their proper share of participation. These institutions must also be more open to public participation and scrutiny. See Yoshiko Kojo's Further Thoughts, "Globalization and International Economic Institutions," on page 166.

Rebuilding the Role of the United Nations

The UN and its agencies, as the most universal and democratic international forum, should be given the opportunity and resources to maintain their identity, have their approach and development focus, as well as reaffirm and strengthen their programs and activities. The recent trend of removing the resources and authority of the UN in global economic and social issues in favor of the Bretton Woods institutions and the WTO should be reversed.

In particular, those Northern countries that have downgraded their commitment to the UN should reverse this attitude and instead affirm its indispensable and valuable role in advocating the social, equity, developmental, and environmental dimensions in the process of rapid global change. The UN could at least be a counterweight to the similar laissez-faire approach of the IMF, World Bank, and WTO.

Strengthening the UN will allow it to play its compensatory role more significantly and effectively. But of course a complementary "safety net" function is the minimum that should be set for the UN. The UN must be able to make the leap: from merely offsetting the social fallout of unequal structures and liberalization to fighting against the basic causes of poverty, inequities, social tensions, and unsustainable development. The more this is done, the more options and chances there are for developing countries and for sustainable development.

There is a danger that some UN agencies (and the Secretariat itself) may be influenced by conservative political forces to join in the laissez-faire approach or merely be content to play a second-fiddle role of taking care of the adverse social effects of laissez-faire policies promoted by other agencies. The UN should therefore keep true to its mission of promoting sustainable development and justice for the world's people and to always advocate for policies and programs that promote this mission; otherwise, it would lose its credibility and its reason for existence.

Reforming the Global Economic System to Benefit the South

Reforming the inequitable global economic system is needed as part of the battle for sustainable development. The substance of the demands for a new international economic order should be seriously addressed instead of being ignored or treated as extremist. Due to the imbalances, the outflow of real and financial resources from South to North far exceeds the flow of aid from North to South. The transfer of resources from the South makes it extremely difficult, if not impossible, for Third World countries to adequately implement sustainable development policies, even if they wanted to. Thus of major importance is the reversal of these South-to-North flows of resources.

A major area for reform is in the terms of trade between Northern and Southern exported products. The poor and deteriorating terms of trade for Third World commodity exports vis-à-vis Northern manufactured exports have been a major source of the lack of foreign exchange and income in the South. The low prices of raw materials have also contributed to the high volume of extraction and production (to maintain export earnings), and thus become a big factor in natural resource depletion. To rectify the unfair economic trade terms as well as reduce resource depletion, the prices of raw materials could be significantly raised to reflect their real and ecological costs. This may require a new round of commodity agreements or other mechanisms.

An enlarged role should be given to a revitalized United Nations Conference on Trade and Development (UNCTAD) and other UN agencies to assist developing countries in areas such as improving commodity prices and building supply capacity, as well as formulating trade, production, and development policies. Another area for reform is the resolution of the external debt burden of poor and middle-income developing countries. Debts of LDCs and other poor countries should be written off so that they can make a fresh start. The recent financial crisis involving high external debts in East Asian countries again highlights the need for countries of the South to guard against falling into a debt trap. A fair resolution to the existing debt problem that would not continue to squeeze Third World economies is important to widening the options of developing countries for the future.

In the area of investment and technology, the South and the UN had in earlier decades tried to establish codes of conduct for TNCs and for the transfer of technology, but eventually these efforts were abandoned in the early 1990s. Instead, the Northern countries are attempting to establish a multilateral agreement on investment rules under the WTO (since their efforts to create one under the Organization for Economic Cooperation and Development [OECD] failed). The investment policy rules sought by the North would largely prevent the developing countries from having meaningful options for policy making over strategic investment and development issues. Developing countries should therefore exercise their membership rights and not allow the WTO to negotiate investment rules. Instead, the right of Third World countries to determine their own economic policies and to have control over their natural resources should be recognized in practice as well as in principle. This would include the right to determine the terms under which foreign companies can invest in a country.

New efforts should be made for codes or arrangements to regulate TNCs and restrictive business practices, and to foster technology transfer to developing countries.

Reviewing the Bretton Wood Institutions and Their Policies

The "globalization" of a particular set of macroeconomic policies was achieved through the structural adjustment programs (SAPs) that the World Bank and IMF designed and exported to more than eighty developing countries. The SAPs led to widespread public discontent, including street riots and demonstrations, in many countries undergoing adjustment, and led to opposition by several people's organizations and NGOs in both the South and the North. The most important issues voiced by developing-country governments and especially by a wide range of Southern and Northern NGOs were the negative economic and social effects of SAPs, the non-accountability of the Bretton Woods institutions, and the need to resolve the South's debt crisis. They have argued that debt and structural adjustment were the most important impediments to social and sustainable development in developing countries. A serious search for the elements of an appropriate approach to macroeconomic policies and development strategies, including the proper balance of roles between the state and the public and private sectors, is essential.

Reforming the World Trade Organization

The WTO should be made more transparent and accountable to the larger international framework of cooperation and sustainable development. This is critical because the rapid developments in the WTO have such major ramifications for sustainable development, and yet there is a lack of information and participation from the public, from many sections of national governments and parliaments, and from other international institutions. There should also be greater internal transparency within the WTO. Developing-country members must have full participation rights in discussions and decision making.

There is a need to assess the implications of existing WTO agreements and to address the imbalances and deficiencies that lead to unequal outcomes at the expense of developing countries. The WTO agreements have on the whole benefited the stronger trading countries much more, and many weaker countries are likely to suffer net losses in many areas. The inequities should be redressed during the review of the agreements that is mandated to take place in the WTO in the next few years.

In particular, the WTO Agriculture Agreement has not taken into account the needs and interests of small farmers, especially the noncommercialized farmers in developing countries that form a large section of the population. The Agriculture Agreement should thus be reviewed and reformed to take into account its impact on small farmers and in the context of food security and sustainable agriculture. See Sohail Inayatullah's Further Thoughts, "Food Politics: A Multi-layered Causal Analysis," on page 168.

A review and reform of Trade-Related Aspects of Intellectual Property Rights (TRIPS) is urgently needed. The problems of implementation facing developing countries should be dealt with as a matter of top priority, and a strengthened special mechanism should be set up to satisfactorily resolve the problems (including through amending agreements) as soon as possible.

The special and differential rights of developing countries should be strengthened and operationalized. In this context, the main operational principle of the WTO, which is liberalization and "national treatment" for foreign products, should be reviewed in light of the experiences of many developing countries, which have suffered adverse effects from liberalizing their imports too rapidly whilst not being able to increase their export capability, access, and earnings. Conversely, the main goal of the WTO is sustainable development, while liberalization is only a means (and should be done appropriately), and this central theme should be operationalized in the workings of the WTO. Developing countries that encounter problems arising from liberalization should be able, in practice, to make use of their right to special and differential treatment so that they can have the option of having the right balance between opening to the world market and promoting the interests of local firms and farms.

Finally, the WTO should not take up issues that are not trade related. The attempts by some countries to introduce such new issues as investment rules, competition policy, government procurement, and labor standards should not be accepted, as developing countries will be disadvantaged by the way the WTO is likely to treat such issues. Moreover, the WTO would be seriously overloaded with such an expanded portfolio when most developing countries are already unable to cope with the current set of agreements and with the present volume of negotiations.

Trade and the Environment

Discussions within the WTO entailing the environmental effects of WTO rules can be beneficial, provided the environment is viewed within the context of sustainable development and the critical component of development is given adequate weight. The principle of "common but differentiated responsibility" derived from UNCED should guide discussions on trade and environment in the WTO and elsewhere.

The Committee on Trade and Environment should orient its work to the more complex but appropriate concept and principles of sustainable development. But there should not be any move to initiate an "environment agreement" in the WTO that involves concepts such as Political Process Models (PPMs) and eco-dumping. Thus there should not be the linking of environmental standards (and the related issues of PPMs and eco-dumping) to trade measures.

Reforming the Global Finance System

Reforms are needed in the global finance system. There should be regulation of capital flows to prevent the disruptive effects and avoid financial crises. Countries that face debt default should be able to have access to debt standstill and debt workout under an international debt arbitration institution. A more democratic system of governance and decision making on international financial matters is also needed.

Technology Assessment and the Precautionary Principle

UNCED did not deal with the theme of assessment and regulation of environmentally unsound technology in a systemic manner. What is required is a competent international center or agency, under the UN, that carries out sustainable-development assessments of technologies, especially new and emerging technologies. The center should establish systems for governing and regulating technologies. The precautionary principle should be applied in technology policy. See Walt Anderson's Further Thoughts, "Biotechnology and Fairness," on page 171.

International Environmental Governance

There are many gaps in the current system of international environmental governance (IEG). There should be better coordination and rationalization among the various multilateral environmental agreements and between these and the United Nations Environment Program (UNEP) as well as the Commission on Sustainable Development (CSD). Future initiatives on environment regulation and on IEG must place the environmental issues within the context of sustainable development so that the development dimension is streamed into environmental policy.

The Search for Alternative Development Strategies

As the UNCED process realized, a reconceptualization of development strategies is required. For example, the recent Asian financial crisis makes it crucial to reflect on the dangers to a country of excessive openness to foreign funds and investors. An important issue is whether developing countries will be allowed to learn lessons from and adopt key aspects of these alternative approaches. For this to happen, the policy conditions imposed through structural adjustment have to be loosened, and some of the multilateral disciplines on developing countries through the WTO Agreements have to be reexamined.

In the search for alternative options for developing countries, approaches based on the principles of sustainable development should be given high priority. The integration of environment with economics, and in a socially equitable manner, is perhaps the most important challenge for developing countries and for the world as a whole in the next few decades. So far there has been a recognition that something should be done, but the real work has only now to begin.

It is crucial that the research in this area be increased. It would be very useful if economic arguments could be put forward to show policy makers that it makes better economic and financial sense to take care of the environment now, even as the country progresses, rather than later. More work needs to be done, including at regional and national levels in developing countries, to produce evidence and to make both the public and policy makers aware that environmental damage is economically harmful and that environmental protection and eco-friendly technology and practices are themselves economically efficient ways of conducting development. It would also be very useful to highlight and draw lessons from examples of successful implementation of sustainable and human development policies and approaches. The emerging "sustainable and human development" paradigm could then contribute to the debate on appropriate macroeconomic policies; the appropriate relations between state, markets, and people; and appropriate development styles and models.

In the ecological sphere, the series of negotiations initiated by UNCED is an opportunity for all countries to cooperate by creating a global framework conducive to the reduction of environment problems and the promotion of sustainable economic models. However, international discussions on the environment can reach a satisfactory conclusion only if they are conducted within an agreed equitable framework. The North, with its indisputable power, should not make the environmental issue a new instrument of domination over the South. It should be accepted by all that the North should carry the bulk of the burden and responsibility for adjustment toward more ecological forms of production. This is because most of the present global environmental problems are due mainly to the North, which also possesses the financial resources and the economic capacity to reduce its output and consumption levels.

There should be much more focus on changing economic policies and behavior in order that the patterns of consumption and production can be changed to become environmentally sound. What needs to be discussed is not only the development model of the South, but even much more the economic model of the North, and of course the international economic order. Key issues to resolve include the following:

1. How to change structurally the Northern model of production and consumption or lifestyles.
2. How to promote ecologically sound and socially just development models in the South.
3. How to structurally adjust the world economic institutions so as to promote fairer terms of trade and reverse the South-North flow of financial resources.
4. How to come toward a fair distribution of the sharing of the burden of adjustment necessitated by ecological imperatives, as between countries and as within countries.

Whilst the international elements of a fair and sustainable global order are obviously crucial, there must also be substantial changes to the national order as a complement. In both North and South, the wide disparities in wealth and income within countries have to be narrowed. In a situation of improved equity, it would be more possible to plan and implement strategies of economic adjustment to ecological and social goals.

In the South, the policy option can be taken to adopt more equitable and ecological models of development. With more equitable distribution of resources, such as land, and greater access to utilities and housing, the highest priorities of the economy should be shifted to the production of basic goods and services to meet the needs of the people. Investments (including government projects) should be channeled toward basic infrastructure and production, in contrast to the current bias for luxury projects and status symbols of progress. Social investment in primary health care, education, housing for people, public transport, and popular cultural activities should also be emphasized, rather than the high-level luxury services that now absorb a large portion of national expenditure. In this social context, changes also have to be made to make the economy follow the principles of ecology. There should generally be a reduction in the extraction and production of primary commodities: this would reduce the problem of depletion of natural resources, such as forests and minerals.

The decline in output and export volume could be offset if commodity prices were to rise, thereby providing a fair value of export earnings. In agriculture, the ecological methods of soil conservation, seed and crop diversity, water harnessing, and pest control should replace the modern, non-ecological methods. With a reduction in production of agricultural raw materials, more land can also be allocated for food crops. There should be as much conservation of primary forests as possible, and the destructive methods of trawler fishing should be rapidly phased out whilst fishery resources are rehabilitated and the environmentally sound fishing methods of small fisherfolk are promoted. In industry and construction, ecologically appropriate forms of production should be given priority. There should be strict limits on the use of toxic substances or hazardous technologies, a ban on toxic products, and the minimization of the volume of toxic waste and pollution. Of course, to make this move toward a better global order possible, there must be people's participation, because the radical changes being called for can be realized only when there is popular will. It is crucial that information be provided to the people through the media and popular education methods and that the people are given the freedom to make their views known to the policy makers and to others.

It should be stressed that the elements proposed here for a fair and sustainable global order have to be taken together, as a package. Social justice, equity, ecological sustainability, and public participation are all necessary conditions for this order, and the change must apply at both national and international levels. Policies that promote equity alone would not necessarily result in a more environmentally sound world. On the other hand, measures to solve the ecological crisis without being accompanied by a more equitable distribution of resources could lead to even greater inequity and injustice.

FURTHER THOUGHTS

Globalization and International Economic Institutions

Yoshiko Kojo

GLOBALIZATION HAS LOTS of meanings depending on people's perspectives. Definitions cover a wide range of today's international phenomena from trade and capital mobility to organized crime and pop culture. Rapid economic flow is one of the most important characteristics of today's globalization.

In the era of today's economic globalization, international institutions have gotten lots of attention. Partly due to the end of the Cold War, the number of international institutions has increased since the late 1980s. Some were newly created, like the North-American Free Trade Agreement (NAFTA) and Asia-Pacific Economic Cooperation (APEC), while some were developed further, such as the WTO. When we observe such increases of international institutions both at global and regional levels, we are wondering how economic globalization has been related to such increases.

Economic globalization has been related to international institutions in two different ways. First, international economic institutions have facilitated economic globalization. After World War II, the Bretton Woods institutions such as the General Agreement on Tariffs and Trade (GATT) and IMF were founded to achieve a "free, open, and multilateral" international economic system. The GATT succeeded in lowering tariffs and facilitated reducing nontariff barriers. After the mid-1980s, the Organization for Economic Cooperation and Development (OECD) and the IMF policies liberalized capital mobility. Also, the regional institutions such as the EU, NAFTA, and APEC have aimed for trade and capital liberalization within each region. These kinds of international economic institutions played a role in facilitating economic globalization by liberalizing each country's economic policy under the name of international rule, although that rule was the product of negotiation among countries. In other words, many countries, mainly industrial ones, made use of international institutions to facilitate a "free, open, and multilateral" international economic system.

The second aspect of the relation between economic globalization and international institutions is that in the face of economic globalization, many governments have begun to recognize that individual governments cannot control the negative consequences of economic globalization, such as a contagious financial crises, environmental pollution, and poverty reduction. In this context, international institutions have been expected to play a role in solving so-called externalities of economic globalization. Proposals for "global governance" in the 1990s emphasized the role of international institutions in global governance. After the Asian financial crisis, the Asian Monetary Fund was under consideration as a new financial lending institution, although it failed. The Basel Accord of banking regulation in the Bank for International Settlement is another example. Even the economic institutions that have promoted economic globalization are asked to play some positive role in solving negative consequences of economic globalization.

Because of these two aspects, international economic institutions are now blamed for their role in facilitating globalization, on the one hand, and yet are expected to play a role in controlling globalization, on the other.

There are now many criticisms toward international economic institutions. Let's look at two such criticisms and see how international economic institutions are responding to them. The first is that international economic institutions failed to deal effectively with the distributional effect of economic globalization among countries. The second is that decision-making processes of international economic institutions are not fair for developing countries.

Developing countries claim that international economic institutions did not effectively deal with inequalities in international society. Responding to such criticism, international institutions have shown some progress, although they are still limited. For example, the World Bank responded to the earlier criticisms of its policy in developing countries by adopting an antipoverty strategy in the early 1990s. It came to emphasize the importance of taking into account each country's domestic social and political situation, as well as its economic one. In particular, the World Bank has been concerned about how to protect vulnerable groups and the poor and what kinds of safety nets can provide an environment in which economic reform is more politically sustainable. To respond to these questions, the World Bank has been seeking an alliance with NGOs in order to reach the poorest more effectively.

The IMF, in the early 1990s, acknowledged the shortcomings of its structural adjustment programs. It emphasized the social and political aspects of adjustment. However, the Asian financial crisis has shown that its policy has been based on the principle that "social development requires a strategy of high quality economic growth," and it is still stuck to a structural adjustment policy.

The WTO situation is rather complex. There, the relation between free trade and social protection has come to the agenda. Greater free trade has produced the recognition that trade liberalization would undermine social protection measures and labor and social regulations and standards. On this issue, developing and middle-income countries were almost universally opposed to the insertion of social clauses in the rules of the WTO, while the United States and France supported it. The former claims that such insertion is an attempt to defend the high-cost economies of the West from international competition and represented protectionism, while the latter claims that the abolition of child labor and free association of labor are fundamental rights.

Regarding the second criticism, there is not much progress responding to the unfair decision-making procedure in international institutions. The problem of the "democratic deficit" has become serious for many international institutions. This deficit means that those who are influenced by their decisions cannot participate in decision making and governance. The IMF and World Bank show no intention of changing their weighted voting systems. However, they try to appeal that their policy programs for individual countries have become more attentive toward the recipient country recently. As for the WTO, many NGOs want to participate in its negotiations.

Despite these steps, international economic institutions are now faced with the difficult task of legitimizing their decisions and policies. Without a sense of ownership of international institutions by every participant, it is getting more difficult for these institutions to play a positive and legitimate role in international society.

Food Politics

A Multilayered Causal Analysis

Sohail Inayatullah

MULTILAYERED CAUSAL ANALYSIS seeks to unpack issues about the future by utilizing four modes of analysis. The first mode is the "litany," or the typical, official, present-based description of the issues. In this mode, concerns about fairness are generally expressed at the individual level: how I was mistreated, how globalization has lead to losses for my business, and how the government is not doing anything about it. These are front-page stories that highlight individual or, indeed, national plights. Success stories abound also: how individuals have done well in globalization or found new exports and/or new trading partners, and how local economic development offices have, in fact, been helpful.

Most popular (and much professional) analysis of futures issues remains locked at the level of "litany" (or "anthem") alone, never going deeper into the underlying causes and solutions.

The second mode of analysis is focused on societal, technological, economic, environmental, and political drivers. Thus changes to public institutions are accomplished through certain systemic changes in policy: a new law, a new procedure, or new modes of access. Farmers in the United States have argued from this perspective and have succeeded in gaining subsidies, for example.

Most policy futures work stays at these two levels: changing how individuals behave and how systems function, but nothing more. However, deeper analysis includes two other levels of understanding and intervention: the worldview level—deeper assumptions on the nature of globalization and fairness—and the myth/metaphor level, or hidden, unconscious stories that give meaning and shape to the worldview, policy, and litany dimension.

In the farming example, there can be a range of worldviews. For example, the Prout model of Indian philosopher P. R. Sarkar argues that globalization is best when conditions of equality (cultural, political, and economic) exist. In conditions of inequity, globalization can hurt individuals and businesses. Thus agriculture should be self-reliant and developed via producer and consumer co-operatives using a mix of organic, high-tech genetics and industrial processes. The issue of subsidies is resolved partly by developing economies that ensure that each nation is agriculturally self-reliant. However, the real unit of the economy should not be only local but, with technological advances, become planetary. If that is the case, then food ceases to be a national commodity and becomes a global right. Switching to this worldview, the intervention needed is a real world food organization with power over nation-states. Thus rethinking the individual and systemic issue through a change in worldviews (using an alternative model of political economy and globality) leads to different solutions, among them fundamentally changing the organizational structure of farming in this example.

Even deeper than the worldview level is the myth and metaphor. For Sarkar, this is like the family traveling in a caravan: there is direction, and if someone falls behind they are picked up. Food politics must thus be both local (local community empowerment) and global (food as a human right).

Alternatively, from the globalized view, subsidies only increase inefficiency. Farming production and prices are best determined by the market. Locating farming at the national level of one nation hurts farmers in other nations. What is needed is a broad agreement on opening up food markets. Sovereignty is not challenged per se, but global institutions should naturally evolve. The story behind this is that the free movement of goods and services leads eventually to the benefit of all. Those who can produce the best and cheapest food should; others should do something else.

Again, if we switch worldviews to the Green-Left perspective, what is important is the quality of the food as well and the impact of certain farming practices on nature. By switching, for example, to a world vegetarian regime, water currently being wasted could be saved, grains currently being used to grow cows for humans to eat could far more efficiently be directly eaten by humans. Thus the current farming discourse is unsustainable for the planet. The issue is not subsidies but changing eating as well as farming practices.

As well, the Green-Left calls for fair trade, not free trade. For them, global trade is skewed toward the rich and powerful and against small farmers from Third World nations. Farming is essentially about power. The powerful should enter new relations with those whose relative (commodity) prices fall in relation to the prices of manufactured goods and services. Farming is structurally unfair. But subsidizing rich American farmers may also not be the best policy. A vegetarian version of this new left may be better.

From a fourth worldview, the issue is not about farming per se but about national-local politics. There is agreement to subsidize farming nationally, knowing full well that such legislation will lead to domestic votes and that the WTO will uphold protests against subsidies. Globalization thus will continue even if it appears that the United States challenges its further development. The story behind this practice is strategic politics—just do what you can to stay in power—essentially, the ends justify the means.

The main point is that there are multiple levels of analysis. Proponents of each worldview seek out "litany" data and statistics as well as policy prescriptions to support their worldview. They are living their story. They use public institutions to realize, via the systemic level of analysis, their worldviews.

For productive pedagogy and analysis, the key is the capacity to move up and down levels, seeking to understand divergent worldviews and the policy and litany statements that result from them. For long-lasting change, however, interventions need to be at every level at the litany, *Time*-magazine level, at the systemic institutional change level, at the worldview, and at the level of myth/metaphor. This might mean an understanding that for farming to be fair, it needs to be (1) local (local community and capacity building), (2) sustainable (mixing types of farming regimes, moving away from meat production and reducing water inputs), and (3) global (food as a human global good and right), and a strong global regime for food production and consumption is needed. This may mean moving toward a "what works" paradigm, that is, which institutional structures work best for prosperity, planet, people, and future generations across civilizations.

Biotechnology and Fairness

Walt Anderson

It is widely accepted that there is a serious "digital divide" in the world, measurable by the enormous disparities in access not only to computers, but also to more basic communications technologies such as telephones and radios. Many different efforts now underway are attempting not only to get communications and information equipment in the hands of people, but also to enable them to use it effectively and gain practical access to the ever-expanding realm of public knowledge.

Less discussed, but no less serious, is what might be called a "genome gap," the inequality of access to the new capabilities of the life sciences and biotechnologies. The promise of new developments along these lines is so great that some people see the beginnings of a new stage in evolution as human beings enjoy health, abilities, and longevity far beyond anything known in the past.

There are many dark sides to this bright picture, the most serious of which are expressed in a simple and obvious set of questions: Which human beings? Whose diseases will be cured? Whose life will be extended? There is already an enormous wealth gap in the world, and inseparable from it is the "health gap": people in the wealthier parts of the world live longer, eat better, are better protected against disease. With new life-extending and performance-boosting enhancements, that gap can grow even wider, to the point that the rich and the poor are hardly the same species.

Such enhancements are already here, and there is no doubt that many more are on the way. Current research and development in biotechnology guarantees that new products will become available, and market conditions (particularly the increasing numbers of older people as the baby-boom generation ages) guarantee a strong demand for them.

Concerns about the safety and efficacy of such products can probably be resolved over time. The more possible it becomes for some people to live longer and function more effectively, the more acute becomes the difference between those who have access to such benefits and those who do not. All of those treatments cost money, and some of them cost huge amounts of it, and it hardly seems likely that publicly funded medical insurance, welfare agencies, NGOs, and international health services are going to bring enhancements to everyone. The best-case scenario (of astonishing breakthroughs in science and technology that fundamentally change human life) can easily become the worst-case scenario of inequalities beyond anything the world has yet seen.

It is a dismal (yet very real) prospect, and one that public policy makers have scarcely begun to think about. Some leaders in the world of science believe it is time they began. Not long ago an editorial titled "Exploring Life as We Don't Yet Know It" appeared in the respected British publication *Nature*. It urged that some organizations (such as the United Nations Educational, Scientific and Cultural Organization [UNESCO]) take on the job of looking at scenarios of likely future developments in the enhancement field, anticipating the time when feats "that are currently regarded as out of bounds have become both practicable and, to some, eminently desirable."

CHAPTER 14

Trends in Bureaucracy, Democracy, and Representation

FRED RIGGS

To understand how globalization affects fairness in public institutions, we need first of all to be clear about the way public institutions are organized. When I use this term, I am thinking not only of the bureaucratic apparatus employed in public administration, but of the control structures that, in a democracy, involve elected assemblies as the source of authority and control. When we conceptualize institutions as government agencies, we are looking at only part of a system.

To understand how globalization and fairness apply to these institutions, we need to visualize them as whole systems. Representative assemblies are as much an integral part of public institutions in a democracy as are its appointed officials. Officials, both elected and appointed, are actors in any system of democratic governance. Of course, the two are linked. We sometimes speak of "representative bureaucracy" referring to the inclusion of minority people in administration, but no bureaucracy can be assuredly representative unless its controlling legislative organs are also representative.

Democratic Paradigm

Globalization compels us to reassess our images of how democracy is constituted or ought to work. Starting at the local level, democratic forms of government evolved, in opposition to monarchic and aristocratic tyrannies, as a form of government based on consensus among all participating citizens. In the context of capitalist and imperialist expansion, bourgeois democracies evolved based on the premise that representative assemblies could govern on behalf of citizens, political expansion making direct democracy impossible. However, the expansion of states also made bureaucracy necessary. Governance in larger states was no longer feasible on the basis of volunteers as implementers of public policy. This generated tensions between the heads of governments and representative assemblies leading to precarious accommodations, first in the format familiar to Americans where a popularly elected president jockeys precariously with an elected Congress, and later in the more stable form based on separation of the roles of head of state and head of government in which real executive power is exercised by a prime minister subject to removal by the assembly.

This paradigm evolved in the context of sedentary populations, typical of agricultural and industrial societies. It never worked in traditional nomadic societies, nor can it work in today's global society where organized groups, often based on the power of glocalizing forces, require recognition and can accept responsibility in concert with organized polities whose representative assemblies are elected by individualized citizens. We typically do not recognize intergovernmental organizations (unions) as truly democratic no matter how democratic may be their goals and legislative processes; the United Nations (UN) provides a salient example. Yet in a globalized world system, we need to recognize and honor a new pattern of democratic organization that links legislative accountability to individuals with group representation. A good example of this design can be found in the European Union, where a council of ministers (representing states) share power with a parliament (representing all the citizens' member states). This new form of democratic organization, which links individual and group representation, still lacks a distinctive name; we need to accept one before it can be widely established in response to the acute requirements of global governance in our synarchic world.

Bureaucratic Accountability

Can any bureaucracy be truly representative if the legislative assemblies that set its agendas and monitor its performance are not also representative? This is an increasingly urgent question throughout the world: more representative legislative bodies entail more diverse bureaucracies. An unrepresentative legislature may support the tokenistic inclusion of a few minority people in the public service, but public bureaucracies will not, I believe, become truly "representative" unless the organs that control them are also representative.

Although our thinking about public institutions typically focuses on the state level, the same principles apply to interstate organizations like the UN. Here, in its most conspicuous form, the representation of states is reflected in the quota system imposed on the UN Secretariat to assure its fairness in dealing with all member states; the principle of group representation is carried to its ultimate level in this context. A more useful model can be found in the design of the European Union, which links a Council of Ministers representing the member states with a European Parliament representing all citizens. The Secretariat of the European Union should, in principle at least, be highly representative of all participating European communities.

Fairness versus Representativeness

Although I have not used "fairness" in this chapter, representativeness and fairness are closely linked. Can anyone count on an unrepresentative bureaucracy (police, teachers, welfare workers, tax collectors, etc.) to treat all communities fairly when they are not themselves fairly constituted? This is apparent in the current war against terrorism, which, in the name of homeland security, has targeted certain minority groups for special attention.[1]

Unfortunately, our theories of representation are one-sided. They provide for the representation of individual voters, but not for the representation of groups, especially communal groups, nor of diasporan citizens living abroad. By contrast, in societies like Afghanistan, it seems clear that group representation is paramount, as in the Constitution of its new interim regime. In traditional societies we see that representation, if it exists, is of communities, not of individuals. These communities include not only those living inside Afghanistan, but Afghans living elsewhere in the world. We may hope that Afghanistan will add the representation of individuals to its Constitution when it adopts a democratic form, but we cannot expect that established tribal organizations and loyalties will vanish or become irrelevant or that they will make a sharp distinction between Afghans at home or in diaspora.

Globalization and Diversity

Conversely, in modern democracies, as they become more multiethnic due to increased flow of migrants boosted by globalization, we need to supplement the representation of individual citizens (now the dominant and, indeed, only recognized form of representation) with representation for groups. This means that reform efforts need to be contextual: in more traditional societies (like Afghanistan), representation for individual citizens needs to become established, but in more industrialized societies, representation for groups also needs to be institutionalized, especially for "indigenous people" as well as for ethnic minority communities. However, there are other unrepresented (or inadequately represented) groups, especially women and children, the elderly, and, indeed, the unborn and the "environment."

Women and children have recently received more attention, but discrimination against them is endemic, reaching acute levels in Afghanistan under the Taliban, as we all know today. As a senior, I am also sensitive to ageism. We tend to equate "people" with the "employed" populations, and retirees are often not seen as real people.

Globalization is not homogenization—far from it! In fact, the spread of global economic, political, informational, cultural, and military forces provokes local glocalizing responses. This is not localization, a purely parochial and natural process as local communities evolve their distinctive practices and ideas. By contrast, in the context of globalization, localities seek to protect their interests and assert their distinctive identities. This glocalizing process generates new phenomena that assert and accentuate local autonomy and leadership. To defend their uniqueness, glocalities evolve products and understandings they view as relevant and important for the rest of the world. Their capacity to influence the world is enhanced by proliferating lines in the global network that enable mobility (the movement of people and information) made possible by new technologies such as the airplane, the Internet, and global English.

The outcome of mobility is diversity and dispersion: every glocality now has increasingly diverse communities, and every locality has become globalized by the dispersion of some of its members. Recognizing this reality, we should not resist globalization; instead, we should encourage constructive glocalization, in Hawai'i and throughout the Asia-Pacific region. This can include the development of local languages, Web sites, cultural practices and products, and truly representative political institutions. It is only fair that people should have the right and opportunity to develop their individual identity and that they should be secure in the process, which requires some kind of global ordering.

The result of globalization and glocalization can be seen in the prevalence of synarchy, a complex networking system that links synthesis and anarchy. Organizational structures that are effective and representative are evolving rapidly to create a global network of linked states, substates, interstate organizations, and a host of nongovernmental organizations at all levels. Corporations, capital flow, and financial institutions are an important part of this network, but they are increasingly countervailed by nonprofit public institutions. In this context, tensions often erupt in civil wars and revolts, even terrorism, leading to the sense of pervasive anarchy. Yet this very anarchy, despite its inhuman costs, also protects zones of autonomy and helps prevent the emergence of authoritarianism, which, at the global level, might create an oppressive and tyrannical form of world empire that we would all abhor.

Virtual Representation

To make this new form of democracy viable, however, it needs to include the virtual representation of "unrepresentable groups," a process that will always be contested yet needs desperately to be addressed. The most obvious category of unrepresentable groups consists of unborn future generations. Who can or should speak for them? All fecund present generations recognize not only the inevitable birth of future generations but acknowledge our obligation to leave or restore a sustainable world for them to live in.

By implication, the earth and all living things are also interested participants; without seeking to reify the environment, it needs to be represented also in global and glocal politics. To do that, we could empower specialized professional and humanitarian groups (associations and institutes) to act on behalf of the unrepresentable. In traditional democracies like the United Kingdom, a House of Peers was established by ascriptive criteria; membership was not representative but rested on status. Today, hereditary peers have been discharged and new forms of representation are being established—they might well include the recognition of unrepresentative categories and the institution of virtual representation to protect these essential interests.

New patterns of democratic governance at all levels (substate, state, and global) are needed if fairness is to be protected with respect to all kinds of minorities (based on age, gender, and ethnicity), if diversity and dispersion are to be safeguarded, and if unrepresentable constituencies are to be given a fair hearing. Unborn generations have no way of securing direct representation, but it is surely possible to give them virtual representation through organized ("futurist") groups able to take a long-term view. The same is true, of course, for the environment, which needs to be respected and conserved despite its inability to speak for itself; there are "ecosophical" groups prepared to reify environmental entities as deserving of representation. We might then think about "virtual" as well as "concrete" representation.

A truly representative bureaucracy that can be counted on to administer public affairs fairly should include members from diverse perspectives. It also needs to manage public affairs in the interest of unrepresented groups, including women, the very young and very old, the unborn, and the environment, including all living creatures.

Note

1. Imtiaz Hussain, a colleague who lives in Mexico and was scheduled to participate in a panel I had planned for the New Orleans ISA conference in March 2002, decided to withdraw for fear that, as a Muslim, he would be mistreated if he came to the United States. His fears may be quite unjustified, but they illustrate the problem of fairness as impacted by globalization.

CHAPTER 15

Civil Society and Governance Reform

JIM DATOR

Evolution of Forms of Governance

For the overwhelming majority of human history, humans lived in very small bands or tribes of from twenty to three hundred people, or in villages of the same size (and only rarely more than one thousand people or so). Even as late as the eighteenth century, "large cities" often had only five thousand to twenty thousand people in them. At the beginning of the nineteenth century the largest city in the world was Tokyo, with slightly over one million people. London, with fewer than one million, was the largest in the West at that time. One of the largest cities in the early twenty-first century is Mexico City, with more than twenty-five million people. A dozen or more other Third World cities are also in this range, and for the first time more of humanity lives in urban areas than rural ones. True, some past civilizations produced impressively large cities and often sustained them for some time, but they were exceptions. "Civilization" itself is only several thousand years old, a blink of the eye for the lifetime of *homosapiens sapiens.*

For most of prehistory, most tribes and bands seem to have been organized "democratically." There were no official leaders, or even permanent "chiefs." Thus it may not be too much to say that humans are "evolved" from small, face-to-face groups where decisions were "democratically" made via discussion and consensus.[1]

Experience from many years of teaching political design courses reveals that most students end up trying to reinvent tribal societies when asked to redesign governance. We all want to be able to participate in matters affecting us. We want to have a fair hand in carrying out group tasks. We want to participate in settling conflicts among our companions.

Well, not everyone does. There are many "libertarians" who believe that life in the "state of nature" was one of free, rugged individuals doing their own thing without the slightest concern about the things that other rugged individuals were doing, and that only recently have governments arisen to steal their natural individual freedom.

Such libertarianism is entirely mistaken, the anthropological evidence shows.[2] Early humans were normally in groups and could scarcely have imagined their independence from their groups. "Individualism" is a recent concept that arose when more and more people did in fact find themselves on their own, without lifetime community attachments, first as a consequence of agricultural, and then especially industrial, processes and institutions. This enabled (required) them to develop ideologies to justify their solitary experiences and to make that experience not only tolerable, but preferable.

Still, the libertarians are right if they mean that humans were not "normally" subject to faceless and remote power figures over which they had no real influence or control. Such dominance clearly is a recently evolved human condition, arising (only several thousand years ago) initially when the first hereditary chiefdoms were established typically by conquest over Others, and then elaborated into the early civilizations, then into extensive feudal arrangements in some parts of the world, then maturing finally into "kingdoms," which, in the European experience, were what so-called "democratic" (really, "representative") forms of government were intended to replace.

As an anonymous pamphlet, *The Genuine Principles of the Ancient Saxon, or English Constitution,* published in Philadelphia in the late spring of 1776, put it, in ancient Saxon times "[m]en became concerned about government because they participated daily in the affairs of their tithings and towns, not only by paying taxes but by performing public duties and by personally making laws. When these tasks were taken out of the people's hands and given to superior bodies to perform, men fell into a political stupor, and have never, to this day, thoroughly awakened, to a sense of the necessity there is, to watch over both legislative and executive departments in the state."[3]

Active participation by people in their own governance was true of humanity everywhere for tens of thousands of years, well before the "ancient Saxons." But "men fell into a political stupor" as local and global populations grew, new technologies (especially first the invention of writing and the printing press) made political control over vast territories, and time, possible, and so empires and eventually nation-states arose that could not be organized on direct, face-to-face bases, but required other means.[4] At first, these means simply required obedience and conformity to the will of the center by those on the periphery through various combinations of religious/ideological and military controls. But as people "awakened to a sense of the necessity . . . to watch over both legislative and executive departments in the state," people began to wonder how self-governance was possible over vast areas of land and among peoples with diverse interests and backgrounds.

An answer was found in the shared philosophy of Locke, Hobbes, Montesque, and Rousseau, and the unprecedented opportunity the American founding fathers had between 1776 and 1789 to turn those philosophies into viable political institutions, resulting in the US Constitution.

So all governments now are still based uncritically on that wonderful eighteenth-century invention, called "constitutionalism," which itself is dependent on Western rationalistic assumptions often called "Newtonianism."[5] Though "constitutionalism" was certainly a stunning, cutting-edge philosophical and technological solution to governance challenges of the time, it is the sad and curious fact that the fundamental epistemological and technological assumptions of constitutionalism have never been challenged, to our knowledge, and certainly never set aside, when new opportunities for designing governance systems arose, as they did first with the creation of socialist systems in the early twentieth century, then during the demilitarization and decolonialization periods at the end of World War II, and more recently with the collapse of socialist systems. Even the American-led "regime change" in Iraq did not result in a fundamentally rethought or contemporary governance structure.

While some accommodations to specific historical and cultural features have of course been made with each new constitution adopted, the basic framework and assumptions of the original US Constitution of 1789 are the bedrock upon which each of the many constitutions created during the twentieth and now twenty-first centuries have rested.

In the first volume of his fabulous science-fiction trilogy set initially in the mid-twenty-first century titled, successively, *Red Mars, Green Mars,* and *Blue Mars,* Kim Stanley Robinson (himself a political scientist by academic training) describes a debate the early settlers of Mars have concerning the creation of a governance system for Mars. Toward the end of the debate one of the settlers, Arkady, cries out in frustration,

> "I can say only this! We have come to Mars for good. We are going to make not only our homes and our food, but also our water and the very air we breathe—all on a planet that has none of these things. We can do this because we have technology to manipulate matter right down to the molecular level. This is an extraordinary ability, think of it! And yet some of us here can accept transforming the entire physical reality of this planet, without doing a single thing to change our selves, or the way we live. To be twenty-first-century scientists on Mars, in fact, but at the same time living within nineteenth-century social systems, based on seventeenth-century ideologies. It's absurd, it's crazy, it's— it's—" he

seized his head in his hands, tugged at his hair, roared "It's unscientific! And so I say that among all the many things we transform on Mars, ourselves and our social reality should be among them. We must terraform not only Mars, but ourselves."[6]

Yes, it is crazy (and "unscientific") indeed. But it is certainly true. Probably the most out-of-date aspects of the everyday world we all live in now are our systems of governance. They are, as the fictional person Arkady says, "nineteenth-century social systems based on seventeenth-century ideologies." And they do have a firm control over our minds and actions.

Structure Matters

Does it matter that all "new" governments of the world are built on cosmologies and technologies almost three hundred years old? It does. First of all, structure itself matters. For example, one of the few clear "laws" of political "science" is that single-member districts (as in the United States) create two-party systems, while multimember districts (found in most of the world) enable multiparty systems.

It is simply not possible for a multiparty system to come into existence in the United States. The single-member district system prevents it. No matter how many minds or wills change, neither a third nor a fourth party can ever compete effectively in the United States as long as the single-member district system remains. Whenever a third party begins to arise, it is either rejected, and so it eventually dissolves and its position (and members) is absorbed by one of the other two major parties, or it replaces one of the two major parties (this has happened in American history, in the nineteenth century). Whatever the outcome, the two-party framework itself is preserved. It is entirely a question of structure.

Indeed, the entire US Constitution is the world's first, and best, example of conscious political design to solve certain "design limitations" that the founding fathers faced in 1787.

1. The "Separation of Power" with "Checks and Balances." How could "evil" men govern? By "separating" "power" and giving specific pieces of it to each of three "independent" yet overlapping branches of government so that "selfish power will balance power," creating social good.
2. The "Division of Power" and "Federalism." How can the thirteen colonies, now newly sovereign nations, be persuaded to join into a closer political union? By "dividing" "power" equally between them and the central government.
3. Bicameralism. But how could populous newly sovereign states be con-

vinced to share power equally with smaller states? By creating a Congress of two "Houses," one in which the states have equal representation regardless of their population and another where the states are represented roughly according to their population size.

4. Presidential Electors. How can a single "president" be chosen for the entire nation? Since the colonies forming the union had no history of political unity and there were no means for creating a national political dialogue at that time (and no great faith in "the people" anyway), how could the people in the widely separated new states possibly know who was nationally the "best man" for president? The founders reckoned they could not, but that they would know their local "best men." So they would choose them, and these local "best men" would go to Washington to choose, after discussion, the national "best man" for president.

5. Presidentialism. But the creation of the presidentialist system itself has behavioral consequences that the founding fathers did not anticipate. Indeed most Americans (even most American political scientists) do not recognize it even now.

There are in the world today basically two governance systems. One is parliamentary and the other is presidential, or, more correctly (according to Fred Riggs), presidentialist.[7] Most countries use a parliamentary form by which the political head of state (e.g., the prime minister) is chosen by, and responsible to, the majority of a representative national assembly (e.g., the Parliament). It is comparatively easy for the national assembly to remove the prime minister from office and install a new one, when there are sufficient policy differences to require it.

However, when the governance system of the United States was created in the late eighteenth century, several design limitations and political considerations led the founding fathers to invent a political system whereby the single chief executive (here, the president) would be elected by a process and constituency completely separate from that of the national assembly (here, the bicameral Congress). Thus the chief executive in the United States is not responsible to and cannot be removed by the national assembly except for extraordinary reasons and by extraordinary measures. This feature often leads to a policy deadlock between the president and Congress that can effectively grind the machinery of governance to a halt. It also allows one man (the president) to gain power during an "emergency" and return it, if at all, long after the emergency has gone.

In the years since 1789, most polities have adopted a parliamentary rather than a presidentialist system when they have had the option. But many have chosen the presidentialist form because of American influence or persuasion. When they have done so, the results have been uniformly catastrophic: all of the thirty nations that adopted the American presidentialist form of government since World War II had, by 1985, collapsed into military dictatorship. For years, the United States itself was the only counter-example of a sustainable presidentialist system. Some might argue that the United States has now finally succumbed to the logic of its structure after September 11, 2001. This remains to be seen.

Of course, this is not to say that some parliamentary systems have not also resulted in military dictatorships. Some have. But the numbers are telling. Only thirteen of over forty regimes (31 percent) established on parliamentary principles had experienced breakdowns by coup d'etat or revolution as of 1985, while all of the presidentialist systems had.

But certainly there must be more alternatives for constituting fair governance than only parliamentary or presidentialist systems! There are very few. At least there is nothing that is not basically a modification of these two. Some suggest that the chief executives of governments should mimic the pluralistic leadership forms of large corporations, with many CEOs for various functions rather than only one for everything (in fact, Benjamin Franklin did suggest a plural executive for the United States). There are also many different forms of relationships between single chief executives and assemblies found in the governance of cities and counties in the United States (strong mayor, weak mayor, mayor/council, city managers, commission form, etc). And France stands as an example of a form that is truly mixed between presidentialist and parliamentarian.

It is high time that new governance design be attempted on the bases of newer scientific and philosophical perspectives (including those of Darwin, Freud, and Einstein, as well as systems theory and chaos theory, for example). It is also time that governance builders affirmatively use their own cultural traditions, modified as necessary for current realities and future possibilities, instead of continuing to rely uncritically on the traditions and beliefs of the West of two hundred plus years ago.

There is no doubt that England, France, and America in the eighteenth century were hotbeds of new political ideas, not only about policies, but especially about structures. All of the structures that are commonplace in governments now—the idea of "constituting" a system of governance by writing down basic rules in a document that was more fundamental than any other; the tripartite separation of governing power into separate but overlapping executive, legislative, and judicial branches; representative legislatures since it was not possible for large numbers of citizens to govern themselves directly; majority rule, federalism, and basic citizen rights that no government (even the majority of citizens) could infringe upon—these and many more ideas and structures were inventions of the seventeenth and especially eighteenth centuries that were practical and effective solutions to "design problems" that faced political designers of the time.

In the two hundred plus years since that time, some of the specific solutions (such as the way the president and vice president were elected, in the American case) did not work and were changed. In addition, many problems and opportunities completely unknown and unknowable two hundred years ago emerged over the nineteenth and twentieth centuries, causing all governments everywhere to develop institutions and processes different from, and often at odds with, those originally invented. Nonetheless, the old fundamental ideas remain essentially unchallenged and certainly unchanged everywhere in the world.

Toward the end of the 1970s and early 1980s I made an extensive survey of the literature on the future of governance—especially governance beyond the nation-state system—that existed at that time.[8] I concluded that there were basically three "piles" of views about the future of governance. One (by far the largest and reflective of most political-science experts and practitioners) assumed without question that the current nation-state system would continue into the foreseeable future with only minor, incremental changes. The second set argued that various forces of globalization (or "planetization" as it was sometimes called then) were rapidly eroding the ability of individual nations, or even international systems, to manage them (whether one likes it or not, and there were some observers who favored the change and others who did not). Of course at that time, hardly anyone imagined that "neoliberalism" would sweep the planet (Ronald Reagan had only begun his first term in office, and the United States was still the number-one creditor nation in the world, a status it lost in three years, becoming the number-one debtor nation as Reaganomics very quickly did its thing). Indeed, globalization then was seen largely (but not entirely) in non-economic terms, being driven by technology, functional necessity, environmental issues, and a growing, positive desire of many people to create a peaceful and diverse world culture in addition to the continuation of local and national cultures.

The third "pile" was composed of normative futures. In contrast to the first two, which simply forecast continuation on the one hand or transformation on the other, the perspectives in the third group contained preferred images of future governance from different ideological perspectives that would require affirmative action to achieve. Among those specifically identified were "socialists, anarchists, libertarians, feminists, liberals, pacifists, [and] mystics. . . . And surprisingly, while they might differ profoundly in their diagnosis of the past and the present, they are astoundingly similar in their preferences for the future as far as the political structure of that future is concerned: decentralized, locally-self reliant, nonbureaucratic, nonhierarchical, anti-statist, and positively anarchistic, yet globally linked and interactive."[9]

The late 1960s and 1970s were a period of considerable interest in new forms of governance, perhaps unsurpassed in America by any period other than that of the founding of the United States itself.[10] However, an important difference between the two periods was that the late eighteenth century was a time when substantially new forms of governance were not only imagined, but also actually created. The 1960s and 1970s were mainly talk (exceptions being experiments with workers' control in Yugoslavia and some communes in Europe and the Americas). But there has been very little talk and little novel action in spite of the creation of many new nations since then. At least in the 1960s and 1970s, some people articulated visions of better worlds to come, a dialogue that has been almost silenced. See Walt Anderson's Further Thoughts, "Global Governance," on page 210.

The major exception to that observation is the creation of the European Union. The governance structure of the European Union certainly is innovative in many ways. It is a grand attempt to create a polity that is in some ways federal, in some ways confederal, and in some ways something unique. Nonetheless, it is a union of sovereign states ("Member States," as the individual European nations are called in the Constitution) and not of the people of the states. According to the Constitution, the basic institutions are

the European Parliament
the European Council
the Council of Ministers
the European Commission
the Court of Justice of the European Union
the European Central Bank
the Court of Auditors

Citizens participate only in electing representatives to the European Parliament from national districts roughly proportionate in population. The European Council consists of the heads of state of the member states, some of whom are elected directly or indirectly by the citizens of the states. Officials of all the other institutions are chosen by representatives of either the Union or the Member States, with citizen input thus only very indirect at best. There is no provision for referendum or any other process of direct citizen initiation, legislation, or recall.

And the Constitution of the European Union is nothing if not wordy. In keeping with most modern constitutions (but in sharp contrast with the original US Constitution), it is extremely long, detailed, and complex, clearly the result of many years of discussions among lawyers, scholars, government officials, and politicians. It is not innovative in any way structurally. In terms of cosmology and technology it could as easily have been written in 1776 as in 2003. The significance of that statement will be made clear later in this chapter.

Also, in terms of our passion about fairness and responsibility toward future generations, it is very disappointing that the document nowhere mentions that concept or concern. There are references to "sustainable development" and laudable emphasis on children's rights, but there is nothing on the obligation of balancing the needs of current generations with those of future generations, and certainly no institutionalized attempts to balance them. From our perspective, however magnificent an achievement it might be in terms of getting the once-fighting nations of Europe to form a single, yet diverse, peaceful, and cooperative political economy, as governance design it is a big disappointment.[11]

Governmental Foresight

Many elected politicians and civil servants have expressed concerns about the future and have been sincerely desirous of acting responsibly toward future generations. Unfortunately, these well-meaning people cannot sustain their good intentions because the pressures and needs of the present always overwhelm their concerns about the future. It is not because these people are insincere or ineffective. Rather, it is because the formal institutions of all governments (especially democratic governments) give weight and legitimacy only to the demands of present generations. They completely discount the needs and desires of future generations. There is no *formal* way that the needs of future generations can or must be taken into account automatically when making decisions in the present. No governmental officer, or even political party, can successfully override those structural impediments to acting on behalf of future generations, no matter how much they might want to do so. The flaw is not in the desires and intentions of the people; it is in the basic structural design of all nations everywhere.

So, beginning with the 1960s and 1970s, advocates for governmental foresight began to try to envision and create new processes and institutions of foresight within existing systems of democratic governance in different parts of the world. These included long-range planning departments, futures commissions, requirements that legislatures conduct future-impact statements on proposed legislation, environmental protection agencies, offices of technology assessment, and the like. Below are examples of actual futures-oriented policies from around the globe.

1. The honor of "the most futures-oriented governance system in the world" may well be accorded to Singapore. The Scenarios Planning Office is a division of the Public Service Division, Prime Minister's Office. The office promotes the use of scenario planning by facilitating the development and dissemination of scenarios to highlight challenges and opportunities facing Singapore. It has published three sets of National Scenarios for Singapore. The 1997 National Scenarios were told from the perspective of the year

2020; the 1999 National Scenarios covered the period 1999 to 2004; and in November 2002, the office developed National Scenarios for 2025.

The Subordinate Courts of Singapore also periodically conduct trend analysis to develop scenarios tailored to the administration of justice, having regard to the larger national and social scenarios. In 1997, it established the Justice Policy Group. This is a strategic think tank that conducts regular environmental scanning. In 2000, the Subordinate Courts completed its first set of justice scenarios and mapped its preferred scenario up to 2020. Efforts such as these have helped the Singapore judiciary to achieve international recognition for the quality of its justice system. Since 1998, Singapore has been rated number one in Asia by the Political and Economics Risks Consultancy. The Switzerland-based International Institute for Management Development, in its World Competitiveness Report, also ranked Singapore number one for legal framework from 1997 to 2000 and again in 2002. The Singapore Subordinate Courts are also recognized by the World Bank as a role model for both developed and developing countries in the field of judicial administration.

2. Currently, Finland may have the most futures-oriented governmental processes in the world. In October 1993, the Finnish Parliament appointed a Committee for the Future on a temporary basis. The purpose of the committee was to assist the Parliament in evaluating and replying to the government's proposals on long-term issues. Because of the usefulness of the committee's work, the Parliament decided that the government should present a Futures Report to the Parliament at least once during each electoral period. This resolution generated a unique political dialogue between the government and Parliament regarding the nation's central future-related issues. In conjunction with a constitutional revision, on December 17, 1999, the Parliament granted the Committee for the Future permanent status.[12]

Slightly earlier, in 1992, with support from the Academy of Finland, the Finnish Ministry of Education created the Finnish Futures Research Center at the Turku School of Economics and Business Administration, with Pentti Malaska the director.[13] The Futures Research Center received its first full professorship, under the Finnish system, beginning in January 2004. Higher education in futures studies in Finland is coordinated by the Finland Futures Academy,[14] part of the Futures Research Center at Turku. Seventeen Finnish universities are affiliated with it, undertaking a variety of futures research and education activities. The academy also participates in several futures research programs within the European Union.

3. During the 1970s, a Secretariat for the Future existed within the Office of the Prime Minister of the Swedish national government, providing an

impressive amount of information about the future for the formal political process. The secretariat became a private think tank during the 1980s.[15]

4. A National Commission for the Future was created in New Zealand in 1980, and a National Commission for the Future was created by the government of Australia in 1986.[16]

5. In 1983, then Senator (and later Vice President) Albert Gore, Jr., and Representative Newt Gingrich, who later became Speaker of the US House of Representatives, introduced legislation to establish an office that would provide the American government with a "national foresight capability." This bill did not become law.[17]

6. Changes were made in the rules of the American House of Representatives in 1974 that required all standing committees of the House (except Appropriations and Budget) to "on a continuing basis undertake futures research and forecasting on matters within the jurisdiction of that committee."[18] The committee report explaining this provision stated, "[T]hese legislative units would have the additional responsibility of identifying and assessing conditions and trends that might require future legislative action. More specifically, this would provide a locus for the systematic, long-range, and integrated study of our principal future national problems. . . . In this way, it is hoped, the House may become more responsive to national needs, anticipating problems before they become crises." Unfortunately, this rule has seldom, if ever, been evoked, and standing committees do not achieve the level of foresight the rule intended.[19] Clem Bezold also discusses the creation and demise of the US Office of Technology Assessment, and the work of Congressman/Senator John Culver of Iowa, who introduced the changes in Senate rules but ultimately was defeated because he "cared more for the future than for corn." Culver also helped establish the US Congressional Clearinghouse on the Future that facilitated futures-oriented discussions among the members of Congress for many years. Bezold also calls attention to various state experiments in "Anticipatory Democracy" in his book, *Anticipatory Democracy: People in the Politics of the Future.*[20]

7. The Office of Planning of the Judiciary of the Commonwealth of Virginia (United States) has probably the most impressive and extensive ongoing system of judicial foresight in the world. Following an impressive statewide futures-visioning process in 1987, the Virginia judiciary established a process within its Office of Planning that assures that actionable parts of the vision are carried out, while new environmental scans are undertaken every year or two so that the original vision is updated and acted on accordingly.[21]

8. Barry O. Jones chaired the Australian House of Representatives committee

for Long Term Strategies, a parliamentary body with specific responsibility for considering the needs of future generations.[22]

9. *Oposa vs. Factoran, Jr.* (1993), decided by the Supreme Court of the Philippines, is the only instance we know of a judiciary organ acting affirmatively on behalf of future generations. In the Oposa case, the Philippine Supreme Court ruled that representatives of future generations have standing and thus can bring legal action to prevent environmental destruction that diminishes the quality of life of future generations. The majority of the Court said, in part,

> Petitioner minors assert that they represent their generation as well as generations yet unborn. We find no difficulty in ruling that they can, for themselves, for others of their generation and for the succeeding generations, file a class suit. Their personality to sue on behalf of the succeeding generations can only be based on the concept of intergenerational responsibility insofar as the right to a balanced and healthy ecology is concerned. Such a right, as hereinafter expounded, considers the "rhythm and harmony of nature." . . . Needless to say, every generation has a responsibility to the next to preserve that rhythm and harmony for the full enjoyment of a balanced and healthful ecology.
>
> Put a little differently, the minors' assertion of their right to a sound environment constitutes, at the same time, the performance of their obligation to ensure the protection of that right for the generations to come.
>
> The *locus standi* of the petitioners having thus been addressed, We shall now proceed to the merits of the petition. . . . After a careful perusal of the complaint in question and a meticulous consideration and evaluation of the issues raised and arguments adduced by the parties, We do not hesitate to find for the petitioners.[23]

It must of course be added that the decision of the Philippines Supreme Court was made much easier by the fact that, unlike the US and most other constitutions, Section 16, Article II of the 1987 Philippine Constitution explicitly provides the following.

> SEC. 16. The State shall protect and advance the right of the people to a balanced and healthful ecology in accord with the rhythm and harmony of nature.
>
> This right unites with the right to health that is provided for in the preceding section of the same article:

> SEC 15. The State shall protect and promote the right to health of the people and instill health consciousness among them.[24]

10. In November 1997, the United Nations Educational, Scientific and Cultural Organization (UNESCO) adopted a "Declaration on the responsibilities of present generations towards future generations." The preamble to the Declaration refers to "the necessity for establishing new, equitable and global links of partnership and intra-generational solidarity . . . the avowal that the fate of future generations depends to a great extent on decisions and actions taken today and that present-day problems, including poverty, technological and material underdevelopment, unemployment and exclusion, discrimination and threats to the environment, must be solved in the interests of both present and future generations."

The twelve articles of the Declaration elaborate proposals on what can be done to safeguard the needs and interests of future generations in the fields of education, science, culture, and communication. Concerning the environment, for example, Article 4 states that "the present generations have the responsibility to bequeath to future generations an Earth which will not one day be irreversibly damaged by human activity. Each generation inheriting the Earth temporarily shall take care to use natural resources reasonably and ensure that life is not prejudiced by harmful modifications of the ecosystems and that scientific and technological progress in all fields does not harm life on Earth." The idea is reinforced in Article 5, which stipulates that the present generations "should ensure that future generations are not exposed to pollution which may endanger their health or their existence itself."

This "Declaration" is the fruit of the labor of many futures-oriented people and institutions. Following the earlier lead of delegates from Malta, in 1979 Jacques-Yves Cousteau initiated the idea of a declaration on future generations. The world campaign he launched gathered 5.5 million signatures. UNESCO's stand on this subject goes back to its first Medium-Term Plan (1977–1982), which mentioned that the recognition of the unity of mankind presupposed "a deliberate choice of fashioning a common destiny with joint responsibility for the future of mankind." The third Medium-Term Plan (1990–1995) stressed the need for ensuring "the sustainability of resources for future generations." UNESCO also cooperated closely with the Foundation of International Studies (Malta), which has created a world network devoted to our responsibilities toward future generations and their environment.

Toward Comprehensive Governance Re-envisioning and Design

So far we have shown that all existing governments find it difficult, if not impossible, routinely to balance the needs of future generations with those of present generations in order to act fairly toward both. Some, of course, do not even strive to "be fair" to all members of present generations. Current governments overwhelmingly ignore future generations, often while privileging certain groups and individuals in the present. Even if individual lawmakers and citizens wish to act fairly toward the future, current structures of governance discount the future so massively that present-oriented structures overwhelm almost any future-oriented intentions.

We then showed that there have been many attempts in recent years to correct this by imagining and attempting to implement various structural changes to existing forms of governance. While some of these have been more or less successful, many of the proposals either were not fully adopted or sustained. When all is said and done, with the collapse of socialist systems in the late 1980s and early 1990s and the creation of new "democratic" governments in their place, most governments have become less futures oriented as they have become more "democratic" over the last decade.

Much more concerted discussion and effort about this is required as present generations appear to "eat up" the future with irresponsible disregard for the needs of future generations, often specifically arguing that future generations can take care of themselves and that we need not worry about them.

There are many "complaints" registered against existing governments. In recent years, I have oriented my graduate course in political design around six of the many complaints levied against existing governments. They are as follows:

1. Bureaucratic: placing the convenience of the governors over the needs of the governed.
2. Nationalistic: privileging the nation-state over both smaller and larger units.
3. Undemocratic: thwarting participation of some groups and individuals while favoring others.
4. Repressive: privileging, using, and causing both direct and structural violence on their own citizens as well as externally.
5. Patriarchal: being created by men, focusing on men's problems and resorting to methods men prefer to use, especially violence, to solve them, while ignoring or marginalizing the participation and perspectives of women.
6. Unfuturistic: discounting the future and concerning themselves with immediate and past problems and conflicts.

Trying to come up with designs of governance systems that rectify even one of these complaints is challenging, but addressing all six is daunting indeed. It is, for example, possible to become "more democratic," but it is difficult to be both "democratic" and "futures oriented," and it certainly is difficult to ensure both without being overly "bureaucratic." However, as far as we know, while there are scholars and practitioners focusing on one or another of these "complaints" (especially that of reducing bureaucracy), no one is trying to address all of the complaints together (and perhaps along with others as well), and yet this is necessary for a design to be credible and effective.

Current Ideas about Governance Reform

At the present time, there are several very different reform discussions going on worldwide. Some of them are focused on issues raised by globalization. Some are entirely inwardly focused, though some of these have recently developed responses to globalization as well. Some are locally focused and thus highly ethnocentric. Others are consistently considered within a cross-cultural perspective. However, none contest the old cosmologies and few contest the old technologies, a point we shall return to later.

One of these discussions is that of the "New Public Management," which Dick Pratt considered in some detail in chapter 9 of this volume. One of the other discussions concerns the idea of a "civil" society located somewhere in between the formal central governing structures and the individual citizen.

Civil Society

One of the most vital discussions about preferred governance currently centers around the notion of civil society. The discussion is in some ways about structure and processes and in some ways about policies and outcomes. One of the seminal books in the field, John Ehrenberg's *Civil Society: The Critical History of an Idea,*[25]

> examines the historical, political, and theoretical evolution of the way civil society has been theorized over two and a half millennia of Western political theory. Broadly speaking, three rather distinct bodies of thought have marked its development. . . . [C]lassical and medieval thought generally equated civil society with politically organized commonwealths. Whether its final source of authority was secular or religious, civil society made civilization possible because people lived in law-governed associations protected by the coercive power of the state. Such conceptions shaped the way civil society was understood for many centuries. As the forces of modernity began to undermine the embedded economies and universal knowledge of the Middle Ages, the gradual formation of national markets and nation states gave rise to a second tradition that began to conceptualize civil society as a civilization made possible by production, individual interest, competition, and need. . . . [I]t was clear that the world could no longer be understood as a system of fused commonwealths. Civil society developed in tandem with the centralizing and leveling tendencies of the modern

state, and an influential third body of thought conceptualized it as the now-familiar sphere of intermediate association that serves liberty and limits the power of central institutions.[26]

However, the concept of civil society entered current political discourse from a very specific set of concerns and actions.

In the early 1980s, a remarkably broad series of civic forums, independent trade unions, and social movements began to carve out areas of free political activity in the Eastern European countries of "actual existing socialism." Their leaders talked of "the rebellion of civil society against the state," and when they started coming to power in 1989 the stage was set for an explosion of interest that has been gathering force ever since. Liberal political theory was revived in demands for "law-governed states" that would protect private life and public activity from the intrusive hand of meddling bureaucracies.[27]

Or as David Crocker put it,

Michael Ignatieff, writing about the aspirations of East European intellectuals in the 1970s and 1980s, tries to capture their ideal of civil society: "the kind of place where you do not change the street signs every time you change the regime." This one-liner nicely captures the antigovernmental approach to civil society. . . . This model usefully provides a basis to undermine state authoritarianism and corporatism, for it envisions a zone of life free of government control.[28]

However, with the rise to dominance of neoliberal ideologies and policies in the United States over the 1980s and beyond, some realized that "civil society" should next come to mean that sphere of life where individuals are free from market totalitarianism and the commodification of everything as well. It seemed that the United States was suffering from a disease opposite to that which plagued "really existing socialist states." Just as socialists came to envision civil society as a place free from governmental definition and control of everything, so "really existing capitalist states" needed places that did not define, reward, and punish everything according to price, profits, and purchasing power.

September 11, 2001, at first seemed to end that concern in the United States. As we have discussed previously, literally overnight, "government" changed from being an evil thing that should be destroyed if possible, and ignored if not, to becoming our best protector in a world teeming with millions, if not billions, of unknown and ever-active terrorists.[29] Money that could not be found for public education, medical care, housing, or transportation was found in abundance for "security," and people who had insisted on privatizing all government services insisted that only government employees could do security jobs reliably. However, the underlying antipathy for government appears not to have abated. Except for the military and government agents of internal surveillance, faith in the market seems undiminished, and so a "civil society" free from both governmental surveillance and control on the one hand and the unfettered marketplace on the other is still contested, in the United States at least.

Indeed, civil society has come to mean one of two different perspectives in the United States, according to Crocker.

> A narrower approach to civil society, which in the US debate has been termed the *associational* model, excludes for-profit groups and commercial organizations and emphasizes private voluntary associations such as churches, self-help groups, amateur sports leagues, and groups pursuing common hobbies. On this view, civil society is a "third sector" different from both state and market. The state coercively protects or promotes the public good. In the market, private producers and consumers freely exchange goods and services. In civil society, private individuals freely join together to pursue some noneconomic common passion or project.[30]

The third model "focuses on the communicative activity generated by civil society's groups and on its potential to strengthen democracy. The continual public conversation generated by civic improvement associations, religious groups, political and social movements, advocacy groups, and the like, filtered through media organs such as newspapers and television, constitute a 'public sphere' that supports the formation of public opinion, a necessary ingredient in democratic politics. This third model has been worked out most fully by Jurgen Habermas, Jean Cohen, and James Bohman.[31] . . . [T]he third model is especially interested in civil society associations whose internal structure mirrors the structure of the public sphere itself: they are egalitarian, democratic, and inclusive. The public sphere model highlights those inwardly democratic, outwardly oriented, nonstate, nonmarket forces that deliberate about and try to protect and extend democratic forms."[32]

This last model is worth considering in some detail. Benjamin Barber, whose earlier work on "Strong Democracy"[33] put forward a progressive view of a more robust, involved, and interactive form of democracy in comparison with the "weak democracy" that characterized the United States and many other "mature" democracies, says that there are three kinds of understandings of civil society in American political conversations: the libertarian view in which civil society is simply a synonym for the private, economic sector;[34] the Communitarian view in which civil society is a synonym for community generally;[35] and his own Strong Democratic view, which sees civil society as the domain between government and the market.[36]

Thus Barber insists that the kind of civil society he promotes should further the goals of Strong Democracy. He lists six arenas for action in support of civil society from the perspective of Strong Democracy.

1. Enlarging and reinforcing public spaces: specifically, retrofitting commercial malls as multiuse and thus genuinely public spaces.
2. Fostering civic use of new telecommunications and information technologies, preventing commercialization from destroying their civic potentials—specifically a civic Internet, public-access cable television; a check on mass-media advertising for (and commercial exploitation of) children.
3. Domesticating and democratizing production for the global economy: protecting the labor market, challenging disemployment practices, making corporations responsible members of civil society without surrendering the government's regulatory authority.
4. Domesticating and democratizing consumption in the global economy: protecting just wage policies, workplace safety, and the environment; the labeling and/or boycotting of goods produced without regard for safety, environment, or child-labor laws.
5. National and community service, service-learning programs, and citizen-nurturing voluntarism.
6. Cultivating the arts and humanities as an indispensable foundation for a free, pluralistic society: treating artists as citizens and citizens as artists in government-supported arts education and service programs.[37]

Barber's perspective is clearly in line with the "third model" that Crocker suggests. In contrast, in June 2003, the American Enterprise Institute (AEI), an influential think tank, sponsored a conference at their headquarters in Washington, DC, titled "We're Not from the Government, but We're Here to Help You. Nongovernmental Organizations: The Growing Power of an Unelected Few." The announcement to the conference stated,

> In recent years, nongovernmental organizations (NGOs) have proliferated, their rise facilitated by governments and corporations desperate to subcontract development projects. While many NGOs have made significant contributions to human rights, the environment, and economic and social development, a lack of international standards for NGO accountability also allows far less credible organizations to have a significant influence on policymaking. The growing power of supranational organizations and a loose set of rules governing the accreditation of NGOs has meant that an unelected few have access to growing and unregulated power. NGOs have created their own rules and regula-

tions and demanded that governments and corporations abide by those rules. Many nations' legal systems encourage NGOs to use the courts (or the specter of the courts) to compel compliance. Politicians and corporate leaders are often forced to respond to the NGO media machine, and the resources of taxpayers and shareholders are used in support of ends they did not intend to sanction. The extraordinary growth of advocacy NGOs in liberal democracies has the potential to undermine the sovereignty of constitutional democracies, as well as the effectiveness of credible NGOs.[38]

Papers presented at the conference and posted on the Web site allege that many NGOs are not dispassionately and fairly interested in the public good, but are merely covers for various discredited "liberal" and "progressive" organizations, attacking the free market and individual enterprise. They lack openness and transparency and are irresponsibly unaccountable to anyone for their actions, often favoring global governance over the sovereignty of nation-states. The AEI and the Federalist Society also announced the creation of a Web site for their new joint project, called NGOWatch,[39] that intends to devote more time and effort to unmasking undesirable NGOs.

Civil Society and Globalization

So far, we have considered civil society only from the point of view of individual countries. But there is also evidence that a kind of global civil society is emerging. Martin Kohler comments,

> There is an abundance of evidence to support the thesis of an emerging global civil society and the formation of a global polity. In many issues of public concern, economic development, peace, social policy, environmental issues, consumer concerns and civil liberties, to name but a few—interest groups are engaged in undertakings which extend beyond borders, building transnational networks to disseminate knowledge, raise consciousness, develop common viewpoints and influence the arena of intergovernmental decision-making in global affairs.[40]

He adds "that it is necessary to relate the phenomenon of the evolving transnational public to the functions and requirements of national public spheres, which are changing as a result of globalization.[41] . . . The very meaning of loyalty might change . . . to include compliance with, on the one hand, a set of globally shared values which affect coalition building, such as human rights, democratic participation, and the rule of law, and, on the other, standards to limit the scope of transnational coalitions and the conflict they may produce, such as respect for social and cultural self-determination."[42]

It is of course precisely this kind of civil society that the AEI and others oppose, as indicated above. Though normally striving to weaken state power while supporting economic enterprise and individual initiative instead, in this instance they favor strengthening the power of certain sovereign states against associations that seek to counter, or find a place free from, the power of the economic sector, globally as well as locally.

Cosmopolitan Democracy

Indeed, considerable discussion of governance (and especially democratic governance and civil society) beyond or across the boundaries of individual nation-states has emerged recently. One of the most interesting proposals is for something termed "cosmopolitan democracy."

Daniele Archibugi defines "cosmopolitan democracy" as "a political project which aims to engender great public accountability in the leading processes and structural alternations of the contemporary world. Not that it is the only project of this kind; many others with similar aspirations (from perpetual peace projects to the World Order Models Project) have been developed over the course of time. We have drawn and learnt a lot from these. The distinctive feature of the model discussed here, however, is that it has made democracy the primary focus and studied the conditions for its applications to states, interstate relations, and global issues."[43]

In the same volume, David Held identifies four features of cosmopolitan democracy.

First, the locus of effective political power can no longer be assumed to be national governments; effective power is shared and bartered by diverse forces and agencies at national, regional, and international levels. Second, the idea of a political community of fate (of a self-determining collectivity which forms its own agenda and life conditions) can no longer meaningfully be located within the boundaries of a single nation-state alone. Some of the most fundamental forces and processes which determine the nature of life chances within and across political communities are now beyond the reach of individual nation-states.

Third, it is not part of my argument that national sovereignty today . . . has been wholly subverted, not at all. But it is part of my argument that the operations of states in increasingly complex global and regional systems both affect their autonomy (by changing the balance between the costs and benefits of policies) and their sovereignty (by altering the balance between national, regional and national legal frameworks and administrative practices). . . . Fourth, over-lapping spheres of influence, interference and interest create dilemmas at the centre of democratic thought. In liberal democracies, consent to government and legitimacy for governmental action are dependent on electoral politics and the ballot box. Yet the [sufficiency of elections] becomes problematic as soon as the nature of a "relevant community" is contested. . . .[44]

Against this background, the nature and prospects of the democratic polity need re-examination. The idea of a democratic order can no longer be simply defended as an idea suitable to a particular closed political community or nation-state. . . .[45]

Cosmopolitan democracy involves the development of administrative capacity and independent political resources at regional and global levels as a necessary complement to those in local and national polities. At issue would be strengthening the administrative capacity and accountability of regional institutions like the EU [European Union] along with developing the administrative capacity and forms of accountability of the UN system itself. [It] would not call for a diminution *per se* of state power and capacity across the globe. Rather, it would seek to entrench and develop democratic institutions at regional and global levels as a necessary complement to those at the level of the nation-state. . . . The case for cosmopolitan democracy is the case for the creation of new political institutions which would coexist with the system of states but which would override states in clearly defined spheres of activity where those activities have demonstrable transnational and international consequences.[46]

Civil Society and Political Design

Most of the literature implies (correctly, we believe) that civil society is a stage of political development, part of the general unraveling of the totalitarian tightness of traditional tribal and small agricultural communities that has been loosening over the last several thousand years as societies have grown more populous, geographically larger, and socially more complex. It is a process driven by developments especially in communications and transportation technologies and the resulting institutions and values that continuously force each of us to be more free than we have ever been before, or might even prefer.

This process was greatly accelerated by the technologies and institutions of industrialism, beginning a few hundred years ago, and is now part of the planetary experience of globalization.

There is of course nothing inevitable about any of this. Entire societies (like China and then Japan for several hundred years each) can and have withdrawn from the process.[47] There are movements toward profound localism and self-sufficiency that very well could carry the day.[48] Catastrophe (whether environmental, economic, military, or political) could halt globalization in all its aspects except the globalization of the catastrophes themselves.[49] These are real alternative futures, and, to many, preferable futures as well.

However, if we can assume the continuation of the unraveling and loosening global processes, then we believe that the kind of Strong Democracy version of civil society that Barber and others envision should be a factor of future political designs. Whenever new forms of governance are being imagined and created, attention should be given not only to the structures of formal governmental (and, we also believe, economic) institutions, but also to the creation of democratically organized spaces between the two. The resulting strong civil society must be hardy enough to negotiate successfully with both in defense of fairness, diversity, and freedom and yet cooperative and communal enough to facilitate both good governance and good commerce.

To do this, several other factors need to be brought into the equation. A feature of Strong Democracy is strong democratic talk (both face-to-face and mediated), mediated both online and interactively as well as through the still-dominant, fundamentally one-way media of television and the press. This idea has received elaboration recently in the guise of "Deliberative Democracy." As John Gastil puts it, "[T]here are two fundamental problems in American politics. The first is that most Americans do not believe that elected officials represent their interests. The second is that they are correct.[50] . . . [A] widespread view holds that the United States needs to implement one of several possible electoral reforms. These include new voting systems (e.g., proportional representation), term limits, public financing or strict regulation of campaign fundraising, voluntary rules of campaign conduct, and the widespread distribution of voting guides."[51]

Gastil supports those efforts but feels they are inadequate in and of themselves. What is needed is something more.

> Some reformers . . . have begun to connect face-to-face deliberation with elections. . . . Programs such as citizen juries and "deliberative polls" bring together representative samples of the public for face-to-face discussions with one another and with expert panels. After a few days of deliberation, these citizen bodies answer survey questions or draft recommendations to tell public officials what policies the larger public might endorse it if had the chance to deliberate. . . .[52]
>
> [F]or random sample forums to create a powerful public voice with significant elector impact, it is necessary to use the existing capacities of the public to connect face-to-face deliberation in small groups with the voting choices of the mass public on election day. . . . My basic recommendation is that voters

should have access to the results of representative citizen deliberation on the candidates and issues that appear on their ballots. . . .[53]

For these citizen panels to achieve their intended purpose, they would have to produce high-quality judgments, and citizens would need to be willing and able to consider panel results when voting.[54]

This proposal is reminiscent of a series of experiments conducted some years ago by Ted Becker, Christa Slaton, and others called "Televote." This has also become an integral part of Becker and Slaton's work with "Electronic Town Meetings" and "Teledemocracy," about which more will be said below.

From Political Reform to Quantum Politics

While we favor the incorporation of many of these ideas and processes into existing governance systems, we still feel that they do not go far enough. They are attempts to make a very old system operate in an environment quite different from that in which it was intended to operate. Merely reforming existing systems of governance to cope with current challenges and opportunities (especially to act fairly toward present and future generations in the face of globalization) is literally like trying to adapt a horse and buggy so it will take off on a jet runway: it might be possible, but it will not be nearly as effective as it would be if we were to abandon the horse and buggy as a once-novel and splendid but now obsolete vehicle and envision, design, and build something intended to operate in the current and future aviation system (and, I might add, the present aviation/transportation system itself desperately needs to be re-imagined and designed as well, but that is another matter!).

Though there are many elements in the civil society, deliberative democracy, and cosmopolitan democracy discussion we greatly admire, as we have suggested throughout, we feel that all current governance reforms are still inadequate on cosmological and technological grounds.

1. They are cosmologically inadequate because they are all based on old "Newtonian" notions of causality and intentionality. It is essential that new forms of governance be based on what the best science and humanities of all cultures can tell us about human and other systems, artificial as well as natural.

2. They are technologically inadequate because they were invented at a time when communications technologies were quite different from what they are now, initially limited to human speech and handwriting, later augmented by the very labor-intensive and slow printing presses of the day. At

that time, literacy was low, books were few and rare, and newspapers little more than a few pages of local announcements and opinion.

Indeed, the specific structures of government adopted a *written* constitution (instead of a mathematically expressed[55] or audiovisual one), voting for "representatives" who would act for you or in your interests (instead of voting directly for yourself via the Internet), the "separation" of "powers" into three—and only three—"branches" (instead of four or more, for future generations, or the media, or education, or CEOs, or the military, or no "branches" at all, recognizing that real governance operates by "Iron Triangles" that cut across the three formal branches), and federalism (the "division" of "power" between a central government and regional polities rather than "non-spatial governance"[56] that facilitates governing functions wherever and however they are performed, rather than privileging the happenstance of geographical place alone). All of these structural features and more can and should be viewed as *"communications technologies"* that were adequate, often brilliant, for their time but are now challenged by newer and arguably better technologies for governance, although their use also needs to be as carefully crafted in accordance with modern scientific and humanistic knowledge and values, and thus "checked and balanced" as appropriate for the present, as were the original design solutions for their time and circumstance two hundred plus years ago.

Why Quantum Politics?

It is typical for technologies, social institutions, human values, and even expressions of art to reflect/be based on the dominant cosmology of the time.[57] Thus ideas of governance and the good life, as well as architectural and sculptural works of the classical Greek period, derived from the philosophical worldviews of that era. The same was true during the Roman and then medieval periods in Europe. In many ways, the best example of this unity was during the early modern period when Newton's ideas of the physical world came to permeate all of the major institutions and cultural expressions of the time.

Since the US Constitution was written during this time by people profoundly influenced by Newtonian ideas, it is not surprising that the Constitution was based upon them as well. However, the dominant intellectual paradigm of our time is quantum physics. There would be no "electronic age" without the discovery and manipulation of the electron. What might be the principles and resulting structures and processes of "quantum politics" based upon quantum physics?

Inspired by some ideas of Glendon Schubert,[58] a group of professors and graduate students at the University of Hawai'i formed a quantum politics study group in the mid- to late 1980s. Members included Glen Schubert, Rudy Rummel, Dick Chadwick, Ted Becker, Christa Slaton, Chris Jones, Sharon Rodgers, Kenn Kassman, Tim Dolan, Jim Dator, and others. Several research projects and publications resulted from this. I wrote two papers[59] and introduced "quantum politics" to my graduate political design courses so that generations of students have subsequently been exposed to the concept and been tempted to develop it. Becker and Slaton did most of the subsequent work, however. Becker edited a volume titled *Quantum Politics*.[60] It contained essays by several of the members of the University of Hawai'i study group and others. Slaton used the theoretical perspective of quantum politics for a book, *Televote: Expanding Citizen Participation in the Quantum Age*.[61]

After a general introduction by Becker, *Quantum Politics* opens with a presidential address to the American Political Science Association delivered by William Bennett Munro in 1927 titled "Physics and Politics: an Old Analogy Revised." Munro himself opened his statement by referring to a book written by the famous nineteenth-century political philosopher Walter Bagehot fifty-five years earlier called "Physics and Politics." Thus we are immediately reminded that this is not a new idea, only a neglected one. Other political scientists who have written about the relation of theories in physics to constitutional and political design include James Robinson, who published an article, "Newtonianism and the Constitution," in 1957,[62] Martin Landau in 1961,[63] and Harvey Wheeler.[64]

Note the title of Robinson's article. It makes clear one of the central points in the quantum politics perspective: that the constitutions of all nations today, beginning with the US Constitution of 1789, derive from a Newtonian worldview dominant in the eighteenth century. This worldview was rationalistic, mechanistic, posited immediate cause and effect, was predictive, and assumed an objective real world that could be objectively observed and measured with no interference or bias on the part of a trained, neutral observer.

This view was further incorporated into the law and legal systems of all nations that assume that humans are rational actors deterred, or encouraged, to obey or defy the law on the basis of a careful, self-interested calculus by which they compare the advantages in breaking or upholding the law with the penalties and punishments for breaking or upholding it each time one acts. Moreover, everyone is supposed to be fully informed of the law and its consequences. "Ignorance of the law is no excuse," assuming that everyone clearly knows what the law is before breaking or abiding by it. Similar assumptions underlie all modern political systems, as well as most theories concerning voting and other political activities (not to mention most modern economic theories).

Most social and behavioral science theories developed since Newton make it clear that these assumptions are not an adequate basis for understanding, controlling, or encouraging actual human behavior. Darwin and Freud, to name two intellectual giants of the nineteenth century, had quite different paradigms that suggest how marginal rationality, predictability, and objectivity are in human decision making and actions. But from the early twentieth century onward, quantum physics and, more recently, related disciplines seemed to go even farther.[65]

Some physicists suggest that there is no real world "out there," or at least no single real world (there may be many worlds, perhaps an infinite number).[66] Moreover, even if a single, objective real world exists that we all inhabit, it is impossible for a human to say anything certain about it (at least at the micro level), because every act of observation and every attempt at measurement disturbs the thing or process being observed. Thus humans participate with the universe and do not just act in it or observe its independent operation.

There may be no immutable natural laws to be discovered. Everything that seems lawful may at best be probabilistic and perhaps fundamentally random. Anything that seems to be immutable may merely be a consequence of the "law" of large numbers and/or the limited time horizon of humans. Little can be predicted with certainty at the micro or meso level (i.e., on a human scale), therefore no "science of the future" that presumes to predict the future of humanity is possible. As we showed earlier, this is importantly the situation on Earth, where if there once ever were "natural" processes that could be observed objectively without human bias or interference, humans by now have so impacted, interrupted, and/or changed them that it is necessary to view all aspects of our environment as "artificial," requiring continual human attention, management, re-imagination, and re-creation.

Another important perspective from quantum physics is *simultaneity,* the validity, or at least utility, of certain contradictory statements about the apparent behavior of a phenomenon. The classic example is that light has observed characteristics of both a wave and a particle. "Common sense" says it cannot be both. Yet which one it appears to be depends on how it is observed.

Moreover, "everything is connected to everything else," so that "action at a distance" (rather than only localized cause-effect) exists in some ways. Yet this is not to say that we simply live in a larger system than we imagined. "System theory" of a mechanistic sort is limited as well. In its place we have "field theory," where the *interaction* of quanta, rather than the operation of *discrete units* in a system, appears to be primary.

Ted Becker, Christa Slaton, and Gus diZerega, each in separate chapters, developed these and other (sometimes competing) notions of quantum physics and quantum politics in contrast to various mainstream political theories based on Newtonian physics. DiZerega also relates them to the ideas of postmodernity, ecology, and Eastern mysticism and attempts to derive a theoretical basis for Green politics. It is worthwhile adding at this point that though there may be no direct genealogical inheritance, these views seem to be in fundamental accord with certain features of the postmodern, deconstructionist school that dominates much of the scholarship of the humanities and social sciences presently.[67] The Green/quantum connection appears a bit more dubious.

A chapter by Laurence Tribe, a distinguished professor of law at Harvard Law School, originally appeared in the *Harvard Law Review* in 1989. Subtitled "What Lawyers Can Learn from Modern Physics," it is the first and only attempt we are aware of to apply quantum physics to law (primarily constitutional law) in the United States. Tribe says that modern physics differs from Netwonian physics in at least two ways that are useful for a better understanding of law and governance. One, at the most macro level, is "that objects like stars and planets change the space around them (they literally 'warp' it) so that their effect is both complex and interactive." The other, at the micro level, shows that "the very process of observation and analysis can fundamentally alter the things being observed and can change how they will behave thereafter.[68] . . . Thus, it is the picture of the court as a largely passive observer, and of the state as a subject exerting force from a safe distance upon the natural world regarded as external and pre-political object . . . that I think can be usefully dissolved, and then helpfully refocused, from the perspective of twentieth-century physics."[69]

Technology and Political Design

As we have said repeatedly, the American Constitution was a brilliant solution that enabled the founding fathers to overcome many of the design problems facing them. For example, even though many citizens of the time preferred to participate in formal political decision making directly themselves—and did so when this was possible—they recognized that this was not possible for the citizens of the vast new nation as a whole *given the communications and transportation technologies of the time.* As Gordon Wood puts it, quoting from political pamphlets of the time,

> Whenever the inhabitants of a state grew numerous, it became "not only inconvenient, but impracticable for all to meet in One Assembly." Out of the impossibility of convening the whole people, it was commonly believed, arose the great English discovery of representation. Through this device of representation, "substituting the few in the room of the many," the people "in an extensive Country" could still express their voice in the making of law and the management of government. . . . The elected members would be . . . "an exact epitome of the whole people," "an exact miniature of their constituents," men whom the people could trust to represent their interest.[70]

Thus representative democracy (citizens participating indirectly in decision making by designating "men they could trust to represent their interest") was seen as a satisfactory solution to the physical impossibility of participating directly. If there had been a technological option (if, for example, modern electric and electronic communications networks had existed), would they have settled for indirect participation through their elected representatives instead? It seems highly unlikely that they would have made election of representatives their primary, much less sole, mode of participation in national politics as it was then, and still is now, in the United States.

However, since the affairs of state are so numerous and complex, it is highly likely that even if these technologies had existed then that the founders would have invented a hybrid system, perhaps similar to that suggested in the Aanivalta proposal in Finland.[71] This system assumes that on many and perhaps most issues citizens are more than happy to choose someone to act on their behalf. But they want to be able to instruct that person directly if they choose to do so and to bestow their mandate on some other delegate at any time if they are dissatisfied with a person they previously designated to act on their behalf. However, knowing that there are some issues on which each citizen might have the knowledge and desire to participate directly, the Aanivalta proposal allows citizens such direct participation in legislation via electronic means whenever they wish, otherwise leaving the details of day-to-day governance to their appointed delegates.

At the very least, direct citizen discussion, debate, involvement, and impact on policy decision making in the way Gastil, Becker, and Slaton propose is possible now in ways that simply were not possible in 1789. So we believe that whenever there is an opportunity or necessity to create new governance systems, or even just to improve old ones, these and future communications technologies should be brought to the front and center of discussions about inventing new processes of governance.

And it is not only in legislative decision making. If direct democracy means allowing citizens to participate directly in policy making, then it also means citizens should be allowed, and expected, to participate directly in all aspects of governance, including "administration" and "adjudication," to restrict ourselves only to the conventional three branches for now.

There has been much more discussion over the years related to direct democracy and much less to "direct administration" and "direct adjudication," but there has been some. Indeed, in some ways, there has been much more actual movement, as well as theoretical discussion, in citizen direct involvement in adjudication. It has been so from the start, with the use of the jury system in the United States and elsewhere. But the entire alternative dispute resolution (ADR) movement is premised on the belief that it is better to enable citizens to settle their own disputes in ways that make sense to them, with the help of skilled mediators, than it is to "go to court" and have an authoritarian (even if compassionate and wise) judge decide the matter for them on the basis of the state's arbitrary and one-size-fits-all "law." Moreover, advances in computer hardware and software, expert systems, online services, and artificial intelligence also are rapidly facilitating this transition.[72]

Do People Want to Participate?

At the outset of this chapter we said, "We all want to be able to participate in matters affecting us. We want to have a fair hand in carrying out group tasks. We want to participate in settling conflicts among our companions." At that point we also said that libertarians who insist on absolute individualism would object to that statement. But there are others who would object to it as well.

We have long argued that there are two kinds of "alienation." One kind, most frequently remarked upon, results when you cannot participate in decisions when you want to. The other, less frequently mentioned, results in being required, or strongly urged, to participate in decisions when you *do not* want to. The extraordinary depth and extent of the second form of alienation, in the United States at least, has recently been well documented in an important book by John Hibbing and Elizabeth Theiss-Morse titled *Stealth Democracy: Americans' Beliefs About How Government Should Work*.[73] It is the product of some excellent empirical work and not simply of speculation and must give pause to anyone who believes citizen participation in politics is good and feasible. The authors state their conclusions very clearly in the introduction to their book.

> The last thing people want is to be more involved in political decision making: They do not want to make political decisions themselves; they do not want to provide much input to those who are assigned to make these decisions; and they would rather not know all the details of the decision-making process. Most people have strong feelings on few if any of the issues the government needs to address and would much prefer to spend their time in nonpolitical pursuits. Rather than wanting a more active, participatory democracy, a remarkable number of people want what we call stealth democracy. . . . The people want democratic procedures to exist but not to be visible on a routine basis.[74]

However, "the people want to be able to make democracy visible and accountable on those rare occasions when they are motivated to be involved. They want to know that the opportunity will be there for them even though they probably have no current intention of getting involved in government or even of paying attention to it."[75]

"Participation in politics is low not because of the difficulty of registration requirements or the dearth of places for citizens to discuss politics, not because of the sometimes unseemly nature of debate in Congress or displeasure with a particular public policy. Participation in politics is low because people do not like politics even in the best of circumstances; in other words, they simply do not like the process of openly arriving at a decision in the face of diverse opinions."[76] The rest of their book documents these conclusions.

It is very important that we keep these facts in mind whenever we turn our attention to political design. However, we believe the evidence clearly shows that structure does matter and that more Americans would participate in political decision making if that participation were made easier, more interesting, and more effective. The Finnish proposal called "Aanivalta" mentioned above, among many others, specifically demonstrates how representative and democratic processes can be effectively and satisfactorily combined in ways that address the concerns of "stealth democracy."

Moreover, Americans do participate in activities that matter to them and if they believe they can influence outcomes by their participation. And they certainly do not shrink from engaging in argument and disputation either, as anyone who has observed parents at their children's soccer practices and games knows very well. But it truly is a strange American indeed who bothers to participate in formal politics, even at the local level, when they are entirely incapable of influencing national decisions (which also have local consequences) at all. Thus the findings of "stealth democracy" should be read as a design challenge to be addressed rather than an eternal verity that must be accepted. Just as we do not want to create alienation by thwarting desired participation, neither do we wish to cause alienation by requiring it when people prefer to be left alone.

So even though most of mainstream political science and administration ignores (when it does not actively ridicule) attempts at electronic democracy,[77] there is a huge and growing body of literature that discusses not just the various proposals and the theories behind them, but also features careful evaluations of numerous actual experiments. And it is a worldwide movement that is helping people learn from each other more rapidly.

Much of this literature was collected and discussed in a book by Ted Becker and Christa Slaton titled *The Future of Teledemocracy*. It, and several other sources, are required reading for anyone interested (even if initially opposed) in understanding how modern communications technologies might be purposely included in new governance designs. It has the additional feature of being based on principles of quantum politics, including the emerging interest in random politics.[78] The Institute for Alternative Futures in Alexandria, Virginia, recently conducted an extensive survey of the use of information and communications technologies (ICT) to support governance. The report determined that currently ICT is used to support governance in five areas.

1. Cyber Administration: Or E-government. The use of the Internet and other information and communications technology to enhance government services. The Internet is helping to expedite a wide range of such services.
2. Cyber Voting: Internet voting for candidates as well as for policies via initiatives and referenda.
3. Cyber Participation: ICT-enhanced citizen interaction and input on policy issues or policy development apart from voting. This would include petitioning legislatures, electronic town meetings, polling and electronically mediated policy dialogues.
4. Cyber Infrastructure: In addition to connectivity, more specific cyber tools used to enhance participation, deliberation, and community building. These tools include groupware and online community development tools, games and simulations, as well as polling and surveys.
5. Cyber Agenda-setting: the use of the Internet and other ICTs to enhance or redirect the political or policy agenda by established groups such as political parties and nongovernmental organizations.[79]

The report also stated that "more than half the US population and three-quarters of European citizens surveyed believe information technology will spark a renewal of democracy and civil society," but at the same time, "with the enhanced connectivity made possible by ICTs come potential privacy violations by 'big brother' governments, corporations, or terrorists; employment discrimination; loss of civic rituals and community; and isolation into one's own political community."[80]

It seems clear to us that electronic communications technologies already are transforming governance in many ways, largely unforeseen and perhaps undesirable, while others appear to be exhilarating and liberating. It is our contention that the conscious, purposeful, and controlled introduction of these and other technologies into the design of future governance systems is an urgent necessity.[81]

In the last chapter of their book, *The Future of Teledemocracy,* Becker and Slaton present what is to us an inspiring and yet responsible and achievable vision of a "Quantum-corrected New Democratic Paradigm." On the basis of years of research and networking in this field, they believe that a "quantum-corrected new democracy" will be characterized by the following features.

1. There will be more community, local, state, provincial, regional, national, transnational, and global direct-democratic movements and governance.
2. There will be more understanding of the common direct-democratic theory that unites them and thus more networking between them.
3. These new direct-democratic systems will use more scientific, deliberative

polling, voting from the home, electronic deliberation, and comprehensive electronic town meeting processes. TV set-computers will become home based, interactive (lateral and two-way) political information and communications systems, eventually assisted by artificial intelligence.

4. Simple majority, win-lose systems will give way to broad-based consensus building as the best way for polities to plan, decide, and administer the public sphere.

5. The use of random sampling will become more common in empowering citizens in self-governance and in influencing representative governments.

6. New forms of electronically based democratic political organizations will emerge that are here today and gone tomorrow—for example, "cyberparties," "citizens initiative networks," "cyberpressure groups," and "virtual communities of political transformation." These will transform representative government into a system much less responsive to traditionally organized pressure groups and more responsive to a broad base of its citizenry.[82]

Concluding Challenge

Responding to globalization with fairness toward present and future generations presents humanity with a new and pressing opportunity: to envision, design, and implement new forms of governance that capture the aspirations for community, identity, and freedom that people have everywhere, but grounded on more appropriate cosmological and technological bases than are current governance systems.

We challenge the readers of this volume, especially those who are in positions of decision influencing and making in East Asia, to accept this challenge and engage in fundamental, culturally appropriate, quantum-informed new democratic governance design. However, as Ian Shapiro and Stephen Macedo point out,

> [A]bstract debates about democratic ideals are of limited value when conducted apart from serious efforts at institutional design, and from serious attention to the varying contexts in which democracy must be realized if it is to be realized at all. Few things are easier than celebrating rule by the deliberate sense of the people, and few things are harder than designing institutions to bring this about in practice.[83]

But (as though illustrating how difficult governance design actually is) in fact there is very little useful information on designing new governance in the rest of their book except for this one sentence by Brooke A. Ackerly in her article, "Designing Democratic Institutions: Political or Economic?" "The history and the present of . . . economics and politics . . . suggest that political reform will not be successful (no matter how coherently designed, no matter how accommodating the political strategies of certain elected officials) if political power continues to be the most sure source of economic gain."[84] We challenge you, in the name of future and present generations everywhere.

FURTHER THOUGHTS
Global Governance
Walt Anderson

FOR MANY PEOPLE the dream of world government has always seemed the key to the future, the only pathway to a world of peace, stability, equity, and fairness. This was the dream expressed by Alfred Lord Tennyson in his poem "Locksley Hall," invoking a future time when "the war-drums throbbed no longer and the battle flags were furled/In the Parliament of man, the Federation of the world."

Today World Federalists carry forth the idea of a global government complete with constitution, capital, and powers to levy taxes and enforce world law. Outside their ranks, many people who are not prepared to go all the way with a complete global state nevertheless advocate a greatly strengthened United Nations or perhaps an elected global parliament.

In striking contrast to this is the worldview of the political theorists and government officials who call themselves "realists" and who see nation-states as the once and future keepers of legitimate power to govern and the realities of world events driven by national interest. From the realist point of view, such a global government is neither practical nor desirable.

A third point of view holds that we already have a system of global governance (not a government, but rather an ever-changing arrangement of governments, intergovernmental organizations, nongovernmental organizations, multinational corporations, regimes, and practices) and that the hope of the future lies in its evolution, variously described as an "ambiguous world order," a "nobody-in-general-charge system," or an "ecology of governance."

Notes

1. Ted C. Lewellen, *Political Anthropology: An Introduction* (Westport, Conn.: Bergin & Garvey, 1992), chaps. 1, 2.

2. D. S. Wilson, "Human Groups as Units of Selection" *Science* 276 (June 20, 1997): 276–277.

3. Gordon S. Wood, *The Creation of the American Republic, 1776–1787* (New York: W. W. Norton, 1969), 228.

4. Jack Goody, *The Domestication of the Savage Mind* (New York: Cambridge University Press, 1977); Walter J. Ong, *Orality and Literacy: The Technologizing of the Word* (London: Routledge, 1982); Eric Alfred Havelock, *The Muse Learns to Write: Reflections on Orality and Literacy from Antiquity to the Present* (New Haven, Conn.: Yale University Press, 1986); Jack Goody, *The Logic of Writing and the Organization of Society* (New York: Cambridge University Press, 1986); Jack Goody, *The Power of the Written Tradition* (Washington, DC: Smithsonian Institution Press, 2000); David R. Olson and Nancy Torrance, eds., *The Making of Literate Societies* (Oxford: Blackwell Publishers, 2001); Marshall McLuhan, *The Gutenberg Galaxy: The Making of Typographic Man* (Toronto: University of Toronto Press, 1962); Elizabeth Eisenstein, *The Printing Press as an Agent of Change: Communications and Cultural Transformations in Early Modern Europe* (New York: Cambridge University Press, 1979); M. Ethan Katsh, *The Electronic Media and the Transformation of Law* (New York : Oxford University Press, 1989).

5. Harvey Wheeler, "Constitutionalism," in *Governmental Institutions and Processes: Handbook of Political Science,* ed. Fred Greenstein and Nelson Polsby (Reading, Mass.: Addison-Wesley Publishing Company, 1975), 5:esp. 6 and 76f.

6. Kim Stanley Robinson, *Red Mars* (New York: Bantam Books, 1993), 89.

7. The following paragraphs are based on Fred Riggs, "Presidentialism: A Problematic Regime Type," in *Parliamentary versus Presidential Government,* ed. Arend Lijphart (Oxford: Oxford University Press, 1992), 217–222.

8. James A. Dator, "Beyond the Nation-State? Images of the Future of the International Political System," *World Future Society Bulletin* 15.6 (November–December 1981): 5–14; and James A. Dator, "Beyond the Nation-State: Three Images of Global Governance," *The Futurist* (December 1981): 24.

9. Dator, "Beyond the Nation-State," 24.

10. Rexford Tugwell, *A Model Constitution for a United Republics of America* (Santa Barbara, Calif.: Center for the Study of Democratic Institutions, 1970); Arthur Waskow, *Running Riot: A Journey through the Official Disasters and Creative Disorder in American Society* (New York: Herder and Herder, 1970); and Alfred de Grazia, *Kalos: What Is to Be Done with Our World?* (Bombay: Kalos Press, 1973), esp. Part V, "Reconstitution" and the "Kalotic Constitution."

11. Draft Constitution CONV 724/1/03, vol. 1, 28 May 2003, available at http://register.consilium.eu.in; and Draft Constitution CONV 802/03, vol. 2, 12 June 2003, available at http://european-convention.eu.in.

12. Available at www.eduskunta.fi/efakta/vk/tuv/tuvesite.htm.

13. Available at www.aka.fi/modules/page/show_page. asp?id=00AE7FC471CD44B 4BC6C508078FF674A&lay out=akatemia-eng&count=1&template=&framename=data _1&tportal.

14. Available at www.tukkk.fi/tutu/tva/bottom_ffa.htm.

15. Ian Lowe, "Governing in the Interests of Future Generations," in *Co-Creating a Public Philosophy for Future Generations,* ed. Tae-Chang Kim and Jim Dator (Twickenham, UK: Adamantine Press, 1999), 140.

16. Barry O. Jones, "Balancing Now and the Future," in *Co-Creating a Public Philosophy for Future Generations,* ed. Kim and Dator, 85–88.

17. H.R. 3070, "A bill to provide for the continuous assessment of critical trends and

alternative futures." Clem Bezold, "Governmental Foresight and Future Generations," in *Co-Creating a Public Philosophy for Future Generations,* ed. Kim and Dator, 92.

18. Staff Report of the Select Committee on Committees, House of Representatives, *Committee Reform Amendments of 1974: Explanation of H. Res 988 as Adopted by the House of Representatives, October 8, 1974.* 93rd Cong., 2d sess., H41-730-O, 56.

19. Bezold, "Governmental Foresight and Future Generations," 92.

20. Clem Bezold, *Anticipatory Democracy: People in the Politics of the Future* (New York: Random House, 1978).

21. Jerome Glenn, Theodore Gordon, and Jim Dator, "Closing the Deal: How to Make Organizations Act on Futures Research," *Foresight* 3.3 (June 2001): 177–189.

22. Lowe, "Governing in the Interests of Future Generations," 140.

23. Supreme Court (of the Philippines), *Reports Annotated,* vol. 224, July 30, 1993, 802f.

24. Ibid., 804.

25. John Ehrenberg, *Civil Society: The Critical History of an Idea* (New York: New York University Press, 1999).

26. Ibid., xi.

27. Ibid., x.

28. David Crocker, "Civil Society and Transitional Justice," in *Civil Society, Democracy, and Civic Renewal,* ed. Robert Fullinwider (New York: Rowman & Littlefield, 1999), 381.

29. John Donahue, "Is Government the Good Guy? After 50 years of Market Ascendancy, Government may be Poised to Reclaim its Role as an Integral and Admirable Part of American Life." Available at www.nytimes.com/2001/12/13/opinion/13DONA .html?todaysheadlines.

30. Crocker, "Civil Society and Transitional Justice," 383.

31. Ibid.

32. Ibid., 384.

33. Benjamin Barber, *Strong Democracy: Participatory Politics for a New Age* (Berkeley: University of California Press, 1984).

34. Ibid., 16ff

35. Ibid., 22ff.

36. Ibid., 33ff; and Benjamin Barber, *A Place for Us: How to Make Society Civil and Democracy Strong* (New York: Hill and Wang, 1998). See also his "Clansmen, Consumers and Citizens: Three Takes on Civil Society," in *Civil Society, Democracy, and Civic Renewal,* ed. Fullinwider, 9–29. Barber's use of the label "clansmen" also critiques the "neutrality" that some uses of "civil society" imply—hate groups like the Ku Klux Klan and/or groups that are internally organized as patriarchal dictatorships, for example, can be understood to be good examples of "civil society" unless a specific value orientation is added.

37. Ibid., 75.

38. Available at http://aei.org/events/eventID.329,filter./event_detail.asp.

39. Available at www.NGOWatch.org.

40. Martin Kohler, "From the National to the Cosmopolitan Public Sphere," in *Re-*

imagining Political Community Studies in Cosmopolitan Democracy, ed. Daniele Archibugi, David Held, and Martin Kohler (Stanford, Calif.: Stanford University Press, 1999), 231.

41. Ibid., 233.

42. Ibid., 247.

43. Daniele Archibugi, David Held, and Martin Kohler, *Re-imagining Political Community: Studies in Cosmopolitan Democracy* (Stanford, Calif.: Stanford University Press, 1999), 4.

44. David Held, "Democracy and Globalization," in *Re-imagining Political Community: Studies in Cosmopolitan Democracy,* ed. Archibugi, Held, and Kohler, 21, 22.

45. Ibid, 22.

46. Ibid., 21–24 passim.

47. On China's destruction of its gigantic exploring sailing fleet and withdrawal into isolation just before Europe set sail for the "New World" in the fifteenth century, see Ben Finney, "The Prince and the Eunuch," in *Interstellar Migration and the Human Experience,* ed. Ben Finney and Eric Jones (Berkeley: University of California Press, 1985), 196–208. On Japan's three hundred years of *sakoku* (isolation), see Chie Nakane and Shinzaburo Oishi, eds., *Tokugawa Japan: The Social and Economic Antecedents of Modern Japan* (Tokyo: University of Tokyo Press, 1990); and Ronald P. Toby, *State and Diplomacy in Early Modern Japan: Asia in the Development of the Tokugawa Bakufu* (Stanford, Calif.: Stanford University Press, 1991).

48. Bill McKibben, *Enough: Staying Human in an Engineered Age* (New York: Times Books, 2003).

49. Martin Rees, *Our Final Hour: A Scientist's Warning: How Terror, Error, and Environmental Disaster Threaten Humankind's Future in this Century, On Earth and Beyond* (New York: Basic Books, 2003).

50. John Gastil, *By Popular Demand: Revitalizing Representative Democracy through Deliberative Elections* (Berkeley: University of California Press, 2000).

51. Ibid., 6.

52. Ibid., 7.

53. Ibid., 8.

54. Ibid., 9.

55. Michael Meyerson, *Political Numeracy: Mathematical Perspectives on Our Chaotic Constitution* (New York: W. W. Norton, 2002).

56. Bruce Tonn and David Feldman, "Non-Spatial Government," *Futures* 27.1 (January/February 1995): 11–36.

57. Jack Burnham, *Beyond Modern Sculpture: The Effects of Science and Technology on the Sculpture of this Century* (New York: G. Braziller, 1968).

58. See, esp., Glendon Schubert, "The Evolution of Political Science Paradigms of Physics, Biology, and Politics," *Politics and the Life Sciences* 1 (1983): 97–110.

59. James Dator, "Quantum Theory and Political Design," in *Changing Lifestyles as Indicators of New and Cultural Values,* ed. Rolf Homann (Zurich: Gottlieb Duttweiler Institute, 1984), 53–65; and Dator, "Confessions of a Quark Smeller: The Implications of Quantum Physics for Political Design," paper for a panel chaired by Ted Becker for the American Political Science Convention, Chicago, September 3, 1987.

60. Theodore Becker, ed., *Quantum Politics: Applying Quantum Theory to Political Phenomena* (Westport, Conn.: Praeger, 1991).

61. Christa Slaton, *Televote: Expanding Citizen Participation in the Quantum Age* (New York: Praeger, 1992).

62. James Robinson, "Newtonianism and the Constitution," *Midwest Journal of Political Science* 1.1 (1957): 252–256; Martin Landau, "On the Use of Metaphor in Political Science," *Social Research* 28 (1961): 331–353.

63. Landau, "On the Use of Metaphor in Political Science," 331–353.

64. Wheeler, "Constitutionalism," in *Governmental Institutions and Processes*, 5:esp. 6 and 76f.

65. For more discussion on the questionable assumptions of rationality underlying law and electoral decision making, see Dator, "Quantum Theory and Political Design."

66. Michio Kaku, *Hyperspace: A Scientific Odyssey through Parallel Universes, Time Warps, and the Tenth Dimension* (New York: Oxford University Press, 1995); Fred Alan Wolf, *Parallel Universes: The Search for Other Worlds* (New York: Simon and Schuster, 1988).

67. Michael J. Shapiro, *Reading the Postmodern Polity: Political Theory as Textual Practice* (Minneapolis: University of Minnesota Press, 1992); Michael J. Shapiro, *Language and Political Understanding: The Politics of Discursive Practices* (New Haven, Conn.: Yale University Press, 1981).

68. Laurence H. Tribe, "The Curvature of Constitutional Space: What Lawyers Can Learn from Modern Physics," in *Quantum Politics, Applying Quantum Theory to Political Phenomena*, ed. Theodore Becker (New York: Praeger, 1991), 171. (Originally published in *Harvard Law Review* 103.1 [1989]: 1–56.)

69. Ibid., 172.

70. Ibid.

71. Jiri Rasanen, "The Platform of Aanivalta (The Finnish Citizens' Power Movement)," unpublished. Contact jiri.rasanen@nic.fi.

72. For more on this, see Jim Dator, "When Courts are Overgrown with Grass: Futures of Courts and Law," *Futures* 32.1 (February 2000): 183–197.

73. John Hibbing and Elizabeth Theiss-Morse, *Stealth Democracy: Americans' Beliefs about How Government Should Work* (Cambridge: Cambridge University Press, 2002).

74. Ibid., 1f.

75. Ibid., 2.

76. Ibid., 3.

77. E.g., even though the titles suggest innovative and unconventional ideas of governance, the authors dismiss the idea of direct democracy without showing any familiarity with the literature on it: Ted Halstead and Michael Lind, *The Radical Center: The Future of American Politics* (New York: Doubleday, 2001), 126ff; Cass Sunstein, *Designing Democracy: What Constitutions Do* (Oxford: Oxford University Press, 2001), 7; and John Haskell, *Direct Democracy or Representative Government? Dispelling the Populist Myth* (Boulder, Colo.: Westview Press, 2001).

78. Lyn Carson and Brian Martin, *Random Selection in Politics* (Wesport, Conn.: Praeger, 1999).

79. Clement Bezold et al., *Cyber Democracy 2001: A Global Scan* (Alexandria, Va.: Alternative Futures Associates, 2001), Executive Summary.

80. Ibid.

81. For more discussion, pro and con, on this issue, see Mark A. Abramson and Therese Morin, eds., *E-Government 2003* (Lanham, Md.: Rowman & Littlefield, 2003); Steve Davis et al., *Click on Democracy: The Internet's Power to Change Political Apathy into Civic Action* (Boulder, Colo.: Westview, 2002); Elaine Kamarck and Joseph Nye, *Governance.com: Democracy in the Information Age* (Washington, DC: Brookings Institution, 2002); Brian D. Loader, *The Governance of Cyberspace* (New York: Routledge, 1997); Michael Margolis and David Resnick, *Politics as Usual: The Cyberspace "Revolution"* (Thousand Oaks, Calif.: Sage Publishers, 2000); Abbe Mowshowitz, *Virtual Organizations: Toward a Theory of Societal Transformation Stimulated by Information Technology* (Westport, Conn.: Quorum Books, 2002); Harold Myerson, "Democrats Campaign Online," *Honolulu Advertiser,* June 19, 2002, A10; Cass Sunstein, *Republic.com* (Princeton, N.J.: Princeton University Press, 2001); and Anthony Wilhelm, *Democracy in the Digital Age* (New York: Routledge, 2000).

82. Ted Becker and Christa Daryl Slaton, *The Future of Teledemocracy* (Westport, Conn.: Praeger, 2000), 211.

83. Ian Shapiro and Stephen Macedo, eds., *Designing Democratic Institutions* (New York: New York University Press, 2000), 15.

84. Ibid., 291.

PART 4

Responding to Globalization in East Asia

This is a very ambitious section. It is the heart and soul of our book. Written for the most part by people living in East and Southeast Asia, it tells how countries in the region have responded to globalization both historically and in the present. Chapter 16, by two young scholars, one from South Korea and the other from Japan, makes it absolutely clear that globalization is nothing new, that it has been a feature of East and Southeast Asia for many thousands of years. Yongseok Seo and Shunichi Takekawa briefly review the history of China, Korea, Japan, Cambodia, and Vietnam, focusing entirely on how each country has been impacted by, responded to, and contributed to globalization from the earliest times to the present.

This is followed by five brief chapters illustrating how China, Korea, Japan, Cambodia, and Vietnam are each currently responding to globalization. Each of these chapters is written by a citizen and resident of the country under discussion. However, each of these authors approaches the task in quite different ways.

In chapter 17, Jingping Ding presents a comparatively detailed overview of how Chinese leaders are committed to economic development through strategic integration into the emerging global economy. This strong commitment has replaced political ideology, even though the Communist Party retains overall control. Issues of fairness are paramount for the country's and the Communist Party's future.

Of all the authors, Yong-duck Jung, in chapter 18, adheres most closely to the direct topic of the book, showing how the government, and primarily the bureaucracy, of South Korea has changed in response to varying external and internal pressures for reform in recent years. Ryo Oshiba, on the other hand, takes a case-study approach in chapter 19 and discusses how even so apparently exclusively "national" a matter such as writing and choosing history textbooks for use in Japanese schools has become a matter of certainly regional and perhaps global concern and interference.

Chanto Sisowath, in chapter 20, considers especially how the younger generation, both formally educated abroad and greatly influenced by transnational media flows at home, is urging substantial change in Cambodia, while Le Van Ahn, in chapter 21, presents a more formal analysis of the many ways Vietnam is seeking to create a viable civil society and to quickly become economically competitive on the world stage.

In between these chapters there are Further Thoughts on civil society in East Asia and on globalization and Japan by Jim Dator and on Cambodia and Vietnam by Yongseok Seo.

Chapter 22, the final one in part 4, by Yongseok Seo, presents the response of East Asian countries to the globalization of culture by examining the changes in East Asian perceptions of culture. He especially focuses on the cultural policy of national governments as a manifestation of East Asian responses to the globalization of culture. This is followed by Further Thoughts by Sohail Inayatullah on globalization and "Asian values" and on generational challenges to Confucian norms.

This section contains rich and varied fare.

CHAPTER 16

Waves of Globalization in East Asia
A Historical Perspective

Yongseok Seo and Shunichi Takekawa

If we define "globalization" as the flow of things around the world, then what we now call globalization is not uniquely modern, nor is it merely a phenomenon of the late twentieth century resulting from new technologies and social systems. Rather, it is a process as old as humanity that began from the earliest days of human existence. Widespread diffusion of culture, religion, technology, and political-economic systems from a few major centers is an ancient phenomenon. The difference that makes contemporary globalization special is its unprecedented speed and the intensity of its flow. The following brief historical survey of China, Japan, and Korea illustrates the way waves of global or regional ideas, institutions, technologies, and people have impacted the three areas and how people in the three areas responded to them.

Four Global Waves of the Premodern Era

The melding, borrowing, and adaptation of external influences can be found in many areas of human life throughout history. East Asia developed its own civilization through frequent contact and exchanges with the outside world. This section will discuss global flows in premodern East Asia, showing how East Asians accommodated, adopted, or rejected outside influences. We will focus on four of the most important global flows in premodern East Asia: Buddhism, Confucianism, Islam, and Christianity.

Buddhism

As one of the world's great religions and philosophies, Buddhism has had a profound impact on all of Asia throughout history. According to legend, Gautama Siddhartha (563–483 BC) founded Buddhism in the northeastern part of India. He later became known as the Buddha and preached paths to achieve enlightenment (nirvana). Buddhism was then transmitted in two major directions:

into Southeast Asia as Theravada Buddhism and into China as Mahayana Buddhism, where it later filtered into Korea and Japan.

CHINA

It is not clear when Buddhism reached China, but historians generally agree that it was via Central Asia (the Silk Roads) around the first century AD. In the beginning, Buddhist practices were resisted by the Chinese in preference to the prevailing Confucianism. However, the demise of the Han Dynasty in AD 220 and the chaotic period that followed facilitated the spread of Buddhism throughout China. By the late fourth century AD, the common people as well as the ruling class began to accept Buddhism. Over time, Buddhism became integrated with local traditions and culture. Although Buddhism had a great impact on the arts and religion of the Chinese people, there is little evidence that Buddhist ideas influenced Chinese political ideology and government institutions. Instead, as we will show, Confucianism played a pivotal role in the governing system of China for two millennia and was not challenged until the Western influence of the late nineteenth century.

KOREA

Buddhism was first introduced to Korea around the fourth century AD from China. Before its arrival, ancient Koreans practiced shamanism that was based on spirits within living things and natural forces. Korea was divided into three separate kingdoms: Koguryŏ, Paekche, and Silla. Buddhism first arrived in the northern kingdom of Koguryŏ and gradually spread to Paekche, in the southwest, finally reaching southeastern Silla in the fifth century AD.

Initially, Buddhism faced great resistance from the indigenous people. In Silla, in particular, the nobles rejected Buddhism and remained faithful to the traditional gods. The Silla court recognized Buddhism only after the martyrdom of Ichadon in AD 527. Eventually, Buddhism became a tool that enabled ruling elites in Silla to gain power and to possess a set of beliefs that enabled them to conquer Paekche and Koguryŏ. After the unification, the ruling class of Silla incorporated Buddhist ideals into Confucianism so that Buddhism was able to maintain its status with little opposition throughout the Unified Silla (668–935) and Koguryŏ (935–1392) periods. However, with the downfall of the Koguryŏ dynasty in 1392, Buddhism slowly declined as the new rulers of the Chosŏn dynasty (1392–1910) adopted neo-Confucianism. This led to the oppression and restriction of Buddhism by political elites of the Chosŏn dynasty.

JAPAN

The formal introduction of Buddhism into Japan was by a Korean king in AD 552, although most historians agree that it was actually present before that time.

The impression of Buddhism held by the imperial court that worshiped Shinto was generally negative, but the head of the Soga families who served the court gained permission from the emperor to adopt Buddhism. However, Buddhism was banned after many people died from an epidemic, of which the Mononobe families claimed Buddhism was the cause. In 587, the Soga, seeking to lead the regime, won the battle against the Mononobe and started to worship Buddhism openly. Subsequently, Prince Shōtoku (574–622)[1] reconciled Buddhism with the native Japanese religion, called Shinto today. Since then, Shinto and Buddhism have coexisted in Japan. However, Buddhism, along with Confucianism, was mostly for the court and aristocrats who used it to sustain their governance and spiritual life during the early days. Being supported by the court and aristocrats, Buddhist art and temple architecture with Chinese traits bloomed in the capital, Heijokyo, located in present-day Nara.

With the decline of the imperial reign and the rise of the samurai warrior class, Buddhism became more popular. During the Kamakura period, the practice of Zen attracted many samurai. Meanwhile, new Buddhist sects, whose monks studied Buddhism in Japan, and not China, emerged and began to disseminate their theories. In particular, monks who developed appealing Buddhist beliefs and practices walked through towns and villages, attracting common people who were suffering from war, natural disasters, famines, and numerous daily problems. Thus Buddhism became domesticated in Japan.

Confucianism

CHINA

Among China's many contributions to globalization, Confucianism has probably had the deepest impact on political and social concepts in East Asia over the last two millennia. Confucianism was founded by Confucius (551–479 BC) and was developed by his successors in ancient China. Unlike Buddhism, Confucianism is a social system and a set of ethical values rather than a religion. It deals with primary values and basic human relationships that originate from an individual's family. Confucianism was transmitted from China to Korea, Japan, and Vietnam and has become an important social and political value system deeply embedded in them. See Jim Dator's Further Thoughts, "Civil Society in East Asia," on page 239.

KOREA

Although Confucianism was introduced into Korea before Buddhism, its ideological flourishing took place later, with the introduction of neo-Confucianism during the late Koryŏ and early Chosŏn periods.[2] However, early Confucianism enormously influenced and transformed Korean society and political systems during the Three Kingdoms era (first through eighth century AD). Unlike the arrival of Buddhism, there was no significant resistance to Confucianism in Korea. Rather, it was effectively used by ruling elites as a means of governing people. Unified Silla adapted Confucianism, merging it with the uniquely Korean monarchical system whereby top administrative positions were given to practicing Confucian officials who had connections with the royal family. In the process of state growth, the Silla class system (known as the "bone-rank" system) began to pose an obstacle to the supremacy of the king. Thus the monarchy introduced Confucianism in order to alter the traditional political processes and to centralize political power, modeled after China.[3] Confucianism flourished in the relatively stable atmosphere of the Unified Silla and Koryŏ dynasty. By the end of the fourteenth century, newly emerged neo-Confucian intellectuals who founded the Chosŏn dynasty collaborated with the military, and the new rulers adopted neo-Confucianism as the governing ideology.

JAPAN

Confucianism was also introduced to Japan via Korea. Prince Shōtoku relied on the essence of Confucianism to build the first centralized state in the Japanese archipelago. His intentions were realized in the so-called Constitution of Seventeen Articles, which stressed that people should live in social harmony. When the imperial family, along with some aristocratic families, revolted against the Soga families and took control of the Yamato court in 645, they planned to build a new state structure by imitating the centralized Chinese imperial dynasty. The idea was spelled out in the Taika administrative and penal code. Under the code, aristocratic family members would serve the court as officials, and ordinary people would become subjects of the court. Yet the imperial family and their governance based on the Chinese Confucian tradition gradually declined, and cultural and commercial exchange with China also diminished. The central government kept its authority but had to rely on local powers. The Heian period (794–1185) also is characterized by "a considerable domestication of imported civilization."[4]

Neo-Confucianism became the official doctrine of the Tokugawa polity (1603–1867). Its emphasis on loyalty and social order was believed to support good governance. The Tokugawa employed Confucian scholars as its officials, preferring the school of neo-Confucianism called Shushi created by the Chinese philosopher Zhuxi (1130–1200), because of its emphasis on loyalty. On the other hand, the Tokugawa banned another school, formulated by the Chinese philosopher Wang Yangming, or Ōyōmei[5] (1472–1529), since the Tokugawa believed that the school's emphasis on independent thought and action would harm social order.

The various branches of Confucianism and Chinese tradition were collectively designated the Schools of Chinese Learning (Kangaku-ha). Japanese Confucianism disregarded some important aspects of Chinese Confucianism, such as the "Mandate of Heaven" and the right of the people to revolt against irresponsible rulers. In this respect, like Buddhism in earlier centuries, Confucianism was also domesticated as a governance tool by the rulers. Yet the ignored aspects of Confucianism gradually came to be known by Japanese scholars and well-educated samurai and eventually were used to support the samurai who opposed the Tokugawa. Meanwhile, Schools of National Learning (Kokugaku-ha) emerged. These schools subsequently provided a theoretical background for the Meiji Restoration and contributed to the rise of modern Japanese nationalism.

Islam

The prophet Mohammed (AD 570–632) founded Islam in 622. Although historians generally regard Islam as the newest among the three major global religions, Muslims believe that Mohammed was just the last of a series of prophets and that Islam existed long before Mohammed.[6] According to Soo-Il Jung, "Islam is a mode of comprehensive life that encompasses politics, economics, society and culture, and is a system of religion and practice that embraces both secular and sacred life."[7]

CHINA

According to historians, Arabian traders first introduced Islam to China in the mid-seventh century via the Silk Road. After that, a number of Muslim merchants, traders, and migrants began to visit China for commercial and religious purposes, and they often returned with Chinese technologies (represented by the Four Great Inventions of paper, printing, the compass, and gunpowder). Muslims who migrated to China had a great impact and influence on the economy as well. Yusuf Abdul Rahman states,

> Muslims virtually dominated the import/export business in China during Sung Dynasty (960–1279 CE). The office of Director General of Shipping was consistently held by a Muslim during this period. During the Ming Dynasty (1368–1644 CE), a period considered to be the golden age of Islam in China, Muslims fully integrated into Han society by adopting Chinese names and some customs while retaining their Islamic mode of dress and dietary restrictions.[8]

Large numbers of Muslims became government officials in the Mongolian-led Yuan dynasty (AD 1279–1368) court. Chinese-Muslim scholars employed ancient Chinese philosophical concepts to explain the principles of Islam and wrote and translated numerous works using Chinese ideographs. In fact, many Han Chinese, as well as Mongolians and Uighurs, converted to Islam. Muslims in China, however, were oppressed later, during the Manchu and communist periods. In 1953, Muslims rose up against communist China in order to build an independent Islamic nation, but they were brutally suppressed. Today, the Muslim population is estimated to be around twenty million and exists among ten distinct ethnic minorities in China.[9]

Korea

According to an Arab record, active trade occurred between the Silla kingdom in Korea and the Islamic world. Ibn Khurdadhibah was the first Arabian geographer to leave records about the exchange between Arab Muslims and Silla. A new era unfolded during the Koryŏ dynasty. A large number of Muslim merchants and traders came to Korea for commercial reasons, and from that time Islamic values and culture began to spread all over Korea. Some Muslim traders and merchants settled in Korea as permanent residents, and Islamic communities were formed in Korea for the first time.[10] However, the impact of Islamic culture on Korean politics and society was relatively limited compared to Buddhism and Confucianism.

Christianity

Christianity is probably the most globalized faith in the world, especially in the last few centuries. It is claimed that "there are about two billion Christians in the world today, of whom 560 million, the largest single bloc, live in Europe. Latin America, though, is close behind with 480 million. Africa has 360 million, and 313 million Asians profess Christianity. North America claims about 260 million believers."[11] However, Christianity may have been even more global in its early period than is realized, and a few historians emphasize the significance of Christian traditions in premodern Asia. In *A History of Christianity in Asia*, Samuel H. Moffett argues that Christianity had been widely diffused in Asia long before the modern missionary movement in the nineteenth and twentieth centuries.[12] Philip Jenkins also observes, "In the thirteenth century, the height of medieval Christian civilization in Europe, there may have been more Christian believers on the continent of Asia than in Europe, while Africa still had populous Christian communities."[13] This section will briefly explore the varied history of Christianity as a global influence as it spread across the East Asian continent.

China

Historians in general agree that Christianity (the Nestorian sect) first reached Asia as early as the seventh century AD and left many unique theological works written in Chinese during the Tang dynasty. Some even argue that the Chinese Christian tradition at that time was more sophisticated than in Europe in terms of scholarly achievement in theology, philosophy, and literature. However, Christianity failed to take root in China due to the strong Confucian tradition and the predominance of Buddhism. The Nestorian and Catholic faiths returned to

China during the Yuan dynasty, and in 1299 the first Roman Catholic church was erected in Beijing. The Mongol dynasty was generous to all religions and even employed Nestorians in its court. After the Chinese expelled the Mongols from China and established the Ming dynasty in 1368, Christianity in China began to decline. Jesuit missionaries came to China during the transitional period between the Ming and Qing dynasties in the sixteenth through seventeenth centuries. Matteo Ricci (1521–1610) was one of the missionaries allowed to live in Beijing. Although some Jesuits tolerated the incorporation of local Chinese religious practices into their liturgies and practices, conflicts between traditional Confucian rituals and Christianity eventually led to the expulsion of Christianity from China.

Korea

In Korea, there is no record of Christianity before the middle of the eighteenth century, when a few Korean envoys to China first introduced Christianity. Matteo Ricci's *Tianzhu* (The true doctrine of the Lord of Heaven) was also promulgated at this time. An intellectual group of *silhak* (practical learning) scholars began to study "the Catholic literature with hopes of learning about Western civilization." By the early nineteenth century, a number of Koreans converted to the Catholic Church, and by 1866 there were eight foreign clerics with more than eighteen thousand believers in Korea. However, Chosŏn government officials feared Christianity would disrupt the basis of Confucian social order, believing that "many elements of Christian doctrine conflicted with the basic ethical and ritual principles of Confucianism."[14] Thus the government issued an edict ordering adherents of the "evil learning" to be treated as guilty of high treason and initiated a series of persecutions. The resulting actions weakened the potential Christian impact until the modernization reforms of 1894.[15]

Japan

Islam never had an impact on Japanese society, but Christianity became a factor that changed medieval Japan drastically. Western Christians brought new technologies that terrorized Japanese leaders. In the sixteenth century, Portuguese traders came to the Japanese archipelago with Christian missionaries, introducing various Western commodities along with a new religion. The Spanish gradually followed the Portuguese. They arrived during the Warring States period (1467–1615), during which samurai warlords fought against each other to protect their territories or to unify the states. The foreign traders were welcomed especially in Kyushu, the southernmost main island of Japan, since they brought useful commodities and technologies such as firearms. A number of warlords converted to Christianity, though some of them reportedly became Christians mainly to increase their trade with the foreigners.

The Warring States period ended with the triumph of three successful warlords. The first, Oda Nobunaga, tolerated Christianity. However, the second, Toyotomi Hideyoshi, at first did not allow the Westerners to preach Christianity, though he did not officially ban it. Then in 1587 Hideyoshi ordered Christian priests to leave Japan. In 1597 he executed Western and Japanese Christians, fearing the political implications of Christianity. The third unifier, Tokugawa Ieyasu, maintained good relations with Westerners, including the Spanish and Portuguese. But the Dutch and English, who did not intend to disseminate Christianity, recommended that Tokugawa abort trade ties with the Catholic countries of Spain and Portugal. Tokugawa began the persecution of Christians, and his successor, Tokugawa Hidetada, executed Christian missionaries and ordered Japanese Christians to convert to Buddhism on pain of death. Subsequently, the Tokugawa regime closed the country to all Westerners except the Dutch.

During the Meiji period, the government lifted the ban on Christianity. It is notable that even though the population of Christians remained small in Japan, some former samurai became Christians and emerged as major political leaders, activists, and educators.

Conclusions for the Premodern Era

The four global waves that swept over premodern East Asia— Buddhism, Confucianism, Islam, and Christianity—either adapted to local cultures through a successful fusion, developed into a unique combination, or perished due to local resistance. Confucianism and Buddhism were successfully localized and deeply embedded in the societies of East Asia. Buddhism developed differently in each country, linking with indigenous values, religions, and belief systems such as Confucianism, shamanism, and Shintoism. East Asian ruling elites often attempted to incorporate Confucianism and Buddhism into traditional political systems and indigenous religious traditions. Accordingly, Confucianism was molded to meet aboriginal needs and tastes and therefore developed differently in China, Korea, and Japan

On the other hand, despite its rich history in seventh- and eighth-century China, Christianity failed to take root as a religious faith. Christianity also encountered strong local resistance, particularly from the ruling elites in sixteenth century Japan and in nineteenth century Korea. Why did Christianity fail to become established in premodern East Asia, while Buddhism, Confucianism, and Islam to some extent took root? Moffett attributes the "failure of Asian Christianity" to "geographical isolation, chronic numerical weakness, persecution, encounters with formidable Asian religions, ethnic introversion, dependence upon the state, and the Church's own internal divisions."[16] Indeed, Christianity, due to its exclusive nature, failed to compromise with the aboriginal cultures and prompted many conflicts, particularly with Confucian traditions. This eventually led to the failure of Christianity to develop as a kind of Christianity with East Asian characteristics.

Global Waves in the Modern Era

The Western concepts "modern" or "modernization"—along with their by-products, Westernization, imperialism, nationalism, capitalism, and communism—were the most widespread ideas in East Asia and the world during the nineteenth and twentieth centuries. This section will survey how East Asians viewed, accommodated, developed, and combined these new values and ideologies.

Response to Western Encroachment in the Nineteenth Century

Although it is difficult to say precisely when "modernity" began, the origin of the modern age is often said to be around the sixteenth century, when Europe experienced unprecedented social, political, and economic transformation. Historians like Elizabeth Eisenstein attribute the transformation to the effects of the printing press on medieval Europe. She argues that the printing press was crucial in enabling the Renaissance, the Reformation, mercantilism, and the Scientific Revolution.[17]

China

As Ming-fong Kuo and Andreas Weiland point out, "the advent of 'modernity' in East Asia is usually connected with the intrusion of the Western imperialist world system."[18] By the early nineteenth century, China began to rapidly lose its supremacy to the modernizing and industrializing West. The initial Chinese response was to reject Western ideas and practices. Although the new world order of the time demanded that China adapt to new circumstances, there was no imperative within the Chinese social system itself to respond to this demand. China's actions were based on an enormous self-confidence that stemmed from "the ideology of the middle kingdom."[19] However, resistance to change only brought humiliation and defeat along with a series of unequal treaties, forcing China to concede a portion of its territory to Western powers.

Japan

Japan also faced Western imperialist intruders in the first half of the nineteenth century. A possible Russian invasion was frequently anticipated by the daimyo. Yet the actual intrusion, with a huge impact, was made by the Americans. Commodore Matthew C. Perry arrived in Tokyo Bay with four warships in 1853 and forced the Tokugawa to open Japan's ports to American vessels. The

Tokugawa made treaties with the United States and eventually opened its ports to other Western countries. Its isolationist policy, *sakoku*, was ended by treaties that resulted in favoring Western countries at the expense of Japan's sovereignty.

In 1867, the Tokugawa renounced the political authority that it had acquired 250 years earlier. The emperor restored his own political supremacy. This power transition was mainly backed by the powerful Satusma, Chŏshu, and Tosa warlords who had been previously subjugated by the Tokugawa. Relatively low-class samurai of those warlords promoted this quasi-revolution and became de facto political leaders of the new Japan. Their pro-imperial movement originally started as actions against the Westerners who had forced the Tokugawa to open the nation. In a sense, the Western intrusion kindled Japan's protonationalism among those samurai who subsequently found their spiritual roots in the imperial family and Shinto. Historians and thinkers, influenced by the Schools of National Learning, provided theoretical reasons to be against Western intrusion. The slogan "Honor the emperor, expel the barbarians" *(Sonnō joi)* represents the view of these samurai. The Meiji Restoration thus was a nationalist movement even though participants were mostly only samurai.

Korea

Korea also felt serious threats from Western imperialist encroachment, and its initial response to the new world system was to resist. During the regency of the Taewongun (Grand Prince from 1864 to 1874), the central government attempted a series of reforms to revitalize the dynasty. "The Taewongun used many devices to strengthen the central administration, the monarchy, and the royal family. . . . He recruited talent much more widely, reorganized the central administration, and revised the law codes. Despite all these efforts to revitalize tradition and even use modern means to defend it, the Taewongun was vigorously exclusionist."[20] In policy struggles, the Taewongun presented resistance to all change in defense of isolationism, Confucianism, and Korean traditions. However, he was overthrown by his enlightened son, King Kojong, and Korea finally was forced to open to the outside world through Japanese gunboat diplomacy in 1875.

Modernization or Westernization?

To counter threats of Western imperialism and to avoid colonization by the West, East Asian leaders recognized that the need to respond effectively was urgent. However, it is doubtful that many East Asian leaders in the late nineteenth century distinguished between modernization and Westernization in their varied efforts to achieve a strong and stable nation-state. Modernization meant Westernization—the process of adapting Western values, ideologies, science and technology, political-economic systems, and, in short, the near-total assimilation of Western culture. As Kuo and Weiland put it,

> The entire frame of reference of the term "modern," the contextual field of the debate within which the term occurs, reflects the immanent assumption that modernity is to be equated with Western modernity and that modernization in East Asia is nothing but the enforcement of a Western (in itself "modern") influence which pushes aside indigenous (per se "traditional") forms of culture.[21]

China

In Qing China (1644–1912), Western science and languages were studied, special schools were opened in the larger cities, and arsenals, factories, and shipyards were established according to Western models. The Qing government also adopted Western diplomatic practices and sent students abroad. The effort to import Western technology into Chinese institutions became known as the "Self-Strengthening Movement" (1860–1895). Han Chinese officials directed this movement and were responsible for establishing Western institutions, developing basic industries, and Westernizing the military. But despite its efforts, the Self-Strengthening Movement failed to recognize the significance of the political and social evolution that had accompanied Western advances and innovations. In one sense, the Chinese Westernizing movement failed because it applied only Western "practical knowledge" while retaining the traditional Chinese mentality of Confucianism. However, Japan's military defeat of China in 1895 was a great shock, particularly to the Chinese traditionalists who had been trying to restore the Confucian tradition. In 1898, the Qing emperor Guangxu (1875–1908) ordered a series of reforms aimed at sweeping social and institutional changes. Kang Youwei (1858–1927) and Liang Qichao (1873–1929) were the principal intellectual architects of these changes. They declared that China needed more than "self-strengthening" and that innovation must be accompanied by institutional and ideological change. The imperial edicts for reform covered a broad range of subjects, including legal systems and governmental structures with Western values and ideology instead of neo-Confucian orthodoxy. However, the reformers' vision ended up being only a vision. The reform plans encountered intense opposition from the conservative ruling elite, especially the Manchu.

Japan

After the Meiji Restoration, in order to prevent the nation from being colonized by Westerners, the protonationalist Meiji leaders drastically Westernized Japanese society. They believed it was the only way to overturn the unequal treaties with the West and to make the country competitive with the Western powers.

Meiji leaders transformed former lords into aristocrats who had no substantial political power while demolishing the differences between the former four classes (samurai, farmers, artisans, and merchants) that marked the Tokugawa period. The privileges of samurai, such as wearing swords, were legally forbidden. More important, their hereditary pensions were terminated, so they had to find jobs or start businesses in order to make a living. Frustrated former samurai joined insurgencies and other anti-governmental movements. Afterward, former samurai became promoters of the people's rights movement and demanded a constitution and parliament. As a result, they also joined the Westernization movement.

Indeed, the Meiji government introduced a constitution, parliament (called the "Diet"), and cabinet system as parts of their Westernization project. But it should be noted that the Meiji leaders did not import everything they found in Western civilization. The leaders carefully studied Western customs, including political, economic, and social systems, and introduced their preferred Western-style organizations while modifying those organizations.[22] They kept some aspects of Japanese tradition and redefined them. They carefully wrote a constitution guided by Western scholars and even redefined the role of the imperial family.[23] Regardless of their intention, the imperial family symbolically and institutionally played a significant role in the creation of a modern nation by making itself visible in public and becoming the backbone of new ideologies.[24]

Meanwhile, Meiji leaders and intellectuals such as Fukuzawa Yukichi urged former samurai, farmers, artisans, and merchants to catch up with the West. Newly established schools and media became tools of Westernization. *Bunmei kaika* (enlightenment and civilization) was a slogan that exhorted people to Westernize and modernize.

Nonetheless, it should be noted that Japanese modernization was not merely a reaction to the Western powers. Modernization had already begun indigenously during the Tokugawa period. Indeed, Japan was in many ways a "modern" nation when Perry arrived. The 250-year-old Tokugawa era generated a nationwide market economy, began to commercialize agriculture, and experienced very significant urbanization.[25] Edo (now Tokyo), the de facto political capital; Osaka, the de facto business capital; Kyoto, the old capital; and castle cities of warlord territories were well connected by roads. Coastal shipping allowed merchants to trade a variety of agricultural and handcrafted products from city to city. The three capitals, Edo, Osaka, and Kyoto, were the world's largest cities by the middle of the Tokugawa period. Wealthy merchants *(gōshō)* who were richer than the small warlords emerged, and some of them became Japanese business conglomerates *(zaibatsu)* after the Meiji Restoration. Literacy and standards of general education were very high—certainly higher than in Europe during the same time. Without the development of these and other factors, Meiji Japan would have taken a different path.

Korea

Modern Western ideas began to exert a powerful influence on a group of *yangban* (Korean aristocracy) officials in Korea. These officials realized that Korea needed to transform its traditional institutions and values into a progressive and Western style. King Kojong and his clique took measures designed to promote "enlightenment" and "self-strengthening," establishing several new government institutions replicating Chinese administrative innovation while sending talented young officials to inspect Meiji Japan's Westernized institutions.[26] Highly inspired by the Japanese version of "civilization and enlightenment," the reform-minded young *yangban* officials attempted a bloody coup d'etat in 1884.[27] As Eckert, Lee, and Lew point out, the coup d'etat "aimed to establish an independent and efficient modern state with an egalitarian social order, to replace the oligarchy, *yangban*-centered socio political structure of the Chosŏn dynasty."[28] However, the coup ended in disastrous failure. It failed not only because of strong resistance from the conservative faction within the government, but also because of lack of popular support from the masses who had a fierce resentment against Japanese imperialism.

Although the coup failed, the promulgation of a fourteen-point reform program showed that there was a strong desire to develop a modern nation. In the document, "the reformers called for the termination of Korea's tributary ties to China, curtailment of *yangban* privileges, appointment of officials on the basis of merit, central control of fiscal and military administration, and the concentration of decision-making power in a state council."[29] The Korean reformist illusion about Japan evaporated with Japan's assertion of its supremacy over Korea in 1905. Korea's dream to become an independent, modern nation-state temporarily ended with Korea's annexation by Japan in 1910.

Communism and Nationalism in East Asia

Nationalism and communism were two dominant ideologies and by-products of Western modernity that emerged in nineteenth-century Europe. Although the definitions of both nationalism and communism are controversial, these two ideologies attained appeal beyond Europe and swept over East Asia in the twentieth century. Even in the twenty-first century nationalism continues to assert its power. People and governments around the world today continue to have a strong sense of attachment to their nation in response to globalization. With the demise of the Soviet empire, nationalism rapidly replaced the communist ideological vacuum in former communist countries. Nonetheless, China, Vietnam, and North Korea continue to identify themselves as communist states as of 2005.

In *Imagined Communities*, Benedict Anderson says that a nation "is an imagined political community," because "members of even the smallest nations will never know most of their fellow-members, meet them or even hear of them, yet in the minds of each lives the image of their communion."[30] Anderson asserts that "the nation's very origins can be traced to the rise of print capitalism and the appearance of mass vernacular newspapers."[31] Books, newspapers, and novels began to be published in vernacular languages with the new, faster, and cheaper method of duplication. This gave readers the idea that they belonged to a shared linguistic and ideological community and made it possible for them to imagine the "nation." Also, a standard national language, either spoken or written, could not have emerged as such before the advent of the printing press. Nationalism was thus, according to Anderson, a socially constructed phenomenon of modernity. By the end of the nineteenth century, nationalistic ideas began to infiltrate East Asia, and the notion of a modern nation-state began to develop in response to Western imperialistic encroachment.

Chinese nationalism

In China,[32] because of the failure of various reform movements from the top and the danger of colonization by the Western (and Japanese) imperial powers, intellectuals and political groups began to acknowledge the need for an "awakening of the consciousness of the nation to its own existence."[33] Chinese nationalism was influenced by a variety of ideological forces including Marxism, American pragmatism, social Darwinism, and traditional Chinese thought. Chinese nationalism presented itself in many different expressions, communism being but one.[34]

The immense expanse and variety of the Chinese nation and of China as a nation-state has been articulated by many intellectuals and political leaders. Sun Yat-sen (1866–1925) was the central figure who attempted to define the nation ethnically. Sun identified being Han with being Chinese and excluded the Manchus from the Chinese nation.[35] For Sun, Chinese of all social classes, including overseas Chinese, made up the nation. According to Fitzgerald, what China needed—and Sun wanted—was control. Later, many of Sun's political ideologies (e.g., advocating one-party rule) were adopted by both Chiang Kai-shek on the right and Mao Zedong on the left.

The peak of Chinese nationalism was the May Fourth Movement. Resentment and disappointment exploded on May 4, 1919, with massive student demonstrations against the incompetent government in Beijing on the one hand and Japanese aggression on the other.[36] The demonstrations, led by nationalistic students and reformist intellectuals, developed into a "national awakening." Students and intellectuals returned from abroad (mainly from Japan and France) and stood at the center of the movement. They blamed Confucianism and China's obsolete value system for China's humiliating defeats at the hands of Western and Japanese imperialists. They advocated Western ideas and ideologies ranging from the "complete Westernization of China" to "socialism" as alternatives to Confucianism. Over the next few decades (from the 1920s to the establishment of the People's Republic of China in 1949), Chinese nationalism was deeply influenced by social Darwinism and Russian ethnographic ideas. During communist rule after 1949, Chinese nationalism further mixed with elements of Marxism and Leninism. The decay of communism and the emergence of global capitalism led to a resurrection of strong nationalism within China.

Chinese communism

Like nationalism, communism was also an invention of nineteenth-century Europe. Communism is a theory and system of social and political organization. Since the second half of the nineteenth century, under the influence of the works of Marx, Engels, and Lenin, "the term *communism* has been used to denote a form of classless society based on common ownership of the means of production."[37] Communism was introduced to China by people like Chen Duxiu and Li Dazhao, both of whom were inspired by the Russian Revolution of 1917. By 1920, people associated with the Comintern (Communist International) were disseminating literature in China and helping to start communist groups, including one led by Mao Zedong. A number of Marxist groups came together and formed the Chinese Communist Party (CCP) in 1921 in Shanghai. Li Dazhao, a leader of the May Fourth Movement and cofounder of the CCP with Chen Duxiu, had a nationalistic view of communism. Mao Zedong also associated nationalism with communism so that he could exclude the bourgeoisie and landlords from the Chinese nation just as Sun excluded the Manchus.

Orthodox Marxism dictated that a communist revolution should begin among urban industrial labor. Li Dazhao, on the other hand, emphasized the role of the peasants in the communist revolution and deeply influenced Mao Zedong. Mao adapted Marxist theory to the underdeveloped conditions of agricultural China, much like Lenin did in early twentieth-century Russia. Mao tried to convince other communist leaders that a revolution on an urban and proletarian basis would not be appropriate in China. As Benjamin Schwartz indicates, Mao was able to realize that China's essential problem was a rural one and that only a revolution with the peasantry as its social basis would succeed.[38]

Korean nationalism

It is generally believed that Korean nationalism stems from the Tonghak (Eastern Learning) religious movement in the 1860s, which was formed in response to Western encroachment.[39] However, recent studies claim that modern Korean nationalism began with "Korea's disengagement from its traditional orientation toward China"[40] in the late nineteenth century. Korean reformist intellectuals who were educated in the West and Japan began to see China as a backward and incompetent state where it had once been perceived as the center of civilization. Andre Schmid argues that it was an important shift that took place in Korean attitudes toward China from "reverence to criticism."[41] Korean reformist intellectuals believed that separating from China was the first step toward reinvigorating Korea's own independent national identity. Nationalistic historians like Sin Ch'aeho assembled a genealogical chart for the Korean *minjok* (nation) and presented a new notion of national identity. This period also observed the sudden public campaign for using the Korean vernacular script *hangŭl*, which had been neglected by Korean intellectuals for several hundred years. Other displays of Korean nationalism during this period included King Kojong's adoption of the designation "emperor" and the promulgation of the Great Korean Empire, along with the introduction of the Korean national flag, *taegŭkki*.[42]

During the Japanese occupation of Korea, Korean nationalists carried out independence struggles against Japanese colonial rule. However, the brutal suppression of the Korean nationalist movement on March 1, 1919, caused many younger Koreans to become militant resistors. Some of them went into China and the Russian maritime province, where they set up resistance forces. Various nationalist groups emerged during this period, including the exiled Korean provisional government in China. It was also from this period that Korean nationalists began to split into right and left nationalist groups. The left-wing nationalist group later developed into the Korean Communist Party.

As Japan's colonial rule over Korea became more established and her aggressive expansion more evident with the Manchuria Incident in 1931, right-wing Korean nationalists became more pro-Japanese and social Darwinists. They believed that the Korean nation had to be assimilated into a greater Japanese nation for the sake of the Korean people. Being influenced by Japanese imperialistic ideology, the right-wing Korean nationalists held a totalitarian perspective with fascist characteristics. This tradition of colonial nationalism continued in both Koreas even after 1945.

Korean communism

The idea of modern communism was first introduced to Korean intellectuals in the early twentieth century, with Korean communists founding numerous circles in China and Russia as well as within Korea. The left-wing nationalists began to resist Japanese colonialism by arming themselves with this strong ideology. By the 1930s, some communists formed armed groups in Manchuria and fought against the Japanese Kwangtung Army by using guerrilla warfare. The most well-known guerrilla leader of this time was Kim Il Sung.

After the foundation of the Democratic People's Republic of Korea (North Korea), a left-wing version of nationalism was combined with communism and became known as Juche (Self-Reliance). The key to Juche ideology is *chajusong* (autonomy or independence). Unlike classical Marxism, which sees the means of production being the key to history, Juche sees self-conscious man as an individual as being key. Each individual possessing independence, creativity, and consciousness creates the future. Moreover, Juche ideology also greatly emphasizes the role of the masses in creating a proletarian revolution, while stressing national self-reliance in politics, economics, and defense. The term *chajusong* itself reveals an essential sentiment of modern nationalism that accentuates the importance of "national independence and sovereignty of one's people."[43] As Kim Jong Il states in *On the Juche Idea,*

> If one is to establish *Juche* in thinking, one must be well versed in one's own thing. . . . Koreans must know well Korean history, geography, economics, culture and the customs of the Korean nation, and in particular our Party's policy, its revolutionary history and revolutionary tradition.[44]

In brief, the Juche ideology emerged in response to global ideologies such as Marxism and Leninism, Christianity, colonialism, and nationalism. It is a unique combination of these global ideas and traditional Korean thought.[45]

Although Korean nationalists and communists in the colonial period had a different vision for the future of Korea, they basically shared the same ultimate goal: independence from Japanese colonial rule and the building of a modern nation-state on the Korean peninsula. Even in the postcolonial era, Korean nationalists in both North and South Korea continue to seek the nation's own identity, along with the importance of the concept of *minjok*—common historiography, culture, language, and territory.

Japanese nationalism

Nationalistic sentiment grew throughout the Meiji, Taisho, and Showa periods. "Rich nation, strong army" *(Fukoku kyōhei)* clearly revealed the nationalistic sentiments of the Meiji leaders. Another Meiji government slogan, "Save capital, develop industries" *(Shokusan kogyo),* showed how to achieve this. They were successful to an impressive degree. Imperial Japan began to compete with Western powers. The victories of the Sino-Japanese War (1894–1895) and the Russo-Japanese War (1904–1905) inflated Japanese nationalistic sentiment. As a result, Japan became expansionist, colonizing Taiwan and Korea and invading China. Ultimately Japan clashed against the rising Western power, the United States, in World War II. In a sense, Japanese nationalism pushed the nation into turmoil and created an unprecedented disaster in Asia.

Indigenous Modernization

China

The Chinese civil war between the communists and nationalists resumed after the war with Japan ended and was won by the CCP. Mao Zedong became chairman of the central government council of the newly established People's Republic of China in 1949. In an attempt to break with the Russian model of communism and to achieve rapid economic modernization, Mao launched the Great Leap Forward in 1958, which ended with a disastrous failure: twenty million people starved, and Mao withdrew from public view. A counter-reaction emerged in the form of the Cultural Revolution. The ostensible reason for the Cultural Revolution was to prevent development of a bureaucratized, Soviet-style communism in China. However, it had its roots in a power struggle between Mao and his political rivals. Through mass mobilization, some of the highest-ranking leaders were removed from power. Deng Xiaoping was among the best-known victims. In 1969, Mao reasserted his party leadership by serving as chairman of the Communist Party Congress, and he was named supreme commander of the nation and army. Mao closed schools and encouraged students to join Red Guard units, which persecuted Chinese teachers and intellectuals. Even Confucius was attacked as having been a hypocritical supporter of the bourgeoisie. The period of the Cultural Revolution (1966–1976) in China is now considered to be the "lost ten years" of building a modern nation. But it was nonetheless a dramatic Chinese attempt to "respond fairly" to some of the ills of globalizing communism of the time.

Deng Xiaoping became the most powerful Chinese leader after Mao. Since earlier attempts at developing China resulted instead in the country falling further and further behind in terms of national wealth and economic power, Deng and his affiliates initiated significant reforms that were labeled the "Four Modernizations" of industry, agriculture, science and technology, and national defense. Deng's reforms in the 1980s were comprehensive and full scale efforts at fundamental transformation of economic, governmental, and political organizations for rebuilding China as a modern socialist nation according to global capitalist standards. The "modernizations" included a program for improving both rural and urban life, the structural adjustment of ownership, and reform of the financial and taxation systems. However, it is important to note that the reforms were made at the administrative level while keeping the overall communist political framework intact. In this context, the reforms in the 1980s had antecedents in the modernization efforts of the late nineteenth century—applying the West's "practical knowledge" while reaffirming the old mentality of Confucianism.

Korea

The initial Korean attempt to build a modern nation in the late nineteenth century failed due to domestic resistance and was later blocked by Japanese colonialists. South Korea began the modernization process only after its liberation from Japan, with the rate accelerating after 1961. Former military generals governed South Korea from 1961 to 1992. At the expense of individual rights, leisure time, and political freedom, the authoritarian military regimes accomplished rapid economic development and pulled the country out of poverty. During this period, the modernization theme was given considerable attention; the term became a popular catch phrase extolling efforts toward achieving self-sustaining economic growth and industrialization. The Japanese modernization model was again depicted as a desirable solution, harkening back to previous attempts in the late nineteenth century. The process of modernization is still ongoing in South Korea, but since the 1990s it has faced the next wave of global pressures (neoliberalism).

Japan

The history of imperial Japan ended in 1945 with the disastrous defeat in World War II. The Allied powers, led by the United States, democratized Japanese political, economic, and social systems, accusing the old systems of being too feudalistic and nationalistic. Nonetheless, Japanese nationalism was still alive, playing a vital role in postwar economic development. Chalmers Johnson regards Japan as a nationalistic developmental state.[46] In contrast to a market-rational state such as the United States, he contends, the developmental state is plan rational and goal oriented, attempting to reform the structure of its domestic industry and promote the nation's economic power. Economic nationalism motivates nationalistic bureaucrats to plan industrial policy and improve the nation's economic competitiveness in the world. Johnson believes this tendency dates back to the Meiji period: national slogans such as "Rich nation, strong army" in the prewar era and "Promote exports" *(Yushutsu shinko)* in the postwar era exemplify Japan's plan-rational and goal-oriented tendency.

From a different perspective, Noguchi Yukio contends that the postwar Japanese economy imitated "the 1940 system" (1940-*nen taisei*) that mobilized Japanese behind the nation's wartime goals.[47] He focuses on the role of both wartime and postwar bureaucrats. The so-called "innovative bureaucrats" *(kakushin kanryo)* played a significant role in the development of the wartime economy during the 1930s and 1940s, while postwar bureaucrats took over the role of reviving the nation's economy around manufacturing and trade. Noguchi says that both Marxism and Nazi corporatism influenced the wartime bureaucrats, while the postwar bureaucrats were socialist oriented. Here again foreign models appeared in Japan-modified versions.

Concluding the Modern Era

Modernization, along with its by-products—nationalism, capitalism, and communism—characterized late nineteenth- and twentieth-century East Asia. As Kuo and Weiland point out, however, "modernization in East Asia is nothing but the enforcement of a Western (in itself 'modern') influence."[48] As the China, Japan, and Korea cases reveal, modernity in late nineteenth-century East Asia was generally equated with Westernization. In the process of "modernization," East Asian societies had to adopt Western values and ideologies, and at the same time they attempted to depart from their traditions (Confucianism in particular) in order to be accepted by the Western powers. In addition, East Asian leaders struggled to build strong nation-states and to create national consciousness through an "awakening nation" in order to avoid colonization by the West. For this reason, nationalism has always been the bottom line in East Asia throughout the centuries, and it continues to assert its existence even today in response to globalization.

Since the 1920s, communism has played a key role in the development of East Asia, particularly in China and Korea. However, we also see that the East Asian communist movement was one way, among many others, of presenting nationalism. Mao Zedong associated nationalism with communism by "awakening the Chinese nation," while left-wing Korean nationalists resisted Japanese colonialism by arming themselves with the strong and more sophisticated ideology of communism. In other words, nationalism and communism in East Asia were not binary; rather, they were hybridized under the processes of colonization and modernization. Communism was used by the early East Asian communist leaders as an ideological tool for building an independent nation-state, rather than as a step toward attaining the world communism that Marx believed would be achieved by historical necessity. In this process, however, both nationalists and communists in East Asia ignored ideals of nonviolence, liberalism, human rights, and democracy, and this vicious tradition continues to suppress people in some parts of East Asia. Nevertheless, the modern period was dramatic, as East Asia attempted to "respond fairly" to globalizing influences of the time.

Concluding Remarks

In this chapter we have examined the responses of three East Asian countries to the waves of globalization throughout history. In the modern era, all three countries have been mostly inward oriented, hence their primary concerns have been domestic politics and economy. The global forces mostly traveled through one-way channels during the premodern period. The global flow of things usually came to China first, then reached Japan by way of Korea or directly from China.

Sometimes they originated from China and reached other parts of the world as well as Korea and Japan.

Political leaders in the three countries sometimes regarded impacts of globalization as welcome gifts, while at other times they attempted to resist them. In particular, the Koreans and Japanese were often receptive to ideologies and culture from China. But it should be stressed that they did not simply absorb the global religions, ideologies, and value systems. Rather, they often selectively adapted and modified them in accordance with their needs and local traditions. Since the early modern era, the pattern of globalization has become more persistent, compulsory, aggressive, and often antagonistic.

Moreover, Japan is no longer merely a receiver of global gifts from China or Korea. It has become an important contributor to the global flow of things, just as China was during the premodern period. To resist or accommodate the new global values—namely modernization, nationalism, and communism—political leaders in East Asia have had to build a nation and a state out of their own domains. It was a process of resistance, selection, imitation, localization, counterblow, and, ultimately, "glocalization."

As of today, the channels of globalization have become more diversified and complicated and, in a sense, reciprocal. We believe that the way the East Asian region "responds in fairness to globalization" will be important for all of humanity. We are hopeful that the resurgence of human and intellectual resources in East Asia—which once had a splendid tradition and made great contributions to humanity—will act as a new alternative foundation for the post-globalized world by interacting with other great traditions everywhere.

FURTHER THOUGHTS
Civil Society in East Asia

Jim Dator

WHAT DOES "civil society" mean within an East Asian perspective? To the extent that East Asian societies are based on Confucian traditions, it might seem at first blush that there is no indigenous concept of civil society in the region. As Nosco and Rosemont tell it, the classical Confucian view of the state is quite similar to what Ehrenberg described, above, about Western ancient and medieval times, a "fused state" in which civilization is made possible only by a strong and all-encompassing government from which there is no legitimate separation or independence.

> The discussion of Confucian perspectives on the boundary between civil society and the state . . . is thoroughly speculative, for classical Confucianism never

envisioned a society inclusive of secular, voluntary associations of the sort suggestive of my understanding of civil society. This kind of society requires not just a sense of the integrity of the individual as an actor capable of negotiating his/her interactions in a responsible and ultimately socially constructive manner (something Confucianism would affirm) but also an acknowledged sphere of privacy granted by the state and society to its individual and corporate members to enable unauthorized voluntary associations, and Confucianism has generally not distinguished between privacy and selfishness in these contexts. (Nosco, "Confucian Perspectives on Civil Society and Government," 337)

The closest classical Confucianism comes to a concept of civil society is in the well-known series of mutual obligations from child to parent upward to the ruler and the ruled. In the family and village/labor community there is a sphere of relations, functionally similar to that of a civil society, but ultimately connected to the emperor, with his Mandate from Heaven at the top.

Confucianism's five relationships (ruler/subject, parent/child, husband/wife, elder brother/younger brother, and friend/friend) explicitly acknowledge the importance and value of such voluntary and consensual relationships. But it is also abundantly clear that Confucianism gives priority to those relationships that are found within the household, and to those relations in which there is a clear benefactor and beneficiary, since these are the relationships that prepare one for citizenship and train one in goodness. (Nosco, "Confucian Perspectives on Civil Society and Government," 343)

In this regard it is important to note that the word for "human being" in Chinese, Korean, and Japanese is composed of two characters. The first is a kind of stylized picture of a single person (pronounced *"ren"* in Mandarin Chinese, *"in"* in Korean, and *"nin"* in Japanese). The second character means "between" and is pronounced *"jian"* in Chinese, *"k'an"* in Korean, and *"gen"* in Japanese—thus *"renjian,"* *"ink'an,"* and *"ningen."* But the point is that to be a "human being" in these cultures, even the written language reminds you, you must be with others. You are not alone. Being human is to be among others, performing your assigned, or assumed, roles. As Rosemont puts it,

If I am the sum of the roles I live, then I am not truly living except when I am in the company of others. As Confucius himself said, "I cannot herd with the birds and beasts. If I do not live in the midst of other persons, how can I live?" While this view may seem strange to us, it is actually straightforward: in order to *be* a friend, neighbor, or lover, for example, I must *have* a friend, neighbor or lover.

(Rosemont, "Commentary and Addenda on Nosco's 'Confucian Perspectives on Civil Society and Government,'" 365)

The classical difference between Western and Eastern political philosophy (and attitudes toward political design) rests in this point. Western (especially American) traditional political philosophy assumes that all humans are evil and self-centered and cannot be fundamentally reformed and certainly not perfected. This point is made throughout *The Federalist Papers* (the seminal document for understanding American political philosophy), but nowhere more vividly than in the following passage from *The Federalist* No. 51.

> But the great security against a gradual concentration of the several powers in the same department, consists in giving to those who administer each department the necessary constitutional means and personal motives to resist encroachments of the others. The provision for defence must in this, as in all other cases, be made commensurate to the danger of attack. Ambition must be made to counteract ambition. The interest of the man must be connected with the constitutional rights of the place. It may be a reflection on human nature, that such devices should be necessary to control the abuses of government. But what is government itself, but the greatest of all reflections on human nature? If men were angels, no government would be necessary. If angels were to govern men, neither external nor internal controls on government would be necessary. In framing a government which is to be administered by men over men, the great difficulty lies in this: you must first enable the government to control the governed; and in the next place oblige it to control itself. A dependence on the people is, no doubt, the primary control on the government; but experience has taught mankind the necessity of auxiliary precautions. (Hamilton, Jay, and Madison, *The Federalist*, 337)

Thus though religion and moral education do the best they can to make humans as good as they can be, they can never be trusted with unrestrained political power. It the words of Lord Acton, which have become a cliché (but nonetheless true), "Power corrupts, and absolute power corrupts absolutely." In creating governance, you must assume evil and self-centeredness, not trust and goodwill. It is only through structural constraints that "good-enough governance" is possible. Structure matters.

In contrast, Nosco points out that "Confucianism fundamentally distrusts such axiomatic propositions in European and North American political culture as the 'rule of law,' instead preferring to foster a sense of self-worth that, it is assumed, will cause individual persons to regard any misconduct as demeaning and shameful" (Nosco, "Confucian Perspectives on Civil Society and Government," 348).

And yet on closer examination, there may not be as wide a gulf between Eastern and Western political theory as was imagined. In East Asia, to be human does not mean to be free to do whatever you want. It is always to be "between" other humans, performing reciprocally beneficial roles.

> Confucianism does not suggest that, for this reason, individuals are in their solitary conditions self-worthy, as others in [the] European classical liberal tradition have suggested. Where classical European liberalism might argue that individual integrity is akin to an inward capacity of the soul, and that persons thus enjoy an inherent measure of self-worth, Confucianism by contrast is uncompromising in its understanding of human worth as something manifested fundamentally in the context of relationship. (Nosco, "Confucian Perspectives on Civil Society and Government," 348)

This is structure! Perhaps structure that works better than the Federalists' "auxiliary precautions," judging by the low levels of crime in East Asian countries compared to the United States.

Rosemont also shows that in addition to the kinds of "space" mentioned so far, there is good reason to say that support for civil society is exemplified by Confucianism itself: "Now if it is free, autonomous individuals who come together in voluntary association—and thus form civil society, it follows that there will not be any voluntary associations of this kind in early Confucian thought (although there were some in practice)" (Rosemont, "Commentary and Addenda," 361). "There were such voluntary associations, one of which is clearly reflected in the *Analects* itself: the association of Confucius and his disciples, who lived, studied, worked, and traveled together. After his death, at least three of the disciples formed associations of their own, as did several of these disciples in turn" (Rosemont, "Commentary and Addenda," 363). Thus Confucianism itself suggests that a kind of civil society existed even in early times.

So far, the discussion has mainly focused on the original Confucian tradition in China from AD 220 until 960. After that, the situation becomes more complex, with varying forms of neo-Confucianism developing in China, Korea, and Japan.

> Historically, however, as societies in East Asia acquired the conditions of early modernity, a kind of "space" did indeed open between the state and the citizen, Confucian misgivings towards such space notwithstanding.
>
> The factors responsible for this development are not unlike those identified

with comparable developments in Europe: increased urbanization, with individuals uprooted from traditional village communities, and endeavoring to create new forms of association to combat the anomie and alienation that accompany such changes; an expansion of surplus wealth and the market, with an ever-increasing volume of transactions, including the commodification of a broad range of cultural products; a developed communication and transportation infrastructure, which contributes to the spread of literacy throughout the society, as well as increased opportunities for personal travel; and in religion, one observes the rise of "protestant" movements in East Asia, as in Europe, such as the Pure Land denominations of Buddhism, which privilege the individual's capacity to negotiate salvation on the basis of personal faith, and which at least conceptually diminish the role of the *ecclesia* as a mediating agency in this process. (Nosco, "Confucian Perspectives on Civil Society and Government," 339)

John Duncan describes the situation in Korea the following way.

[W]e can see that just as anti-Confucianism has been used by a wide variety of people for what are often diametrically opposite purposes, so, too, has pro-Confucianism been used by different groups and individuals for mutually contradictory goals. In some cases, . . . this may mean nothing more than the cynical manipulation of Confucian values for crass political purposes. But in other instances, such as those . . . who criticized one strand of Confucian learning while upholding others, it hints at the richness of the Confucian tradition, which included many different schools and many competing ideas about how best to order society. In short, what we call Confucianism is complex, difficult to define, and subject to appropriation for a wide range of political and social purposes. (Duncan, "The Problematic Modernity of Confucianism," 41)

In "Civil Society in East and West," Bruce Cumings points out that some American scholars are quite critical of civil society in the United States today, saying it is but a sham and shadow of what it once was, Robert Putnam's famous *Bowling Alone* being the most well-known. At the same time, there is a strand of American scholarship that praises the West, and especially the United States, as the pinnacle of social, economic, and political development, beyond which there can be nothing better. Samuel Huntington's *The Clash of Civilizations* and Francis Fukuyama's *The End of History* are prime exhibits. Similarly, there are Western scholars who criticize Asian societies for not being like America or the West generally, Karel van Wolferen's *Enigma of Japanese Power* being Cuming's main example. Cumings writes,

In this discourse, which is quite common in the US, the ills and pathologies of American civil society curiously disappear, to be replaced surreptitiously by an idealized construction drawn from Locke and Tocqueville. Of course no one can claim that East Asian countries have the social pathology obvious on almost any street in any American city, and recent elections in Korea and Taiwan had rates of voter turnout and exuberant participation far above those of American elections. But all that is forgotten in the conjuring of a Western civil society where well-informed citizens debate the important questions of politics and the good life without fear or favor, in contrast to the limited democracies, authoritarian systems and general illiberalism of East Asia, with the People's Republics in China and North Korea taking the cake as the worst-case outcomes of the pathologies of Asian politics. (Cumings, "Civil Society in East and West," 14)

Cumings further argues that using Anglo-American/French history as the best or only model of the pathway to economic and political "development" and thence to "civil society" is misleading, especially in the case of East Asia. He argues that Germany is the better example.

The Germans invented the fused state not to solve the problems of liberty, equality, and fraternity at the dawn of the industrial epoch, but to solve the mid-nineteenth century problems of the second industrial revolution and, more importantly, to catch up with England. A fused state is one that both subsumes civil society, and tries to build it up, but not if these efforts get in the way of industrialization.

Here, in short, is a political theory of late development that put off to a distant future the magnificent obsession of the Anglo-Saxon early industrializers with questions of popular will, democratic representation, public vs. private, or state vs. civil society. It is also a theory that explains much about East Asia's democratic trajectory: Japan, a democracy after 1945 but only after the cataclysm of war and occupation; South Korea, a democracy in 1993 but only after the cataclysm of revolution, war, division, and decades of military dictatorship (1961–1987) and sharp political struggle; Taiwan, a democracy in 1996 but only after a revolution, war, national division, and forty years of martial law (1947–1987). . . .

We had the fused state in South Korea and Taiwan, and now we have a limited form of procedural democracy—just like Japan and Germany. But the path to this end was hardly smooth: instead it was filled with decades of torment and turmoil, *Sturm und Drang*, and then—and only then—democracy. (Cumings, "Civil Society in East and West," 25)

Nosco shows that during the last decades of the seventeenth century and first decades of the eighteenth, Tokugawa Japan was under the influence of a liberal kind of Confucianism during which civil society flourished. Shogun Tsunayoshi "sponsored debates among various schools of Confucianism, and even lectured on the classics before assembled audiences of feudal lords and scholars" (Nosco, "Confucian Perspectives on Civil Society and Government," 341). A wide variety of unofficial cultural forms were permitted as long as they did nothing to disturb the peace. So, for example, "the government . . . showed itself to be utterly unconcerned about either Kabuki staging or the content of its repertoire" (Nosco, "Confucian Perspectives on Civil Society and Government," 342). However, toward the end of the eighteenth century, Matsudaira Sadanobu introduced a severely puritanical form of Confucianism that censored the same activities that had been supported, or permitted, a few decades earlier (Nosco, "Confucian Perspectives on Civil Society and Government," 346f).

In Japan's case as well, from the Meiji Restoration onward, in spite of some occasional liberal periods, the sphere of civil society in Japan was comparatively restricted. As Keiko Hirata explains, "The developmental state paid little attention to noneconomic affairs in the realm of civil society, such as respect for individuals' rights, since the state's primary goal was rapid economic development. . . . To maintain state control to promote economic growth, the developmental state regulated civil society activities by imposing strict legal restrictions on citizens' associations" (Hirata, *Civil Society in Japan*, 22).

However, things are different now.

The developmental state, which brought about spectacular economic success in Japan, was eventually eroded by two very powerful forces. One of these was internal, a maturation of industrialization that weakened the need for a developmental system. The second was external, a process of globalization that brought powerful new external forces to bear on Japan's political economy society and culture. Together these factors have contributed to profound structural and normative changes in Japan, contributing to the rise of Japanese civil society. (Hirata, *Civil Society in Japan*, 26)

Notes

1. Prince Shōtoku became regent under the Empress Suiko, his mother, who was a daughter of the Soga. Prince Shōtoku was said to be extremely gifted, but some historians argue that he did not exist at all.

2. Neo-Confucianism was developed in the twelfth century by Zhu Xi, who synthesized Taoist cosmology and Buddhist spirituality with the core Confucian values. Neo-Confucianism became a dominant ideology in the intellectual and spiritual life of East Asian literati in the premodern period.

3. See Sohn Pow-key, Kim Chol-choon, and Hong Yi-sup, *The History of Korea* (Seoul: Korean National Commission for UNESCO, 1984).

4. P. H. P. Mason and J. G. Caiger, *A History of Japan* (Boston: Tuttle Publishing, 1997), 65. The court moved its capital from Heijokyo in Nara to Heiankyo in Kyoto in 794. The Heian period begins with this capital transformation. Both capitals were designed according to the Chinese style. However, many temples and other constructions in Heiankyo represent Japanese traits, while those in Heijokyo embody Chinese styles.

5. "Wang Yangming" in Chinese characters is pronounced "Ōyōmei" in Japanese.

6. Details available at www.chaplaincare.navy.mil/Islam.htm.

7. Soo-Il Jung, "Exploring 1200 Years of Korea and Islam Interchange," *Sindonga* (May 2001): 424.

8. Yusuf Abdul Rahman, available at www.islamic-world.net/islamic-state/islam_in_china.htm.

9. Ibid.

10. Jung, "Exploring 1200 years of Korea and Islam Interchange," 425–426.

11. Philip Jenkins, *The Next Christendom: The Coming of Global Christianity* (Oxford: Oxford University Press, 2002).

12. Samuel H. Moffett, *A History of Christianity in Asia* (Maryknoll, N.Y.: Orbis Books, 1998).

13. Jenkins, *The Next Christendom*, 23.

14. Andrew E. Kim, "History of Christianity in Korea: From Its Troubled Beginning to Its Contemporary Success," available at www.kimsoft.com/1997/xhist.htm.

15. Ibid.

16. Quoted in Moffett, *A History of Christianity in Asia*, 503–509.

17. Elizabeth L. Eisenstein, *The Printing Press as an Agent of Change: Communications and Cultural Transformations in Early Modern Europe* (New York: Cambridge University Press, 1979).

18. Ming-fong Kuo and Andreas Weiland, "Modern Literature in Post-War Taiwan," *Intercultural Studies* no. 1 (Spring 2003). Available at www.intercultural-studies.org/ICSI/Kuo.htm.

19. Belief in the cultural superiority of Chinese civilization and that they are the center of the world.

20. John K. Fairbank, Edwin O. Reischauer, and Albert M. Craig, *East Asia: Tradition and Transformation* (Boston: Houghton Mifflin, 1989), 612.

21. Kuo and Weiland, "Modern Literature in Post-War Taiwan." Available at www.intercultural-studies.org/ICSI/Kuo.htm.

22. D. Eleanor Westney, *Imitation and Innovation: The Transfer of Western Organizational Patterns to Meiji Japan* (Cambridge, Mass.: Harvard University Press, 1987).

23. Emiko Ohnuki-Tierney, *Kamikaze, Cherry Blossoms, and Nationalisms: The Militarization of Aesthetics in Japanese History* (Chicago: University of Chicago Press, 2002), chap. 2.

24. Carol Gluck, *Japan's Modern Myths: Ideology in the Late Meiji Period* (Princeton, N.J.: Princeton University Press 1985); and Takashi Fujitani, *Splendid Monarchy: Power and Pageantry in Modern Japan* (Berkeley: University of California Press, 1998).

25. Andrew Gordon, *A Modern History of Japan: From Tokugawa Times to the Present* (Oxford: Oxford University Press, 2003); and Nobuyuki Yoshida, *Seijukusuru Edo: Nihon no rekishi,* vol. 17 (Tokyo: Kodansha, 2002).

26. Carter J. Eckert et al., eds., *Korea, Old and New: A History* (Cambridge, Mass.: Harvard University Press, 1990), 203–204.

27. Although the West was conceived as the most advanced and civilized entity, the Korean reformists were greatly influenced by the idea of "the Japanese Imperial Pan-Asian Alliance" against the threats from the West and believed that this was the best way eventually to catch up with the West.

28. Eckert et al., eds., *Korea, Old and New,* 210.

29. Ibid., 210–211.

30. See Benedict Anderson, *Imagine Community: Reflections on the Origin and Spread of Nationalism* (London: Verso, 1983).

31. Ibid., 5–6.

32. Although there was a traditional Chinese concept of state, it was primarily based upon the "Middle Kingdom Principle." The Chinese saw the state *(kwuo)* as a "cultural community" rather than as a sovereign entity.

33. John Fitzgerald, *Awakening China: Politics, Culture, and Class in the Nationalist Revolution* (Stanford, Calif.: Stanford University Press, 1996).

34. Ibid.

35. After the 1911 Revolution, the official definition of "Chinese" was expanded to include non-Han ethnicities.

36. The May Fourth Movement is the name given to the student demonstrations against the Paris Peace Conference's decision to hand over former German concessions in the Shantung Province to Japan instead of China.

37. Available at Wikipedia Encyclopedia, http://en.wikipedia.org.

38. Schwartz suggests that communism outside the Soviet Union did not follow the blueprints for revolution as designed by Marx, nor was there a master plan determined by the Comintern. Benjamin Schwartz, *Chinese Communism and the Rise of Mao* (Cambridge, Mass.: Harvard University Press, 1951).

39. Throughout the Japanese colonial period, Tonghak played a significant role in maintaining the nationalistic consciousness, such as the mass demonstration of March 1, 1919.

40. Andre Schmid, *Korea Between Empires: 1895–1919* (New York: Columbia University Press, 2002), 11.

41. Ibid.

42. Ibid.

43. Kim Jong Il, *On the Juche Idea* (Pyongyang: Foreign Languages Publishing House, 1982), 41.

44. Ibid., 38.

45. Along with Confucianism, the Christian tradition was quite strong in the northern region of the Korean peninsula prior to 1945.

46. Chalmers Johnson, *MITI and the Japanese Miracle: The Growth of Industrial Policy, 1925–1975* (Stanford, Calif.: Stanford University Press, 1982).

47. Noguchi Yukio, *1940-nen Taisei: Saraba "Senji Keizai"* (Tokyo: Toyo Keizai Shinposha, 1995).

48. Kuo and Weiland, "Modern Literature in Post-War Taiwan." Available at www.intercultural-studies.org/ICSI/Kuo.htm.

CHAPTER 17

Globalization, Fairness, and Public Institutions
A Chinese Perspective

Jingping Ding

Societal Challenges to China's Public Institutions Due to Globalization

From the Chinese perspective there are at least three big differences between earlier forms of globalization and its present stage. First, there is a huge amount of short-term capital moving around the world facilitated by information technology, providing investors with greater flexibility. Large quantities of information flow in the world through various means, such as the Internet, intranet, media, e-commerce, and so on, providing investors with many choices.

Second, there are many restrictions on the free movement of regular labor, but fewer restrictions on the movement of talented people. For instance, the United States always gives priority to talented people who want to stay in that country. Many countries in Europe, such as the United Kingdom and Germany, also have started to give citizenship to talented foreigners in recent years.

Finally, the most important and obvious difference in globalization today is the deeper and broader involvement of multinational companies (MNCs). As corporations expand their markets globally, they also try to optimize their resource allocation and production globally. As a result, production elements, including capital, highly educated people, technology, and materials, are being mobilized all over the world. To some extent, globalization can be described as the process of MNC expansion.

Why is there such concern about globalization? Loss of national sovereignty is one reason. Since it is driven by the developed countries, mainly the United States, many people believe globalization is Americanization. Signs for Starbucks, McDonald's, KFC, Baskin-Robbins, Dunkin Donuts, Levis, and many others can be seen all over the world, including China. Local cultures are threatened. People in these countries cannot see themselves as different from others anymore. They worry about who they will become in the future.

Another worry is about the loss of original personal interests. Among the losers to globalization in China are the state-owned enterprises (SOEs), agriculture producers, and other less-competitive producers. This not only creates unemployment, but also causes a growing gap between rich and poor, with the poor becoming more marginalized, especially in the rural areas.

There also is concern about the loss of talented people. Foreign companies are more attractive to local talent than are most domestic firms. They can provide higher compensation and benefits, training opportunities abroad, and a more transparent environment for personal development. Talented people quickly move to the MNCs when they come into the Chinese market. Local firms face a talent war, and the technological gap between local businesses and MNCs widens.

Along with economic globalization, linkages between countries also become extremely tight. If one country catches cold, other countries also will cough. Asia's economic "flu" was a clear example. Today concerns about the US economy also are seriously impacting the world economy. In terms of drugs and AIDS, China has been in a serious situation since the opening of its economy during the early 1980s. Southwest China is next to the major drug production area of the so-called "Golden Triangle." Drugs pour into China, making it one of the highest drug-using countries in Asia, next to India, Thailand, and the Philippines.

AIDS also has been expanding rapidly in China since the early 1980s. China discovered its first AIDS carrier in 1985. Now it has reached the fast-growing period of the disease. The number of cases is increasing rapidly each year. In geographical terms, almost all provinces and autonomous regions have AIDS carriers. Since many do not know they are carriers or do not report to doctors, these figures show only a small part of the picture. Experts believe there are at least six hundred thousand people with AIDS in China.

More recently, SARS has become a classic case of how disease is globalized, demonstrating that the Chinese government needs to learn how to respond fairly (for the benefit of the world as well as its own people) to what once might have been seen as strictly a local/national concern.

Other issues cannot wholly be attributed to globalization, but can be partially. Globalization and other changes in society mix together. For instance, the income gap between people was bound to grow once China started to move to a market economy. However, the negative impacts from openness and MNCs cannot be ignored.

Globalization's Effects on Chinese Ideas of the Purpose of Public Institutions

Globalization, information flow, the market system, and democracy are four major trends in today's world. Interactions among them are driving society into a new and rapidly changing era. They are also heavily impacting public institutions and the role of government in China.

With globalization, the scale and ways of moving commodities, services, production elements, and information freely across boundaries and around the world makes all national economies heavily reliant on one another. This complex of activities generates more and more regulations and a need for coordinating organizations to strengthen their international economic activities. The World Bank, International Monetary Fund (IMF), and General Agreement on Tariffs and Trade (GATT) created the systemic foundation for international economics and trade. The replacement of GATT by the World Trade Organization (WTO) enhanced the freedom of global trade, investment, and finance. More and more countries, including China, have become members of the WTO and thus have accepted the rules of globalization.

Under these circumstances, governments play more and more important roles in the global economic environment. Their traditional functions have to change from a primary focus on domestic issues to a focus on international issues. Various interactive activities in each country push governments to be at the forefront and to deal with each other internationally. There are more demands for negotiation and coordination among countries today than at any time before. In this sense, governments play an increasingly important role at the global level.

This is true for the Chinese government too. Because of engagement in the global economic environment, traditional government functions have to be shifted. Many governmental functions have to be transferred to other public institutions, such as industrial associations, foundations, and other nongovernmental organizations (NGOs), and ruled by law, not because these issues are less important, but because these are more efficient ways to manage them.

A fundamental change is that globalization requires more efficient ways of doing business. However, one of the major roles of government is to see that all sectors of society are treated fairly. Governments today have to continuously balance efficiency and fairness. Efficiency should always be the first priority of enterprises. But government must select fairness as its first priority.

Globalization's Impact on the Notion
of Fairness in Chinese Society

Social fairness has been a controversial topic in China throughout its long history. One of the major driving forces causing the overthrow of one dynasty and the creation of another has been the quest for "fairness." "Fairness" in the Chinese mind always means sharing everything equally.

Before China's reforms and opening, state-owned enterprises played the major role in guaranteeing social fairness. They performed many social functions, such as providing day-care centers, schools, hospitals, and apartment buildings for all while assuring that everyone was paid a similar salary. Once the economic system changed to a market economy, these firms could not compete with others if they still had to maintain social fairness.

In a market economy, fairness has a different meaning from what it meant in a planned economy. There is now more emphasis on equal opportunities, not on equal sharing outcomes. The work of guaranteeing fairness therefore has to be taken over by the government directly, and not left to enterprises. For instance, giving everyone an opportunity to be educated, promoting more opportunities for everyone to develop him or herself, and providing special assistance to disabled people are now government responsibilities. Actually, the Chinese people accepted the new concept quickly because they received a lesson from the Cultural Revolution (1966–1976). After that, most Chinese people realized that "equal sharing fairness" could not make any sense if there is nothing for them equally to share.

Once MNCs came to China, the new meaning of fairness immediately showed itself to the Chinese people. That is, the better-educated or more skillful people had the opportunity to be hired by McDonald's. These people generally earn much higher salaries. The principle of "pay for performance" that the MNCs implemented is completely different from "pay for job" or "pay for relations" that many local companies had previously implemented.

Globalization changed the meaning of social fairness in China through job opportunities and payment. The average annual salary in different companies varies widely, especially between fully foreign-owned companies and local enterprises for the same position.

In addition, the capital market also forced China to change its fairness functions from a focus on individual enterprises to society as a whole. For instance, a company that wants to be listed publicly (whether on the foreign or domestic stock market) lists only the most valuable assets for the market, not its social facilities and related costs. If it did not do this, no one would buy its stocks. In order to utilize the capital market efficiently, a company has to first separate its core business and non-core business. Social functions have to be taken care of by the government or other organizations.

China's acceptance into the WTO will certainly break old concepts of fairness, but it also will give new meaning to the term. In the past, all personnel in state-owned businesses could share benefits equally whether or not they met their performance goals. That cannot happen today. For the losers in a competition, this is unfair. But it will seem very fair to the winners.

China's Response to the Challenges of Globalization

China's response to the challenges of globalization can be explored in three ways: in terms of its national interests, finances, and immigration policy. China's national interests should be the guiding principle for responding to challenges from globalization. Today, the first priority for China is economic development. This basic principle, made by Mr. Deng Xiaoping in 1979, is not to be changed for another century. Everything China does today should follow from this. Accordingly, China made a detailed strategic plan stating that by the end of 2000, China should reach its goal of a fourfold increase in gross domestic product (GDP). Then it would double its GDP within the next ten years, from 2000 to 2010. After that and through the end of 2020, China should achieve the goal that everyone can live a "fairly comfortable life." Finally, by the year 2050, China should reach the goal of a standard of living equal to that of middle-level developed countries.

This is a clear goal, and China now is fully utilizing all resources and efforts to achieve it. From the beginning of its opening and reform in the 1980s until now, China always has used these criteria to measure the advantages or disadvantages in both domestic and international matters. With these basic criteria, China can measure and deal with challenges actively rather than passively. Anything that can bring clear benefit to China will be adopted. Otherwise, it will be modified or rejected.

Having a clear goal is a good beginning for a long march. In order to reach the final destination, society also needs a strong government, especially a large country like China, with its huge population. It must implement the principle of "the minority obeys the majority" and of "crossing the river without touching the stones." Debate among people is always necessary, but debate cannot be a reason for stopping action. Otherwise, there will be no movement forward.

Of course, the way to realize goals is also very controversial. This requires a strong government with efficient tools. Moreover, the proper way to respond to challenges is also critical. China has adopted a progressive way rather than a radical one. Unlike the former Soviet Union, China opened its doors to the outside cautiously, and not all at once. China does not like the "shock treatment" approach, but moves gradually. Geographically, China started from some "Special Economic Zones" in the coastal areas and then expanded them to some inland areas or big cities, and only then to the rest of China.

On the industrial side, China opened its doors first to those industries that were comparatively weak, such as high-tech manufacturing and export-oriented ventures, and then expanded to infrastructure, service industries, and other relatively weaker enterprises.

In the second kind of response to globalization, the financial side, China encouraged foreign direct investment in manufacturing and services rather than more speculative and short-term indirect investment in banks, funds, or stocks. There is no way to speculate since all investment is in real production or services. Borrowing foreign loans is tightly controlled by the central government. Plus, Chinese currency is not convertible. These are the reasons China was not hurt so much by the Asian financial crises.

Finally, with its immigration policy China does not completely prohibit people from immigrating, even though it already has a large population. People with certain skills are always welcome. Every year, China invites more than ten thousand foreign experts to work in such areas as education, medicine, scientific and technological research, and many production industries. Foreign experts coming with MNCs are also welcome. These people give the Chinese modern knowledge and skills. Some of them have received "honorary citizenship" from the government since they have made a big contribution to Chinese society. They can come and stay in China anytime, or forever.

There are many related issues that China needs to deal with in order to respond to globalization fairly. The most important of these can be summarized in four areas: ensuring economic growth, establishing a modern legal system, providing a complete social security system, and improving the education system.

Ensuring Economic Growth

The economy is a society's foundation. It is also the fundamental strength from which to respond to the challenges from globalization. If there is no economic strength, there will be no capability to respond to the challenges.

Therefore, doing good homework so that China will grow stronger economically makes more sense than just arguing with others. The year 2001 was a slow one for economic growth throughout the world. The events of September 11, 2001, in the United States made the world economy even worse. The Chinese economy also was seriously impacted. However, the annual growth rate of China's economy has remained stable and high at around a 7 percent increase annually.

China's economic growth basically depends on expanding domestic demand. The government has invested in many huge projects to stimulate domestic market demand. The demands for housing, vehicles, and durable consumer goods are the main drivers of economic growth.

Other good things happened in 2001 too. These included China winning the right to host the 2008 Olympic Games, its acceptance into the WTO, and its hosting of the Asia-Pacific Economic Cooperation (APEC) conference in Shanghai. All suggest a bright future for China. They were new elements that stimulated investment and people's demands.

A Complete, Modern Legal System

An efficient market economy requires the support of a strong and complete legal system. Throughout its long history, Chinese society has been ruled essentially by a nonlegislative system. Policies and regulations were not transparent because an individual ruler, such as an emperor, made them. Under the planned economy, there was no need for a sophisticated legal system because all businesses belonged to the government. A big improvement occurred at the end of the Cultural Revolution. The market economy broke up single ownership, which made a modern legal system a basic condition for economic development. However, the existing legal system is still far from what a model society needs. It cannot fully support the needs of the market economy, especially after the acceptance of China into the WTO. In order to provide a fair competitive environment to all types of business owners and fair protections for domestic businesses, a complete and transparent legal system must be one of the fundamental elements for China.

The central government and all levels of local government are clearing up old policies and regulations. Many of them have been removed because they conflict with WTO requirements. For instance, the State Planning and Development Commission (SPDC) has declared that projects investing in five specific categories do not need to be approved by the SPDC in the future. These projects are city infrastructure construction; agriculture, forest, and water irrigation systems; large culture and entertainment projects; housing construction; and a trading market. Meanwhile, some new laws and regulations have been introduced. For example, a regulation on "anti-dumping" was made in the middle of December 2001 to protect domestic industries within the WTO frame.

Completing the Social Security System

The social security system is very young and weak in China. There still is a long way to go in setting up a complete social benefit system that covers the entire society. Such a social security system is important for a society to gain stability and to realize social fairness. A lot of effort has been made since the early 1990s, when social functions were separated from state-owned enterprises. Since then, several insurance systems have been built, including retirement, medical care, unemployment compensation, and accident and basic life insurance for urban areas.

Improving the Educational System

Education for training and for giving more capabilities to the younger generation was originally driven by the need for national development. However, globalization stimulates even more demand for talent. Education is also a fundamental and strategic countermeasure for China's future development that cannot be ignored. Education plays a significant role in teaching people both how to think and act globally, and is of great importance in showing how to accept the new meanings of fairness, both spiritually and materially.

Changes have been made in the content of education at all levels in order to meet the demands of a competitive economic environment. A good example of changed teaching content is providing the younger generation with the ideas and the capability to live independently. Another example is the implementation of a new national examination for students who apply for college. Not everyone takes the same examination, but everyone is given the same opportunity.

Foreign-language education has become more and more critical and practical. Junior high school requires foreign-language education, but it also is expanding to primary education in the big cities. In high school, not only grammar and writing but also speaking and listening to foreign languages are now required. Computer capability also has become a basic skill at all levels of education. Along with it, knowledge of network and information technology has become a necessity for the younger generation.

China and the Challenges of the World Trade Organization

Membership in the WTO was a milestone for China in dealing with the challenges of globalization. The Chinese government saw that membership in the WTO is an efficient means to improve the competitive capabilities of the nation. For many years, the entire Chinese economy was fully controlled by the state government, but a highly centralized economy has comparatively low efficiency in the long run. It cannot meet ambitious development goals. China has had to select efficiency rather than equality as its first priority. The only way to do that is to create competition within the economic area and society. The WTO as an external force can help China to strengthen real competition.

Changing the nature of state-owned businesses was necessary for China to join the WTO. Since most of the assets belong to the state, managers of state-owned firms do not really care about competition. Other personnel do not want to change because they have gotten used to a noncompetitive environment. Meanwhile, welfare systems created under the old system, such as schools, housing, and hospitals, are burdens on the firms. The most efficient way to force the old system to change is to engage the Chinese economy with the global market. That is why the Chinese government joined the WTO.

Membership in the WTO is a two-way street. It brings real challenges to Chinese society. The biggest impact is to the Chinese government itself. It forces the government to change its functions to fit into the WTO framework. It has to reposition its roles and responsibilities within the market and individual enterprises. Under the planned economy, the government was both a direct conductor and a participant in the national economy. It made plans, allocated various resources to each enterprise, and met individual needs. The market had a very limited role to play. Enterprises were just the means for implementing the government's plans.

Within the WTO framework, the government has to be an indirect controller, such as setting up macroeconomic adjustment mechanisms based on economic and legal systems, not on administrative convenience. It must coordinate state-owned enterprises by policies and regulations, not through direct commands. And it must open most economic areas to private and other nongovernmental business. The market allocates all natural and social resources by the "invisible hand." In this environment enterprises must become responsible for their own profits and losses.

The government also should facilitate foreign trade, foreign currency exchange, and foreign economic management processes that are in accord with WTO regulations. The WTO requires transparency and nondiscrimination, which means there should be low national tariffs, a system of accessible "internal documents," and no regional trade barriers, resulting in uniform "national treatment" being given to all foreign-invested firms.

According to the commitment to the WTO, all existing Chinese laws, regulations, and policies need to be completely cleaned up to enhance their alignment and transparency and avoid hidden "internal" policies. This means that nontariff barriers, restrictions on foreign investment and local private business, the proportion of foreign investment in each project, awarding foreign investment national treatment, and protecting intellectual propriety rights all need adjustment. Administrative law to regulate governmental authorities and actions is also being developed. A law for unified and consistent administrative processes is an urgent issue for the nation. Without it there is no way to improve efficiency and transparency and to avoid corruption.

It also is necessary to create a fair, competitive environment for all types of enterprises. So far, there is substantial discrimination against local private businesses in China. For instance, in industrial sectors where SOEs are allowed to enter, it is often the case that foreign investment can be made, but private businesses are not allowed to enter.

Next, reform and restructuring of public areas and so-called "natural monopolies" such as telecommunications, power generation, petrochemicals, railroads, and civilian aviation need to be speeded up. Commercialization of these industries has been implemented in different ways. Meanwhile, restructuring state-owned businesses, especially large-scale SOEs, by making them public is becoming more and more popular. Unlike small or medium-size businesses, restructuring large SOEs needs to attract big investors with global business experience. Mergers and acquisitions done by MNCs and non-state-owned businesses are now being recommended.

Finally, the gap between rich and poor needs to be narrowed. One way to do this is to develop the western part of China. The government has been increasing the amount of investment in western China since 2000; in recent years, more than 40 percent of the central government's annual investment has been in the west. Another way is to increase rural residents' income by reducing prices, developing processing industries for agriculture products, promoting loans to rural areas, reducing taxes and fees for rural residents, and speeding up urbanization. Tightening personal income tax collection also has become a more and more efficient way of narrowing the income gap in recent years.

In terms of actions taken, as soon as it joined the WTO, China made much progress toward implementing its commitments. In commodity trade, since January 1, 2002, China has reduced its tariffs on more than five thousand commodities. The total rate of tariffs is down. In nontariff areas, China has abolished import licenses for many products such as grain, cotton, and chemical fertilizers.

China has published serious regulations for opening service areas to foreign investment, including law offices, telecommunication services, financial firms, securities companies, insurance companies, and new travel businesses. Foreign investment now can enter these areas according to the new regulations.

In intellectual property rights, China has set up several laws to protect these rights since 2000, including a patent law, a trademark law, a copyright law, a computer software law, an integrated circle design protection regulation, and many more.

In foreign investment, China revised three basic laws: the joint venture law, the foreign corporation law, and the exclusive foreign investment law. The basic goal is to provide national treatment to foreign investors. Foreign investors and visitors can get the same treatment as local people in most areas. In addition, an "Industrial Guiding Category for Foreign Investment" has been published.

As far as transparency is concerned, as a result of their commitment to the WTO, China's Ministry of Foreign Economics and Trade set up a new bureau, the so-called Notice and Consulting Bureau. Its purpose is to provide consulting to both foreign and local firms or individuals to answer questions relating to international trade. All these efforts show that China is moving in the direction that the WTO requested.

Current and Future Obstacles for Public Institutions

Nothing can be smooth on the path to development. There are many critical obstacles for China to overcome in order to implement what is desirable for social fairness. These include

> how to maintain a relatively high economic growth rate to reach the goal
>   that China has designed for both the short and long term;
> how to create more opportunities for unemployed people;
> how to reduce income gaps;
> how to educate and retain talented people for China's development; and
> how to deal with problems of increasing corruption and crime.

Economic growth is the foundation for social fairness. There will be many difficulties for China to maintain a relatively high growth rate while the rate of the rest of the world is slowing. As mentioned before, China has to maintain a relatively high growth rate to reach its development goals. However, there are so many uncertainties in the future. These uncertainties will impact the Chinese economy, since China is going to be tightly entwined in the global economy. Dealing with global uncertainties will be a challenge for China.

The world economy remains slow, especially in developed countries such as the United States, western Europe, and Japan. There is no clear evidence of recovery in the near term. This will have negative impacts on Chinese economic growth since these are major export markets. China's economic growth still has to depend on the expansion of domestic demand. However, which factors will stimulate domestic demand is a big question. Peoples' deposits in banks have increased substantially. However, most deposits have been associated with long-term concerns, like housing, medical services, children's education, and retirement. How to bring these deposits to real consumption is another big question.

Economic restructuring still has a long way to go in China, especially for those SOEs that are losing money. Efficiency also remains a big problem. The capabilities of technology-intensive industries are still low. The knowledge-intensive economy is still far from what is desired. Patents are few; "intellectual property rights" (IPR) has low recognition.

Non-state-owned economies have much potential that has not yet been realized. Many areas have been opened to non-state-owned business, such as automobile manufacturing, infrastructure construction, and finance. Stimulating these businesses in order to let them play a more important role is also a critical challenge.

Job creation and employment are the toughest problems for China to solve fairly since it has the largest population in the world. The overall unemployment rate in 2003 was estimated at 20 percent, with unemployment and underemployment considerably higher in rural areas than in urban areas, where the rate was 9.8 percent. It is estimated that there are between 100 and 150 million surplus rural workers adrift between the villages and the cities, many subsisting through part-time, low-paying jobs.[1] According to ministry statistics, more than 26 million workers were laid off from state-owned enterprises between 1998 and 2002. Many are still jobless because of the number of new jobs—24 million in 2003— that would be needed to absorb them.[2]

The income gap directly reflects social fairness. While China is growing economically, expansion of the gap has become a critical problem. It widened in the first quarter of 2005, with 10 percent of the nation's richest people enjoying 45 percent of the country's wealth. The Xinhua News Agency cited a survey by the National Bureau of Statistics showing that China's poorest 10 percent held only 1.4 percent of the nation's wealth. China's richest 10 percent had disposable incomes 11.8 times greater than the lowest 10 percent at the end of the first quarter of 2005.[3] In urban areas, the gap between the poorest and richest also is expanding. The increase in the rate of the highest income group from 1997 to 1999 was 18 percent, compared to only 8 percent for the lowest income group.[4]

There are many people in China living on the margins of society, although the lives of most people have improved. The size of this marginal group is not as big as it was several years ago, but there still are about thirty million people with very low living standards (less than RMB200, or US$25, per person per month). This will be a problem for China to deal with in the next few years.

Three of the most critical obstacles are related to human resources. First, China lacks talented people, especially in new competitive areas. Many of China's senior executives are not familiar with management regulations. They should understand how to play in various domestic markets. Second, China lacks high-quality personnel who are good at international business practices and foreign languages. And third, most Chinese students who have studied abroad stay abroad; only about one-third return to China. According to statistics provided in 2001 by China-InfoBank, an information Web site in China, among the two hundred thousand professional engineers working in Silicon Valley, California, sixty thousand were Chinese. Eighty two percent of the graduates from Tsinghua University and 76 percent of the graduates from Beijng University, two top universities in China, now are working in the United States.[5] However, America's new regulations regarding foreign workers, made in response to September 11, has put an end to this, and most Chinese students now must go to other countries to study.

Politically, the most serious obstacles will be leadership formulation, legislation building, and anti-corruption. A large country like China needs a strong and outstanding leading team. Weak government definitely will not help a nation handle such complex tasks as avoiding an Asian economic crisis, maintaining a high growth rate, and reforming the economic system. However, selecting outstanding persons from the huge population, or from the ruling party, in order to maintain strong capability for all levels of government is an elusive problem. In other words, how China can move from a "rule of man" country to a "rule of law" country is a tough and urgent issue.

Corruption has become one of the most critical issues in China today. How to reduce corruption and supervise leadership effectively is a vital matter. The market economy needs a democratic system to supervise public managers and to protect the public's interests. Right now, the media play an important role, but expanding to other channels and finding the most efficient way to implement democracy must be on the agenda.

Other problems like drugs, AIDS, and prostitution are also damaging society. Increasingly, crimes are threatening peoples' lives. These are problems that China should not ignore because they are the factors causing social instability.

Domestic Forces Shaping the Responses of Public Institutions

The forces that can help China create effective responses are the large Chinese conglomerates, private businesses, information and Internet technologies, the transportation system, and Chinese NGOs.

Increasing the size of conglomerates is one of the ways China can deal with globalization. Some Chinese companies have been listed among the top five hundred by *Fortune Magazine* in recent years. These include the Bank of China, the Industrial and Commercial Bank of China, PetroChina, the China National Petrochemical Corporation (SINOPEC), the China National Cereals, Oils and Foodstuffs Corporation (COFCO), and others. Besides them, there are over three hundred super-scale enterprises whose gross industrial output value (GIOV) was 35 percent of the total SOEs' GIOV in 2000. Following that, there are 2,308 large-scale enterprises whose GIOV was 34 percent of the total SOEs' GIOV. Together, large-scale and above SOEs account for almost 70 percent of the total GIOV.[6]

Booming private business is another force that can help China deal with globalization. Private businesses, which employ 24 million people, have generated about one-third of China's GDP since 2000. Their registered capital reached RMB1.331 billion, but less than RMB100 million in loans were provided to them. Their taxes also provided 10 percent of the government's business tax. In many cities in south China, 80 percent of the government's tax is from private business. After twenty years (1980–2000), private business has been growing very rapidly. It plays a more and more important role in China.[7]

Information and Internet technologies certainly can help a developing country like China to leap over some traditional steps of industrial development. China has been the largest country in the world in terms of users of both fixed-line telephones and mobile phones. In transportation, the Chinese railroad system today is more than seventy thousand kilometers long. Paved roads, highways, and air transportation have also quickly expanded.

Development of telecommunications and transportation not only reduces the distance between people, but also increases information flow and changes people's behavior and mindset. They are efficient tools for making things more transparent, encouraging the possibility of the right types of decisions for both doing business and creating democracy.

The emergence of Chinese NGOs is another new force for facilitating the desired responses of government. China now has approximately two thousand voluntary associations. About another three hundred associations have been created by the government. Many of these shifted from being governmental bodies in recent years. For instance, in 2001 China completely restructured nine industrial ministries as associations, including the ministries of textiles, machinery, chemicals, light, electricity, and others. Besides industrial associations, there are other NGOs, such as poverty-alleviation, animal protection, and environmental protection organizations.

Formulation of large-scale, state-owned enterprises, rising non-state-owned businesses, developments in telecommunications and transportation, especially Internet networks, and the emergence of NGOs are the new forces in China. They are playing positive roles in changing China's society and in responding to the challenges brought by different aspects of globalization. It is foreseeable that within a not-too-long period Chinese society will experience even more dramatic change and will present a brand-new China to the world.

Critical Issues Relating to Reform in China

Government structural reform also has been implemented from top to bottom. Since 1998 government bodies have been reduced from forty to twenty-nine at the ministry level. In each remaining ministry, 25 percent of the departments have been removed. Hundreds of administrative functions in the ministries have moved to nongovernmental institutions such as associations, NGOs, and enterprises. Half of all government employees have been laid off. From 2000 to early 2001 similar reforms expanded to the provincial level, and it is moving down to county-level government as well.

Due to the popularity of the Internet, e-government also has to be encouraged in order to meet the needs of society. In fact, it is one of the five most fundamental Internet networks being built by the government (the other four being e-commerce, long-distance education, long-distance medical treatment, and e-entertainment). In China, the government holds 80 percent of all valuable information and more than three thousand information databases. However, most of this information is not well utilized by the public. Since 1999, an e-government project has been conducted. Most of the ministries, provincial governments, and city governments have set up Web sites.

Chinese e-government projects will have three phases: setting up Web sites for each level of government and sharing information partially with the public; linking all Web sites and realizing office automation; and promoting all other related matters to be "e" and working online as much as possible.

However, government reform still has a long way to go. Direct interference with business operations, especially of state-owned businesses, is still too great. An efficient system for managing state-owned assets has not been completed yet. The inspection and approval system by government, formed in the planned-economy period, still exists in many areas. For instance, government restrictions on private business are still heavy. Fair competition between SOEs and non-SOEs is still far away.

The ability of the government to regulate and manage the market is not strong enough either. Legal systems in the business area are relatively weak, especially in the area of credit. The credit crisis is becoming a cancer that is poisoning society. Even enforcing existing laws is difficult because there are no heavy penalties. Local protection is still very strong and causes a breakdown of the unification of the national market.

Education, Training, and Research

A series of issues, obstacles, and responses have been discussed in this chapter. Some are more theoretical problems while others are more immediate and practical. Public institutions undertaking education, training, and research activities must focus more on the theoretical problems for the long run of society. The problems that should be studied are

how to distinguish between globalization, Westernization, and
    Americanization;
how to recognize the trends of globalization and regionalization and their
    relations;
how to retain a desired growth rate within a globalizing and competitive
    environment;

how to balance globalization and domestic development;

how to evaluate the role of MNCs in globalization;

how to educate and retain talented people in China;

how to set up an efficient political system to ensure economic goals and
social stability;

how to balance foreign culture and local culture;

how to balance fairness and effectiveness; and

how to balance the collective and the individual.

The more practical and immediate problems that need to be studied are

how to face challenges from globalization: actively or passively? Radically
or progressively?

how to make economic structural reforms and system reforms;

how to attract foreign investment and utilize it efficiently;

how to complete an effective social security system with limited resources;

how to retain a strong and effective leadership for a very large country like
China; and

how to deal with population problems, such as job opportunities and
unemployment.

These important issues should be introduced to ordinary people in order to change their attitudes toward such things as competition, the WTO, human resources, and privacy. In the meantime, since the social environment has changed dramatically, some new explanations should be given for the meaning of social fairness, the collective, the individual, and so on. Globalization creates many new concepts that ordinary people in China do not understand. In order not to fail, education, training, and research institutions should study them and give people a better education while they are facing these challenges.

As an example, the Chinese people do not have much experience with competition because China did not have a real capitalist period. For thousands of years the Chinese mind was ruled by feudalism, which promoted noncompetition in the form of forbearance, humility, and cooperation.

The market economy system, on the other hand, needs competition. The motivation for competition is personal interest. Personal interest should be put in the center while competition is encouraged. Otherwise, there will be no motivation for people to compete with each other. The foundations of a market economy are totally different from a nonmarket economy. Personal interest has to be recognized while the market economy is being implemented.

At the same time, there still will be need for traditional concepts like forbearance and humility. The problem is how to balance traditional and modern concepts that are in conflict. There is no perfect system for all types of societies because of differences in history, culture, tradition, level of economic development, and education. Every country is looking for a more suitable way for itself.

No matter how these contradictory elements are weighed and balanced, one thing is clear: it is not a good idea to mix all the concepts in one arena. For example, competition should be implemented in business, but not in places where social fairness should be emphasized, namely the community and the family.

The WTO represents another new concept that provides an important milestone in modern Chinese history. China started to implement economic reform and an open-door policy in 1979. The idea was to combine the planned economy with a market economy. The planned economy was still the main base. This was the first milestone of historical change. The second milestone was when China announced its decision to implement a market economy in 1991. The principle was to let the market play the dominant role in the Chinese economy. China's acceptance into the WTO in late 2001 forces China into a complete market economy and forces it to be fully engaged with the global economy.

The WTO not only impacts the Chinese economy, but also the Chinese political and social structure. The old bureaucratic system has to be changed from its foundation. The social structure must be fundamentally changed as well. Since the economic system (the foundation of human society) has changed, other systems such as the political, legal, cultural, and educational have to be changed too. The impact will be so significant that the whole society, including lifestyles and working behavior (even ideology), will be different from that which currently exists. Unfortunately, not many Chinese realize the significance of their country's membership in the WTO.

The human resources issue also is a new concept in China. A talent war started as soon as the door began opening. China had no "human resources" concept until the middle of the 1990s; there was only manpower or labor resources. The value of talented people was not so obvious, since everything was highly controlled by the government. Meanwhile, the labor-intensive industrial structure also made it less important to be highly talented. The importance of labor seemed more obvious in a centrally controlled system.

Since more and more MNCs have come to China, two fundamental changes are happening. One is that they have brought the new concept of "human capital." Another is that they have created a talent war. Historically, China never saw human resources as "capital," but merely as a "cost." The old system very much emphasized obedience: no matter where I put you down, you should listen and work well there, like a "brick." Personal initiative was not encouraged. Today competition is breaking down the passive human resources management system. Talented people are leaving for new places where they can work more actively, such as in the open areas and non-state-owned sectors.

Collectivity and the individual, as two contradictory concepts, also have different meanings in the new environment. For thousands of years Chinese culture and ethics promoted the value of collectivity in society, not individuality. Now competition encourages individuality. If collectivism played a positive role in traditional manufacturing industries, it will have a very limited role in a "knowledge economy" that heavily depends on individual knowledge and capability. Since China intends to move its industry to "knowledge-oriented" and labor intensive, it has to give more attention to individuality. Collectivity can still play important roles in the sense of "teamwork," but the individual's role must dramatically change from what it was before.

Another severe problem that China should address is quality of education. Improving education, especially at the college level, so as to improve people's capabilities in a competitive environment, is one of the most urgent issues facing China. All of the new concepts that need to be introduced into the society can be done through education. It is an efficient and fundamental process for all people—not only for the next generation, but also for all existing generations.

Over 90 percent of the graduates of primary schools enter junior high, but only about one-forth of junior-high graduates enter senior high schools. Only about one in four graduates from senior high school enter college, according to statistics.[8] In 1990 only a fraction, 1,071 per 10,000, had at least a primary-school education. That rose to just 1,076 by 1999. The proportion of people with a secondary-school education was 447 in 1990, but rose to 636 by 1999. Only the proportion of college and university students rose, from 18 out of every 10,000 persons in 1990 to 32.8 in 1999.[9] The level of education will be a serious barrier to becoming a "New Economy" and to competing with MNCs in the future.

Conclusion

Globalization is a multifaceted process with complex and varying impacts. It must be looked at from multiple perspectives. The key determinants of impact are, first, governmental capabilities. A strong, stable, and popular government is better able to manage the impact of globalization. Weaker leading domestic companies are at risk if their government does not have the knowledge, tools, or skills necessary to manage globalization's impact.

Second, decisions about the positive or negative impact of globalization are not absolutes. Each society must decide for itself, based on its values and culture. One important thing learned from the Chinese experience is that a society should have a clear goal for all the people to reach. Discussing, exploring, and arguing are always necessary, but none of them should be an excuse for stopping real action. Society should allow mistakes to be made in order to find a suitable way forward. Otherwise, there will never be any improvement.

Third, it is most important that we realize that globalization (as well as regionalization) cannot really be stopped. A good society must find better ways to manage both and try to expand its own advantage by forming "win-win" partnerships with other countries.

Finally, China is one of few developing countries that seems to be benefiting by engaging globalization positively. Its experience could be a reference for others. However, there is no unique model suitable for everyone. The only way to be successful in dealing with globalization is to use one's own talents to face and challenge globalization, and not try to avoid it.

Notes

1. Central Intelligence Agency, available at www.cia.gov/cia/publications/factbook/geos/ch.html.

2. "China Faces Uphill Battle to Create Jobs," available at www2.chinadaily.com.ch/en/doc/2003-08/26/content_ 25834.htm.

3. "Income Gap in China Widens in First Quarter," available at www.chinadaily.com.cn/english/doc/2006-06/19/content_452636.htm.

4. *China Statistical Yearbook* 2000, 315.

5. China-InfoBank, available at www.chinainfobank.com.

6. *China Statistical Yearbook* 2001, table 13-1.

7. Available at www.chinainfobank.com.

8. *China Statistical Yearbook* 2000, table 5.

9. Ibid., 656.

CHAPTER 18

International Competitiveness, Fairness, and Public Institutions in the Era of Globalization

A Korean Perspective

YONG-DUCK JUNG

In 1995, Korea ranked eleventh in world trade, had a per capita national income exceeding $10,000, and became the twenty-ninth member of the Organization for Economic Cooperation and Development (OECD). In 1997, however, seven of the thirty largest businesses went bankrupt. In November 1997, the Korean government had to request bailout loans from the International Monetary Fund (IMF) because of a lack of foreign exchange reserves. The per capita national income dropped to about $6,700, which sharply lowered credit ratings. The number of jobless and the level of income inequality rapidly increased during and after the IMF structural adjustments (see table 18.1).

The currency crisis of 1997 and subsequent economic difficulties have caused most Koreans to regard globalization as a new international order that represents more unforeseen dangers and challenges than potential opportunities. It seems that the current economic difficulties, which began with the currency crisis at the end of 1997, are the result of a failure to properly respond to the globalization phenomenon. To Korean social scientists other than neoclassical economists, globalization seems to be "a new kind of imperialism" that a small country cannot avoid.[1]

In August 2001, the government completed its repayment of the IMF loans three years ahead of schedule, making Korea the first among the countries hit by the 1997 Asian financial crisis to fully repay those loans. The GDP growth rate in 2001 was 3.1 percent. Yet the negative rather than positive Korean sentiments toward globalization have been reinforced since the terrorist attacks on the United States on September 11, 2001. The tragic events made the American economy sluggish, and this in turn made Korean economic prospects all the more gloomy. In addition to the economic effects, the events of September 11 dramatically illustrated the turbulent nature of globalization and how complicated it is to forecast and understand its vicissitudes, and underscored the vulnerability of this

Table 18.1 Economic Growth, Unemployment, and Inequality in Korea

YEAR	GDP GROWTH RATE (%) (1995 PRICES)	NI PER CAPITA ($) (CURRENT PRICES)	UNEMPLOY- MENT RATE (%)	JOBLESS (1,000 PERSONS)	GINI CO- EFFICIENT (URBAN HOUSEHOLDS)
1996	6.8	11,385	2	435	0.291
1997	5.0	10,315	2.6	568	0.283
1998	-6.7	6,744	7	1,490	0.316
1999	10.9	8,595	6.3	1,374	0.32
2000	9.3	9,770	4.1	913	0.317
2001	3.1	9,000	3.8	845	0.319
2002	6.3	10,013	3.1	708	0.312
2003	–	–	3.4	777	0.306

Source: Bank of Korea, each year, http://ecos.bok.or.kr; National Statistics Office, each year. Available at www.nso.go.kr/newcms/help/faq; http://kosis.nso.go.kr.

"global, open society where virtually anything can be transmitted, good and bad, very quickly."[2]

Globalization may have resulted from the conscious efforts of certain leading countries and multinational corporations. It also may be an inevitable phenomenon at this stage of human history with the admixture of information technology development and the "end of ideology."[3] Whatever its origins, a small country like Korea cannot be so much an innovator as it can be a beneficiary of the globalization phenomenon. Considering the unhappy legacy of recent history and the consequent mutual mistrust in East Asia, at least for the foreseeable future, globalization will have a more difficult task advancing regional cooperation to mitigate its shocks and challenges in Asia than in European countries.[4] It is inevitable, then, that Korean public institutions adapt aggressively to the globalization phenomenon.

After the financial crisis of 1997, public policy makers realized that the country's existing governance system did not fit well with globalization, hence it invested considerable effort to reform public institutions to adjust to globalization. The outcome, however, was not satisfactory and left the existing core institutional structure of government intact. Moreover, the reform efforts were an insufficient response to globalization in terms of their goals and scope. The government focused primarily on enhancing international competitiveness and restructuring its governance system appropriate to globalization, as it had done in the earlier period of rapid industrialization. Other than these narrow goals and scope of reform efforts, focused mainly on pro-market governance, the government has paid scant attention to the issues of fairness, an issue that globalization may worsen both within Korean society and between Korea and other societies.

International Competitiveness

As globalization proceeds, the world becomes integrated "through explosively increasing material, ideal and human flows across the borders of the nation states and to processes whereby social relations acquire relatively placeless, distanceless and borderless qualities."[5] Therefore, globalization requires a country's public institutions to adopt global standards. As a small, export-dependent country, Korea is no exception and is rather more vulnerable to this new challenge of globalization.

Korea is a "developmental state" that uses considerable state interventions in the market and civil society. Most of these interventions focus on rapid industrialization and economic development. State interventions maintain a high level of state autonomy and policy capability by institutionalizing a governance system of executive dominance, centralized central-local government relationships, a highly integrated bureaucracy, and corporatist government-business and government-nongovermental organization (NGO) relationships.[6]

Many Korean policy makers and social scientists believe that such a governance system contributed much to the country's rapid economic growth, at least until the 1980s. Even the pro-market international organizations such as the World Bank praised the governance system as unique and a great contributor to the country's rapid economic development.[7] Since the currency crisis of 1997, however, the governance system has been criticized as one of the main causes of the economic crisis: the Korean mode of governing and its institutional structure have become more and more unsuited to global standards.

In fact, Korea has been recently evaluated as a country with a low level of international competitiveness. The World Economic Forum (1996), for example, ranked Korea 20th among forty-nine countries in level of competitiveness.[8] It might be understandable that Korea was outranked by Singapore (1st), Hong Kong (2nd), Luxembourg (5th), and Switzerland (6th) in the international competitiveness index because such small and open economies specialize in providing trade and financial services to the rest of the world. Considering its rapid economic growth during the last several decades, however, it is rather hard to understand why Korea was also outranked by its Asian neighbors, the so-called newly industrializing countries (NICs) of Taiwan (9th), Malaysia (10th), Japan (13th), and Thailand (14th).[9] Why did the country rank so low in competitiveness?

A partial explanation can be found by examining the methodology used to create an international competitiveness index, which applies eight clusters of structural characteristics to each country, as follows:

1. Openness of the economy to international trade and finance: i.e., the extent to which a country's goods and financial markets are linked to worldwide markets, with the expectation that the more open the market, the more competitive it is.
2. Role of government budget and regulation: i.e., the intrusiveness of government spending and taxation and economic regulation, with the expectation that the lower the level, the better for competitiveness.
3. Development of financial markets: i.e., the development and efficiency of banking and stock markets, with the expectation that the more underdeveloped or burdened by government regulation they are, the worse it is for competitiveness.
4. Quality of business management: i.e., the capacity of business leaders and business organizations to respond to new market opportunities in a creative and flexible manner.
5. Labor market flexibility: i.e., the extent of government restrictions on labor flexibility, the distortion of taxation on labor, and the quality of industrial relations, expecting that the more flexible, the less taxation, and the more smooth industrial relations are, the better for competitiveness.
6. Quality of judicial and political institutions: i.e., the extent to which the legal and political systems provide for low "transactions costs" in writing and defending contracts and in protecting property rights.[10]
7. Quality of infrastructure: i.e., a county's systems of transport, communications, power, and other infrastructure services.
8. Quality of technology: i.e., a country's capacity in basic and applied sciences.

The main indicators of higher levels of competitiveness are neoliberal prescriptions such as openness, flexibility, and small government. This explains why in the competitiveness index Anglo-Saxon countries like New Zealand (3rd), the United States (4th), Canada (8th), Australia (12th), and the United Kingdom (15th) outrank most European Union member states other than the open and small ones. This also explains why Japan and Germany, the two most competitive countries in the latter half of the twentieth century, ranked only 13th and 22nd, respectively. These countries retained characteristics such as relative closure to international trade, big government, and labor market inflexibility.[11]

Consequently, some analysts consider the relatively low level of Korea's competitiveness as merely the result of neoliberal biases in the measurement index. They may analogize this with the case that it is hard for non-Western participants to win international beauty contests because of the bias for Western standards of beauty. Such an analogy is not very persuasive, however, considering that the higher the rank in the competitive index, the higher the economic growth during the same period.[12] It is inevitable, then, that a country must restructure its governance system to become more open, flexible, and smaller if it wants to achieve better economic performance.

Reform Efforts and Institutional Path Dependency

After it required IMF loans at the end of 1997, the Korean government concentrated its efforts on the reform of public and private institutions. Public institutions have been both an initiator and an object of such reforms. On the one hand, public institutions have been a subject for conducting structural adjustments in the private sector, including financial, corporate, and labor sectors. On the other hand, public institutions have also been an object of reform.

To reform public institutions, the Korean government has applied the so-called "New Public Management" or "Entrepreneurial Government," which stresses a "small but efficient government."[13] By introducing pro-market governance models, the government tried to become smaller, more open, flexible, and market-like competitive. The post-IMF reform efforts include a wide variety of re-organizations and deregulations of public institutions (see tables 18.2 and 18.3).[14]

The results of these reform efforts were unsatisfactory in at least two aspects. First, the goal itself of a market-like government was not relevant enough to reform the Korean government. This will be discussed in some detail in the next section. Second, even the goal of reforming public institutions by applying a market-like governance model was not achieved satisfactorily, for reasons that will follow.

As indicated above, the Korean government has put forth considerable effort in restructuring its public and private institutions by applying pro-market models. However, the role the government played in the process of the post-IMF structural adjustments was not much different from its past economic management.[15] While it is true that after the currency crisis the government's primary economic goals changed from promotion of rapid industrialization to making structural adjustments to the free market economy, the government still played the role of the "developmental state." The government has not only enforced structural adjustments to overcome the economic crisis, but also worked on industrial policies to foster certain industries.

A telling example is the information-communication industry. Right after the currency crisis, the Kim Dae-jung government initiated the so-called "knowledge-based society" and strategically supported the information-communication industry. The government also selected and supported many venture

Table 18.2 Changes in Korean Central Government Positions (1993–2001)

GOVERNMENT	YEAR	MINISTER & VICE- MINISTER LEVEL	DIRECTOR- GENERAL (GR-1, 2, 3) LEVEL	DIVISION CHIEF (GR-4) LEVEL	LOWER THAN GR-5 LEVEL	TOTAL
Kim Young-sam	1993	-4	-8	-15	-112	-139
Government	1994	-5	-31	-112	-854	-1,002
	Total	-9	-39	-127	-966	-1,440
Kim Dae-jung	1998	-14	-70	-115	-7,442	-7,641
Government	1999	2	0	0	0	2
	2000	4	-90	-200	-2,436	-2,722
	2001	6	-2	17	99	120
	Total	-2	-162	-298	-9,779	-10,241

Sources: Ministry of Government Affairs & Home Affairs, *Annual Report.*

Table 18.3 Reductions of Korean Public-Sector Staff (1998–2000)

	PLAN (A)	ACHIEVEMENT (B)	B-A
Total	130,278	131,082	804
Central Government	21,858	21,356	-502
Local Governments	49,506	49,506	0
Public Enterprises	41,234	41,704	470
Subsidiaries	17,680	18,515	836

Source: Ministry of Planning and Budget, Annual Report, 2001.

businesses to foster the growth of medium- and small-sized enterprises. Thus the main changes were that the targeted industrial sector was to be supported by a mercantilist approach. Specific sector support that had shifted from the import substitution industries in the 1960s to the heavy chemical industries in the 1970s was now concentrated in information-communication industries.

The post-IMF restructuring process shows, therefore, that at least in the short term, globalization has sustained and reinforced the institutional structure of the "strong state." In the name of "restructuring," the government conducted numerous interventions in the areas of finance, industry, and labor. The schemes to restructure both the public and private sectors have not been very different from the "reform from above" of Korea's previous era of rapid industrialization. Although the Korean government publicized its structural adjustments as New Public Management, its real efforts have been at maintaining and reinforcing the institutional structure of the strong state. The reform efforts have been bureaucratically initiated, directed, and controlled by the top-down approach of the core executive. There have been no provisions for significant change to the mechanism by which the government wields its corporatist control over the "quagos" and "quangos" (quasi-autonomous NGOs) that function as intermediaries between the state and society. Some of the main factors that contributed to the maintenance and reinforcement of the institutional structure of the strong state in Korea are listed below.

First, the economic debacle resulting from the dramatically changed international environment of globalization has led the Koreans to prefer a strong state. Along with the democratic transitions that have occurred since the late 1980s, decentralization of the state apparatus and management has made considerable progress. While experiencing an economic crisis since 1997, however, Koreans have implicitly agreed that in order to be more responsive to both the crisis and globalization, they need to restructure the state and society under the strong and able leadership of the president. Since 1998, the establishment of the Planning Budget Commission (PBC), which was renamed as the Ministry of Planning and Budget (MPB) in 2000, as a core agency of the administration was supported by the public's nostalgia for the former Economic Planning Board (EPB), the pilot agency of the Korean developmental state (1961–1994).[16] Many people fondly remember the EPB's powerful role during Korea's rapid industrialization.

Second, the institutional characteristics embedded in the state apparatus have also had consequential effects. The traditional top-down approach to government reform eventually creates favorable conditions for central agencies to sustain their power. The establishment of the PBC and the attempts to upgrade it to the MPB are the result of the united front taken by former EPB officials (see table 18.5 below). The resurrection of the EPB would not have been possible without the sophisticated bureaucratic politics of former EPB officials in the face of opposition political parties.

The institutional persistence of the Korean state apparatus is not constrained by the adoption of the pro-market governance models like the New Public Management. While the model reflects a strong orientation toward a pro-market state, it runs the risk of centralizing political power in the core executive. By applying this reform model to the Korean government, it is quite likely that the core executive would maintain its dominance over the policy-making process, hence supporting the "imperial presidency."[17]

This shows that reforming public institutions is a difficult task; it is difficult to change existing public institutions because of their tendency to reproduce well-established patterns. Korean public institutions differ significantly from the neoliberal market-oriented institutions such as are found in some Western countries. It is difficult to change the existing public institutions because of special interests within the bureaucracy. Such institutional persistence limits the possibilities of future changes to public institutions that would make for better adaptation to globalization.

Great Policy Failures

The reform efforts conducted by the Korean government have been limited to the narrow goal of pro-market governance. Besides the challenges attributed more to such exogenous factors as globalization, Korean public institutions need to be reformed because their policy failures can be attributed to more endogenous factors. The Korean government conducted a number of large-scale public projects, some of which resulted in great policy failures or disasters. Naturally, such failures and the resultant severe side effects contributed to negative feelings toward the government. Examples of some recent monumental policy failures are followed by a discussion of their root causes.[18]

The construction of Cheongju International Airport from 1992 to 1997 cost the Korean government US$93 million. However, the number of flights handled by the airport the year after construction was remarkably low. International flights, which represented only 7 percent of all flights, ceased operation after 1997, leaving only one domestic line in operation. The project represented a giant loss, which was caused by a poor estimate of demand.

The government formally announced a cable TV network project in 1990 by providing free programming to over 10,000 households as an experiment. During 1993 and 1994, the government selected the Program Providers (PPs) and Network Operators (NOs), but the original plan to begin paid services in 1994 was delayed for almost two years due to lack of preparation. The original estimate was that about 500,000 households would subscribe to pay cable TV networks. In reality, only about 230,000 households subscribed. With such a low subscription rate, it was hard for the PPs and the NOs to earn income from advertisements, which are the primary sources of revenue. There were approximately 860,000 subscribers in 1999, but only 3 out of 29 PPs earned a profit, and each of the 46 NOs were in the red. By forcing public and private enterprises to cooperate in the project, the government was responsible for a heavy financial burden on the participating cable TV networks.

The Seoul-Busan High-Speed Railway project was to construct a 450-km railway connecting Seoul to Busan, with an investment that totaled 5,800 billion won (US$7.3 billion) between 1991 and 1998. However, the original budget had increased threefold by 1998, increasing the debt to 18.4 trillion won and extending the date for completion to 2010. Again, the government's failure was caused by an inaccurate estimate of both the cost and time necessary for completion.

The Korean government enacted the National Welfare Pension Act in 1973 but had to delay it due to a recession that occurred after the oil shock of 1974. In 1986, the government enacted the National Pension Act, which was applied to companies with ten or more employees. It was extended to firms with five or more employees in 1992, to farmers and fishermen in 1995, and, finally, to the entire population in 1999. Ineffective fund management caused the earning rate to spiral downward. This raised concerns about the stability of the fund. In 1999, less than 30 percent of the self-employed covered by the National Pension System willingly reported their income, and only about 60 percent of them paid their insurance bills. Due to rising criticisms over unfairness of the rates charged, insurers began to reject payments. According to a survey, only 19 percent of those covered expected the National Pension System to be helpful during their retirement, and only 4 percent considered salaried workers and the self-employed to be co-expense sharers.[19]

In 1987, the objective of the Sihwa Lake Project was to form 17,000 hectares of reclaimed land by investing 899 billion won (US$2.4 billion) in the project by 1998. At a cost of 528 billion won, by 1994 it was supposed to provide 180 million tons of agricultural and industrial water by building a 12-km tide embankment and making 69.1 sq km of the Sihwa Lake. Polluted water from surrounding farms and factories flowed into the lake and forced the government to build a sewage disposal plant in 1996 at a cost of an additional 449.3 billion won. However, the damage had been done. Research conducted in 1997 reported that the lake was severely polluted. Eventually, the government abandoned the project. A further 2,348.3 billion won (US$2.9 billion) was invested to reclaim the land. The results of this project: a polluted lake and a destroyed marine environment.

The Korean government's policy failures had some common characteristics. First, each was a large-scale public project with a huge budget. Each raised questions of whether, at the time, these large-scale public projects fit both Korea's social efficiency and national priorities. Second, the public policies were pushed forward without proper preparation and were based on unreasonable expectations of production costs and the demand of policy outputs. Thus there were repeated trials and errors in the process of implementing the projects, which resulted in a longer term for completion and a larger budget than anticipated.

Such large-scale policy failures were caused by political factors. One is that public policies were created to fulfill the private agendas of political leaders in government. These leaders initiated the projects in order to demonstrate their ambitious spirit to the public and to cultivate popular support. They rushed to announce their grand plans and paid scant attention to the monumental demands of each project. Worst of all, these political leaders tried to satisfy their own interests by various forms of corporate patronage.

The difficulty of policy coordination among the administrative agencies that were responsible for the projects was another major cause of failure. When the Republic was established in 1948, Korea's public administration was structured to perform the basic functions of building the nation. During the authoritarian regime of President Park Chung-hee (1961–1979), the state began to play a greater role in economic development. This basic structure has been maintained over the past forty years and has been supplemented only by "patchwork" reforms to meet proposed deadlines. The partial and incremental growth of the administrative apparatus for the past forty years has created serious functional overlaps among the various agencies. Such functional and organizational overlaps have made policy coordination among agencies difficult.[20]

Ironically, policy coordination among the administrative agencies has become more difficult as Korean democratization has developed. Policy coordination may have been more effective under authoritarian governments. Political leaders, with the assistance of powerful central agencies like the EPB, could easily coordinate policies between administrative agencies using top-down approaches. Politico-administrative democratization has provided some discretionary power to individual agencies, but new pluralist collective decision-making processes have not yet been institutionalized.

Neoliberalism and Equality of Opportunity

In addition to international competitiveness, Korean public institutions have been faced with issues of fairness and other issues attributed to globalization. In all societies, the norms of fairness evolve, although each society may differ substantially from others in its perspectives of fairness. There are at least three different norms of fairness, including egalitarian, meritorious, and need-based conceptions of distributive justice.[21] A society that has developed an egalitarian value system will focus on the equal distribution of social values. A society developed on a meritorious value system will focus less on the level of equalization of social values as an end state and more on the equalization of opportunity. A society with a need-based value system will consider the fundamental deficiencies in meeting human needs. Any of the three norms of fairness will be affected by globalization. It is necessary, therefore, to consider fairness as an important issue in reforming public institutions with respect to globalization.

According to the meritorious principle, the end state of income distribution is not the focus of concern. It is important instead to focus on the fairness of procedures—that is, whether everyone is provided with an equal opportunity, such as the chance to develop his or her abilities and capacities and to succeed

Table 18.4 Korea's Corruption Perceptions Index (CPI)

YEAR	NUMBER OF COUNTRIES EVALUATED	RANK OF KOREAN GOVERNMENT	CPI
1995	41	27	4.29
1996	54	27	5.02
1997	52	34	4.29
1998	85	46	4.20
1999	99	50	3.80
2000	90	48	4.00
2001	91	42	4.25
2002	102	40	4.50

Source: www.transparency.de/documents/cpi.html.

through effort. Thus in evaluating a country's fairness, the principle of equal opportunity can be applied to the extent to which there are illegitimate barriers to improving incomes or to which opportunities are available to some groups but not others.

According to the meritorious criteria, Korean public institutions have practiced a considerable number of unfair procedures and policies. The Korean government has intervened in civil society and the market numerous times and has had a significant impact on the redistribution of social values. The government permitted large firms to conduct monopolistic pricing in the name of encouraging economies of scale and enhancing competitiveness in international markets. Government policies were more beneficial to profit earners and to expert-oriented industries than to wage earners and domestic consumption-oriented industries. They also benefited larger-sized firms rather than small- or medium-sized ones, and men more than women. The list goes on.[22]

Perhaps more worrisome has been the unending corruption and favoritism of public institutions. While administrative corruption by street-level bureaucrats has declined significantly, political corruption remains static. As seen above, the free election process requires a tremendous amount of politically raised money, which in turn encourages politicians to amass private political funds illegally. Such illegal private fund-raising forces political leaders to practice favoritism, resulting in a reduction of the state's legitimacy and policy capability. This explains why the Korean government has been ranked low (27th among 41 countries in 1995 and 40th among 102 countries in 2002) in the Corruption Perceptions Index (see table 18.4). As noted above, political-administrative corruption contributed much not only to the great policy failures, which reduced the country's international competitiveness, but also to procedural unfairness in Korean society.[23]

Fortunately, globalization may contribute to improving procedural fairness in Korea. By pursuing "one global market," globalization nudges every society toward a neoliberal value system, which, although it disregards the end state of distribution of social values within the country or between countries, is coincident with a meritorious notion of fairness. If public institutions adopt especially the elements of "good governance," it is hoped that Korean society will improve its procedural fairness more effectively.

Inequality and a Social Safety Net

The norm of equal distribution of social values as an end for the state appears to have a place in the social ethic of any society. Every human being is equally human, and that minimum qualification entitles all to share equally in certain human rights. In addition to civil rights such as freedoms of speech, press, and assembly, people are entitled to certain economic rights such as food, shelter, and education. Consequently, the greater the equal distribution of social values as an end for the state, the higher its achievement of fairness. On the other hand, the needs-based norm of fairness prescribes that social values should be distributed on the basis of individual needs. In most forms, the norm of fairness shares common ground with the other two social values and hence is a method of mediating the application of the egalitarian and meritorious norms of fairness.

Fortunately, inequality of income and wealth has not been particularly severe in Korea, with the exception of the rapid industrialization period of the 1970s. Its Gini coefficient, one of the reliable measures of income inequality in a society, was .36 until the 1960s, increased to the .40s during the rapid industrialization of the 1970s, reflecting greater inequality, but has lowered to less than .30 during the 1980s and 1990s.[24] As the post-IMF restructuring proceeded, however, income inequality rapidly increased to over .30 (see table 18.1).

Moreover, as the post-IMF structural adjustments have proceeded, the unemployment rate and the number of jobless have rapidly increased (see table 18.1). From 1997 to 1998, unskilled, low-income workers were particularly affected as job losses for clerical and operative workers exceeded twelve million.[25] The Korean government increased the budgets for national pension and welfare to assist the unemployed. However, only 7 percent of the total unemployed have benefited from unemployment insurance, and less than 9 percent of the unemployed have benefited from the public assistance programs. This means that more than 90 percent of the jobless are outside the social safety net.[26] Therefore, the Korean government needs to include in its reform goals the establishment of greater social safety nets to secure basic needs for the jobless and to mitigate the increasing income inequality.[27]

In this context, many Koreans fear that the so-called "20:80 society" will emerge with the advance of globalization.[28] As is often pointed out, globalization may influence the "distribution of power and wealth within and between countries."[29] A gloomy prediction on this impact is that 20 percent of the population will garner and enjoy most of the benefits of globalization, while the remaining 80 percent will be insulated from them.[30] The wealthiest 20 percent of Koreans account for 39.3 percent of the total national income. Fortunately, this is a relatively lower level of inequality when compared with 40.2 percent for France, 40.3 percent for Switzerland, 43 percent for Britain, and 46.4 percent for the United States.[31]

A Confucian value system such as prevails in Korea may conflict with the neoliberal individualism of globalization: the former has a more egalitarian orientation and emphasizes social harmony within the community, while the latter is more meritorious and emphasizes individual competition in one global market. Korean society needs to reconcile adopting global standards for globalization with building democratic consensus for national priorities for fairness. It will not be an easy task because what is considered good for the former is not necessarily considered good for the latter.

Political and Educational Implications

Considering the tasks of public institutions in the era of globalization, Korea needs first to accelerate the speed of its democratic consolidation. After more than four decades of authoritarian rule, Korea has been in the process of democratic transition since the late 1980s. Now, political regimes change by free popular elections, and local self-government can be formed by the will of residents. In spite of such progress in democratization, the country still needs to reform public institutions to overcome their authoritarian ways of governance with core executive dominance and top-down bureaucratic management approaches.

In this context, globalization and democratization can be of mutual benefit in the future. On the one hand, as democratization proceeds, the government will be able to increase its legitimacy and policy capabilities, which are necessary to conduct reforms more effectively with the goal of good governance. On the other hand, as globalization deepens, the country is forced to adopt global standards, which can be summarized by the concept of "good governance."[32] This will make the Korean policy-making process more accountable and transparent, which will result in improved democracy.[33]

One of the significant developments since the late 1980s is the rapid growth

Table 18.5 Growth of NGOs in Korea

Source: Citizen's Movement Communication Center, Directory of Korean NGOs, 2000

of civil society, which has contributed to the accumulation of important social capital. More than half of all NGOs have been established since 1990 in Korea (see table 18.5). Also, the NGOs established after 1990 differ from the previous ones in terms of their goals and relationships with government. The former pursue a more reformist agenda and are critical of or independent from government, while the latter have a mainly pro-government orientation. The former pursue policy goals such as democratization, environmental protection, gender equality, and civil rights, rather than pro-market economic liberalization.

The growth of NGOs will be an important factor in improving fairness and the equitable distribution of social values. However, NGOs will not necessarily be a contributing factor to the reform of government institutions when these institutions move to adopt and adapt to pro-market global standards.

Relevant education and research will be another important factor for Korea's effective adoption of globalization. During the last several decades, the Korean people's desire for high levels of education, investment, and performance brought about rapid economic development. Korean parents send their children to school even though they do not have an automobile or a house. This is an invaluable element of the Confucian value system. The problem is the content of the education. The younger generation, especially those who are interested in solving public-policy problems, need to be educated in understanding, thinking, and acting globally. In order to overcome the obstacles to globalization, it is necessary to provide the ideas, theories, and techniques of good governance to the incumbent and future public administrators and NGO activists. These administrators and activists need to learn how to collaborate to define and solve public-policy issues. Public administrators need to recognize that the NGOs are important partners in the co-production of public goods. Traditionally, public administrators have regarded NGOs as an arm of government to be mobilized for effective policy implementation. NGO activists, most of whom were former political activists against authoritarian political regimes, also must learn to consider public servants as counterparts in solving public-policy issues, not as "enemies" to oppose at every turn. Public institutions and education for public service are related. A telling example is the civil-service recruitment system. Public service is still regarded as one of the most prestigious careers in Korea. However, those who want to become civil servants must pass civil-service examinations, which mostly are written. Students used to memorize textbooks and thus prefer traditional types of lectures to seminars, case studies, and internship training. Educational institutions, therefore, contribute to limiting the more dynamic curricula and teaching methodologies.

Fortunately, the government introduced an open recruitment system for about 20 percent of the higher-level civil-service positions (i.e., director generals), which has encouraged the government to scout for personnel in the private sector and abroad as well as within the traditional base. Some fear that an open, competitive, contract-based recruitment system will weaken the institutionalized civil service that has been considered desirable for state capabilities during the last several decades. However, applying an open recruitment system, at least for a proportion of public positions, will stimulate civil service. Moreover, practicing open civil-service recruitment will force Korean students who want to become civil servants to pursue diversity in their education and training. As this case shows, quality public institutions require quality education, and vice versa.

Every society will change as globalization proceeds, but there will be a variance in the speed, style, and content of changes, depending on the society. Considering the institutionalized pattern of the Korean governance system, it is unrealistic to expect that the Anglo-Saxon model of governance, the one most suited to global standards, can be reproduced in precisely the same way in Korea.

The ultimate goal of reform is to institutionalize a "Made in Korea" model of governance that is suited to global standards as well as to a locally built consensus of values and culture. In the era of globalization, as in the past eras of modernization or industrialization, the issue of relevancy must be emphasized. To monitor, predict, evaluate, and revise the reform processes and plans, it is necessary to conduct research in comparative perspectives. It is also necessary to learn about and compare the cultural and institutional developments of different countries. Furthermore, international cooperation is required in order to conduct comparative research, to develop curricula, and to offer educational and training programs that focus on the future of globalization.

Notes

1. Korean Political Science Association, "The Korean Political Economy: Crisis and Response," proceedings of the Special Conference of the Korean Political Science Association, Seoul, March 21, 1998 (in Korean).

2. R. Ghere, "Globalization, Public Service Ethics, and Public Trust: Some Directions for Inquiry," paper presented at the 63rd National Conference of the ASPA, March 23–26, 2002, Phoenix, Arizona, 6.

3. D. Bell, *The End of Ideology* (Glencoe, Ill.: Free Press, 1960).

4. Korean Political Science Association, "The Korean Political Economy."

5. J. Rosenau, "Letter from James N. Rosenau," *Fairglobe-1* (2001). Available at www.fairglobe. hawaii.edu.

6. Y. Jung, "The Territorial Dimension of the Developing Capitalist State: Measuring and Explaining the Centralization in Korea," *International Review of Administrative Sciences* 53 (1987): 128–153.

7. World Bank, *World Development Report: The State in a Changing World* (Oxford: Oxford University Press, 1997).

8. Korea was even ranked as low as 23rd in 2001. See World Economic Forum, *The Global Competitiveness Report 1996* (Geneva: WEF, 2001).

9. The Asian NICs that Korea outranked included Indonesia (30th), the Philippines (31st), and China (36th), all of which have maintained a relatively low level of per capita income or have recently liberalized markets. See F. Hu and J. Sachs, "Executive Summary," in World Economic Forum, *The Global Competitiveness Report 1996*, 15.

10. Ibid.

11. Ibid.

12. J. Sachs and A. Warner, "Why Competitiveness Counts," in *The Global Competitiveness Report 1996*, 10–11; and Hu and Sachs, "Executive Summary," 16–17.

13. Jon Pierre and B. Guy Peters, *Governance, Politics and the State* (New York: St. Martin's Press, 2000).

14. Even before the post-IMF restructuring by the Kim Dae-jung government (1998–2003), the previous governments conducted a number of governmental reforms by establishing the Presidential Committee on Administrative Reform (PCAR), including President Roh Tae-woo (1988–1993) and Kim Young-sam (1993–1998). The PCARs of the three governments proposed reform goals such as promoting democratization, social justice, and welfare in the 1980s and pursuing a more market-oriented governance system in the 1990s. The reform committees put forth a lot of effort, which included reorgani-

zation and deregulation of the central and local governments, to achieve their goals. I believe, however, that the financial crisis of 1997 and the economic difficulties since then were caused, at least in part, by the unsuccessful results of the previous administrative reforms.

15. Y. Jung, "Institutions, Interests and the Post-IMF Structural Adjustment in Korea," *Korean Journal of Policy Studies* 16.1 (2001): 11–22.

16. Y. Jung, "Globalization and the Institutional Persistence of the Developmental State in Korea," *Korean Journal of Policy Studies* 15.2 (2000): 27–40.

17. Ibid.

18. Ibid.

19. *The Chosun-Ilbo,* April 26, 1999, 7

20. Jung, "Globalization and the Institutional Persistence of the Developmental State in Korea."

21. Y. Jung and G. Siegel, "Testing Perceptions of Distributive Justice in Korea," *Journal of Northeast Asian Studies* 2.2 (1983): 45–66.

22. Ibid.

23. Y. Jung, "Great Policy Failures, Public Administration's Credibility, and Good Governance in Korea," *International Review of Public Administration* 5.1 (2000): 152–159.

24. Such a relatively low level of income inequality is due to various historical and cultural factors, including the almost total destructions caused by Japanese colonial rule and the Korean War and the Confucian value system, which emphasizes social harmony. The Korean government's efforts to develop social welfare programs, including national pension, health insurance, etc., as the country became more industrialized in the 1980s are also contributing factors. See Jung and Siegel, "Testing Perceptions of Distributive Justice in Korea."

25. S. Park, "Labor Market Policy and the Social Safety Net in Korea: One Year after 1997 Crisis," *Korean Policy Studies Review* 9.2 (2000): 294.

26. Until the mid-1960s, the "absolute poverty" group in Korea comprised about 40 percent of the total population. This declined to 15 percent in the mid-1970s and has more significantly declined since then due to the rapid economic growth. See ibid., 291–318.

27. A telling example of the necessity for Korea to build a social safety net is the disastrous subway blaze in Daegu Metropolitan City in February 2003, which left at least 198 people dead, 145 injured, and about 160 missing. That tragic accident was the result of arson by an unemployed taxi driver in his mid-fifties. *The Korea Times,* February 18, 2003, 1.

28. H. Martin and H. Schumann, *Die Globalisierungsfall* (Hamburg: Rowohlt Verag GmbH, 1997).

29. D. Held et al., *Global Transformations: Politics, Economics and Culture* (Stanford, Calif.: Stanford University Press, 1999).

30. Martin and Schumann, *Die Globalisierungsfall.* E.g., in the United States from 1950 to 1979, the real revenue of households in the richest quintile increased by 99 percent, while the average income of the poorest fifth of the population increased by 99 percent. However, the 20 percent of the poorest sector of the population accounted for

a mere 3.7 percent of national income (against 5.5 percent in 1970), while the richest quintile accounted for an unprecedented 50 percent. Other statistics show that the average income gap between people living in the most advanced countries and those living in the poorest is greater today (74 to 1) compared to 1960 (30 to 1) See P. Golub, "Globalization and its Discontents." *The Donga-Ilbo,* August 16, 2001, A7.

31. *The Korea Herald,* March 7, 2003, 5.

32. For the concept of "good governance," see Asia Development Bank, *Annual Report 1998,* available at www.adb.org/Governance/default.asp.

33. Jung, "Great Policy Failures, Public Administration's Credibility, and Good Governance in Korea."

CHAPTER 19

Globalization and Education in Japan
The Case of Junior High School History Textbooks

RYO OSHIBA

Importance of the History Textbook Issue

History education and textbooks have been used as tools for building national identity among people in many countries. This is particularly true in the case of Japan, where the government has adopted a screening system for primary and junior high school textbooks. The screening system is a governmental device for educating people about national memory and creating national identity. As a result, junior high school textbook issues have been politicized in Japan. The Ministry of Education (MOE), teachers' unions, parent-teacher associations, nationalist groups, local civic groups, and transnational gender networks joined the political game of the textbook issue while all of those actors have been influenced by multidimensional globalization. I will examine the Japanese junior high school textbook issue of 2001 in order to examine the role of public institutions—the MOE and education committees—in the globalization process. See Jim Dator's Further Thoughts, "Globalization and Japan," on page 296.

Screening Process for Junior High School Textbooks

The screening process for Japanese junior high school textbooks consists of two stages: an approval process and a selection process. The MOE provides guidelines for editing textbooks and writing content. Textbook writers and publishing companies submit their draft textbooks to the MOE for approval. Then, screening officers appointed by the MOE examine incorrectness and appropriateness of expression. China, South Korea, and Vietnam bitterly criticized Japanese history textbooks in 1982, and the MOE decided to take into consideration the relationship with Asian countries in screening history textbooks.

The selection process commences after textbooks are approved by the MOE. The education committees in individual municipalities officially have the right

Table 19.1 Textbook Screening/Authorization System in Major Countries

| | | PUBLISHER | | SCREENING/AUTHORIZATION | |
		Government	Private Publisher	Screening by National Government	Authorization by Local Authorities or Civil Organization
Asia	Japan		○	○	
	Korea	○	○	○	
	China	○	○	○	
	Thailand	○	○		
	Malaysia	○	○	○	
	Singapore	○	○		
Europe and North America	UK				
	Germany		○	○	
	France		○		
	Sweden		○		
	US		○		○
	Canada		○		○

Source: Ministry of Education, Culture, Sports, Science and Technology, www.mext .go.jp/a menu/shotou/kyoukasho/gaiyouK020901c.htm

to decide which textbooks are to be used in their districts. Members of education committees are appointed by the executive heads in individual municipalities. The education committees usually ask their own subcommittees, which are composed of schoolteachers, to undertake a detailed examination of textbooks for all subjects published by all companies. The education committees have usually followed the recommendations of the subcommittees.

Politics Over Junior High School Textbooks in Japan

The problematic history of the junior high school textbook can be classified into three periods. The first period is characterized by the so-called Ienaga court trials. Ienaga Saburo, a professor of Tokyo Education University, brought this issue to trial in 1955.[1] Ienaga alleged that the official screening system was unconstitutional under the Japanese Constitution. This trial ended in 1997, and the details will be described later. The second period began in 1998, when historians and educators shifted their concerns to monitoring the management method of the official screening system rather than criticizing the system itself. The third period began in 2000, when the Atarashii Kyokasho wo Tsukurukai (New History Textbook-Making Group, hereafter Tsukurukai), established in 1997, submitted their own junior high school textbook, which led to great controversy and public debate.[2]

The First Period (1955–1997): Views of the Left

Professor Ienaga brought the problem of his junior high school textbook on Japanese history to trial in 1955. He pointed out that the system for official screening of textbooks infringed upon the Japanese Constitution. Ienaga also claimed that the MOE's examiners went beyond their jurisdiction in screening the content of his junior high school textbook.

In the cases of 1980 and 1983, Ienaga and the MOE clashed over the following issues.

1. Ienaga wrote that Japanese Combat Unit No. 731 engaged in medical experiments using live bodies, but the MOE examiners criticized this argument as lacking wide academic support. (In 1997, the Supreme Court decided that MOE's request to delete this sentence went beyond MOE's jurisdiction, since there was no strong academic opinion to negate the existence of Combat Unit No. 731 when the textbook was written.)
2. MOE examiners requested that Ienaga add the following sentence: "Collective suicide in Okinawa was one of the most decisive factors in increasing the number of deaths in Okinawa." (The Supreme Court accepted MOE's opinion as reasonable because the collective suicides, as well as the killings of residents in Okinawa by Japanese soldiers, were important events for demonstrating the disaster of the Okinawa battle.)
3. MOE examiners requested that Ienaga delete the expression "Korean people's resistance to Japan" because this simple expression is ambiguous. (The Supreme Court also saw it as vague in 1997.)
4. MOE examiners advised Ienaga to change the expression "Aggression into China" to "Advance into China." (The Supreme Court approved the MOE's behavior as legal because it was advice rather than a request.)
5. MOE examiners requested that Ienaga change the expression "Nanjing Massacre and other cruelties committed by the Japanese military." (The Supreme Court decided the MOE's request was illegal because it went beyond the MOE's jurisdiction.)

The Second Period (1998–2000):
Shift to the Viewpoint of Global Civil Society

The second period began in 1998, when historians and educators established a new group for monitoring the textbook screening process. This group undertook three functions. First, it aimed at checking whether or not MOE examiners' requests and advice were within the MOE's jurisdiction. Second, it examined how to reform the textbook selection process. Third, the group demanded an increase in the transparency of the MOE's screening system and the selection process for junior high school textbooks.

The major issues being debated in this period were as follows.

Appropriateness of topics for junior high school students

MOE examiners were reluctant to include the description of "comfort women" in junior high school textbooks. When discussion of this topic appeared in textbooks for the sixth grade in 1999, MOE examiners judged it inappropriate for boys and girls under fifteen years old. The MOE said that it suggested revisions rather than requested them, but most textbook publishers said that there was no big difference between suggestions/advice and requests.[3]

Changing original expressions in literature

Words that discriminate against minorities and/or the handicapped are not permitted in junior high school textbooks. How, then, do we treat those words or expressions when they are written in historical documents and/or classic literature?

Twice between the years 1998 and 1999 MOE examiners requested that publishers change the word *Shina* (a derogatory word for China) to *Chukoku*, the official name for China. Nosaka Akiyuki, a writer, used *Shina* in his novel *Hotaru no Haka* (Tomb of firefly), and a part of this novel was quoted in a Japanese textbook. The publisher followed the MOE's advice and changed it without the permission of the author in 1998. The same word—*Shina*—was also used in a Japanese textbook in which a part of *Kinosaki nite*, written by Shimazaki Toson, was printed.

MOE examiners saw their advice as appropriate, but some people argued that those words should be printed in their original form because such words and expressions were frequently used at that time. They insisted that it would be more effective for students to understand what happened in the past.

The national flag and national anthem

The problem of the Japanese national flag and national anthem has been a controversial topic in Japanese politics since the end of World War II. Though widely used as such, there was no legal rule declaring that *Hinomaru* be the national flag and *Kimigayo* the national anthem. However, nationalism in Japan has been strengthened by globalization. The National Flag and National Anthem Act was passed in August 1999.

Following this, MOE examiners requested that all publishers include a photo of the Japanese emperor in textbooks for sixth graders. Two publishers refused to follow this request, saying they did not have any pictures of the emperor that could be used for explaining his role. Then, MOE examiners requested a revision because the MOE's *Shido Yoryo* (Course of study) asked writers to describe respectfully the emperor's role in order to understand it better. Once these two publishers included a picture of the emperor, the MOE approved their two textbooks.

The Third Period: (2000–2001): Rise of the Nationalistic Viewpoint

Approval Process

The representative of Tsukurukai, Professor Nishio Kanji, of the University of Electoro-Communications, and his nationalistic group submitted its textbook to MOE for approval in April 2000, leading to great controversy.[4]

The textbook had the following characteristics: first, it describes in detail the Japanese origin myth. National myths are generally used as a symbol of national integration, and in fact these myths were much described in the history textbooks of prewar Japan. Second, it stresses the role of race. For example, the Russo-Japanese War is described as a conflict between races, ignoring its aspects as an imperial war. Third, World War II is described as an imperial war, ignoring the fact that Western countries appealed to the principles of self-determination and democracy in their colonies, even if it was a matter of "lip service." Western democracies could not help but appeal to these principles in order to mobilize the support of people in their colonial areas, while Japan did not appeal to the principles of democracy to justify the war.[5] In December 2000, MOE examiners requested that the publisher of the textbook written by Tsukurukai make 137 revisions. The supporters of this nationalistic textbook insisted that various interpretations of history should be accepted. Even so, the publisher revised its textbook in February 2001.

On the other hand, left-wing groups were critical of the textbook. They warned that the MOE would be criticized by China and South Korea if it officially accepted the Tsukurukai textbook. They insisted that the MOE must be responsible for the content of textbooks that it approves, since the MOE maintains an official screening process.

A third group criticized the left wing as well as nationalistic textbook writers. They saw the role of the Left as critics to be solely confined to the Cold War period. They believed that it was more important to help students become members of a "global" civil society through education in the twenty-first century, rather than educate children as members of nation-states. They argued specifically that textbooks should describe the historical facts that are empirically tested. They also insisted that teachers should teach the traditional interpretations of historical facts while also informing them of alternative interpretations. Multiculturalism is important in interpreting historical facts.

China and South Korea bitterly criticized the description of the following topics in the nationalistic textbook.

1. The Nanjing Massacre. The Tsukurukai textbook argued that killing people is unavoidable during war and that the incident in Nanjing was totally different from the Holocaust. However, they deleted this sentence after MOE examiners requested a revision. The final expression was, "There are various opinions over the incident in Nanjing and the debate over it still continues."

2. The number of people killed in the Nanjing Massacre. Those who criticize the Japanese government often argue that 200,000 Chinese people were killed in the Nanjing Massacre, but the Tsukurukai textbook is skeptical of this figure. They argued that the population of Nanjing was around 200,000 at the time and that the population increased to 250,000 one month after the Japanese attack on Nanjing. They argued that it is unlikely that 200,000 people were killed.

3. View on war. The Tsukurukai textbook argues that it is difficult to judge what constitutes a "just" war, although many people in Japan are critical of this way of thinking because it can be used to justify prewar Japanese aggression.

4. The Pacific War. The textbook stated that the Japanese did not choose the option of "surrender without fighting with the U.S." After being criticized, they revised this to "Let's think over the reason why Japan engaged in a war against the U.S."

5. The Western colonial powers and Asia. The textbook emphasized that Japan recognized the independence of Asian countries from the Western colonial powers.

6. Annexation of Korea. The textbook stressed the legality of Japan's annexation of Korea. It also argued that there was no alternative for Japan but to become a great power like the European countries had been in the late nineteenth century. The MOE advised the group to take into consideration

the fact that Japan promoted the policy of assimilation after colonizing Korea. The publisher then revised the expression as follows: "Japan developed railway networks and irrigation water systems in Korea. However, Japan pursued assimilation policies such as teaching Japanese to Korean people, which caused anti-Japanese feeling among the Korean people."

The Korean parliament also passed a resolution not to support Japan as a permanent member of the United Nations Security Council because of the nationalistic history textbook. Korea warned that it would reverse its policy of opening the Korean market to Japanese cultural products unless the nationalistic textbook was revised more thoroughly. On the other hand, Korean academics and students seem to have different attitudes. They were highly critical of the Tsukurukai textbook, but they were also critical of the Korean textbook system and the content of those textbooks.

The Chinese government showed ambivalent attitudes. On March 7, 2001, China warned that the nationalistic junior high school textbook would negatively impact China-Japan relations unless more corrections were made, but on March 16, 2001, China announced that China-Japan relations as a whole should be separated from the textbook issue.

Selection Process

Tsukurukai criticized the selection process: they demanded that education committees select textbooks by themselves rather than choose textbooks based on the recommendations of their subcommittees, which are mainly composed of left-wing teachers.

As in the Cold War period, liberals such as Ohe Kenzaburo (a Nobel Prize-winning writer), Miki Mutsuko (wife of a dovish former Liberal Democratic Party prime minister of Japan), and Inoue Hisashii (supporter of the Communist Party) urged the MOE not to approve the nationalistic textbook. They also requested that the selection process be more transparent.

Recently, local communities have played important roles in the selection process as well, changing the politics over textbook issues in the post–Cold War period. Many people in local areas attended the education committee meetings as observers and issued information about what was going on in their local education committees on their individual Web sites. This led to the development of anti-nationalistic textbook networks among local people and groups.

In addition, various kinds of transnational networks have helped the anti-nationalistic textbook movement. In particular, transnational networks of women such as the Violence against Women in War Network (VAWNET) have contributed to clarifying the situation of "comfort women" or "sexual slaves" to the world. These networks have helped women around the world share historical memory based on the perspective of gender. This transnational group has provided strong support to the critics of the nationalistic textbook.

In the end, Tsukurukai's textbook was adopted by seven private schools and three special public schools in Tokyo (whose governor is Ishihara Shintaro, a famous right-wing politician). The percentage of the share of the nationalistic textbook was 0.039. The number of students who use this history textbook is 521. The majority of Japanese people were critical of the nationalistic history textbook, which explains the low adoption ratio. However, the debates in individual education committees were heated, and the opinions of education committee members were split in many districts.

As a result, textbooks whose content was relatively moderate were more likely to be selected (table 19.2). The textbook by Nihon Shoseki is the most liberal. It uses the term "comfort women" and describes the issue of war compensation for a full page, but its share dropped from 13.7 percent in 2001 to only 5.9 percent in 2002. Alternatively, the textbook of Teikoku Shoin, liberal but more moderate, increased its share from 1.9 percent to 10.9 percent. All textbooks by Kyoiku Shuppan, Osaka Shoseki, and Tokyo Shoseki, which avoided using the terms "comfort women" or "comfort facility," can be seen as falling in the middle. The textbooks of the first two look relatively liberal when they refer to the issue of war compensation, while Tokyo Shoseki's textbook made no mention of the problem. However, the shares of Kyoiku Shuppan and Osaka Shoseki dropped from 18 percent to 13 percent and from 19 percent to 14 percent, respectively, while Tokyo Shoseki increased its share from 40 percent to 51 percent. This finding is based on a preliminary analysis, but there is a clear tendency to select moderate textbooks.

To summarize the history of the textbook issue, in the first period ideological conflicts affected the textbook issue: pro-Marxist writers and teachers' unions challenged the MOE's textbook screening system. In the second and third periods, after the Cold War, nationalists rather than left-wingers challenged the MOE's screening system. Further, the left-wingers appealed to the MOE not to approve a nationalistic textbook in its textbook screening system.

Conclusion: Seeking a Transnational History in the Age of Globalization

Globalization may contribute to an increase in the number of people who behave as members of global civil society when a country is on the winning side of globalization. However, nationalism is likely to rise to the surface when a country is on the losing side. Japan has suffered from an economic recession since its "bubble economy" burst. That may explain why Tsukurukai published a nationalistic history textbook when it did.

Table 19.2 Comparison of Textbooks by Seven Publishers: Description of War Responsibility Issues and Share of Textbooks

PUBLISHER

TOPIC		Nihon Shoseki	Teikoku Shoin	Kyoiku Shuppan	Osaka Shoseki	Shimizu Shoin	Tokyo Shoseki	Nihon Bunkyo
Nanjing Incident	Does the textbook describe that Japanese were not informed at that time?	Yes	Yes	No	Yes	Yes	Yes	Yes
	Does the textbook describe that Japanese celebrated the fall of Nanjing to the Japanese Army?	No	No	Yes (by photo)	Yes (by photo)	No	No	No
	How does the textbook describe the number of victims	200,000 people killed	Many	Many	Many	Many	Many	Number of victims uncertain
War Compensation	Does the textbook describe this problem under a headline?	Yes	Yes	Yes	Yes (in a column)	No	Yes (explanation of photo)	No
	How much space does the textbook give to this topic?	One page	Half page	One page	Two lines	None	None	None
"Comfort Women"	What words does the textbook use for this topic?	Comfort women	Comfort facilities	None	None	Comfort facilities	None	None
Share	% of share in 2001 before the Tsukurukai proposed its textbook	13.7	1.9	18.0	18.8	3.9	40.4	3.2
	% of share in 2002 after the Tsukurukai proposed its textbook	5.9	10.9	13.0	14.0	2.5	51.2	2.3
	Change in shares between 2001 and 2002	Down (-7.8%)	Up (9%)	Down (-5%)	Down (-14.8%)	Down (-1.4%)	Up (10.8%)	Down (-0.9%)
Overall Impression		Liberal (radical)	Liberal (moderate)	Middle (radical)	Middle (radical)	Middle (moderate)	Middle (moderate)	Conservative

Source: Table created by the author. N.B. Overall impression is mainly based on the two factors of "comfort women" and war compensation.

However, their textbook was adopted by only a small number of districts/schools. What are the reasons? First, Japanese people, in fact, fear globalization, but neither anti-foreign attitudes nor protectionism of trade dominate their thinking.[6] Japanese interests have already been structured around the globalizing economy, and many people perceive that Japan will not be able to achieve its interests without reforming its public/corporate governance appropriate for the globalized economy.

A change in the perception of "nation" is another reason for the Japanese to reject the nationalistic textbook. A nation is not composed of just majority groups; minorities are now perceived as an important part of the "nation." As a result, there has gradually developed a movement to guarantee the rights of Korean residents and other foreign people in Japan. The participation of foreign residents in local politics is now being examined. At the same time, the number of people who have dual nationality is increasing. They are ethnically Japanese, but they behave unlike traditional Japanese people. Many Japanese people are facing the question of who is "Japanese" and what is "Japan."

Tsukurukai's textbook gave no answer to these questions but reasserted simple and traditional arguments of the "nation." It failed to address new ideas of "Japan" as a nation and the "Japanese" as a people in a globalizing world.

Can we share historical perceptions between nations if globalization develops further? Multiculturalism is often mentioned as a way to stimulate the reinterpretation of national history. However, Laura Hein and Mark Selden suggest that revising the interpretation of the Vietnam War or the atomic bombings of Hiroshima and Nagasaki is still very difficult in the United States.[7] This suggests that multiculturalism can change historical memory as far as it relates to domestic issues, but it faces difficulty in providing a new interpretation when it relates to U.S. foreign policy.

Globalization of the economy will contribute to the gradual expansion of multiculturalism, even in Japan, but, as the American case suggests, the spread of multiculturalism is not always effective in the reinterpretation of national history.

We may develop a viewpoint of global/human history because globalization of information presents us all with common problems. For example, conflicts in Rwanda were reported by CNN and the genocide in Kosovo was broadcast around the world so that people everywhere discussed the legitimacy and effectiveness of humanitarian intervention.

Can we reinterpret national history and share historical memory as we accumulate our common experiences of current events? The idea to publish a common history textbook in Asia is often proposed for this purpose. The European experience suggests that it is not an easy task, however.

The case of the Japanese history textbook issue suggests that sharing historical perceptions between transnational groups is possible even if building a global/human history is still unrealistic. In fact, various kinds of transnational networks have developed. For example, as we have said, VAWNET has contributed to clarifying the situation of "comfort women" or "sexual slaves" to the world. It may help women around the world share historical memory based on the perspective of gender.

Democratization around the world can help build a transnational history. For example, democratization of Asian countries in the 1990s has stimulated the growth of pluralistic societies in Asian countries. People in these countries have developed critical views of their governments as well as of the nationalistic textbooks in Japan. For example, Koreans criticized the nationalistic textbook and the MOE's approval of it in Japan, and yet at the same time they were also critical of their government's textbook policy. Textbooks of Korean language, social studies, and ethics are published by the government in Korea. Critics see the history in these textbooks as an "official" history, and they raise questions of whether or not it is a "public" history. The answer depends on the definition of "public," which is usually used in three contexts: "official," "common," or "open." Is the history contained in Korean textbooks commonly shared by many Korean people?

National governments have used history textbooks as a tool for building national identity among people, and they have developed screening/authorizing systems. History textbooks screened/authorized by public institutions are assumed to reflect the public memory, or commonly shared historical perceptions. The history textbook issue has not been politicized in the United States, where public memory of major wars is established, but it has been a big political issue in Japan because Japan has no single public memory of World War II.

Under this situation, it is difficult for Japanese to build a shared memory with people of other nations. Creating a transnational history is a realistic alternative beyond national history in the age of globalization, and it is a first step toward building a public memory in the Asia-Pacific region.

FURTHER THOUGHTS

Globalization and Japan

Jim Dator

JAPAN IS ONE of the few countries in the world that has had two chances to respond to massive global pressures for governance reform. The first opportunity, already discussed briefly in chapter 16, was in the second half of the nineteenth century, when Japan was forced to end its centuries-long self-imposed global isolation and transform itself into a modern nation against its will. Japan accomplished the feat extremely effectively and in an extraordinarily short period of time by inviting in scores of foreign experts on all aspects of society (and then escorting them all home within a decade), while also sending young Japanese observers overseas to study what were then the "best practices" of nations around the world, especially in Europe and North America.

As a consequence of these rapid and profound internal reforms and the foreign policies flowing from them, Japan quickly became a major global military power in the twentieth century and (emulating and exceeding its tutors' most extravagant expectations and outrageous examples) adroitly attacked and conquered surrounding nations until it eventually overreached and was devastatingly defeated in World War II.

Subsequently, it was immediately provided a second chance at major governance reform via global pressure. Taking advantage of an extraordinarily open, but brief, window of opportunity, Japanese constitutional lawyers in 1947 quickly drafted, adopted, and implemented what some scholars have convincingly argued is the "best" constitution in the world of the many created during the twentieth century (e.g., Beer and Maki, *From Imperial Myth to Democracy: Japan's Two Constitutions*). However, the major lesson that Japan learned from its defeat in World War II was that while imperialistic military might define a powerful nation in the nineteenth and early twentieth centuries, the future belonged to economically powerful nations. And so Japanese decision makers consciously set out to make Japan a leading economic power. "For example, 'Long Range Prospects of the Japanese Economy' published in August 1960 by the Economic Council is the first result of future research activities by the government in postwar Japan. On October 27, 1965, officials of the Economic Planning Agency blue-printed 'A Vision of Affluent Japan after Twenty Years' " (Yujiro Hayashi, "Japan Society of Futurology"). To imagine in the 1960s that Japan would be "affluent" by the 1980s was certainly audacious, but indeed as early as 1970 futurist Herman Kahn published a book titled *The Emerging Japanese Superstate: Challenge and Response*. This was followed later, in 1979, by Kahn's and Thomas Pepper's *The Japanese Challenge: The Success and Failure of Economic Success*—the same year that respected Japan scholar Ezra Vogel published *Japan as Number One: Lessons for America*.

Japan was indeed a (if not *the*) major economic superpower over the 1980s, with Japanese banks as well as automotive and electronic corporations ranked among the top five or ten in the world. Some observers even anticipated that the yen would replace the dollar as the world standard. And then the bubble burst (as bubbles do), and Japan entered a prolonged economic stagnation that persists to the present time. A great many words have been written about the wretched condition of the Japanese economy and how unemployment (virtually unknown from the mid-1950s) and crime were both on the rise. Countless foreign advisors from the IMF, World Trade Organization, World Bank, and the like have urged Japan to adopt the draconian policies that they inflicted elsewhere.

But the Japanese have steadfastly refused. Did they refuse because of the entrenched and fossilized bureaucracy and political system? That is what almost all observers contend. Or did they refuse because of their wise realization that slowing the transition from myriad "mom and pop" factories and retail outlets to offshore factories and a few externally controlled "box stores" is better for Japan, politically and culturally, than the humiliating and severe "shock treatments" endured by Russia, Brazil, Thailand, Korea, and many other places (as I feel very strongly is the case)? It is a subject to debate.

From my point of view, Japan, along with Malaysia and Singapore, both of which consciously learned from Japan in their own way, are, by and large, three excellent examples of how political institutions in Asia might "respond to globalization in fairness." The Japanese economy is, after all, still the second largest in the world, while the standard of living of most Japanese is the envy of everyone in many aspects. Would that all economies were so "stagnant"!

However, in his contribution to our volume, Professor Oshiba shows that "responding to globalization in fairness" is much more than merely an economic issue. There are cultural dimensions as well, largely devoid of any economic import whatsoever. His example is the extremely interesting and complex issue of how officially recognized secondary-school history textbooks (intended only for Japanese students) deal with Japan's role in World War II. It is an issue that not only has profound implications for future generations of Japanese themselves, but also for relations between Japan and its neighbors presently. Something seemingly as utterly "local" as a few words in a nation's school textbooks has substantial and unintended global ramifications.

Notes

1. All Japanese names will be written in Japanese style, i.e., surname then first name.

2. Nishio Kanji, ed., *Atarashii Rekishi Kyokasho* (New history textbook) (Tokyo: Fusosha, 2001).

3. MOE examiners raised the question of appropriateness of topics for junior high school textbooks when we were faced with discussions of increasing numbers of divorce, single mothers, and the system of husband and wife retaining separate family names. According to MOE examiners, recent textbooks on home economics tended to emphasize the importance of individuals too much, while placing less importance on family values.

4. Nishio, ed., *Atarashii Rekishi Kyokasho*.

5. Yui Daizaburo, *Nichibei Senso Kan no Sokoku—Masatsu no Shinso Shinri* (View of war in Japan and the US: Psychology of U.S.-Japan frictions) (Tokyo: Iwanami Shoten, 1995).

6. Abe Kiyoshi, *Samayoeru Nashonarizumu* (Whither nationalism?) (Kyoto: Sekai Shiso-sha, 2001).

7. Laura Hein and Mark Selden, eds., *Censoring History: Citizenship and Memory in Japan, Germany, and the United States* (Armonk, N.Y.: An East Gate Book, 2000).

CHAPTER 20

Globalization and Generational Change
The Evolution of Cambodia's Social Structure

CHANTO SISOWATH

The Origin of State Legitimacy: The God King

In order to appreciate the impact of globalization on Khmer society it is necessary to grasp the fundamental political and social values of Cambodia. Cambodian culture has been very resistant to change, showing strong reverence for the monarchy and the ways of antiquity. In traditional belief, the king was the sovereign ruler whose divine right legitimized his authority to rule over all social and political institutions.[1] See Yongseok Seo's Further Thoughts, "A Brief History of Cambodia," on page 307.

In the context of state and social relations, the origin of Khmer political and social values is found in the decisions of the God King, who wielded absolute authority. The culture of divinity has made an everlasting impact on the social values of Khmer society, the most visible impact being the application and administration of power. For instance, during the height of the Khmer Empire (6th through 13th centuries), the king was the center of Khmer culture and might, and his legitimacy was broadly revered by the religious sector and the general population. Starting from this premise, the king held absolute power, and although he granted some autonomy to local authorities, the royal court made the final decisions on policies about the development of the kingdom.[2] As a result, there was no separation of governmental powers that permitted the ministries to function independently, a problem that this present generation must overcome. When the kingdom started to establish foreign relations with European and neighboring countries, the monarchy had many difficulties in consolidating and protecting its absolute right to power as well as administrating and implementing policy.[3] For example, by the eighteenth century, a time when the rest of the world was evolving from absolute monarchy toward constitutional monarchy, the kingdom of Cambodia was thwarted by external challenges, especially the rising power of Thailand and Vietnam.[4] Confined by institutional weaknesses, Cambodia was contained within its own kingdom, isolated from international politics and the forces of modernization. The entire kingdom was almost lost.

Perhaps the reason the king resisted modernization was that the monarchy felt that it had the responsibility of protecting the political and cultural sovereignty of the kingdom. The fact is that the king was the state, and the state was the king, so whose sovereignty was at stake?[5] By failing to provide the legal right for social participation in nation-state building, the state ignored public opinion in the process of public-policy formulation.[6] It was the failure to recognize the right of participation and the value of political diversity that prompted a breach of trust between the state and society.

In addition to that, the monarchy also overlooked the important role of the bourgeoisie and the merchant class in nation-state building. In the case of Cambodia, the bourgeoisie and aristocrats composed the elite (landlords, provincial governors, and the military) who legitimized royal decrees. They were the buffer between the ruler and the ruled. When compared with their European counterparts, Cambodian elites did not seek a political and commercial revolution. Instead, they survived by feeding off the monarch. The primary concern of the aristocrats and the bourgeoisie was to embrace the royal culture and benefit from it.

By neglecting to recognize the importance of social and political diversity, the ancient regime created a system of class supremacy and alienation. Cambodia has inherited this legacy while it is trying to democratize its social institutions. The inherent challenge is not only that Cambodia has been a post-conflict society since the Paris Peace Agreement of 1991 ended the Cambodian civil war, but also that the norms of social mobility continue to distance the majority from social advancement because these norms undermine fair opportunities and competition. As a result, Cambodia faces the problem of political and social inequity, especially in this age of globalization.

Entering the Free Market System: Directional Change

Although Cambodia gained full sovereign status from France in 1954, the political system remained exclusive. Cambodia has never gone though a social revolution but is now gradually undergoing a paradigm evolution due in part to globalization and in part to the erosion of traditional values. Cambodian society has never been comfortable with an open political system because its social values and institutions have not come to terms with liberal democracy.[7]

It was not until 1993 that Cambodia opened up to the global system and thus was able to accommodate some of the values and practices of liberalism. At the end of the Cold War, Cambodia was able to focus on economic development and strengthening its national identity. The fall of communism meant a reduction in the Soviet Union's assistance to the communist states in Indochina, including Cambodia.[8] However, the end of the Cold War also ushered in a different kind of challenge to Cambodia, namely an international political economy that demanded simultaneous reform of both the economy and the polity.

In the economic sphere, the World Bank and the International Monetary Fund (IMF) required Cambodia to make structural reforms and replace the indigenous economy with the mechanisms of a liberal market economy. In the political sphere, Cambodia was expected to liberalize its political system and guarantee civil liberties. By entering the market system Cambodia had to make directional changes, transforming a post-conflict society into a market society through structural reforms. After years of international isolation and extensive internal strife, Cambodia has no choice but to accommodate the international system, making economic, political, and social reforms in order to integrate into and benefit from the global community.[9]

But first, Cambodia had to manage and resolve its own internal differences. It successfully achieved national reconciliation through the 1991 Paris Peace Agreement on a Comprehensive Settlement for the Cambodian Conflict. Following the 1991 Paris Agreement, Cambodia wanted to accomplish national unity followed by national rehabilitation, and ultimately combat poverty and improve the living standard of its citizens.[10] When the four rival political parties (namely the Cambodian People's Party; the Royalists-United Front for the Independent, Neutral, Peaceful and Co-operative Cambodia; the Buddhist Democratic Liberal Party People; and the People Democratic Kampuchea)[11] signed the 1991 Peace Agreement, they agreed on a process of national reconciliation and adopted a pluralistic democratic constitution. The Paris Peace Agreement uniquely focused on the principle of human rights, especially the components of the United Nations Universal Declaration of Human Rights and the International Covenant on Economic, Social and Cultural Rights. In addition, the four major political parties agreed to cooperate with the United Nations Transnational Authority in Cambodia (UNTAC) and to be subject to UN-sponsored national elections in 1993. The presence of the UN Peace Keeping Force and national elections organized and monitored by UN personnel were historic events. More important, the very fact that the four contending parties gave up armed competition in favor of a national election and accepted conditions set by the international community, emphasizing the importance of human rights and democracy, was indicative that Cambodia was moving toward a new era of nation-state building.

For any developing country or country with post-conflict experience, the process of democratization is challenging, and Cambodia is no exception. One dilemma is whether to pay more attention to democratization or to poverty reduction. Professor Jeffrey Sachs, an economist from Columbia University, argued that for Cambodia at the early period of post-conflict recovery, it is necessary to tend to the challenges of poverty, especially food security, and then gradually turn its attention to building democracy.[12] Local and international nongovernmental organizations (NGOs) also often argued that democracy and poverty reduction should be achieved simultaneously because the two are indivisible. For the average Cambodian, having access to public services such as health care, food, and education is most important for daily life, but at the same time they do not discard their desire for democratization.[13]

For many Cambodians, democracy is necessary for two fundamental purposes: for enabling equitable growth and protecting political rights and civil liberties, and for the prevention of a political and economic monopoly. In this context, the correlation of democratization with poverty reduction is very crucial for a post-conflict society because a responsible and accountable political system is a prerequisite for social development. Interfacing with the global system means reforming civil administration so that both the private and the public sectors accommodate the market system. This emerging process is mainly channeled by civil society, which includes international development institutions and agencies such as the World Health Organization (WHO), United Nations Development Program (UNDP), United Nations Children's Fund (UNICEF), United Nations Educational, Scientific and Cultural Organization (UNESCO), United Nations Food Program (UNFP), United Nations Human Rights Commission (UNHRC), World Bank, IMF, and International Labor Organization (ILO), in addition to myriad local and international nonprofit organizations and religious establishments.

Civil society has impacted the country considerably, particularly by raising awareness of human rights, equality, equity, poverty alleviation, preventive medicine, birth control, HIV/AIDS prevention, planning parenthood, children's rights, gender equity, and workers' rights. In many ways, nonprofit organizations are liberating people from the shackles of state-made decisions by empowering the grass-roots levels with practices and information necessary to manage their own lives.

From another perspective, the fusion of global communications and integration processes continues to change Cambodia's social structure.[14] For instance, globalization demands competitiveness, but competitiveness has been defined in terms of creativity rather than capital and by intangible assets such as knowledge rather than tangible assets. Cambodia has been compelled to respond to the paradigm change rather than having been persuaded by it to reform its social and political philosophy and economic practices.

However, even if globalization is thought to improve the distribution of resources within nation-states or within the global community, the reality is that only a few profit, while the benefits of globalization remain out of the reach of most people.[15] An imbalance in access to public services and opportunities remains for many Cambodians. But regardless of the debate on how globalization is to benefit Cambodia, it is a fact that globalization is a catalytic factor and has compelled Cambodia to readjust its social structure. Global politics and international relations are negotiated in terms of investments, cost and profit, production, competitive advantage, labor, tariffs, and the market. Market access and investments have become the means of peaceful cooperation for coexistence and co-prosperity. In this age of globalization, the law of supply and demand knows no boundary, nationality, or race.

At the present, Cambodia is facing what Ross and Trachte describe as "the irony of the new leviathan." The new leviathan of global capitalism does not defend the citizens of a nation from foreign invasion, as Hobbes imagined. The old leviathan emphasized the state's legitimacy to exercise its authority. State sovereignty and power were defined in the context of self-preservation and order. In Hobbes' *Leviathan,* the state's primary instrument for social order was force. The new leviathan's idea of social order is rational calculation, individual interest, capitalism, investments, specialization, and employment. In the age of a global economy, national security encompasses the idea of protecting the domestic economy and industrial development.[16] Principles of property rights, ownership, commerce, and trade are issues that complicate administration. And even if the global economy culminates in interdependency, it is not necessarily a prelude to commercial and political harmony, a point that political economists such as Giplin, Wallerstein, and others have made.

Globalization: The Contesting Process

In addition to the increasing presence of democratic values, decentralization and deconcentration, and the modernized development model, information technology (IT) and information and communications technology (ICT) have affected and shaped how Cambodia and Cambodians behave and respond to the impact of globalization.[17] For the past eleven years, Cambodian youth have been enjoying a wealth of information. If this process continues, it is probable that a new social paradigm and values will emerge within this generation. Cambodia recognizes the influence of Western economic and political models because the market economy demands structural reform to succeed. This means that if Cambodia wishes to accelerate its poverty reduction goals and benefit from globalization, it must simultaneously reform its political practices through decentralization and deconcentration of power by rearranging the structure of the state for more flexibility and efficiency.[18] On the other hand, the essential requirement to benefit from this emerging paradigm is to give priority to human resource development and access to technical information that will be useful for decision making. The advent of technological transfer, as well as skills transfer, has helped reshape the way people work, think, play, and interact internally and externally.[19] The present generation has much more exposure to developmental information than its predecessors. The increasing acquisition of analytical tools and the understanding of technological application helps the process of nation-state building as well as social mobility. Today, Cambodian youth are exposed to updated information, particularly on democratic processes, and the functions of the market economy, medicine, engineering, liberal arts, and international cultures. Cambodian youth are now able to evaluate the credibility and legitimacy of the state while at the same time being less receptive to state propaganda and more responsive to the importance of human rights and intellectual development. As a consequence, state propaganda and the feudal system have lost their potency, and so the culture of divinity is facing an institutional crisis. Similarly, Cambodia's patriarchic system is beginning to fade as the mystique of the God King, feudalism, and nepotism all gradually lose functionality and the support from the younger generation, especially since the current generation is suffering from low employment opportunities.

While the state is steadfast in protecting its own prerogatives, privileges, and power, the private sector continues gradually to erode the functions and authority of the state. This means that the state has had to become more cooperative with the private sector and finally accept its significant role and function in nation-state building. In this age of globalization, the Cambodian state has to become more open and transparent, which in many ways demystifies the power of the state. This enables people to become more aware of their rights and to recognize the limitations on the power of the state.

The Information Market: Education as a Main Driver

Cambodia's educational process is gearing the next generation toward the market economy. Privately owned educational establishments are flourishing across the country, providing the younger generation with technical skills so they will be better prepared for the market system. As the success of the market is driven by financial interests, the state has recognized that private education may provide the needed services and values, namely *marketable skills*. Liberalizing the economy and furthering education promotes competition and competitive advantage, strengthening knowledge and employment prospects for the younger generation. Although at the moment public-information management is usually confined to state ministries, access to public information through the Internet and Web sites provides the younger generation with a better understanding of the role and function of state institutions.[20] Moreover, as youth from elite families receive education abroad, they are returning home better prepared for administration and management. Local institutions such as the National Institute of Management (NIM), the Royal University of Phnom Penh (RUPP), Norton University (NU), and the Royal Academy of Administration (RAA) are the four main accredited educational institutions that produce future leaders. International nonprofit organizations such as the Japan International Cooperation Agency (JICA) and the Japan International Cultural Exchange (JICE) promote technical and infrastructural development such as water plants, power plants, roads, education, schools, irrigation engineering, telecommunications, broadcasting systems, satellite operation and broadcasting, cultural preservation, environmental engineering, and development of the legal infrastructure.[21] Cambodia's RUPP is well known for its science and technology department, while NIM specializes in economics and international business. NU focuses on foreign languages, especially English, and RAA is responsible for producing top-notch administrators.

Globalism: Challenging Conventional Wisdom

Since the 1991 Paris Peace Agreement, Cambodia has been preoccupied with internal politics. To prevent the return of conflict, the government had to sideline public services, administrative reform, and good governance initiatives. Consequently, Cambodia has made limited progress on human resource development, which eventually complicates its ability and opportunity to harness external and internal resources for nation-state building.[22] As a result, in comparison with Vietnam, Cambodia is facing the problem of development gaps because Cambodia failed to sustain the competitive advantages needed to attract foreign direct investments and loans. While it is true that globalization offers numerous possibilities, it also narrows opportunities by raising the levels of competition, standards, and expectations. For Cambodia to harness the benefits and opportunities of globalization, it must redefine its own working culture, social relations, modes of production, finances, legal system, civil and state relations, and international relations. An important example of this occurring is in the military, which continues to work on improving civil relations by educating junior- and high-ranking officers on the role and function of the military in conflict resolution and constitutionalism,[23] while the Ministry of Defense continues to implement exchange programs and sends attachés to Western institutions.

More generally, to keep pace with development and institutional changes, Cambodia is gradually changing its social values and state relations. State centrism, an idea that once dominated the social and political landscape of Cambodia, is being redefined and eventually will be restructured toward accommodating the ideas of individualism, liberty, and economic and political rights.

Expectations and Realities

Opponents of globalization argue that the process of globalization creates development gaps and increases inequity. Yet there are many positive opportunities for developing countries, including Cambodia, to benefit from the process. However, before Cambodia puts all of its expectations and faith in the global system, it needs to have a model that is compatible with globalization. This is where the problem lies. For Cambodia, in particular, the main question is how to construct and finance development or create a development model that is compatible with its own social values and practices.[24] What are Cambodia's development options, and which can Cambodia afford? Like many developing and post-conflict countries, it is the international financial institutions (IFIs) and international economic institutions that influence national development models. The former expects the latter to implement structural reform and complex technical operations to accommodate the market economy.[25] This in many ways increases the burden of policy and financial planning. IFI policy planners need to keep in mind that the majority of the developing nations are not able to build or accommodate the market economy overnight without risking political and social instability. In such a case, the market system coerces developing countries with market pressure and eventually co-opts them into crippling economic and political debts.

Conclusion

Globalization is causing Cambodia to adjust its social and political values. The state, while retaining its legitimacy, finds that its credibility, functionality, and efficiency are challenged by the market system, global information, and the rising level of knowledge. It is the duty and opportunity of Cambodian youth to find the successful balance of traditional and global for their future.

FURTHER THOUGHTS

A Brief History of Cambodia

Yongseok Seo

Indian Influence in Premodern Cambodia

THE FIRST WAVE of global influence in early Cambodia came from India. According to Chinese records, Funan, located in modern Cambodia, was the first ancient kingdom to appear in Southeast Asia. The kingdom of Funan flourished as a strategic place of maritime trade between India and China from the first to the end of sixth century. Indian cultural influence on the Funan kingdom was conspicuous, including the foundation myth of the kingdom that has persisted as the legend of Cambodia's origins.

Angkor was one of two Indianized states in Southeast Asia in the ninth century that represented Hindu religious views (see Osborne, *Southeast Asia: An Introductory History,* 21–22). (The years between AD 802–1431 in Cambodian history were called the Angkor period. Angkor maintained a huge imperial image from the eleventh century and ruled over a large region of Southeast Asia. Angkor Wat is a temple that has Indian/Hindu architecture.) Most of the kings during the Angkor period followed Hindu rituals (Coedès, *The Indianized States of Southeast Asia*). Angkor flourished until the end of the twelfth century, when it began to receive pressure from Thailand. As Thailand's influence on Angkor grew, the Khmer gave up Angkor and moved their capitol to Phnom Penh. At the end of the fifteenth century the Angkor kingdom in Phnom Penh collapsed as the result of a Vietnamese invasion, and Cambodia fell under the influence of Vietnam. For the next several centuries, external pressures from both Thailand and Vietnam caused the gradual decline of the Cambodian kingdoms and ultimately led to Cambodia becoming a French protectorate in 1863.

The West's Encroachment and French Colonial Rule

Like other East Asian countries, Cambodia had to face pressure from Western imperialism in the nineteenth century. In the early 1880s, France diverted its attention to Cambodia after colonizing Vietnam. In 1884, the French colonial government in Cochin China forcefully required the Cambodian king to sign an unequal treaty that seriously undermined the sovereignty of Cambodia. However, the French had to face a nationwide demonstration of Cambodians who rallied against the treaty. France's reputation was heavily damaged by the demonstrations, and nationalism took root among the Cambodian people after this uprising.

From Independence to Civil War

Cambodia was under Japanese control during the Pacific War. In March 1945, the Cambodian prince Norodom Sihanouk declared independence, but France did not recognize it. After a series of struggles, Cambodia was granted independence by the Geneva Agreement in July 1954. It was, however, a prelude to tragedy for the Cambodian people. Cambodia, like many other East Asian countries, became an arena of competition of Western ideologies. Global pressure forced newly reborn Cambodia to choose communism or capitalism as their national ideology. Although Prince Sihanouk initially established a communist autocracy after independence from France, he attempted to maintain a neutral position for Cambodia by taking sides with neither China nor the United States as the Vietnam War broke out.

However, in 1970, while Sihanouk was on a foreign tour, a military coup took place in which right-wing military general Lon Nol took power. As a result, a pro-Western military government was established in Cambodia in 1972. Lon Nol's government was unstable from the beginning. The leftist Khmer Rouge guerillas began a civil war against the Nol government in 1975. At the end of the Vietnam War, the Khmer Rouge overthrew the American-backed Nol government. Supported by China, the Khmer Rouge established a communist government, headed by Pol Pot. The Pol Pot government was a brutal autocracy that killed millions of innocent people, including many noncommunist political, military, and religious leaders as well as the bourgeoisie. It is estimated that more than two million people were killed between 1975 and 1979 (Osborne, *Southeast Asia: An Introductory History,* 199).

In 1978 Vietnam invaded Cambodia with the support of Cambodian communists who opposed Pol Pot. Vietnam pulled its troops out of Cambodia in 1988, and the UN Security Council approved a plan for a UN-monitored cease fire and elections. This was the first time that global pressure brought about peace (instead of war) in Cambodia. A peace agreement was signed in Paris, and UN Peace Keeping Forces entered Cambodia to enforce the armistice in 1991. Under UN supervision, an election occurred in 1993, and the current government was elected. Despite its splendid history and culture, Cambodia is a country that has been the victim of external pressures. Of all countries in the region, Cambodia has probably had the bitterest experiences with "globalization" over the centuries.

Notes

1. Gabriel Quiroga de San Antonio, *A Brief and Truthful Relation of Events in the Kingdom of Cambodia* (Bangkok: White Lotus Co., 1998). The God King theory originated in India, but the Khmer adopted this divine theory as the foundation of their sociopolitical civilization. Currently, Cambodia's political practice is a hybrid of Confucianism and Buddhism as the country emerges from inner conflict. However, the advent of globalization is challenging both philosophies.

2. Ibid., 74.

3. Ibid., 78.

4. See also David P. Chandler, *The History of Cambodia* (Boulder, Colo.: Westview Press, Inc., 1998).

5. J. T. McAlister, Jr., *Southeast Asia: The Politics of National Integration* (New York, NY: Random House, 1973), 74-90.

6. Michael Vickery, *Cambodia, Cambodia: 1975-1982* (Chiangmai: Silkworm Books: 1999).

7. David P. Chandler, *The Tragedy of Cambodian History: Politics, War, and Revolution Since 1945* (New Haven, Conn.: Yale University Press, 1991), 14–46.

8. Charles Twining, "The Economy," in *Cambodia 1975–78*, ed. Karl Jackson (Princeton, N.J.: Princeton University Press, 1989), 150.

9. William Shawcross, *Cambodia's New Deal* (Washington, DC: Carnegie Endowment for International Peace, 1994).

10. Ibid.

11. These were the four political regimes of Cambodia prior to the Vietnamese invasion in 1979. Each of the regimes believes that its legitimacy was forcefully deprived by the other regimes and that Cambodia's problems are rooted in foreign intervention. It is also important to note that these four contentious groups were not simply political parties—they were political regimes that sought to regain their legitimacy.

12. CICP, Special Lecture Series, *Democracy and Development* (Phnom Penh, Cambodia: 2002).

13. CICP/World Bank Institute, "Development Debates and Poverty Reduction: Policy Dialogue," presented at the National Conference on Sustainable Development, Poverty Reduction and Good Governance in Cambodia (September 20–21, 2001), Government Palace, Phnom Penh, Cambodia.

14. Joel S. Midgal, Atul Kohli, and Vivienne Shue, *State Power and Social Forces: Domination and Transformation in the Third World* (Cambridge: Cambridge University Press 1994), 143–155. In many ways, this process co-opts the technical aspects of a centralized administration regime, but it does not co-opt the patriarchal tradition. In the case of Cambodia, globalization is severely testing the administrative and political structure of the Cambodian operating system. The political elite continue to informally consolidate their power to withstand the external challenges from the global system.

15. J. S. Robert Ross and C. Kent Trachte, *Global Capitalism: The New Leviathan* (Albany: State University of New York Press, 1990), 1–65.

16. Ibid.

17. Royal Government of Cambodia, *SEILA Program Document 2001–2005* (Phnom Penh: December 2000).

18. Jeffrey A. Kaplan, "As Cambodia Considers AFTA," *The Cambodian Journal of International Affairs* 1 (Fall 1996): 20–28.

19. UNDP, "A Breakthrough in Cambodian Election Broadcasting," *Equity News* (Cambodia, August 2003), 1–24.

20. Cambodia Development Resource Institute (CDRI), "A Study of the Cambodian Labor Market: Reference to Poverty Reduction, Growth and Adjustment to Crisis," *Working Paper* no. 18 (Phnom Penh: August 2001).

21. JICA, *The Kingdom of Cambodia: From Reconstruction to Sustainable Development* (Tokyo: JICA, 2002), 11.

22. Ibid.

23. Ministry of Defense, *The White Paper 2002* (Phnom Penh: MOD, 2002).

24. Prime minister of Cambodia Hun Sen's speech, "At the Consultative Group

Meeting" (Phnom Penh, 2002), 6. In this speech, the prime minister identified three areas for building the foundations for pro-poor development: (1) fiscal policies that enhance revenues and direct expenditure in favor of pro-poor public investment; (2) assurance of sustained economic growth and macroeconomic stability; and (3) formulating and implementing appropriate sector policies, including attention to social development via increased investment in health and education, mainstreaming gender issues, ensuring the development of ethnic minorities, land reform, and sustainable development

25. IMF has been working on restructuring Cambodia's economy since 1994. Basically, the Enhanced Structural Adjustment Facility (ESAF) is to deconstruct the traditional economy and substitute the old economic regime with the free market economic system. In most developing economies in Asia, the five-year plan is incompatible with the current market model, especially after the fall of communism. Given the pattern of the global trend, capital flow, technological acceleration, and market development, a country such as Cambodia cannot accommodate anything less than a five-year plan.

CHAPTER 21

Adapting to Globalization in Vietnam
Seeking Development in the Global Economy

LE VAN ANH

P romoting international cooperation and integration has become a major feature in the renovation process in Vietnam. Since 1991, our country has consistently implemented the policy that "Vietnam wants to befriend all nations of the world and strives for peace, independence and development." With this policy, Vietnam has gained a number of major economic, cultural, and social achievements. The living standard and infrastructure throughout the country have gradually improved. The country is approaching the national goal of "a wealthy people, a powerful nation, a fair, democratic and civilized society." See Yongseok Seo's Further Thoughts, "A Brief History of Vietnam," on page 316.

Economic Globalization and Socialist Markets

We are aware that economic globalization is a natural trend, a development of production forces and transnational, transregional, and global economic relationships in which goods, capital, information, and labor all naturally circulate and in which regional and national economic relationships intertwine as individual economies gradually expand and become interdependent.

Our economy has shifted from a centrally planned economy to a socialist-oriented market economy. Though laws of market value and competition have tremendous importance in a market economy, the state will continue to play an important role in planning and monitoring these laws. Thanks to our own advantages, we hope to exploit the efficiency of our economy and, with international market cooperation, enjoy the latest technological achievements and cultural essences of all nations of the world. We need valuable and efficient support from friends all over the globe. Therefore, just as we formerly participated in SEV (the former socialist Union of Mutual Economic Assistance), so now we are reinforcing international integration and cooperation, especially with the countries in the region through the Association of Southeast Asian Nations (ASEAN).

Provincial Connections to Globalization

Fostered by this national policy, and thanks to different cooperative relationships and international integration, Thua Thien Hue Province has been making use of its own advantages for expanding development. Though our production is still underdeveloped and limited, we have already sold several products on the international market—for example, sea products, garments, mineral and agricultural products, and handicrafts have all been sold to Japan, China, America, and Europe with a modest turnover of US$25 to 40 million per year.

Though situated in a less-favorable location in terms of weather, our province has implemented some projects with foreign investment in cement production and other construction materials for hotels, breweries, and so forth. At the same time, Thua Thien Hue has received funding from Official Development Assistance (ODA) and nongovernmental organizations (NGOs) in order to further improve the infrastructure and social welfare system. With the additional comparative advantage of being a "world cultural heritage" area, with beautiful natural landscapes and unique cultural traditions, we have attracted visitors from all over the world, gradually promoting tourism, services, and international cultural exchanges.

We have involved ourselves recently in urbanization and have continued more extensive participation in international urbanization. Hue City maintains close relationships with such organizations as La Fédération Mondiale des Cités Unies (FMCU), CITYNET (a network of local authorities for the management of human settlements in the Asia-Pacific region), the city of New Haven, Connecticut, in the United States, and various cities in France, Italy, Portugal, Japan, and China. We share experiences in urban management, such as cultural heritage development and maintenance, infrastructure building, and waste treatment. In addition, we cooperate technically in the fields of health, culture, foreign languages, and administration.

As a very small area in Vietnam with an adverse climate, we have to make every effort to develop actively and to participate in economic cooperation and integrate with other countries so as to create new opportunities for local development.

Challenges from the Global Market

Like other developing countries, we face many challenges as we try to integrate into the global economic community. With small-scale production and poor productivity due to old-fashioned technology and equipment, we can hardly compete in strict markets. It is extremely difficult for our key products to have access to suitable foreign markets. Farmers and fishermen usually suffer losses when farm products (including seafood), animal husbandry, agricultural, and forest products undergo difficulties in both the production conditions of harsh weather and foreign market integration. This consequently has negative effects on living conditions.

As a developing country, we face a fundamental lack of understanding of international markets and poor managerial capacity. This increases the risks of economic integration. In addition, with powerful economic potential and hundreds of years of business experience, big companies and corporations from many countries have easily established themselves and become extremely competitive in our own small market, retarding the development of our domestic production. Moreover, with the boom of information technology, the Internet, international telecommunications, and the rapid development of television and radio corporations, our traditional culture is quite vulnerable to foreign influences. The penetration of drug trafficking and addiction, prostitution, and crime into the country requires integrated approaches for resolution. In some cases, foreign influences have threatened the stability of the local community. This is one of the challenges that we constantly have to cope with in our new world.

In the market economy, the commodification of all goods and the law of competition have intensified inequality among the different classes. The poor are getting poorer as they no longer enjoy social subsidy. This is one of the most difficult social problems our state has to tackle. We must, therefore, adopt different macro policies.

The Role of the State in Fairness

In order to achieve sustainable development in the pursuit of international integration, we are, step-by-step, promoting the role of three partners: the state, enterprises, and the people.

Together with careful planning and monitoring of the whole process of economic, cultural, and social development, the state will strengthen legislation, economic institutions, and policies, thus creating fair regulations so that all economic organizations and sectors can have fair and healthy competition. The state will take different measures in order to create a necessary power of its own during the process of integration. These measures will also do away with any obstructions in international affairs in accordance with signed agreements and will facilitate all economic sectors to fully utilize their potential for development. It will create favorable conditions for promoting various forms of training, including jurisprudence, business management, and the technical professions, so that all citizens can improve their knowledge through learning. The state will perfect domestic markets, provide support for foreign market expansion and guidelines, build up suitable relations and attitudes toward multinational corporations and regional economic organizations, as well as set up an attractive environment for trade and investment. The state will also provide legislative guarantees and support enterprises so as to raise their global competitiveness through policies, financial assistance, and credit.

Enterprises from all economic sectors are pioneering toward international economic integration. At present, under the leadership of the state, enterprises in all economic sectors are making arrangements for suitable reform, gradually reducing their reliance on the state and accepting the competition of the market. Our state policy is to facilitate the development of all economic sectors and to encourage healthy competition in order to create motivation for development. As transnational companies hold most of the key markets of the world, Vietnamese enterprises have to find suitable solutions for an effective connection on the basis of improving their quality and impact in the marketplace.

The community plays an important role in the national economic integration process. Currently in Vietnam different social strata have different views on globalization. Some do not see its adverse side. Therefore, through mass media it is necessary to help people to understand globalization better and to take more responsibility in this process. Since the public is the beneficiary through the consumption of material, cultural, and spiritual products, the people have rights to fair selections without any restrictions. In addition, it is the public who works directly for the state, enterprises, and social organizations. The role of these people will decide the actual results in all fields during the process of global economic integration.

Balancing Development and Fairness

In order to respond to the challenges and foster Vietnam's integration into the economic globalization process, we have concentrated on human-resource training. We have made significant advances in education. We have almost achieved universal primary education, and we hope to complete universal junior-high-school-level education soon. In our province, five universities, many high schools, and vocational training and education facilities improve the knowledge and skills of our people. Focusing on international cooperation in human-resource training, we have recently had access to the modern science and technology of other countries. This is an important element for the success of economic integration.

With state and local investment and the creative cooperation of mass organizations such as youth unions, women's associations, trade unions, farmer's associations, and war veteran's associations, poor households have been effectively supported in the production of knowledge, advanced technology, and capital. Furthermore, the state also has special programs that invest in remote and isolated areas—for instance, by building rural roads, houses, and clean water supply systems, and by providing medical assistance, books, and notebooks for education. As a consequence, the living conditions of the poor have notably improved, poverty rates have decreased from 32 percent to 17.6 percent, and there are no longer households in hunger. The economic gap between areas and localities is relatively small. We are striving to build a society without poor people.

In order to overcome and prevent an increasing gap between the rich and the poor, we have successfully implemented hunger and poverty eradication policies at both national and local levels.

Although the quality of material life in general is still not very high, the government has paid much attention to building a better spiritual life for the community. Cultural institutions have been supported. Democratic regulations at the grass-roots level continually build up the people's role. Cultural villages are created that are self-managed in accordance with village traditions. The purpose of all this is to preserve national identity. We do not want our people and their culture to be eroded by the process of international integration.

We believe that the above-mentioned issues are simultaneously our solutions, our achievements, and our lessons during the international economic integration process that is essential for our development.

Further Thoughts
A Brief History of Vietnam

Yongseok Seo

The First Wave of Global Pressure:
Sinicization and Indianization

Vietnamese history is a story of the struggle to develop a sense of identity and to maintain it against external pressures. The first major external pressure to Vietnam's existence was the conquest of the Red River Delta by Han China (206 BC–AD 220) in the first century BC. Vietnam was under Chinese control for the next millennium. The Vietnamese response to Chinese rule was twofold. On the one hand, they developed a national consciousness. On the other hand, they accepted various Chinese cultural practices such as political ideologies, administrative styles, and Chinese written characters. Despite this extensive accommodation and borrowing, "there has been a significant tension between the claims of non-Chinese elements in Vietnamese life and the claims of the Chinese elements" throughout Vietnamese history (Osborne, *Southeast Asia: An Introductory History*, 31). Paradoxically, the Sinicization process created a national consciousness in Vietnam that enabled the Vietnamese to resist Chinese political domination in later centuries. By the end of the Tang dynasty in China, there was frequent resistance by a strong anti-Chinese group in Vietnam that overthrew Chinese rule in 939. Yet Chinese cultural practices persisted.

Another wave of global force hit the southern part of Vietnam during the first millennium. The Sinicization of Vietnam was limited to the Red River Delta in the north. Maritime trade with India flourished in the south, and an array of goods and ideas, such as Hinduism and Buddhism, reached Vietnam during this period. Anthropologists generally agree that the Chams, who occupied the middle part of Vietnam, are ethnically and culturally different from the Viets in the north. The Chams accommodated Indian culture and created their own civilization. As a result, while present-day Vietnam is politically one state, culturally it is divided into two areas, the northern area above eighteen degrees latitude belonging to the Chinese cultural sphere and the southern area belonging to the Indian cultural sphere.

Pressure from the West and French Colonial Rule: Westernization

A new type of external pressure reached Vietnam in the seventeenth century, when European missionaries and merchants became important factors in Vietnamese life and politics. Although foreign merchants and missionaries arrived by the early sixteenth century, neither had much impact on Vietnam before the seventeenth century. (The best known of the early missionaries was Alexandre de Rhodes, a French Jesuit who is credited with perfecting a romanized system of writing the Vietnamese language *[quoc ngu]*.) Western influence became a more serious problem for Vietnam during the Nguyen dynasty (1802–1945) as European imperialists sought to exploit and secure colonies in Asia and other parts of the non-Western world.

From the middle part of the nineteenth century, Vietnam faced a formidable challenge from French colonialists. Between 1858 and 1873, the French conquered Vietnam and divided it into three parts: Cochin China, Annam, and Tonkin. France colonized Cochin China in 1867, while Annam and Tonkin were added to France's protectorate in 1883. From the beginning of colonial intrusion the Vietnamese struggled for their independence against French colonialism. French colonial rule was, for the most part, politically repressive and economically exploitative. In the political sphere, a modern French administrative system was introduced to run the new colony. The Vietnamese people had no part in it, as they were limited to the lower levels of the bureaucracy. Economically, the French exploited Vietnam for rice and rubber. Most of the rice produced in the Mekong Delta was exported to Europe in spite of serious food shortages in Vietnam.

In the midst of this harsh French colonial rule, the notion of nationalism and the modern nation-state emerged among Vietnamese intellectuals as a response to French colonialism. Many Vietnamese nationalists came from a Western-educated middle class. They involved themselves in study groups, demonstrations, and acts of terrorism with a vision of an independent Vietnam as their goal. Nguyen That Thanh, later known as Ho Chi Minh, was one of them. Like many other East Asian nationalists of the time, Ho was greatly impressed by the Russian Revolution, while also holding mixed values of Confucianism and nationalism. After World War I, when the principle of self-determination swept over the whole of East Asia, nationalist sentiments in Vietnam strengthened even further. Despite all the insurrection and efforts, the Vietnamese nationalist movement failed to gain independence from the French. Given this failure, Vietnamese nationalists like Ho Chi Minh began to realize the need to involve the masses in a successful anti-colonial movement.

After the defeat of Japanese invaders in the Pacific War, the Vietnamese nationalistic communists under Ho quickly seized control in northern Vietnam, but they soon had to confront the returned French colonialists. Finally, Vietnam secured its independence and expelled French colonialists. However, the 1954 Geneva Conference divided Vietnam, with Ho Chi Minh's communist government ruling the north and Ngo Dinh Diem's regime, supported by the United States, ruling the south. Another two decades of bitter conflict ensued before Vietnam was unified as an independent nation. After a short period of recovery from the horrors of protracted war, in 1986 the Vietnamese government commenced an omnidirectional reform program known as the "Doi Moi." It aimed at "stepping in the general development trend and the process of gradual globalization and regionalization" (see www.vietnamembassy-usa.org/learn/history .php3). By the mid-1990s Vietnam was ready to reclaim its status as a major player in Southeast Asia.

CHAPTER 22

East Asian Response to the Globalization of Culture

Perceptional Change and Cultural Policy

YONGSEOK SEO

This chapter focuses on East Asia's responses to a particular aspect of globalization, namely the globalization of culture. While that response is manifested in many ways, consideration is given mainly to the cultural policies of national governments.

Changes in East Asian perceptions of culture from the late nineteenth century onward will first be examined and compared. How these perceptional changes were articulated in the cultural policies of various government bodies in selected East Asian states is then discussed. At the end of the chapter, the effectiveness and durability of state subsidization of culture and other cultural policies is briefly explored. See Sohail Inayatullah's Further Thoughts, "Asian Values and Generational Challenges to Confucian Norms," on page 329.

East Asian Understanding of Culture in the Age of Modernization

Culture has been used to denote various concepts. In general, scholars divide the notion of culture into either a broad or a narrow sense. In the broad sense, culture is defined as a "patterned way of life," which includes shared social practices such as language, family norms, ethics, religious practices, institutions, and manners.[1] The narrow sense of culture usually refers to "the expression of internal emotion and aesthetic expression of mind or thoughts." Culture in the narrow sense often is what is called "art" in that it refers to creative products that stimulate and entertain humans. The narrow sense thus includes both what is called "low" (or popular) culture and "high" culture.

Culture in both meanings is not static. It develops through interaction with other cultures. Most of the aspects of any single culture may have a long history of many hundreds to thousands of years prior to their incorporation into any specific culture. As Tyler Cowen notes,

If we consider the book, paper comes from the Chinese, the Western alphabet comes from the Phoenicians, the page numbers come from the Arabs and ultimately the Indians, and printing has a heritage through Gutenberg, a German, as well as through the Chinese and Koreans. The core manuscripts of antiquity were preserved by Islamic civilization and, to a lesser extent, by Irish monks.[2]

East Asia also developed its own civilization through frequent cultural exchanges with the outside world. China played an important role and had many opportunities to interact with foreign civilizations. Land and sea routes (particularly the Silk Roads) made great contributions to the development of world culture by facilitating interchange between East and West. Through these trade routes, ancient Chinese culture was introduced to the Western world. Likewise, the religious and philosophical concepts of Islamic and Western civilization were transmitted to East Asia as well as China. As a consequence, East Asia became a region of diversity in which each country has its own highly hybridized culture: a combination of Buddhism, Hinduism, Confucianism, Islam, Christianity, and local traditions.[3] If the notion of globalization is equated with hybridization rather than homogenization, then East Asia is a much more globalized region than Europe or America, where the Christian tradition is predominant.

The Wave of "Civilization and Enlightenment"

The process of cultural exchange in the premodern era was reciprocal, and the diffusion of foreign culture in society was slow and steady in terms of intensity and speed. Thus East Asians had enough time to accommodate and modify foreign culture in accord with their needs and local traditions. However, ever since the Industrial Revolution, the development of modern transportation and communication such as steamships, railroads, and the telegraph brought a great increase in interaction among people and countries. More significantly, the rise of Western powers and their encroachment into East Asia in the late nineteenth century brought dramatic changes in the East Asian perception of culture.

After a series of unequal treaties with the West and the threat of colonization, East Asian leaders began to believe that assimilation into Western culture was an urgent task. In order to achieve this goal, East Asia had to adopt Western values, ideologies, and institutions while abandoning local traditions, in order to be accepted by the Western powers. It was also a period in which the global wave of "civilization and enlightenment" began to permeate East Asia along with Western imperialism, while the notion of "nation" and "national culture" also came into being. East Asian intellectuals and reformists realized that "awakening the nation" and reinvigorating "national culture" was important to unify and mobilize the masses against Western imperialism.[4] They attempted to define the "nation" based on ethnicity and sought to find their own independent national identity. It was in this milieu that a new notion of "national culture" appeared for the first time in East Asia. This phenomenon is well observed in Meiji-era Japan. Tomooka, Kanno, and Kobayashi state,

> The origin of cultural policy in Japan can be traced to the beginning of the modern nation-state in 1868, when the country's new leaders were faced with the problems of assimilating and adapting to Western influence after the Meiji Restoration. Like many other non-Western countries during that period, the Japanese saw Western culture as a reference point for evaluating their own culture. Since Japan was eager to emulate Western modernized countries, the government's industrial policy focused on rapid modernization, and cultural policy was formed and transformed in accordance with this goal. In a sense, the Japanese government's orientation toward culture at that time was based on the goal of promoting national integration and improving the international reputation of the nation.[5]

Nationalistic historians throughout East Asia tried to emphasize their unique national culture and sought to renew their national history based on genealogical charts. This period also observed public campaigns to use local vernacular scripts (e.g., Korean *hangŭl*) and other cultural symbols (national flags).[6] With the exception of Japan, however, East Asian countries' attempts to build a "national culture" in the late nineteenth century evaporated due to colonization. Nonetheless, the sense of "national identity" and "national culture" was preserved by the local nationalists and provided major momentum for national independence movements in many countries in East Asia.

Postcolonial Era and Culture in Establishing Nationhood

Through the long experience of colonialism and the process of Westernization, East Asian societies came to realize that their own traditions had been eliminated, damaged, or distorted. Hence the recovery of traditions and the establishment of national culture with modernization became a nationwide business in many East Asian countries in the postcolonial era. With this recognition, the governments in East Asia attempted to renew their cultural heritage and to rediscover national culture. Accordingly, state influence and intervention into cultural domains was overwhelming. Governments made conscious efforts to support the revitalization, preservation, and strengthening of national culture and identity.

At the ministerial level, many East Asian states established a Ministry of Culture or similar institution in order to accomplish the goal of national unity. In South Korea, for instance, the Office of Cultural Assets was installed under the auspices of the Ministry of Culture, which designates selected persons as intangible cultural assets because of their contribution to the maintenance of national culture. Government support for both tangible and intangible cultural assets, in many cases, was in the form of patronage. In addition, a considerable amount of money was spent in support of museums, national parks, libraries, national archives, tangible and intangible cultural properties, and protection of the national environment and endangered species.[7]

Several countries in Southeast Asia show a similar pattern to that of Korea. Jennifer Lindsay writes,

> The new postcolonial Southeast Asian nations with government portfolios specifically set up for culture indicates the importance placed on culture in establishing nationhood. From the outset, culture was identified as a state-directed tool of national identity. In Indonesia, where the debate about cultural heritage and national identity had been raging long before independence, the government department for culture was established immediately in 1945. In Malaysia, the first full agency for culture at the ministerial level was established in 1964, seven years after independence. . . . In the case of Thailand, the only non-postcolonial nation among those discussed here, the government agency for culture (Department of Fine Arts) was established in 1933 as part of the new system when the absolute monarchy was overthrown, with an emphasis not on the creation of something new, but on turning into public property a cultural heritage that was previously attached to the institution of the monarchy. In 1942, this department became the Bureau for Culture, and was upgraded to a ministry in 1952.[8]

Post-colonial Chinese cultural policy is also primarily based on the perception of "cultural heritage" and "national culture." As Mao Zedong pointed out, "China's long feudal society created a splendid ancient Culture. In inheriting the Culture, discarding the feudalist dross and selecting the democratic essential is the necessary condition for developing a new national Culture and improving the nation's self-confidence."[9]

Unlike other East Asian neighboring states, government intervention in culture in postwar Japan was relatively weak. Tomooka, Kanno, and Kobayashi interpret the reason in the following way.

> Cultural policy in the postwar period was slow to develop, in part because of the history of government control of the arts and culture that began in the Meiji period and intensified during the years prior to World War II and during the war itself. Performing arts and the media were regulated and cultural activities were used to mobilize the public for the war effort. Since the Japanese term for

cultural policy before 1945 could be interpreted as "control of culture," the use of the term was avoided . . . and it was difficult to support the arts on a national level.[10]

In regard to the foreign cultural influx, East Asian governments have attempted to "control the types of channels and types of content that enter and leave their territory."[11] Nonetheless, each East Asian government has managed the influx differently depending on the origin of the culture and has selectively controlled it within the scope that it does not undermine the political and social stability of the nation. In sum, the basic direction of East Asian cultural policy in the postcolonial era was based on the notion of "revitalizing cultural heritages" and "rebuilding national culture and identity." As a result, the cultural policies of East Asia reflected these basic directions systematically under the process of establishing nationhood. East Asian governments made great effort to promote, preserve, and protect the cultural values and assets of the nation, while also attempting tightly to manage foreign cultural influx. These two basic directions of cultural policy continued up until the late 1980s.

The Global Tsunami of "Neoliberal Capitalism"

Since the late 1980s, East Asian perceptions of culture have begun to shift once again and have been greatly influenced by the new global wave of neoliberalism.[12] Neoliberalism has so profoundly influenced East Asia that the notion has expanded into all aspects of society. Adapting to globalization has become the primary direction of all areas of governmental policy.

In the area of culture, the new digital technology and the revolution of communication devices "has made cultural exchanges continuous at a planetary level with unprecedented rapidity and amplitude."[13] One conspicuous feature under these circumstances in the cultural domain is the commercialization of culture and the emergence of a cultural industry.[14] Since the early 1990s, cultural industries worldwide have grown rapidly and cultural markets are becoming increasingly global, with the development of new information technologies and the diffusion of worldwide deregulatory policies.[15] These new environments caused drastic change in the perception of culture, and East Asian governments began to undertake very different cultural policies based on new notions and technologies. Those East Asian governments that earlier opted for the notion of "nationhood," which has aimed to revitalize national cultures, shifted to the new approach. In this basic response toward the new wave of globalization, culture came to be acknowledged as a consumer commodity. More significantly, cultural policies started to relate closely to industrial policies. Consequently, there began to be a focus on how to protect domestic cultural markets and industries from powerful foreign cultural products, as well as on how to increase the competitiveness of domestic cultural products and industries.[16] Culture, which once was treated as a "state-directed tool of national identity," now has reached the point of being considered an essential component of the economy.

South Korea is on the cutting edge of this recognition. There, various support plans for the development of domestic cultural products and industries began to be proposed at the institutional level in the mid-1990s. The Cultural Industry Bureau was created in 1994 within the Ministry of Culture and Sports. The South Korean government began to recognize that "the cultural industry is an important sector providing an infrastructure to the society and therefore care should be taken at the government level."[17] According to the *White Paper on Cultural Policies* (2001), released by the Ministry of Culture and Tourism,[18] several policy initiatives (mainly regarding the features of the cultural industry and the necessity of policy intervention) have repeatedly been proposed. This includes "the establishment of an organization to manage and coordinate the cultural industry, the necessity of gaining support for the cultural industry through public funding, a policy catering to the new-media industry, and the development of domestic culture."[19]

The emergence of the Hanryu (lit. "Korean Wave") phenomenon[20] in the late 1990s further encouraged the South Korean government to become involved in the cultural sector via a commercial approach. The Korean National Tourism Organization attempts to use Hanryu as a marketing strategy in tourism by trying to "promote active and continuous marketing to maintain Hanryu fever."[21] According to a high government official in the Korea Culture and Contents Agency (KOCCA) under the Ministry of Culture and Tourism, in order to "secure well-qualified personnel in related fields and educating them to be professionals, KOCCA has drawn up a comprehensive plan to cultivate specialized human resources, and has put it into action to produce experts with creativity and practical skills, which is the core infrastructure of the culture content industry." He also said that "within 10 years, the cultural content industry will grow to be the leading industry of the country."[22] South Korean President Roh Moo-hyun recently announced that "his administration would exert efforts to turn the nation into one of the world's five major cultural industry powers within five years." Moreover, Roh asserted, "I will also present various policies and institutional devices to promote the arts and Korea's traditional culture, which form the basis of cultural industries."[23]

Elsewhere in East Asia, in spite of its open-door policy since the late 1970s, Chinese communist leaders have persistently stressed the concept of a unique Chinese socialistic spiritual culture. They believe that "popular culture under the socialist market system should always be in the faithful service of the people, and that it should not follow the way of the capitalistic popular culture in the

Western countries."[24] Western popular culture (American culture in particular) is considered the evil side of capitalism and Westernization.

The new global trend of neoliberal capitalism and the commercialization of culture, however, have considerably changed the perception of Chinese party leaders. Chinese premier Wen Jiabao stated that "the people's intellectual and cultural needs are constantly increasing along with the economic development and social progress in China, so the government must attach greater importance to cultural development." Wen also said in his report on the work of the government, delivered at the opening of the Second Session of the Tenth National People's Congress, "[W]e should promote the reform of the system and innovation of the mechanisms of the cultural industry, give more support to non-profit cultural undertakings, and improve our policy for the cultural industry to give a greater role to the market and ensure the simultaneous development of cultural undertakings and the cultural industry."[25]

Given this acknowledgment, the Chinese government rigorously encourages the domestic development of cultural commodities by formulating a development strategy at the national level. The government, for instance, "encouraged the formation of large corporate groups in the print media sector by merging several newspapers in 1998 in order to prepare for the challenge of the foreign media after China's entry into the WTO. Similar strategies were adopted in the publishing, movie, television, and fast food industries during 1998 and 1999."[26] According to the *Beijing Times,* "[F]or the first time, the Chinese government included the cultural industry in its five-year economic and social development plan which outlined a clear strategy for the boosting of the industry."[27] Newspapers also offered comments by an expert in the Chinese cultural industry sector: "China's emerging cultural industry should be growing more rapidly in order to meet the challenges arising from China's access to the World Trade Organization."[28] In sum, the cultural policy of China in the late 1990s became closely related to economic rationale and national industry.

The Singapore government seems to have had the earliest and the most aggressive plan for development of the cultural industry since the early 1990s. The study of the cultural policy of Singapore by Kwok and Low shows how Singaporean policy makers understand cultural globalization and perceive it economically. They state,

> One key to understanding the thrust of cultural policy in the 1990s is that policy makers had by then come to appreciate the economic value of the arts. . . . For example, under the leadership of the Ministry of Trade and Industry, a number of key agencies, namely the Economic Development Board, the Trade and Industry Board, and the Singapore Tourism Board "facilitate the introduction of galleries, dealers, and value-added, export-ready products and productions into

the business community, publicizing events at home and abroad, structuring tax incentives and promoting investment" (*Strait Times*, April 1, 1998). . . . In a word, Singapore's cultural policy has everything to do with staying on top as a focal node in the late-capitalist world system of the new millennium.[29]

The Malaysian government also recognizes that culture is important to economic development. The Ministry of Culture, Arts and Tourism was established to make the cultural industry one of the nation's pivotal industries. The Malaysian government made a special effort to promote the film industry by passing the National Film Policy in 1997. According to the Malaysian Ministry of Culture, "[I]t aims to raise the standard of Malaysian films in terms of their aesthetics, quality and the industry to international standards. Among its objectives is to create the catalyst for the development of the Malaysian film industry."[30]

As far as the foreign influx of culture is concerned, East Asian governments have taken different approaches and strategies into account, notably the readiness of the market and industry, origin of cultural products, and potential impact on political and social systems.[31] East Asian states used to intervene heavily against the influx of certain foreign cultural products by controlling the degree and speed of the cultural market opening. This approach is closely related to protectionism. While regulations and controls in certain areas were put into place in order to protect vulnerable domestic industries, at the same time states focused on how to increase the competitiveness of domestic industries.[32] This approach is a typical industrial policy for embryonic industrial development that has been utilized by many East Asian countries. Some East Asian governments are still applying such policies in the area of culture.

However, this protectionist approach is also being challenged by the wind of neoliberal globalization.[33] The process of globalization is significantly alleviating and eliminating systematic governmental regulations on the circulation of capital, goods, services, and cultures. The series of international negotiations on free trade agreements and the rapid development of information and communications technology (which has radically lessened transaction costs) are two driving forces that have facilitated this process. At the last round of General Agreement on Tariffs and Trade (GATT) talks[34] and at the Doha development agenda of the World Trade Organization (WTO) in 2001, it was discussed whether cultural products should be included in free trade agreements.[35] This suggests that the commercialization of culture and the free flow of cultural products has become a hot issue in international trade negotiations. At the same time, the development of new digital communications technology and broadcasting of mass media enables the rapid increase of the transmission of cultural products (computer software and games, electronic books and magazines, and digital films and music files) across borders through computer networks. With respect to the process, "the capacity of national governments to control the dissemination of culture within their borders had been greatly diminished."[36] These are two major global issues that continue to press East Asian states to open their markets and societies to the world.

A Lesson from Japanese Cultural Policy?

Unlike other East Asian countries, Japan does not have any specific cultural policy or cultural industrial policy at an institutional level to deal with cultural globalization or the production of popular culture. As Tomooka, Kanno, and Kobayashi have observed, "Japanese cultural policies are still focused on high culture and have not supported popular culture and the culture industries seriously."[37] Nevertheless, Japanese pop culture and cultural products have been vigorously produced and exported to overseas markets.[38] Japanese cultural products have not only exercised dominant power in Asia, but "Japanese cultural products are now appreciated even by major Western countries."[39] Japanese cartoons are broadcasted in European countries such as Italy and France and in the United States. Japanese TV animation and its derivative products are prevalent all over the world. Douglas McGray describes the influence of Japanese cultural power as follows: "Japan's global cultural influence has quietly grown. From pop music to consumer electronics, architecture to fashion, and animation to cuisine, Japan looks more like a cultural superpower today than it did in the 1980s, when it was an economic one."[40]

Japanese cultural products and cultural industry are among the most recognizable in the global cultural market in terms of quality and quantity. Nonetheless, the government has not led the development of the Japanese cultural industry. More significantly, the competitiveness of Japanese cultural products in the global market has not been achieved by government intervention. Rather, it was developed by the private sector and attained its global competitiveness without government guidance. Tomooka, Kanno, and Kobayashi describe this phenomenon as "ironic" in that "Japanese popular culture, which has been neglected by government policymakers, has been produced and exported very successfully by Japanese cultural industries (producers)." It is, however, too parsimonious to refer to the phenomenon as "ironic." Questions then arise as to why the Japanese government did not (or could not) become involved in the cultural industry, unlike other industrial sectors. Why there have been different orientations to the cultural industry in Japan is a complex question that needs a full-scale study. Nonetheless, it might be assumed that the Japanese policy makers recognized that those kinds of efforts would be in vain. They probably concluded that state intervention in culture would be doubtful in terms of effectiveness and durability because of the unique nature of popular culture. If this is so, are there certain kinds of unique market networks or structures that are deeply embedded in cultural markets that are quite different from those of other conventional industrial sectors? The Japanese case may provide a warning to those East Asian governments who are actively involved in promoting their cultural industry.

Concluding Thoughts

East Asia developed its own civilization through frequent cultural exchanges with the outside world. Among other things, the development of new technology played an important role in this process. Following the Meiji Restoration in 1868, East Asia was obsessed for nearly a century with the notion that its "national culture" must be kept pure and protected from foreign contamination, no matter the cost. Just as the global wave of "civilization and enlightenment" did in the late nineteenth century, the new global wave of "neoliberal capitalism" in the late twentieth century drastically changed the perception of culture so that many East Asian states began to perceive it in terms of the capitalist world system: the commercialization of culture. Just as the inventions of paper, the compass, the printing press, and the galleon greatly contributed to cultural exchange among regions in the premodern era, and just as the steamship, railroad, and electronic communications devices had done so in the early modern era, so have the new digital technologies and the revolution of communications devices caused a radical shift in the East Asian perception of culture. Global cultures and new technologies have constantly changed East Asian perceptions of culture, and the perceptional change has often been expressed through cultural policies. As a result, the impetuses of East Asian cultural policies since the late nineteenth century have been deeply rooted in then-contemporary global ideology, value, and technologies.

From the viewpoint of fairness and globalization, cultural exchange between East and West was reciprocal at least up until the mid-nineteenth century. Cultural globalization since the Meiji Restoration has been largely from West to East and thus is an unfair, abnormal, and quite unusual phenomenon when we reflect on the long history of humankind.

If we believe that cultural globalization should not be mere homogenization and the domination of one culture over all others, then the West has not fully enjoyed the benefits of globalization, while East Asia has savored the diverse choices of the global cultural menu.

An Indian friend studying in Hawaiʻi recently said something very interesting. According to him, there seem to be more people interested in yoga in the United States than in India. It is quite true that some Americans have learned to enjoy Asian culture. As the aesthetic values, artistic creativity, and cultural output of Asia rise rapidly, Japanese animation, Chinese and Indian cinema, and

Korean soap operas and electronic games, among many other things, are becoming popular in the United States. In this respect, perhaps the globalization of culture has just begun in the United States (or has returned to past patterns of reciprocity). This would be an important step toward the fair and genuine globalization of culture. The resurgence of Asian culture will further this process. The future of cultural globalization, therefore, should be fairer, reciprocal, and hybridized, rather than unfair, one way, and homogenized. This certainly is our preferred future.

FURTHER THOUGHTS

Asian Values and Generational Challenges to Confucian Norms

Sohail Inayatullah

AT ONE TIME, "Asian values" meant a concern for a slower time, a concern for spiritual factors, a concern for community. "Asian values" were thus trumpeted as that which was nonnegotiable in economic development. Indeed, with the rise of Japan, there was interest in seeing if there was an Asian ethic (similar to the "Protestant ethic" in the West) that could explain Far Eastern capitalism. But while there is an economic dimension to Asian values, generally "Asian-ness" is seen as existing in counterpoint to the secularism, crass commercialization, and sexualization of the West.

However, in recent times, Asian values have also been used as a defense for all sorts of human rights abuses. Asian values have moved from being an ethical framework for day-to-day behavior to becoming a political instrument used against the West and indeed against Asia itself. Former Prime Minister Mahathir of Malaysia, for example, played the Asian values card in his brutal sacking of former Deputy Prime Minister Anwar Ibrahim. Mahathir claimed that Ibrahim had to be stripped of his position because he was allegedly a homosexual.

To protect his own local capitalism cronies, Mahathir again evoked Asian values, that is, "we must protect our own." And yet while billionaires were protected from the Asian financial crisis, small shopkeepers were not. The Association of Southeast Asian Nation's (ASEAN) defense of Burma also has been based on "Asian values." (ASEAN criticized Burma's human rights record in the summer of 2003 in one of the organization's rare moments of boldness.) Asians are different and thus have different politics.

While there is certainly some truth to cultural differences focusing on a slower time and long-term relationship building, destruction of the environment, injustice toward the poor, and torture of unpopular individuals (to mention a few actions committed in the name of Asian values) should not and cannot be tolerated.

We should not be surprised by the hijacking of Asian values. While once it meant a call to civilizational dialogue, when few weapons were available for Asian leaders (with a desire to be prime minister for life), Asian values have since become the cynical tool of choice. The degradation of civilizational dialogue to mere West versus non-West politics has a number of ramifications. First, Asian values themselves are not questioned, but are seen as a priori instead of situational and evolutionary responses to the human condition. This does not mean that they are not universal, but that their universality must be seen in a historical context. Second, those who in fact live Asian values are denigrated as their framework is politicized, used as a way to attack others instead of as a guiding ethical framework, much as the way bin Laden and others have hijacked Islam. Third, once politicized, the possibility of real dialogue decreases.

Asian Values and Innovation

And it is real dialogue that is necessary in East Asia. For example, East Asian nations have prospered by essentially copying Western products. This strategy of producing Western goods at a lower cost has worked so far, but as Singapore has understood, there are real limits to this. The next phase in development requires innovation, experimentation, and creativity—all values that are not generally associated with the timelessness and feudalism of Asia. While younger East Asians may be quite ready to adopt these values (accepting them as global via music television and the brain-gain returning to home countries after receiving advanced degrees in the United States and the United Kingdom), middle-aged managers have not. The managers have succeeded in the old feudal hierarchical system. This is not a plea totally to tear down the vertical relations that are central to Asian universities, businesses, and government, but rather to keep the notion of "wise elder" while augmenting it with notions of flat, adaptive, learning organizations and communities. Thus the elder stays to provide vision and direction but not to skew economic and social opportunities. The elder essentially knows when it is time to flatten the organization and when it is time to leave.

The appropriation of "Asian values" by economic and political interests ensures that the elite in Asia stay too long and that the needed social transformation to create learning communities and nations does not occur. And that is why efforts to resist the hijacking of Asian values are crucial for Asia to transform from within.

Generational Challenges

Part of this tension is being resolved through age-cohort changes. For example, in research on how youth in Taiwan envision the future, there are marked generational differences. The elder generation's identity was largely created through the split with mainland China and thus sees the world through the strategic discourse with China to be feared. Younger Taiwanese (in their forties) have been concerned with notions of Taiwanese identity and with a stable economy and nation. But the younger age-cohort (teens and twenties) has even more different concerns. First, while they sense the tenuous relationship with China (like being a bird in a cage; like walking a tightrope with the United States on one side and China on the other, they remarked in a visioning workshop), they see the solution as partly achieved through globalization. That is, revolutions in science, technology, and air travel may create one world, where national identity is far less important.

But at the same time, the image of the past as the future also has currency. This is expressed as the desire to return to the farm, engage in organic farming (but of course, Internet connected and mobile-phone linked) and live a quieter and softer life.

Age-cohorts also see basic issues such as sexuality differently. In one focus group of Taiwanese students (mostly male), all but one saw their preferred and likely future of sex as virtual plus robotic (sex with robots who look like humans). Only one preferred sexual relations through marriage. Older age-cohorts are unlikely to know what virtual sex is, much less prefer it. The model they have is sex for life with a marriage partner. Of course, those at the top of the system can take a second wife or engage in sexual relations outside marriage. This is accepted as part of male feudal relations. For the younger generation this is not accepted, while virtual sex might be.

The yet unanswered question is that as young cohorts age, will these new values gained from the globalization of travel, media, and technology hold sway, or will the institutional constraints of Confucian feudalism dominate? This is partly a question of aging but also a central economic question. For East Asia to continue to prosper, it must both retain its Asian-ness and deeply transform it. It must retain respect for the elderly, respect for tradition, and yet also find ways to innovate, to engage in creative destruction. There is no easy answer to this. While Singapore seeks legislative creativity, other East Asian nations are still focused on the old "development" game. Until 9/11, the American system had deep openness, letting the outsider in, and even if the American flag was high, multiculturalism had become part of the discourse. Can Asia follow suit? Will American openness return to America or will "American values" take over that once open country?

Notes

1. Joan Leopold, *Culture in Comparative and Evolutionary Perspective: E. B. Tylor and the Making of Primitive Culture* (Berlin: Dietrich Reimer Verlag, 1980).

2. Tyler Cowen, *In Praise of Capitalism* (Cambridge, Mass.: Harvard University Press, 1998), 6.

3. E.g., South Korea is a typical multi-religion country where there is no predominant religion. According to the Korean National Statistic Office (1999), Koreans identify themselves as Buddhist 26.3 percent, Protestant 18.6 percent, Catholic 7 percent, and other religions 1.3 percent. Source: The Korean National Statistic Office, available at www .nso.go.kr/.

4. See Benedict Anderson, *Imagine Community: Reflections on the Origin and Spread of Nationalism* (London: Verso, 1983); John Fitzgerald, *Awakening China: Politics, Culture, and Class in the Nationalist Revolution* (Stanford, Calif.: Stanford University Press, 1996); Takashi Fujitani, *Splendid Monarchy: Power and Pageantry in Modern Japan* (Berkeley: University of California Press, 1996); and Andre Schmid, *Korea Between Empires: 1895– 1919* (New York: Columbia University Press, 2002).

5. Kuniyuki Tomooka, Sachiko Kanno, and Mari Kobayashi, "Building National Prestige: Japanese Cultural Policy and the Influence of Western Institution," in *Global Culture: Media, Arts, Policy and Globalization,* ed. Diana Crane et al. (London: Routledge, 2002), 49.

6. For instance, "Japanese cultural policies were established in the Meiji era to give 'distinction' to Japanese society by creating cultural symbols that contributed to national prestige." Ibid.

7. Korean Ministry of Culture and Tourism. *White Paper on Cultural Policies* (2001). Available at www.culturelink.or.kr/policy_korea.html.

8. Jennifer Lindsay, "A Drama of Change: Cultural Policy and the Performing Arts in Southeast Asia," in *Global Culture,* ed. Crane et al., 65.

9. Culturelink, available at www.culturelink.or.kr/policy_china.html.

10. Tomooka, Kanno, and Kobayashi, "Building National Prestige," 52.

11. Diana Crane, "Culture and Globalization: Theoretical Models and Emerging Trends," in *Global Culture,* ed. Crane et al., 12.

12. Key to this notion is deregulation, non-intervention, and liberalization.

13. Jean Tardif, "The Hidden Dimensions of Globalization: What is at Stake Geoculturally," ATTAC's (an international movement for democratic control of financial markets and their institutions) International Portal, May 29, 2002. Available at http://attac .org/indexen/index.html.

14. The definitions of "cultural industry" are diverse. For instance, Benjamin Walter understood cultural industry as mass culture, in which reproduction and technical tools destroy the authenticity of the works of art. Benjamin Walter, "The Work of Art in the Age of Mechanical Reproduction," in *Illuminations,* ed. (with intro) Hannah Arendt, trans. Harry Zohn (New York: Schocken Books, 1968). At present, "it is generally agreed that this term applies to those industries that combine the creation, production and commercialization of contents which are intangible and cultural in nature. . . . The notion of cultural industries generally includes printing, publishing and multimedia, audio-visual,

phonographic and cinematographic productions, as well as crafts and design." Quoted in "What Do We Understand by 'Cultural Industries'?" in *Culture, Trade and Globalization: Questions and Answers* (Paris: UNESCO Publishing, 2000), 19. See also D. Thorsby, *Economics and Culture* (Cambridge: Cambridge University Press, 2001).

15. See "What is the Market Structure of Cultural Industries?" in *Culture, Trade and Globalization*, 19.

16. The purpose of industrial policies in general is to protect and foster the growth of industry by providing various means of support. The government (not the market) decides if a certain industry is to devote limited human and capital resources for the growth of the industry. The industrial policies of East Asian countries have their origins in Japanese industrial policy. See Chalmers Johnson, *MITI and the Japanese Miracle: The Growth of Industrial Policy, 1925–1975* (Stanford, Calif.: Stanford University Press, 1982); and Bruce Cumings, "The Origins and Development of the Northeast Asian Political Economy: Industrial Sectors, Product Cycles, and Political Consequences," *International Organization* 38 (Winter 1984): 1–40.

17. Korean Ministry of Culture and Tourism, *White Paper on Cultural Policies*.

18. The Ministry of Culture and Sports was renamed The Ministry of Culture and Tourism in 1998 in the midst of the Asian economic crisis. The ministry is the major department responsible for national cultural policy and for the promotion of culture, arts education, cultural industry, preservation and conservation of cultural heritage, national historic sites and natural treasures, as well as international cultural exchange.

19. Korean Ministry of Culture and Tourism, *White Paper on Cultural Policies*.

20. Since the late 1990s, Korean movies, popular songs, fashion vogues, and particularly Korean soap operas have become increasingly popular in China, Taiwan, Vietnam, Singapore, and even Japan. See Jim Dator and Yongseok Seo, "Korea as the Wave of a Future: The Emerging Dream Society of Icons and Aesthetic Experience," *Journal of Futures Studies* (August 2004): 31–44.

21. "Hanryu Tourist Marketing," available at www.knto.or.kr/eng/hallyu/hallyu.html.

22. Yong-Sung Lee, "KOCCA Expects Cultural Content Industry to Be Leading Business," *The Korea Times*, September 19, 2003, 14.

23. "Roh Vows to Build Korea into Cultural Power," available at www.kois.go.kr/menu/government/newscontent.asp?Number=20030901008.

24. Quoted in Cheng Daixi, "Dazhong Wenhua Tan" (Telling the popular culture), *Qiushi* 96, no. 4, in Kim Yeongku, "The Meandering Chinese Culture Industry: The Beclouded Drift of Publishing and Cinema," *Journal of International and Area Studies* 4.1 (1997): 55–72.

25. "Premier Urges Cultural Development," *People's Daily*, March 5, 2004, available at http://english.people.com.cn/200403/05/eng20040305_136608. shtml.

26. See Yunxiang Yan, "Managed Globalization," in *Many Globalization: Cultural Diversity in the Contemporary World*, ed. Peter L. Berger and Samuel P. Huntington (Oxford: Oxford University Press, 2002), 42.

27. "Experts Discuss Chinese Cultural Industry," *People's Daily*, May 23, 2002, available at http://english.people.com.cn/200205/23/eng20020523_96327.shtml.

28. Ibid.

29. Quoted in Kian-Woon Kwok and Kee-Hong Low, "Cultural Policy and the City-State: Singapore and the 'New Asian Renaissance,'" in *Global Culture,* ed. Crane et al., 152. As the Singapore case shows, cultural policy during the 1990s unfolded in a way that all relevant ministries, departments, and other government bodies were involved in the development of the cultural sector. The multi-ministry collaboration included ministries ranging from culture, commerce, trade, industry, tourism, foreign affairs, and education, to other government agencies responsible for customs, information and communications, as well as the postal service. Once united, the representatives of these various ministries collaborated together in supporting the multi-faceted strategic problems involved in promoting cultural industry.

30. Culturelink, available at www.culturelink.or.kr/policy_malaysia.html.

31. E.g., South Korea has remained closed to the inflow of Japanese popular culture for more than a half century since the establishment of the Republic of Korea in 1948. This is mainly due to Japan's colonization of Korea (1910–1945), which included an attempt to replace the Korean language and Korean culture with that of Japan. The official reason for South Korea's ban on Japanese popular culture was "anti-Japanese sentiment," which was still widely prevalent in Korea. The government officials argue that Japanese popular culture would "evoke bitter memories of colonial subjugation and cultural assimilation under Japanese colonial rule" ("KOCCA Expects Cultural Content Industry to Be Leading Business," 14). Another protective measure of South Korean cultural policy is the "screen quota system," which obligates film theaters to set aside a certain amount of screening time for Korean films. Enacted in 1963, the "screen quota" was originally designed to guarantee the showing of all films produced in South Korea in the context of revitalizing and promoting national culture. Since the mid-1990s, the nature of the screen quota system began to shift to an economic rationale in that the goal of the system would be to protect the local film industry and markets from powerful Hollywood films. The screen quota policy was successful to some degree in that the local film industry was revitalized and has become competitive against Hollywood movies in the local market.

32. Since the beginning of the 1990s, the debate over Japanese popular culture began to shift from historical matters to economic concern. South Korean policy makers have been concerned about powerful Japanese cultural products that would potentially sweep over the whole of the fragile Korean cultural market and industry. The general consensus of the government, local cultural industries, and research institutes is to remain closed to Japanese popular culture until Korea attains a certain level of competitiveness against Japanese cultural products.

33. E.g., the South Korean government faced a strong demand from the US government in the late 1990s to abrogate its screen quota policy. In order to cope with American pressure, the South Korean government attempted to abolish the screen quota system, but it soon faced fierce resistance from local filmmakers. They saw the colossal power of the Hollywood film industry as destroying the fragile Korean film industry. Film directors and actors (some of the most famous artists in Korea) took the most extreme forms of action, such as shaving their heads. The debate over whether to abrogate the screen quota is ongoing, even inciting sharp confrontation between the Ministry of Culture and Tourism and the Ministry of Foreign Affairs and Trade. While the latter argues that opening

the domestic films market is an inevitable global trend, the former insists that the screen quota must be maintained in order to protect the local film industry.

34. The United States, which possesses the foremost popular culture and cultural industries, tried to stop European states from protecting and subsidizing their film industries.

35. E.g., as joining of the WTO reveals, Chinese leaders seem to believe that China is greatly exposed to the outside world and that integration into the global economy is an ineluctable part of a nation's future. Chinese leaders are well aware that protective measures may still be possible in certain cases, but protectionism is a temporary solution to to the issue of cultural globalization. They are deeply concerned that the Chinese cultural industry will be faced with numerous challenges after China's entry into the WTO.

36. Crane, "Culture and Globalization," 12.

37. Tomooka, Kanno, and Kobayashi, "Building National Prestige," 53.

38. Ibid., 60; see also Douglas McGray, "Japan's Gross National Cool," *Foreign Policy* (May/June 2003), 45–54.

39. Koichi Iwabuchi, "From Western Gaze to Global Gaze: Japanese Cultural Presence In Asia," in *Global Culture,* ed. Crane et al., 268.

40. McGray, "Japan's Gross National Cool."

∽ PART 5 ≈

Conclusions

CHAPTER 23

Education, Training, and Research

CHRISTOPHER GRANDY AND DICK PRATT

The authors of this chapter are colleagues in the Public Administration Program at the University of Hawaiʻi, Mānoa. Dick Pratt has been with the program since its inception in the mid-1980s and comes from a background in political science. Chris Grandy has taught in the program for a number of years and was trained as an economist. These differing backgrounds give rise to differing perspectives on many issues in their classes and, as might be imagined, sometimes lead to lively debate. For example, they have differing, though not necessarily incompatible, views on public institutions.

Pratt understands public institutions foremost as arenas in which public-regarding principles compete with various interests to shape, for good or ill, actions that have public authority. He values a competitive market, but sees its limitations. He thinks that public life is valuable in itself and is not just another kind of market activity. Grandy sees public institutions as mechanisms for resolving problems that arise from, or are poorly handled by, markets. He shares the value of competitive markets and the recognition of its limitations. He sees public life as the place where those limitations are dealt with. For Grandy, public authority provides a necessary framework within which private arrangements can promote people's well-being. For Pratt, that framework can often be co-opted for special, as opposed to general, interests. Their perspectives also differ in several respects on the net effects of globalization. Grandy tends to see the positive effects, while Pratt is less enthusiastic, though neither sees the globalization issues as black-and-white.

Introduction

Globalization is a pervasive force for the foreseeable future, and both public administrators and public administration education must adapt and respond to that force. This chapter begins by reviewing some current thinking about the issues that globalization presents to public administration education and training. Next is a proposal for the content of that education, followed by an argument about what should be beneath the provision of content. Finally, the chapter concludes with a pedagogical illustration of what this looks like in practice.

Globalization and Public Administration Education: Some Issues

This section briefly reviews some current thinking about the issues that globalization presents to public administration education as a prelude to the proposals we offer in the next section.

In the early 1990s, Morton Davies and his colleagues conducted an international survey to assess the degree to which public administration education was being changed by the new managerialism that had become a global phenomenon.[1] They surveyed 141 institutions engaged in education and training. While the response rate was only 21 percent, the results were provocative.

The authors found a wide variation in curriculum content, reflecting change, new terms masquerading as change, and insufficient attention to emerging issues. A "managerial revolution" had, in fact, impacted the education and training of many institutions. At the same time, it appeared that fashionable terminology was being used to describe classroom practices that had in fact not changed. They referred to this difference between rhetoric and reality in education and training as an "implementation gap" that might affect the ability of administrators to deal effectively with globalization-related changes.[2] Finally, the authors questioned the degree to which appropriate information technology training, women's perspectives, and the administrative aspects of environmental concerns were finding their way into the cores of curricula.

In 2001 Nick Manning came to somewhat different conclusions with respect to the managerial revolution. A senior public-sector management specialist with the World Bank, Manning's review of the impact of the New Public Management (NPM) in developing countries serves as a useful follow-up to the earlier work of Davies et al. Manning wanted to know whether "in a fashion-prone industry does [NPM] stand out from the other relatively minor twists and turns of public management?"[3] He concluded that NPM has not become the dominant school of management thinking and has not been nearly the cure-all that some of its proponents forecasted. Indeed, he argued that we have been lucky that NPM's sometimes formulaic approach to complex problems has not actually damaged public organizations. Manning did note that NPM succeeded in broadening the range of choices, opening up "interesting, albeit untested, possibilities."[4]

Donald Kettl highlighted the emerging need for indirect management tools as a result of globalization.[5] Kettl, who has written extensively about changes in public administration and public affairs internationally, observes that globalization has meant that more government programs are being offered through nongovernmental partners. This implies the need for indirect management tools. These "indirect tools of government require different management approaches, and those approaches are substantially different from the traditional authority-based models that dominate the study and teaching of public administration."[6] Lester Salamon's large collection of essays underscores these themes and offers a common set of criteria to describe and assess a range of approaches to both direct and indirect government.[7]

Ali Farazmand urges a more comprehensive response to globalization by public administration educators and practitioners.[8] He sees the need for education and training that

> helps engage citizens in the work of public institutions while maintaining a balance between serving the economic interests of national or global corporations and broader public interests;
>
> makes visible the high performance capabilities of public organizations and the failures of the private sphere;
>
> carries a strong public service ethic that is resistant to forms of corruption that might accompany privatization;
>
> does not allow the idea of "citizen" to be replaced by the idea of "consumer";
>
> is more sensitive to the differing forms of administration that may prove successful in diverse cultural and societal contexts; and
>
> acts as a conscience and protector of "global community interests" against inequities and political repression that globalization may spawn or not undo.[9]

How educators provide information can be as important as the content. The familiarity of Marshall McLuhan's phrase "the medium is the message" suggests that we understand this point, but the insight, for a number of reasons, often is ignored in practice. During much of the post–World War II period in the United States, little attention was given to the significance of how to deliver education. That began to change in the 1980s, and today phrases like "designed learning environments," "student-centered learning," "teaching versus learning," and "active learning" are fairly common throughout the educational system.

Sensitivity to the impact of delivery on learning (what we might label the process issues) is less common elsewhere. Often both content and delivery are relatively unchanged over time. In places where content is altered to incorporate new knowledge (perhaps knowledge made available through globalized networks), the way teachers communicate that knowledge to learners remains unchanged.

Yong-duck Jung in this volume (chap. 18) addresses this issue and its significance for responding to factors associated with globalization. He observes that students being prepared for work in public institutions in South Korea still must memorize what is written in textbooks and write down what they are told by lecturers. The type of exams required to enter civil service reinforces this system. Jung observes that this method of learning is incompatible with the kind of critical and innovative thinking necessary for public institutions to effectively function in an era of globalization.

Public Administration Education and Training in a Globalizing World: A Proposal

Given the reality of globalization-induced changes, the role public institutions might play in shaping those changes in socially valuable directions, the need for new institutional forms and the idea of a response to globalization appropriate to a specific social-cultural-institutional setting, and the difficult choices about the most needed education and training, what do people in public roles need to know to be effective in the face of increasing globalization?

Our response to the question comes in two parts. The first part addresses content areas; the second deals with the educational process or orientation to content.

With respect to content, we suggest nine areas of special importance in the face of globalization.

1. *Critical economics.* Though other factors are important in globalization, the pursuit of economic interests and the interpretation of globalization by mainstream economic analysts are central. By "critical economics" we refer to an understanding of the primary tenets of mainstream, contemporary economics, as well as an awareness of the field's assumptions and values (both explicit and implicit) and their limitations.[10] We also emphasize the differences between economics and business as fields of study and practice, in particular in their orientation to the role of the market and their differing focus on societal versus individual outcomes. For example, where the field of business education may focus on how to increase profits by moving production away from the host country, the field of economics would focus on whether the net benefits (benefits less costs) to society are positive or negative as a result.

2. *Organizational capacity.* Globalization is associated with changes in the resources available to public institutions as well as ideas about how public organizations should operate. By "capacity" we refer to knowledge that

is most likely to maintain or create public organizations, especially governmental organizations, capable of balancing the conflicting values of responsiveness, public accountability, and equity. We emphasize learning that contains positive images of public organizations appropriate to local environments as well as knowledge of strategies most likely to give those images reality. For example, opportunities for higher-quality training and education in public-service work, enabled by exposure to international programs, will encourage employees to become constructive change agents in their organizations.

3. *Inter-organizational relations.* Globalization will present more social problems that require coordinated responses among public agencies, both governmental and nongovernmental. Often these problems reach across national boundaries, originating in one nation-state but heavily impacting others. This learning emphasizes how to create effective vertical and horizontal partnerships and responding to the challenges of collaboration while maintaining core organizational functions. For example, environmental nongovernmental organizations (NGOs) concerned with the destruction of unique natural habitats may work with local governments to regulate, or provide new economic incentives that ameliorate, environmental damage from economic activities.

4. *Public-private relations.* In a world reshaped by the dynamics of globalization, public organizations increasingly will find themselves in a variety of working relationships with private organizations. These relations take many forms and are heavily couched in contractual language. Taken together they are called indirect or third-party government.[11] Whatever the specific form of the relationships, if they are to be effective and public regarding, then public officials will require new kinds of knowledge. Such knowledge will include the ability to recognize the incentives and likely outcomes embedded in privatization contracts and generate ideas for realigning incentives in poorly designed contracts to support socially desirable outcomes.

5. *Partnering and citizen empowerment.* Broad citizen involvement will prove critical in maintaining legitimacy if public institutions are to respond appropriately to narrow, but powerful, global economic interests. Such involvement will also give authority to local priorities in relation to global initiatives. This learning focuses on the importance of organizational transparency and citizen participation, as well as the ways in which public organizations can encourage public deliberation and develop citizens as partners. For example, in the environmental arena, international agreements can put transnational corporations on collision courses with

local communities over restrictions on business activities. People in public positions must play a delicate role in sorting through the laws, interests, and values, while legitimating citizen involvement in the future of their community.

6. *Public-service ethics.* Ethics studies the ways in which value conflicts are handled, especially the conflicts among values held by a single individual or group (e.g., the choice between duty to one's workplace or one's family, or between loyalty to the group and the desire for promotion). The focus here is on the value conflicts that globalization's differentiated rewards raise for people in public-service roles and the tools that can be used to help resolve those conflicts in publicly responsible ways. For example, conflicts arise between the desire to protect cultural values from global homogenization and concerns that "local values" may merely cover specific parochial interests.

7. *Futures orientation.* Because globalization is a powerful, far-reaching, and (potentially) long-lasting force, it is in many ways about competing views of the future. Will globalization lead to as yet unimagined prosperity for all? Or will it bring environmental catastrophe and huge gaps in income and wealth? Learning in this area focuses on developing capacity for futures-oriented thinking, a sensitivity to identifying alternative futures in a globalizing world, and how public institutions can help move toward futures seen as desirable from the largest number of perspectives.

8. *Technology for public purposes.* Individuals in public roles can be taught to use information technology in ways that serve several purposes especially significant in a globalizing world. One purpose is to help individual organizations that are moving toward greater connectivity to share information and coordinate actions. Another purpose is to link practitioners to methods in other places that may deal more effectively with common public problems. For example, it is now possible for someone in Mongolia to learn about reform initiatives in Great Britain and to communicate with a knowledgeable official about specifics of the initiative's outcomes. A third, and emerging, purpose for information technology is to link together individuals in different parts of the world in their citizen roles, thereby helping to create a basis for global public interests and global citizenship.

9. *Indigenous issues.* Nowhere does the local/global dichotomy emerge with more force than with respect to the issues of indigenous peoples. Indeed, in a real sense, the effects of globalization define indigenous issues. How do we balance the interests and duties of indigenous and other citizens when responding to globalizing forces? Concerns of temporal and spatial priority arise in conjunction with conflicts among unique cultures, justice, and responses to external influences. Public administrators must become adept

at seeing issues from indigenous eyes and learn to develop and manage processes that resolve conflicts in ways that build communities and a shared sense of citizenship.

Despite its importance, the content of curricula is only part of the education and training challenge; the other part requires ways of thinking that give public administrators the skills to successfully respond to situations their teachers have not yet imagined. This shift of focus to look beneath the content of public administration training and education comes in reaction to what we observe in many education and training settings: after going through an education or training program, individuals find themselves acting in ways that do not support, or even undermine, what they have learned. This pattern may develop especially in places where the organizational and/or professional subcultures emphasize top-down relations, the importance of certainty, and avoiding public differences of opinion. However, as we have shown, individuals in public roles can expect to deal with an increasingly complex, multilayered environment that demands an equally complex outlook to be effective. This means that we need to understand how people obtain this mental complexity and build its attainment into public service education.

There are a number of ways of understanding how human beings shift from more rigid, categorical ways of thinking about the world toward more complex processes capable of sorting through conflicting information, values, and emotions to reach decisions and take action.[12] We find especially helpful the understanding that William Perry, Jr., developed initially to describe how young adults who were facing an increasingly pluralistic world adapted, or failed to adapt, their mental structures to that world.[13]

In Perry's interpretation, all of us have the potential to evolve the way we view our environments—what he referred to as our mental structures. He described this evolution as going from "dualistic thinking" to "committed relativism." Dualistic thinking is an orientation that divides issues into good or bad, right or wrong, true or false and relies heavily on authority figures for The Answer.

"Committed relativism" denotes an orientation that views the world as highly contextual and in which change is continual. This is an outlook that contains a self-understood capacity to make meaning and, in the light of that meaning, to take action. Here, as in dualism, authority and shared meanings provide an important source of knowledge and understanding, but there is no expectation that authority can, or should, know everything or that shared meanings lie beyond question.

Perry places "relativism" between dualism and committed relativism. A person oriented to the world through relativism is neither dualistic nor capable of sorting through different ways of seeing things. As a consequence, a relativist is left to make choices on the basis of what is personally, socially, or politically comfortable or expedient.

For example, it is not difficult to find individuals who embrace globalization as all "Good" or reject it as all "Bad." Others are unable to figure out exactly what they think or how to act: a person may read about child labor in a clothing factory one day and buy an inexpensive shirt imported from that factory the next. Committed relativists will see the same, or more, complexity in the issue, but have the inclination and the tools to come to their own conclusions. Thus a committed relativist may favor this instance of globalization because it provides higher wages but be keenly aware of the possibilities of abuse and the need for some regulations.

An orientation of committed relativism contains two qualities especially important for public administration roles in a globalizing environment. The first quality is the convergence of intellectual and ethical development. These two go together because a committed relativist neither depends upon authority figures to know what to think nor feels overwhelmed by contradiction, ambiguity, or change. Instead, opinions and actions are self-consciously connected to a process for understanding. For example, a committed relativist would neither completely rely on nor dismiss the official interpretation of a cross-border transmission of disease. Instead, one would deliberately go through a process that weighs other relevant information before coming to one's own opinion. It is this process and the taking of personal responsibility that makes the orientation ethical.

We refer to the second quality as "committed openness" (a slight but, we think, useful variation on Perry's committed relativism). In committed openness the meaning of action has changed. Where a dualist finds certainty in what an authority advocates and a relativist relies on familiarity or expediency, committed openness creates a state of tension. The tension lies between the need to make meaning and take action in complex situations and the need, because of that very complexity, to remain open to reconsideration of what is thought and done. Opinions and decisions are taken seriously but are not considered final. They instead are the result of a process the individual "owns" that necessitates both commitment to one's views and openness to changing them.

The movement from dualism to committed openness, as portrayed by Perry, takes place through a series of steps that do not occur simply as part of aging or physical/emotional maturation. It happens because the way the individual sees things (the mental structure) is challenged. A person living in a world of homogeneous values, shared interpretations, and unquestioned authority is not likely to change the way she or he thinks. On the other hand, the same individual living in a more pluralistic, change-oriented world will be challenged. Because of globalization, more and more of the world's population will be confronted with challenges to how they view their world. This is especially true, and socially significant, for those who work in public-service positions. Creating education and training environments that recognize and help individuals to creatively deal with these challenges will help foster movement toward committed openness.

Fair Trade

In this section we illustrate our suggestions for public-service education using an important issue associated with globalization. The phrase "fair trade" gained public prominence during the events surrounding the 1999 World Trade Organization (WTO) protests in Seattle, Washington. The phrase is commonly posed as an alternative to the "free trade" slogan that has played an important part in economists' thinking since the days of Adam Smith and David Ricardo.

We refer to fair trade as a set of "side agreements" to international trade compacts that attempt to ameliorate what some see as the negative consequences of international trade. The most familiar of these agreements are labor, and environmental standards. Labor agreements include measures governing working hours, child labor, and working conditions. Environmental standards such as carbon emissions restrictions also could be made part of such agreements. From an economic perspective, fair trade refers to any terms attached to trade agreements that add conditions or regulations concerning the indirect effects of trade. From a political perspective, "fair trade" denotes rules attached to economic transactions that influence the way the benefits and costs of those transactions are distributed.

A Dualistic View

As an illustration of dualistic thinking about fair trade, consider two opposite positions on the issue. A dualist might argue that any side agreements are inappropriate because they reduce the optimal benefits provided by free trade and market-based economies.[14] This view supports a strongly pro-market orientation and sees little or no role for the public sector, especially in international trade agreements. A person holding this view, not uncommon among the owners or managers of businesses, would object to any international framework and would simply support direct negotiations between firms or countries (bilateral trade negotiation).

Another dualistic view, quite different from the first, sees unregulated free trade leading to unambiguously negative consequences for the world. In this orientation, side agreements are required if trade is to have socially positive outcomes.[15] This was the view of some of those protesting in Seattle. This perspective might also be consistent with those who argue that international trade simply benefits large corporations and makes the rich richer. Indeed, one can imagine that those advocating this view might see international trade as so biased that it would be better to halt all of it so that countries would move toward self-sufficiency.

Both of these examples present extreme positions, which allows us to make another point. We do not argue that extreme positions are necessarily dualist. It is possible to adopt an extreme position after having considered the issues and having constructed good arguments against the alternatives. At the same time, moderate positions are not synonymous with committed openness. A dualist might adopt a "reasonable" position merely because an authority figure has espoused it or it is dominant peer opinion.

We work hard in encouraging students to self-consciously adopt differing perspectives as lenses through which they can interpret complex issues. One way we do this is to link the "economic perspectives" and "political perspectives" learning using a modular format. Using this format we ask students to apply some of the tools of economic and political analysis to a single topic, such as fair trade. At the end of the first of these two modules the participants write a "thought piece." This relatively informal, analytic piece allows them to develop an understanding of the module's major concepts when applied to fair trade.

At the end of the second module, the participants write a more formal paper in two parts. The first part also applies that module's major analytical concepts to fair trade. The second part of the paper asks the writer to think about the similarities and differences in interpretation and possible action steps suggested by the two disciplines. In short, we want them to be skilled in using different perspectives and to be aware of what it means to do this.

We now summarize the process we use to accomplish these goals.

Economic Perspective

We start the economic perspectives module by reminding participants of mainstream economic arguments for free trade. This involves a discussion of "comparative advantage" and the argument that specialization combined with trade can make all countries better off in the specific sense that world production of goods and services rises and each country ultimately gets more of each good to consume.

We then begin to look at the economic concepts that are relevant to criticisms of trade (which also apply to market transactions more generally). For instance, one participant routinely will ask about the potential environmental costs of trade that occur, for example, when a less-developed country specializes in mining activity. This might lead to a conversation about externalities and how economists think about unintended environmental damage that arises from market transactions.

We would point out that a well-accepted role for government in this area involves either imposing emissions taxes on activity that generates pollution or granting subsidies for limiting pollution. We might then discuss the possibility raised by the Coase Theorem for resolving such problems via negotiation and that this might be possible within the bargaining over an international trade agreement. Thus we might find ourselves talking about an approach that looks something like "fair trade." The negotiations over environmental issues may not lead to government-like regulation, but may still involve negotiations over how environmental costs will be borne.

Other questions may focus on labor issues, such as child labor, or even slavery. This could lead to a discussion of market power on the employer's side, the employees' side (unions), or both, and the question of whether existing alternative economic activity in less-developed countries makes some types of child labor desirable. The discussion of slavery also provides the opportunity to emphasize the voluntary nature of market transactions, making the point that by definition slavery is not voluntary for the enslaved. Thus slavery would fall outside the boundaries of the usual positive welfare conclusions of mainstream economics because it violates the fundamental premise of voluntary exchange.

Political Perspective

We ask students to continue thinking about issues raised in the economic perspectives module as they move to the political perspectives module, but now we ask them to apply the conceptual tools of principles, interests, and strategies to examine issues, including fair trade.

We commonly start by noting that political analysis and political action are about how things of importance are distributed in society. We point out that trade is a good place to ask the fundamental political question: who gets what, when, and how?

Within this context we begin by identifying the most organized and influential players involved in the fair trade issue: developed-country corporations, unions, environmentalists, less-developed-country businesses, unions, national governments of various types, the WTO, and so on. We encourage students to understand that all of these players (and others not listed) have particular interests at stake in the fair trade debate. These players also will espouse value-based principles that they adhere to, or at least put forward. Some of them will act strategically, that is, with a considered course of action, as they engage in the debate and as they pursue their interests. We point out the importance, and the difficulty, of separating principles from interests and of identifying strategies that must be concealed in order to be effective.

In considering the environmental standards component of fair trade we might note the interests of some of the parties: higher profits and/or management income for multinational corporations, environmental cleanup for users of natural resources in a developing country, profits and income for developing-country companies, jobs for workers in both developed and developing countries, and so on.

We would then try to identify the various principles put forward by the parties. Multinational corporations might argue for the virtues of free trade, unimpeded by "government bureaucracy." Developing-country companies and unions might argue for the right of open access to developed-country markets and the rights of sovereignty of each country to manage their resources as they see fit. Environmentalists and users of natural resources from developing countries might raise the issue of ecological sustainability and the value of preserving plant and animal species.

In discussing labor issues through the political lens we might contrast the principle of voluntary associations in a labor market put forth by economists with the interest employers have in retaining enough control over the labor force to keep employee costs low. We introduce the idea of "structural coercion" and encourage a discussion of whether a person with no employment options who must accept low wages and poor benefits can no longer be said not to have a voluntary choice.

For each topic students would be encouraged to identify the strategies used by the parties and the likely sources of power. We might point to lobbying, campaign contributions, and efforts to influence rule making as some of the strategies of multinational corporations, thereby implicitly recognizing the power of income and wealth. We might note the use of publicity by environmentalists in appreciation of their power that comes from use of the mass media and the appeal to "universal" interests. And we might note the use of the free-market argument by developing-country companies and unions to gain access to developed-country markets and the power derived from the position of the "underdog."

A Committed-Openness View

We believe this process helps bring our students to an outlook that incorporates the processes associated with committed openness. Of course, there is no single "committed openness" view on fair trade (or, indeed, on any complex issue). People may agree completely or disagree sharply, but we would hope they do so after looking at the issue from a variety of perspectives and engaging the compelling arguments on other sides.

So it is quite possible to find someone coming out of this process dedicated to the position that, suitably structured, free trade agreements are desirable. This person may recognize that economic incentives can lead to environmental degradation or unsafe working conditions. But they may see the imposition of blanket trade conditions as undermining the economic possibilities of poorer countries. The person may believe that many of the environmental and labor-condition issues will resolve themselves as income and wealth are produced through open international trade.

A colleague may disagree, arguing that environmental degradation may be irreversible and must be prevented. The individual may note that the "winners" of free trade agreements in developing countries are a small subset of the local population and that income and wealth inequalities will only become exacerbated in the absence of appropriate side conditions, a development that can undermine the possibilities for open and democratic societies.

The two people defending these views may or may not find resolutions to their disagreements. Yet being openly committed to their positions means that they listen carefully to each other's arguments and attempt to honestly address them from their perspectives. Where appropriate, each may modify their position in light of the arguments put forward by the other or by new information they encounter at a later date.

Conclusion

Factors associated with globalization are having, and are likely to continue to have, profound effects on the size, form, and purpose of public institutions. Whatever those effects, these institutions will play a critical role in determining who benefits and who loses from globalization, both within nations and between them. That is, public institutions will help shape the public consequences of globalization.

How public institutions engage fairness in the face of globalization will depend on a number of factors, some of which are seemingly beyond anyone's control. One of the factors we can control is how we educate and train people in public roles. Globalization will make the work of public administrators more complicated, while at the same time increase the demands for leadership at all levels. Paying careful attention to the content of public-service education, as well as the more subtle but powerful process issues associated with that education, can have large public benefits.

Notes

1. Morton R. Davies, John Greenwood, and Lynton Robins, "Public Administration Education and Training: Globalization or Fragmentation," *International Review of Administrative Sciences* 61.1 (March 1994): 73–78.

2. Ibid., 77.

3. Nick Manning, "The Legacy of the New Public Management in Developing Countries," *International Review of Administrative Sciences* 67 (2001): 297.

4. Ibid., 308.

5. Donald Kettl, *The Global Public Management Revolution: A Report on the Transformation of Governance* (Washington, DC: Brookings Institution Press, 1999).

6. Ibid., 215.

7. Lester Salamon, ed., *The Tools of Government: A Guide to the New Governance* (Oxford: Oxford University Press, 2002).

8. Ali Farazmand, "Globalization and Public Administration," *Public Administration Review* 59.6 (November/December 1999), 509–522.

9. Ibid., 517–519.

10. For an example of work that lends itself to a critical discussion of economics, see Elinor Ostrom, "Collective Action and the Evolution of Social Norms," *Journal of Economic Perspectives* (Summer 2000): 137–158.

11. Salamon, ed., *The Tools of Government.*

12. Jean Piaget, *The Origins of Intelligence in Children* (New York: International University Press, 1952); and Carol Gilligan, *In a Different Voice: Psychological Theory and Women's Development* (Cambridge, Mass.: Harvard University Press, 1982).

13. William Perry, *Forms of Intellectual and Ethical Development in the College Years: A Scheme* (New York: Holt, Rinehart and Winston, 1970).

14. Perhaps as in Adam Chacksfield, "Why We Should Concentrate on Free Trade and Stop Worrying About the Balance of Payments" (1993), available at www.moneyweb.co.uk/essays/politecon/balance.html.

15. Perhaps as in Shay Cullen, "Fair Trade and Social Justice" (1996), available at www.preda.org/fairtrading/ftpapr01.htm.

CHAPTER 24

Conclusion

JIM DATOR, DICK PRATT, AND YONGSEOK SEO

This book was inspired by a "dialogic" conference to which selected international scholars and practitioners were invited, primarily from East Asian countries. Participants were asked to reflect on and discuss to what extent public institutions in East Asia act so that the advantages and disadvantages of globalization, broadly defined, are widely distributed—what we have referred to as "public regarding." We also asked participants to say whether a concept such as "fairness" is used in making such an assessment and whether advantageous and disadvantageous impacts are and can be considered not only concerning people living now, but also for future generations and for the environment.

In the first several chapters of this book we explained what we meant by fairness, globalization, and public institutions. Globalization was agreed to involve more than economic issues. Cultural, political, environmental, security, mobility, popular culture, and many other factors were also important, independent of their strictly economic impact. Similarly, we tried to show that "fairness" should be widely construed and that other concepts, such as "harmony," might be more appropriate in some Asian contexts. Finally, we argued that public institutions mean much more than the formal institutions of government. They include informal social networks, national and international nongovernmental organizations, and many aspects of civil society as well.

Our Conclusions

On the basis of what is contained within the confines of this book, our conclusions would have to be generally negative: with only a few exceptions, we would have to conclude that, no, public institutions in East Asia generally have not played a significant enough role in seeing that the impacts of globalization are fairly distributed among persons living now; that public institutions have not acted seriously enough on behalf of environmental values or concerns; and that

353

public institutions have not been at all concerned about the needs and desires of future generations.

Globalization and Public Institutions

With some exceptions noted below, the evidence in this book is that public institutions in the Asian countries represented here have felt obliged to embrace globalization and to try to find a way to gain their own niches within it, leaving it up to future generations to sort out the environmental and other future impacts. For now, public institutions act as though they are open to new ideas, values, and institutions, either embracing them sincerely in their typically syncretic way or else pretending to accept them until each specific fad of the present passes, as they know, from centuries of experience, it eventually will.

One reason for this might be that Asians (more than Europeans or North Americans) are much more comfortable with globalization. Westerners have basically ruled the world and its current globalization processes for the past several hundred years. As long as Westerners believe they control globalization, and as long as some of them clearly profit from it, most of them are more or less happy with it. It is only when globalization is guided by Others, and on the behalf of Others, that globalization becomes problematic for most Westerners, it seems. Current discussions and reconsiderations of "free trade" and agricultural policy hint at this.

But to most Asians, globalization per se is nothing new—the values and institutions of all of the Asian nations under consideration here have been profoundly influenced by wave after wave of external, often global, forces, virtually since the beginning of human history. While they each have their own culture, they recognize that it is largely syncretic and not primarily indigenous. Certainly at the present time, all Asian values and institutions stand profoundly influenced by "foreign" ideas, beginning with the very concept of "nation" and the ideology of "nationalism" all the way down to today's institutions of governance, economics, education, and pop culture. While each country under consideration has its own unique history, all of them to a large degree have been made what they are by having endlessly had to deal with powerful ideas, values, and institutions from the "outside" as well as from the "inside."

Moreover, unlike the West, the cosmologies of Asia tend to enable Asians to handle apparent contradictions with greater ease. It is possible for many Asian societies to be Buddhist, Confucian, Christian, and animist all at the same time or to adopt European clothing and customs for certain situations while at the same time retaining clothing and customs from their own past for others—clothing and customs that themselves might well have been introduced from abroad at an earlier time.

In this context, globalization—including such specific factors as the New Public Management—is seen as just the most recent in a very long set of waves that rush toward them, lifting them up for a while and sending them off in a different direction from their original heading, but eventually setting them back down in an area of relative calm so that they can integrate the new with the old in ways that do justice to both. This process mystifies many Westerners who are accustomed to determining "right" from "wrong" and "good" from "bad" and then choosing the former while firmly rejecting the latter. Asians are more content with finding a middle way.

At the same time, some of the authors affirmatively embrace globalization as a solution to what they consider to be the dysfunctional, unfair systems left over from the past. They believe that external pressures, while having their own problems, are necessary in order to get rid of undesirable values and institutions still lingering from that past. It is too difficult and too costly to try to transform their societies from within. In this context globalization is a big help.

Finally, we find that the events of September 11, 2001, and America's responses to them have placed the post–World War II understandings of globalization into a context it has not had before. With the events both before and certainly after 9/11, and then following the narrow but more legitimate reelection in 2004 of George W. Bush as president of the United States, that nation has discarded the kind of globalization that marked the world since World War II and has embarked on something quite different.

America was a dominant nation globally after World War II, becoming the single hegemon after the collapse of the Soviet Union and its allies by 1990. While America never engaged in practices clearly contrary to its national interests, and while it did embark on many misguided, and worse, misadventures, it could, in its best moments, be viewed as a leading participant in a globalization process ultimately intended (within the capitalist paradigm) to favor all people in all nations. Americans were always on, and usually in charge, of any committee concerned about the future of the world. But people from many other cultures and classes were on those committees too, and their words and concerns were important, if seldom finally determinative.

When George W. Bush won the disputed American election of 2000, his administration immediately began a process of militarization and unilateralism wholly unprecedented in American history. Both processes, now internally as well as externally applied, characterized their response to 9/11.

Bush of course favors globalization, but it is no longer the neoliberal, mildly free-market kind. Rather it is much more aggressively American-centric. Trade agreements are made between the United States and other nations solely on the basis of whether the nation supports or does not support current American foreign policy and especially military actions. While we have very serious doubts about the utility, much less the morality, of this policy, Bush has interpreted his (re)election as a mandate to pursue his domestic and global ideological visions, and is doing so vigorously. To date there has been nothing within the United States that can stop him, despite substantial efforts. Those who oppose US policy, whether within the United States or abroad, will be ignored when convenient, discredited if persistent, and crushed if possible.

This may result in a long-term American global imperium, all denials of such an intention notwithstanding. We, however, expect that America's heavily indebted economy, increasing dependence on outsiders, and growing internal divisions, on the one hand, and looming environmental crises, emergence of competing supereconomies, and growing global resentment, on the other, make a long American rule unlikely.

Whatever the longer-term prospects, among the many consequences of America's new policies is a revival of narrowly nationalistic perspectives not only at home, but elsewhere as well. Whereas a decade ago scholars could write convincingly of the end of the nation-state system and the emergence of some kind of cooperative global governance system beyond that of the United "Nations," most scholars now see the reemergence of nationalism instead.

And whereas once upon a time some people could dream of a world without war, made so in part by the belief that "freely-trading democracies do not fight," now, with the possible de facto end of free trade, wars between nations seem more likely, even as security forces still are unable to cope with "terrorism" launched by nonstate actors.

Japan appears to be preparing itself to become what is frighteningly said to be "a normal nation" once again. It is very likely to have a full-fledged military able and willing to fight anywhere in the world to advance its national interests and not merely for "national defense." China is no longer the sleeping giant, but is stretching its muscles as a manufacturing and, perhaps soon, agricultural power. Its economic ambitions are charged by a deep desire to never again be anyone's victim.

While currently preoccupied with the quagmire of Iraq, US policies aim to be able to defeat militarily any nation it declares to be an enemy, whether it be North Korea today, China tomorrow, or Russia the day after. War is no longer the last method used to advance policies. It has become the second—to be used immediately if threats fail.

But whatever form it takes—neoliberal and more or less equitable, or imperial under American hegemony—globalization does not seem to be a big deal for Asia. And now they are preparing to deal with the opportunities and threats contained in China's economic, political, and cultural emergence. They have seen it all before, and somehow coped. They expect to muddle through—if not triumph—this time as well.

Fairness and Public Institutions

As Edgar Porter, Sohail Inayatullah, and others have said, it is not clear that "fairness" is the most useful term for most Asian contexts. "Harmony" seems to be better. But even "harmony" is in doubt. In East Asia (at least in Japan and Korea) the term was often used in the phrase "harmony within hierarchy" when national leaders (or heads of organizations) wanted to emphasize national or social unity over individual rights during the recent developmental era. For many young people in East Asia today the term "harmony" implies the sacrifice of individual rights, exploitation through mass mobilization, and something very unfair. It has come to have more negative connotations than positive ones.

In any event, "fairness" always arises within a cultural context, one of which might make "harmony" the goal of fairness.

Consider the issue of who cuts the cake and who takes the first piece that was discussed in chapter 3, "What Is Fairness?" The riddle is based on the assumption of individual selfishness: we expect the person who takes the first piece of cake to choose the bigger piece for herself. In order to "be fair," someone else must cut the cake so each piece is as equal as possible. So even if the chooser wants to be selfish, she can't. And that is fair.

But imagine you are in a culture where deference to others is so important that the first chooser is annoyed, if not insulted, by not being able to take a smaller piece so the next person can have a bigger one. How should the cake-cutter cut then, in order to do so fairly?

Or imagine a world (as some think it was for a very long time) in which one would be embarrassed to have something that others did not have, or to have more than others have, and thus would do everything she or he could to see that scarce things were shared equitably in order to suppress envy and preserve the harmony of the group as a whole.

Moreover, recent comparative research, discussed in chapter 3, suggests that in fact almost no people prefer to act greedily. Even with strangers, but certainly among friends, they want to be able to share—to be fair—and so they often chafe at institutions or situations that require them to act selfishly. Humans are fully capable of selfishness (as they are of killing), but which they do—cooperate or appropriate, kill or embrace—often depends on the social situation they find themselves in. Neoliberalism presumes and rewards selfishness—makes it a profound virtue and mocks altruism as a pathology. Any good human can be made into a neoliberal, given enough time and the proper ration of rewards and punishments, but it seems more likely that, left to their own devices, most people would prefer harmony and identity within some group, whether it be family, community, church, sports club, criminal gang, or corporation, over self-centered individualism.

These general points about fairness are connected to the tensions between economic values and other social values in the post–Cold War era. Economic analysis focuses on whether or not aggregate wealth is increasing. From an economic perspective the issue is largely or exclusively the degree to which total global or national wealth is increasing. If it is increasing, the global or national system is working. If it is not, we are falling back.

The economic lens gives much less attention to how wealth is distributed. To begin with, "politics" and "policy" are matters to which the tools of economic analysis lend themselves less well. More generally, things that are done to distribute wealth more evenly are often seen to be in competition with processes that maximize its creation (i.e., killing the goose that laid the golden egg).

In the post–Cold War environment we are, often unwittingly, witness to a striking variety of experiments in capitalist systems of wealth making. They include the Scandinavian countries, Canada, Japan, China, Korea, Singapore, Thailand, and many others. These experiments give differing priorities and attention to the creation versus the distribution of wealth. Each seeks a somewhat different balance along a continuum that ranges from, at the one end, a "market society" and, at the other, a "social economy."

One way to view the questions raised in this book about fairness, globalization, and public institutions is this: what form of society—market society or social economy—will emerge as dominant, and what network of global rules, also affecting fairness and the public benefits of globalization, will be created by it?

Perhaps the most common expectation is that the American model, moving ever farther in the direction of a market society, will prevail. There are a number of reasons to doubt this. The United States has created great wealth and is justifiably proud of its democratic traditions. At the same time, it is not hard to make the case that America today has done something never before accomplished in human history: created fabulous wealth and widespread abundance amidst impoverished lives.[1] The impoverishment derives from not only the fact that many are excluded, but it is also based in the personal anxiety and stress, environmental dangers, and intergenerational risks created by the relentless pursuit of more of everything, and from the erosion of institutional safety nets dictated by economic efficiency rationales.

The American paradox of impoverished abundance creates a social and political space in which to reconsider American capitalism. Something else helps to create that space: the collapse of the Soviet Union. Its demise removed a comparison that had reinforced and legitimated the priorities of the American form of capitalism. With the Soviet Union no longer available to hide the shortcomings of the American model, self-assessments and comparisons take on a different appearance.

If this view is at least partially correct, then our focus must shift. We must adopt a more globalized perspective on changing institutions, one that gives legitimacy to diverse experiments. How do these emerging social economy experiments strike the balance between wealth's creation versus its distribution, or between the goals of a market society versus those of a social economy? Equally important, how are public institutions used to strike and maintain those balances?

Fairness to the Environment and to Future Generations

Almost none of the authors in this book (except the organizers of the conference itself) seem particularly concerned about environmental problems or about balancing the desires of current generations with those of the environment now and later. Martin Khor is a clear exception.[2] The only others affirmatively to raise the issue in this book are Ivana Milojevic and, to some extent, Sohail Inayatullah.

No one breathed a word of concern for future generations except for (again) Milojevic and Inayatullah, who have been long-time participants in various activities sponsored by the Future Generations Alliance of Kyoto, Japan. As we noted above, there was an episode during the conference when some participants were concerned that if China were to achieve a Western standard of living soon that the environmental impacts would be disastrous.

The Chinese participants immediately said this was not fair! Unless the West was willing to give up its wealth and live far more modestly, China and other developing nations have the right to develop as quickly and as fully as they wish. Everyone seemed to agree with this to the extent that no one stood squarely behind the right of the environment to be saved from devastation.

And no one asked what future generations—in China and elsewhere—might think if the price for enabling China to become wealthy now meant that future generations everywhere would be poor.

We live in a world where few care enough to act on behalf of tomorrow and yet where many proclaim their support for "family values." A strange paradox indeed.

Final Observations

So we are left both hopeful and concerned about the future of the region.

We seem worried about war, global warming, global economic depression, global population aging, and the militarization of space. But most of our respondents seemed convinced that Asian interests will adapt, as they have always done, and perhaps even, in this new environment, prevail.

This may come to pass. Yet we know the grim times East Asians have been through, often as a consequence of an earlier wave of globalization. We do not want that for their—or our—future generations. As we confront the challenges and opportunities of the new manifestations of globalization, we are well advised to keep in mind the linkages between fairness, globalization, and public institutions.

Notes

1. For a detailed example of this perspective, see William Greider, *The Soul of Capitalism* (New York: Simon & Schuster, 2003).

2. Khor did not actually attend the conference, though invited. He did allow us to edit a chapter for inclusion in the volume, and we are grateful.

Bibliography

Abdul Rahman, Yusuf. "Islam in China." Available at www.islamic-world.net/islamic-state /islam_in_china.htm.

Abe Kiyoshi. *Samayoeru Nashonarizumu* (Whither nationalism?). Kyoto: Sekai Shiso-sha, 2001.

Abramson, Mark A., and Therese Morin, eds. *E-Government 2003.* Lanham, Md.: Row-man & Littlefield, 2003.

Afshar, H., and S. Barrientoes, eds. *Women, Globalization and Fragmentation in the Devel-oping World.* London: Macmillan, 1999.

Agh, Attila. "Globalization and Regionalization in Central Europe: Positive and Negative Responses to the Global Challenge." In *Demystifying Globalization,* ed. Colin Hay and David Marsh. London: Macmillan Press, 2000, 127–146.

Akira, Suehiro. "Asian Crisis and Economic and Social Governance: Americanization and Social Governance." In *Developing Economies in the Twenty-First Century: The Challenges of Globalization,* ed. Ippei Yamazawa. Tokyo: Institute of Developing Economies, 2000.

Amin, Samir. *Capitalism in the Age of Globalization: The Management of Contemporary Society.* London: Zed Books, 1997.

Anderson, Benedict. *Imagine Community: Reflections on the Origin and Spread of Nation-alism.* London: Verso, 1983.

Appadurai, Arjun. *Modernity at Large: Cultural Dimensions of Globalization.* Minneapo-lis: University of Minnesota Press, 1996.

Archibugi, Daniele, David Held, and Martin Kohler. *Re-imagining Political Community: Studies in Cosmopolitan Democracy.* Stanford. Calif.: Stanford University Press, 1999.

Argyriades, Demetrios. "Values for Public Service: Lessons Learned from Recent Trends and the Millennium Summit." *International Review of Administrative Sciences* 69.4 (December 2003): 521–533.

Armstrong, Charles K., ed. *Korean Society: Civil Society, Democracy, and the State.* New York: Routledge, 2002.

Arner, Douglas, et al. *International Financial Sector Reform Standard Setting and Infra-structure Development.* New York: Kluwer Law International, 2002.

Arquilla, John, and David Ronfeldt. "A New Epoch—and Spectrum—of Conflict." In *In Athena's Camp: Preparing for Conflict in the Information Age,* ed. J. Arquilla and D. Ronfeldt. Santa Monica, Calif.: RAND, 1997, 1–20.

Asia Development Bank. *Annual Report 1998.* Available at www.adb.org/governance/default.asp.

Bacevich, Andrew J. *American Empire: The Realities and Consequences of US Diplomacy.* Cambridge, Mass.: Harvard University Press, 2002.

Bagong, Alysang, ed. *Alternatives to Globalization: International Conference on Alternatives to Globalization, 7–10 November 1998.* Tagaytay City, Philippines: Development Academy of the Philippines, 1999.

Ban, Carolyn. "The Changing Public Affairs Community." Presidential address at the National Association of Schools of Public Affairs and Administration, Washington DC, October 2001.

Barber, Benjamin. "Clansmen, Consumers and Citizens: Three Takes on Civil Society." In *Civil Society, Democracy, and Civic Renewal,* ed. Robert Fullinwider. New York: Rowman & Littlefield, 1999, 9–29.

———. *A Place for Us: How to Make Society Civil and Democracy Strong.* New York: Hill and Wang, 1998.

———. *Strong Democracy: Participatory Politics for a New Age.* Berkeley: University of California Press, 1984.

Barlett, Christopher A., and Sumantra Ghoshal. *Managing across Borders: The Transitional Solution.* 2d ed. New York: Random House Books, 1998.

Bartkowski, F. *Feminist Utopias.* Lincoln: University of Nebraska Press, 1989.

Bauer, Joanne, and Daniel A. Bell, eds. *The East Asian Challenge for Human Rights.* Cambridge: Cambridge University Press, 1999.

Baumol, William J. *Superfairness.* Cambridge, Mass.: MIT Press, 1986.

Beck, Ulrich. *What Is Globalization?* Malden, Mass.: Blackwell, 2000.

Becker, Theodore, ed. *Quantum Politics: Applying Quantum Theory to Political Phenomena.* Westport, Conn.: Praeger, 1991.

Becker, Theodore, and Christa Daryl Slaton. *The Future of Teledemocracy.* Westport, Conn.: Praeger, 2000.

Beer, Lawrence W., and John M. Maki. *From Imperial Myth to Democracy: Japan's Two Constitutions, 1889–2002.* Boulder: University Press of Colorado, 2002.

Beeson, Mark. "The Political Economy of East Asia at a Time of Crisis: Responses to Globalization." In *Political Economy and the Changing Global Order,* ed. Richard Stubbs and Geoffrey Underhill. Oxford: Oxford University Press, 2000.

Bell, D. *The End of Ideology.* Glencoe, Ill.: Free Press, 1960.

Bello, Walden F., and Anuradha Mittal. *The Future in the Balance: Essays on Globalization and Resistance.* Oakland, Calif.: Food First Books, 2001.

Bendz, Fredrik. "Morality as Fairness" (1997). Available at www.update.uu.se/~fbendz/philo/fairness.htm.

Benyon, John, and David Dunkerley. *Globalization: The Reader.* New York: Routledge, 2000.

Berger, Peter L., and Samuel P. Huntington. *Many Globalizations: Cultural Diversity in the Contemporary World.* Oxford: Oxford University Press, 2002.

Bezold, Clement. *Anticipatory Democracy: People in the Politics of the Future.* New York: Random House, 1978.

————. "Governmental Foresight and Future Generations." In *Co-Creating a Public Philosophy for Future Generations,* ed. Tae-Chang Kim and Jim Dator. Twickenham, UK: Adamantine Press, 1999, 89–97.

Bezold, Clement, et al. *Cyber Democracy 2001: A Global Scan.* Alexandria, Va.: Alternative Futures Associates, 2001.

Bhatta, Gambhir, and Joaquin L. Gonzalez. *Governance Innovations in the Asia-Pacific Region: Trends, Cases and Issues.* Brookfield, Vt.: Ashgate, 1998.

Blau, Peter. *The Dynamics of Bureaucracy.* Chicago: University of Chicago Press, 1963.

Bok, Derek. *The Trouble with Government.* Cambridge, Mass.: Harvard University Press, 2001.

Bonnett, Thomas. W. *Competing in the New Economy: Governance Strategies in the Digital Age.* Washington, DC: National League of Cities, 1997.

"Boom in World Tourism Called Threat to Culture and Ecology." *International Herald Tribune,* July 12, 2000, 2.

Bordo, Michael D., Barry J. Eichengreen, Douglas A. Irwin, and National Bureau of Economic Research. *Is Globalization Today Really Different Than Globalization a Hundred Years Ago?* Cambridge, Mass.: National Bureau of Economic Research, 1999.

Bornstein, David. "A Force Now in the World, Citizens Flex Social Muscle." *New York Times,* July 10, 1999, B7.

Boulding, E. *Building a Global Civil Culture: Education for an Interdependent World.* New York: Teachers College Press, 1988.

————. "Women's Visions of the Future." In *Visions of Desirable Societies,* ed. E. Masini. Oxford: Pergamon Press, 1983, 9–24.

Bowden, Bradley, and Bob Russell. "Benchmarking, Global Best Practice and Production Renorming in the Australian Coal Industry: The Impact of Globalization." In *Globalization and Its Discontents,* ed. Stephen McBride and John Wiseman. New York: St. Martin's Press, 2000, 97–110.

Boyer, Robert, and Daniel Drache, eds. *States against Markets: The Limits of Globalization.* New York: Routledge, 1996.

Brah, A., Mary J. Hickman, and Mairtin Mac an Ghaill. *Global Futures: Migration, Environment, and Globalization.* New York: St. Martin's Press, 1999.

Braithwaite, John, and Peter Drahos. *Global Business Regulation.* Cambridge: Cambridge University Press, 2000.

Brecher, Jeremy, et al. *Globalization from Below: The Power of Solidarity.* Cambridge, Mass.: South End Press, 2000.

Brinkerhoff, Derick W., and Jennifer M. Coston. "Globalizing the Theory and Practice of Public Administration." In *Public Administration in the Global Village,* ed. Garcia-Zamor, Jean Claude, and Renu Khator. Westport, Conn.: Praeger, 1994.

————. "International Development Management in a Globalized World." *Public Administration Review* 59.4 (July 1999): 346–363.

Brook, Timothy, and B. Michael Frolic. *Civil Society in China.* Armonk, N.Y.: M. E. Sharpe, 1997.

Brown, Ronald C. "Employment and Labor Law Considerations in International Human

Resource Management." In *Global Perspectives Human Resource Management.* New York: Prentice-Hall, 1995.

Bryant, William R., Jr. *Quantum Politics: Greening State Legislatures for the New Millennium.* Kalamazoo: Western Michigan University, 1993.

Burchill, S., and A. Linklater. *Theories of International Relations.* New York: St. Martin's Press, 1996.

Burnham, Jack. *Beyond Modern Sculpture: The Effects of Science and Technology on the Sculpture of this Century.* New York: G. Braziller, 1968.

Busch, Andreas. "Unpacking the Globalization Debate: Approaches, Evidence and Data." In *Demystifying Globalization,* ed. Colin Hay and David Marsh. London: Macmillan Press, 2000, 21–48.

Caiden, G., and Y. Kitaguchi. "Promoting Good Governance." *Korean Journal of Policy Studies* 14.1 (1999): 1–13.

Cairns, John, Jr. "Equity, Fairness, and the Development of a Sustainability Ethos." *Ethics in Science and Environmental Politics* 1 (February 2001): 1–7.

Cambodia Development Resource Institute (CDRI). *A Study of the Cambodian Labor Market: Reference to Poverty Reduction, Growth and Adjustment to Crisis.* Working Paper no. 18. Phnom Penh: CDRI, August 2001.

Camerer, Colin. "Strategizing in the Brain." *Science* 300 (June 13, 2003): 1673–1675.

Canto, Victor A., et al. *Foundations of Supply-Side Economics: Theory and Evidence.* New York: Academic Press, 1983.

Carson, Lyn, and Brian Martin. *Random Selection in Politics.* Wesport, Conn.: Praeger, 1999.

Castells, M. *The Rise of the Network Society: The Information Age, Economy, Society, and Culture.* Vol. 1. Malden, Mass.: Blackwell Publishers, 1996.

Central Intelligence Agency. Available at www.cia.gov/cia/publications/factbook/geos/ch.html.

Cerny, Philip G. "Restructuring the Political Arena: Globalization and the Paradoxes of the Competition State." In *Globalization and Its Critics: Perspectives from Political Economy,* ed. Randall D. Germain. London: Macmillian, 2000, 117–138.

Chacksfield, Adam. "Why We Should Concentrate on Free Trade and Stop Worrying about the Balance of Payments" (1993). Available at www.moneyweb.co.uk/essays/politecon/ balance.html.

Chan, Steve, and James R. Scarritt. *Coping with Globalization: Cross-National Patterns in Domestic Governance and Policy Performance.* Portland, Oreg.: F. Cass, 2002.

Chandler, David P. *The History of Cambodia.* Boulder, Colo.: Westview Press, 1998.

———. *The Tragedy of Cambodian History: Politics, War, and Revolution Since 1945.* New Haven, Conn.: Yale University Press, 1991.

Chang, Kenneth. "I.B.M. Creates A Tiny Circuit Out of Carbon." *New York Times,* August 27, 2001, 1.

Chao, Linda, and Ramon H. Myers. *The Divided China Problem: Conflict Avoidance and Resolution.* Hoover Institution Working Papers. Stanford, Calif.: Hoover Institution, 2000.

Chase-Dunn, C., and T. D. Hall. *Rise and Demise: Comparing World-Systems.* Boulder, Colo.: Westview Press, 1997.

Chau, Dao Minh. "Administrative Concepts in Confucianism and Their Influence on Development in Confucian Countries." *Asian Journal of Public Administration* 18.1 (June 1996): 45–69.

Cheng Daixi. "Dazhong Wenhua Tan (Telling the popular culture)." *Qiushi* 96, no. 4, in Kim Yeongku, "The Meandering Chinese Culture Industry: The Beclouded Drift of Publishing and Cinema." *Journal of International and Area Studies* 4.1 (1997): 55–72.

"China Anti-Drug Status is Critical." *Beijing Evening News.* December, 30, 2001, 3.

"China Faces Uphill Battle to Create Jobs." Available at www2.chinadaily.com.cn/en/doc/2003-08/26/content_258354. htm.

China People Statistical Yearbook. 2000.

China Statistical Yearbook. 2000.

CICP. Special Lecture Series. *Democracy and Development.* Phnom Penh, Cambodia, 2002.

CICP/World Bank Institute. "Development Debates and Poverty Reduction: Policy Dialogue." Presented at the National Conference on Sustainable Development, Poverty Reduction and Good Governance in Cambodia, September 20–21, 2001, Phnom Penh, Cambodia.

Citizen's Movement Communication Center. *Directory of Korean NGOs.* Seoul: Citizen's Voice, 2000.

Clammer, John. "In But Not of the World? Japan, Globalization and the 'End of History.'" In *Demystifying Globalization,* ed. Colin Hay and David Marsh. London: Macmillan, 2000, 147–167.

Clinton, William Jefferson. "China's Opportunities, And Ours." *New York Times,* September 24, 2000, section 4, 15.

Coedès, G. *The Indianized States of Southeast Asia.* Ed. Walter F. Vella, trans. Susan Brown Cowing. Honolulu: East-West Center Press, 1968.

Cohen, Joshua. *For Love of Country: Debating the Limits of Patriotism.* Boston: Beacon Press, 1996.

Compton, Robert W. *East Asian Democratization: Impact of Globalization, Culture, and Economy.* Westport, Conn.: Praeger, 2000.

———. *Transforming East Asian Domestic and International Politics: The Impact of Economy and Globalization, The International Political Economy of New Regionalisms.* Burlington, Vt.: Ashgate, 2002.

Coontz, Stephanie. *The Way We Never Were: American Families and the Nostalgia Trap.* New York: Basic Books, 1992. (As adapted in *Harper's Magazine,* October 1992, 13–16.)

Corwin, Edward. *The President: Office and Powers, 1789–1984.* New York: New York University Press, 1984.

Coser, Lewis A. *Masters of Sociological Thought: Ideas in Historical and Social Context.* 2d ed. New York: Harcourt Brace Jovanovich, 1977.

Cowen, Tyler. *In Praise of Capitalism.* Cambridge, Mass.: Harvard University Press, 1998.

Crane, Diana. "Culture and Globalization: Theoretical Models and Emerging Trends." In *Global Culture, Media, Arts, Policy and Globalization,* ed. Crane et al. (London: Routledge, 2002), 1–25.

Crane, Diana, Nobuko Kawashima, and Kenichi Kawasaki. *Global Culture: Media, Arts, Policy, and Globalization*. New York: Routledge, 2002.

Crocker, David. "Civil Society and Transitional Justice," in *Civil Society, Democracy, and Civic Renewal*, ed. Robert Fullinwider. New York: Rowman & Littlefield, 1999, 375–401.

Cullen, Shay. "Fair Trade and Social Justice" (1996). Available at www.preda.org/fairtrading/ftpapr01.htm.

Culturelink. Available at www.culturelink.or.kr/policy_china.html.

Culturelink. Available at www.culturelink.or.kr/policy_malaysia.html.

Cumings, Bruce. "Civil Society in East and West." In *Korean Society: Civil Society, Democracy and the State*, ed. Charles K. Armstrong. New York: Routledge, 2002, 11–35.

———. "The Origins and Development of the Northeast Asian Political Economy: Industrial Sectors, Product Cycles, and Political Consequences." *International Organization* 38 (Winter 1984): 1–40.

Cvetkovich, A., and D. Kellner. *Articulating the Global and the Local*. Boulder, Colo.: Westview Press, 1997.

Dao, Minh Chau. "Administrative Concepts in Confucianism and Their Influence on Development in Confucian Countries." *Asian Journal of Public Administration* 18.1 (June 1996): 45–69.

Dator, James A. "Beyond the Nation-State? Images of the Future of the International Political System." *World Future Society Bulletin* 15.6 (November–December 1981): 5–14.

———. "Beyond the Nation-State: Three Images of Global Governance." *The Futurist* (December 1981): 24.

———. "Bright Future for Democracy?" In *The Future of Democracy in Developing Countries*, ed. Jim Dator et al. Islamabad, Pakistan: National Book Foundation, 1994.

———. "Confessions of a Quark Smeller: The Implications of Quantum Physics for Political Design." Paper presented for a panel chaired by Ted Becker for the American Political Science Convention, Chicago, September 3, 1987.

———. "Quantum Theory and Political Design." In *Changing Lifestyles as Indicators of New and Cultural Values*, ed. Rolf Homann. Zurich: Gottlieb Duttweiler Institute, 1984, 53–65.

———. "When Courts are Overgrown with Grass: Futures of Courts and Law," *Futures* 32.1 (February 2000): 183–197.

Dator, Jim, and Yongseok Seo. "Korea as the Wave of a Future: The Emerging Dream Society of Icons and Aesthetic Experience." *Journal of Futures Studies* (August 2004): 31–44.

Davies, Morton R., John Greenwood, and Lynton Robins. "Public Administration Education and Training: Globalization or Fragmentation." *International Review of Administrative Sciences* 61.1 (March 1994): 73–78.

Davies, S., and N. Guppy. "Globalization and Educational Reforms in Anglo-American Democracies." *Comparative Education Review* 41.4 (1997): 435–460.

Davis, Steve, et al. *Click on Democracy: The Internet's Power to Change Political Apathy into Civic Action*. Boulder, Colo.: Westview, 2002.

de Grazia, Alfred. *Kalos: What Is to Be Done with Our World?* Bombay: Kalos Press, 1973.

DeMartino, George F. *Global Economy, Global Justice: Theoretical Objectives and Policy Alternatives to Neoliberalism*. London: Routledge, 2000.

de San Antonio, Gabriel Quiroga. *A Brief and Truthful Relation of Events in the Kingdom of Cambodia*. Bangkok: White Lotus Co., 1998.

Dickens, William T., and James R. Flynn. "Heritability Estimates versus Large Environmental Effects: The IQ Paradox Resolved." *Psychological Review* 108.2 (2001): 346–369.

Dierckxsens, Wim. *The Limits of Capitalism: An Approach to Globalization without Neoliberalism*. London: Zed Books, 2001.

Donahue, John. "Is Government the Good Guy? After 50 Years of Market Ascendancy, Government May Be Poised to Reclaim Its Role as an Integral and Admirable Part of American Life." Available at www.nytimes.com/2001/12/13/opinion/13DONA .html?todaysheadlines.

Donnelly, Thomas, et al. *Rebuilding America's Defenses: Strategy, Forces and Resources for a New Century*. Washington, DC: The Project for the New American Century, September 2000. Available at www.newamericancentury.org/RebuildingAmericas Defenses.pdf.

Dower, Nigel, and John Williams, eds. *Global Citizenship: A Critical Introduction*. New York: Routledge, 2002.

Doyle, Charles. "The USA PATRIOT Act." Library of Congress, Congressional Research Service, April 18, 2002. Order Code RS 21203. Available at www.fas.org/irp/crs/ RS21203.pdf.

Drewry, G., and C. Chan. "Civil Service Reform in the Peoples Republic of China: Another Mirage of the New Global Paradigm of Public Administration?" *International Review of Administrative Sciences* 67.3 (2001): 461–478.

Dror, Yehezkel. *The Capacity to Govern: A Report to the Club of Rome*. London: Frank Cass, 2001.

D'Souza, Dinesh. "In Praise of American Empire." *Christian Science Monitor,* April 26, 2002. Available at www.csmonitor.com/2002/0426/p11s01-coop.html.

Duncan, John. "The Problematic Modernity of Confucianism: The Question of 'Civil Society' in Choson Dynasty Korea." In *Korean Society: Civil Society, Democracy and the State,* ed. Charles K. Armstrong. New York: Routledge, 2002, 36–56.

Dunn, Douglas. "Economic Justice & Fairness." 1999. Available at www.wordwiz72.com/ econ.html.

Eckert, Carter J., et al., eds. *Korea, Old and New: A History*. Cambridge, Mass.: Harvard University Press, 1990.

Edwards, R., and R. Usher. *Globalisation and Pedagogy: Space, Place and Identity*. London: Routledge, 2000.

Ehrenberg, John. *Civil Society: The Critical History of an Idea*. New York: New York University Press, 1999.

Eisenstein, Elizabeth L. *The Printing Press as an Agent of Change: Communications and Cultural Transformations in Early Modern Europe*. New York: Cambridge University Press, 1979.

Eisler, R. *The Chalice and the Blade: Our History, Our Futures*. San Francisco: Harper & Row, 1987.

―――. "Riane Eisler: Dominator and Partnership Shifts." In *Macrohistory and Macrohistorians: Perspectives on Individual, Social, and Civilizational Change,* ed. J. Galtung and S. Inayatullah. Westport, Conn.: Praeger, 1997, 141–151.

―――. *Sacred Pleasure: Sex, Myth, and the Politics of the Body.* San Francisco: Harper Collins, 1995.

―――. *Tomorrow's Children: A Blueprint for Partnership Education in the 21st Century.* Boulder, Colo.: Westview Press, 2000.

Elazar, Daniel J. *American Federalism: A View from the States.* 3d ed. New York: Harper and Row, 1984.

Elkington, John. *Cannibals with Forks: The Triple Bottom Line of 21st Century Business.* London: New Society Publishers, 1998.

ERIC Digests. "Gender Bias and Fairness." Available at www.ed.gov/databases/ERIC_ Digests/ed328610.html.

Evans, Peter. "The Eclipse of the State? Reflections on Stateness in an Era of Globalization." *World Politics* 50.1 (1997): 62–87.

"Experts Discuss Chinese Cultural Industry," *People's Daily,* May 23, 2002. Available at http://english.people.com.cn/200205/23/eng 20020523_96327.shtml.

FAIR: National Media Watch Group. Available at www.fair.org/whats-fair.html.

Fairbank, John K., Edwin O. Reischauer, and Albert M. Craig. *East Asia: Tradition and Transformation.* Boston: Houghton Mifflin, 1989.

Falk, Richard. *Human Rights Horizons: The Pursuit of Justice in a Globalizing World.* New York: Routledge, 2000.

―――. *Law in an Emerging Global Village: A Post-Westphalian Perspective, Innovation in International Law.* Ardsley, N.Y.: Transnational, 1998.

―――. *Predatory Globalization: A Critique.* Malden, Mass.: Blackwell, 1999.

―――. "The Quest for Humane Governance in an Era of Globalization." In *The Ends of Globalization: Bringing Society Back In,* ed. Don Kalb et al. Oxford: Rowman & Littlefield, 2000, 369–382.

―――, ed. *Religion and Humane Global Governance.* Houndmills, UK: Palgrave, 2001.

Falk, Richard, and Andrew Strauss. "Toward a Global Parliament." *Foreign Affairs* 80.1 (January/February 2001): 212–220.

Farazmand, Ali. "Globalization and Public Administration." *Public Administration Review* 59.6 (November/December 1999): 509–522.

Featherstone, Mike, ed. *Global Culture: Nationalism, Globalization, and Modernity.* London: Sage, 1990.

Feldman, Allan M. "Welfare Economics." In *The New Palgrave, A Dictionary of Economics and the Law,* ed. John Eatwell, Murray Milgate, and Peter Newman. New York: The Stockton Press, 1987, 889–895.

Fingleton, Eamonn. "The Other Deficit." *The Atlantic Monthly,* April 2002, 32–33.

Finney, Ben. "The Prince and the Eunuch." In *Interstellar Migration and the Human Experience,* ed. Ben Finney and Eric Jones. Berkeley: University of California Press, 1985, 196–208.

Fitzgerald, John. *Awakening China: Politics, Culture, and Class in the Nationalist Revolution.* Stanford, Calif.: Stanford University Press, 1996.

Flynn, James R. "Searching for Justice: The Discovery of IQ Gains Over Time." *American Psychologist* 54 (January 1999): 5–20.

Foley, Duncan. "Resource Allocation and the Public Sector." *Yale Economic Essays* 7 (Spring 1967): 45–98.

Foltopoulos, Takis. *Towards an Inclusive Democracy.* New York: Cassell, 1997.

Friedman, Thomas L. *The Lexus and the Olive Tree.* New York: Anchor Books, 2000.

Friedmann, John, and University of British Columbia Institute of Asian Research. *Urban and Regional Governance in the Asia Pacific.* Vancouver: Institute of Asian Research University of British Columbia, 1999.

Fuerth, Leon. "An Air of Empire." *Washington Post,* March 20, 2003, A29.

Fujitani, Takashi. *Splendid Monarchy: Power and Pageantry in Modern Japan.* Berkeley: University of California Press, 1998.

Fujiwara Kiichi. *Senso wo Kioku Suru: Hiroshima, Holokosuto to Genzai* (Memorizing wars: Hiroshima, Holocaust and the present). Tokyo: Kodansha, 2001.

Fukuyama, Francis. *The End of History and the Last Man.* New York: Free Press, 1992.

Fullinwider, Robert K., ed. *Civil Society, Democracy, and Civic Renewal.* Oxford: Rowman & Littlefield Publishers, 1999.

Gallicchio, Marc. "Memory and the Lost Found Relationship between Black Americans and Japan." Paper presented to the Conference on Memory in US-Japan Relations, Honolulu, Hawai'i, March 25–26, 2001.

Garcia-Zamor, Jean-Claude, and Renu Khator. *Public Administration in the Global Village.* Westport, Conn.: Praeger, 1994.

Garreau, Joel. *The Nine Nations of North America.* Boston: Houghton, Mifflin, 1981.

Gastil, John. *By Popular Demand: Revitalizing Representative Democracy through Deliberative Elections.* Berkeley: University of California Press, 2000.

Germain, Randall D. "Globalization in Historical Perspective." In *Globalization and Its Critics: Perspectives from Political Economy,* ed. Randall D. Germain. London: Macmillian, 2000, 67–90.

Ghere, R. "Globalization, Public Service Ethics, and Public Trust: Some Directions for Inquiry." Paper presented at the 63rd National Conference of the ASPA, March 23–26, 2002, Phoenix, Arizona.

Gilligan, Carol. *In a Different Voice: Psychological Theory and Women's Development.* Cambridge, Mass.: Harvard University Press, 1982.

Gills, Barry K. *Globalization and the Politics of Resistance.* New York: St. Martin's Press, 2000.

Gilpin, Robert, and Jean M. Gilpin. *The Challenge of Global Capitalism: The World Economy in the 21st Century.* Princeton, N.J.: Princeton University Press, 2000.

Glenn, Jerome, Theodore Gordon, and Jim Dator. "Closing the Deal: How to Make Organizations Act on Futures Research." *Foresight* 3.3 (June 2001): 177–189.

Gluck, Carol. *Japan's Modern Myths: Ideology in the Late Meiji Period.* Princeton, N.J.: Princeton University Press, 1985.

Golding, Peter, and Phil Harris. *Beyond Cultural Imperialism: Globalization, Communication and the New International Order.* Thousand Oaks, Calif.: Sage Publications, 1997.

Golub, P. "Globalization and its Discontents." *The Donga-Ilbo,* August 16, 2001, A7.

Goodsell, Charles. *In Defense of Bureaucracy.* 2d ed. Chatham, N.J.: Chatham House Publishers, 1985.

Goody, Jack. *The Domestication of the Savage Mind.* New York: Cambridge University Press, 1977.

———. *The Logic of Writing and the Organization of Society.* New York: Cambridge University Press, 1986.

———. *The Power of the Written Tradition.* Washington, DC: Smithsonian Institution Press, 2000.

Gordon, Andrew. *A Modern History of Japan: From Tokugawa Times to the Present.* Oxford: Oxford University Press, 2003.

Gorman, Brian. "The Massachusetts Burma Law." *Villinova Law Review* 45 (2000): 137–154.

Greider, William. *The Soul of Capitalism: Opening Paths to a Moral Economy.* New York: Simon & Schuster, 2003.

Grondine, Robert F. "An International Perspective on Japan's New Legal Education System." *Asia Pacific Law Journal* 2.2 (Spring 2001). Available at www.hawaii.edu/aplpj.

Griller, Stephan. "Judicial Enforcement of WTO Law in the European Union," *Journal of International Economic Law* 3 (2000): 441–462.

Gummett, Philip. *Globalization and Public Policy.* Cheltenham, UK: E. Elgar, 1996.

Hacker, Kenneth L., and Jan van Dijk. *Digital Democracy: Issues of Theory & Practice.* London: Sage Publications, 2000.

Hahm, Sung Deuk, and Kwang Woong Kim. "Institutional Reforms and Democratization in Korea: The Case of the Kim Young Sam Administration, 1993–1998." *Governance: An International Journal of Policy and Administration* 12.4 (October 1999): 479–494.

Halbert, D. *Feminist Fabulation: Challenging the Boundaries of Fact and Fiction. The Manoa Journal of Fried and Half Fried Ideas.* Honolulu: Hawai'i Research Center for Futures Studies, 1994.

Halstead, Ted, and Michael Lind. *The Radical Center: The Future of American Politics.* New York: Doubleday, 2001.

Hamilton, Alexander, John Jay, and James Madison. *The Federalist. A Commentary on the Constitution of the United States. Being a Collection of Essays Written in Support of the Constitution Agreed upon September 17, 1787, by the Federal Convention.* New York: Random House Modern Library Edition, 1937.

Han, Sung-Joo, ed. *Changing Values in Asia: Their Impact on Governance and Development.* Singapore: Institute of Southeast Asian Studies, 1999.

"Hanryu Tourist Marketing." Available at www.knto.or.kr/eng/hallyu/hallyu.html.

Hanson, Victor Davis. "A Funny Sort of Empire: Are Americans Really So Imperial?" *National Review,* November 27, 2002. Available at www.nationalreview.com/hanson/hanson112702.asp.

Haraway, D. *Simians, Cyborgs, and Women: The Reinvention of Nature.* New York: Routledge, 1991.

Harcones, Los. "Personalized Government: A Governmental System Based on Behavior Analysis." *Behavior Analysis and Social Action* 7.1–2 (1989): 42–47.

Harris, Errol E., and James A. Yunker. *Toward Genuine Global Governance: Critical Reactions to "Our Global Neighborhood."* Westport, Conn.: Praeger, 1999.

Haskell, John. *Direct Democracy or Representative Government? Dispelling the Populist Myth.* Boulder: Colo.: Westview Press, 2001.

Havelock, Eric Alfred. *The Muse Learns to Write: Reflections on Orality and Literacy from Antiquity to the Present.* New Haven, Conn.: Yale University Press, 1986.

Hay, Colin, and David Marsh. "Introduction: Demystifying Globalization," in *Demystifying Globalization,* ed. Colin Hay and David Marsh. London: Macmillan Press, 2000, 1–17.

Hayashi, Yujiro. "Japan Society of Futurology." In *Japan Society of Futurology 4, Challenges from the Future: Proceedings of the International Future Research Conference.* Tokyo: Kodansha, 1970.

Hayduk, Ronald, and Kevin Mattson, eds. *Democracy's Moment: Reforming the American Political System for the 21st Century.* Lanham, Md.: Rowman & Littlefield, 2002.

Hein, Laura, and Mark Selden, eds. *Censoring History: Citizenship and Memory in Japan, Germany, and the United States.* Armonk, N.Y.: An East Gate Book, 2000.

Held, David. *Democracy and the Global Order.* Stanford, Calif.: Stanford University Press, 1995.

———. *Models of Democracy.* Oxford: Polity Press, 1987.

Held, David, and Anthony McGrew, eds. *The Global Transformation Reader: An Introduction to the Globalization Debate.* Malden, Mass.: Blackwell Publishers, 2000.

Held, David, et al. *Global Transformations: Politics, Economics and Culture.* Stanford, Calif.: Stanford University Press, 1999.

Helu, I. F. *Tradition and Good Governance.* Canberra: Australian National University, 1997.

Henderson, Hazel. *Beyond Globalization: Shaping a Sustainable Global Economy.* West Hartford, Conn.: Kumarian Press, 1999.

———. *Building a Win-Win World: Life Beyond Global Economic Warfare.* San Francisco: Berrett-Koehler Publishers, 1996.

Henrich, Joseph, Robert Boyd, and Samuel Bowles, eds. "In Search of *Homo Economicus:* Behavioral Experiments in 15 Small-scale Societies." *American Economic Review* 91 (May 2001): 73–78.

Herod, Andrew, Gearaoid Tuathail, and Susan M. Roberts. *An Unruly World? Globalization, Governance, and Geography.* New York: Routledge, 1998.

Heyzer, N., S. Kapoor, and J. Sandler, eds. *A Commitment to the World's Women.* New York: UNIFEM, 1995.

Hibbing, John, and Elizabeth Theiss-Morse. *Stealth Democracy: Americans' Beliefs about How Government Should Work.* Cambridge: Cambridge University Press, 2002.

Hirata, Keiko. *Civil Society in Japan: The Growing Role of NGOs in Tokyo's Aid and Development Policy.* 1st ed. New York: Palgrave/Macmillan, 2002.

Hoffman, Stanley. "Clash of Globalizations." *Foreign Affairs* 81, no. 4 (July–August 2002): 104–115.

Hollis, D. W. *The ABC-CLIO World History Companion to Utopian Movements.* Santa Barbara, Calif.: ABC-CLIO, 1998.

Holm, Hans-Henrik, and Georg Soensen. *Whose World Order? Uneven Globalization and the End of the Cold War.* Boulder, Colo.: Westview Press, 1995.

Hosoya Chihiro, Iriye Akira, and Oshiba Ryo, eds. *Kioku to Shiteno Pā-ru Hā-bā* (Pearl Harbor as memory). Kyoto: Minerva, 2004.

Hu, F., and J. Sachs. "Executive Summary." In World Economic Forum, *The Global Competitiveness Report 1996.* Geneva: WEF, 1996, 14–19.

Hubbard, Barbara Marx. *Conscious Evolution: Awakening the Power of Our Social Potential.* Novato, Calif.: New World Library, 1998.

Huddleston, Mark. "Onto the Darkling Plain: Globalization and the American Public Service in the Twenty-First Century." *Journal of Public Administration Research and Theory* 10.4 (October 2000): 665–684.

Hun Sen. Prime Minster of Cambodia's Speech. Phnom Penh, 2002.

Huntington, Samuel P. *The Clash of Civilizations and the Remaking of World Order.* New York: Simon & Schuster, 1996.

———. *Who Are We? The Challenges of America's National Identity.* New York: Simon & Schuster, 2004.

Hurrell, Andrew, and Ngaire Woods, eds. *Inequality, Globalization and World Politics.* Oxford: Oxford University Press, 1999.

Hveem, Helge, and Kristen Nordhaug. *Public Policy in the Age of Globalization: Responses to Environmental and Economic Crises.* New York: Palgrave/Macmillan, 2002.

Ikenberry, W. John. "America's Imperial Ambition." *Foreign Affairs* 81, no. 5 (September/October 2002): 44–60.

———. "The Myth of Post-Cold War Chaos." *Foreign Affairs* 75 (May/June 1996): 79–91.

"Income Gap in China Widens in First Quarter." Available at www.chinadaily.com.cn/english/doc/2005-06/19/content_452636. htm.

Ingraham, Patricia W. *The Foundation of Merit: Public Service in American Democracy.* Baltimore, Md.: Johns Hopkins University Press, 1995.

Iriye, Akira. "Modernization, Globalization, and World War." Paper presented to the Conference on Memory in US-Japan Relations, Honolulu, Hawai'i, March 25–26, 2001.

Isbister, John. *Capitalism and Justice: Envisioning Social and Economic Fairness.* Bloomfield, Conn.: Kumarian Press, 2001.

Ishii, Osamu. "Arrogant Japanese, Angry Americans: Economic, Cultural and Social Frictions between Japan and the United States in the late 1980s and early 90s." Paper presented to the Conference on Memory in US-Japan Relations, Honolulu, Hawai'i, March 25–26, 2001.

Iwabuchi, Koichi. "From Western Gaze to Global Gaze: Japanese Cultural Presence in Asia." In *Global Culture: Media, Arts, Policy and Globalization,* ed. Diana Crane et al. London: Routledge, 2002, 256–273.

James, Jeffrey. *Globalization, Information Technology and Development.* New York, St. Martin's Press, 1999.

Jenkins, Philip. *The Next Christendom: The Coming of Global Christianity.* Oxford: Oxford University Press, 2002.

JICA. *The Kingdom of Cambodia: From Reconstruction to Sustainable Development.* Tokyo: JICA, 2002.

Johnson, Chalmers. *Blowback: The Costs and Consequences of American Empire.* New York: Henry Holt, 2000.

———. *MITI and the Japanese Miracle: The Growth of Industrial Policy, 1925–1975.* Stanford, Calif.: Stanford University Press, 1982.

Jomo, K. S., ed. *Tigers in Trouble: Financial Governance, Liberalisation and Crises in East Asia.* London: Zed Books, 1998.

Jones, Barry O. "Balancing Now and the Future." In *Co-Creating a Public Philosophy for Future Generations,* ed. Tae-Chang Kim and Jim Dator. Twickenham, UK: Adamantine Press, 1999, 80–89.

Jones, D. A. F. *Women of Spirit.* Sudbury, Mass.: Visions of a Better World Foundation, 1995.

Jones, R. J. Barry. *The World Turned Upside Down? Globalization and the Future of the State.* Manchester: Manchester University Press, 2000.

Jreisat, E. Jamil. *Comparative Public Administration and Policy.* Boulder, Colo.: Westview Press, 2002.

Jun, S. Jong, ed. *Rethinking Administrative Theory: The Challenge of the New Century.* Westport, Conn.: Praeger, 2002.

Jun, S. Jong, and Deil Spencer Wright. *Globalization and Decentralization: Institutional Contexts, Policy Issues, and Intergovernmental Relations in Japan and the United States,* Washington, DC: Georgetown University Press, 1996.

Jung, Soo-Il. "Exploring 1200 Years of Korea and Islam Interchange." *Sindonga* (May 2001): 424–431.

Jung, Y. "Globalization and the Institutional Persistence of the Developmental State in Korea." *Korean Journal of Policy Studies* 15.2 (2000): 27–40.

———. "Great Policy Failures, Public Administration's Credibility, and Good Governance in Korea." *International Review of Public Administration* 5.1 (2000): 152–159.

———. "Institutions, Interests and the Post-IMF Structural Adjustment in Korea." *Korean Journal of Policy Studies* 16.1 (2001): 11–22.

———. "The Territorial Dimension of the Developing Capitalist State: Measuring and Explaining the Centralization in Korea." *International Review of Administrative Sciences* 53 (1987): 128–153.

Jung, Y., and G. Siegel. "Testing Perceptions of Distributive Justice in Korea." *Journal of Northeast Asian Studies* 2.2 (1983): 45–66.

"Justice & Fairness." Available at www.calvertnetk12.md.us?instruct/jusfair.shtml.

Kagan, Donald, Gary Schmitt, and Thomas Donnelly. *Rebuilding America's Defenses: Strategy, Forces and Resources for a New Century.* Washington, DC: The Project for the New American Century, September 2000.

Kahn, Herman. *The Emerging Japanese Superstate: Challenge and Response.* Englewood Cliffs, N.J.: Prentice-Hall, 1970.

Kahn, Herman, and Thomas Pepper. *The Japanese Challenge: The Success and Failure of Economic Success.* New York: Crowell, 1979.

Kaku, Michio. *Hyperspace: A Scientific Odyssey through Parallel Universes, Time Warps, and the Tenth Dimension.* New York: Oxford University Press, 1995.

Kamarck, Elaine Ciulla. "Globalization and Public Administration Reform." In *Governance in a Globalizing World,* ed. Joseph Nye, Jr., and John D. Donahue. Washington, DC: Brookings Institution Press, 2000, 229–252.

Kamarck, Elaine, and Joseph Nye, Jr. *Governance.com: Democracy in the Information Age.* Washington, DC: Brookings Institution, 2002.

Kamppinen, Matti, et al. "Citizenship and Ecological Modernization in the Information Society." *Futures* 33.3–4 (April–May 2001): 219–370.

Kang Sang-jung. *Nashonarizumu* (Nationalism). Tokyo: Iwanami, 2001.

Kang Sang-jung and Shunya Yoshimi. *Guro-baruka no Enkinho* (Globalization in Perspective). Tokyo: Iwanami, 2001.

Kaplan, Jeffrey A. "As Cambodia Considers AFTA." *The Cambodian Journal of International Affairs* 1 (Fall 1996): 20–28.

Kaplan, Robert. "Supremacy by Stealth: Ten Rules for Managing the World." *The Atlantic Monthly* 292, no. 1 (July/August 2002): 65–83.

Kaspersen, Lars Bo. *Anthony Giddens: An Introduction to a Social Theorist.* Malden, Mass.: Blackwell Publishers, 2000.

Katsh, M. Ethan. *The Electronic Media and the Transformation of Law.* New York: Oxford University Press, 1989.

Katz, Ellen. "Private Order and Public Institutions: Comments on McMillan and Woodruff's 'Private Order Under Dysfunctional Public Order.'" *Michigan Law Review* 98 (2002): 2481–2494.

Katz, Richard. *Japan, The System That Soured: The Rise and Fall of the Japanese Economic Miracle.* Armonk, N.Y.: M. E. Sharpe, 1998.

Kay, Charles. "Justice as Fairness" (1997). Available at truth.wofford.edu/~kaycd/ethics/justice.htm.

Keane, John. *Global Civil Society? Contemporary Political Theory.* Cambridge: Cambridge University Press, 2003.

Kelsay, John. "Civil Society and Government in Islam." In *Civil Society and Government,* ed. Nancy L. Rosenblum and Robert C. Post. Princeton, N.J.: Princeton University Press, 2002, 284–316.

Kennedy, Paul, et al. *Global Trends and Global Governance.* London: Pluto Press, 2002.

Kenny, Mel. "Globalization, Interlegality and Europeanized Contract Law." *Pennsylvanian State International Law Review* 21 (2003): 569–620.

Keohane, Robert, and Helen Milner, eds. *Internationalization and Domestic Politics.* New York: Cambridge University Press, 1996.

Keohane, Robert O., and Joseph S. Nye, Jr. "Introduction." In *Governance in a Globalizing World,* ed. Joseph Nye, Jr., and John D. Donahue. Washington, DC: Brookings Institution Press, 2000, 1–41.

Kettl, Donald F. *The Global Public Management Revolution: A Report on the Transformation of Governance.* Washington, DC: Brookings Institution Press, 2000.

———. "The Transformation of Governance and Public Affairs Education." *Journal of Public Affairs Education* 7.4 (October 2001): 213–217.

Khagram, Sanjeev, et al. *Restructuring World Politics: Transnational Social Movements, Networks and Norms.* Minneapolis: University of Minnesota Press, 2002.

Khor, Martin. *Rethinking Globalization: Critical Issues and Policy Choices, Global Issues.* New York: Zed, 2001.

Kim, Andrew E. "History of Christianity in Korea: From Its Troubled Beginning to Its Contemporary Success." Available at www.kimsoft.com/1997/xhist.htm.

Kim Jong Il. *On the Juche Idea.* Pyongyang: Foreign Languages Publishing House, 1982.

Kim, S. Samuel. *East Asia and Globalization, Asia in World Politics.* Lanham, Md.: Rowman & Littlefield Publishers, 2000.

———. *Korea's Globalization, Cambridge Asia-Pacific Studies.* New York: Cambridge University Press, 2000.

King, D. Anthony. *Culture, Globalization, and the World-System: Contemporary Conditions for the Representation of Identity.* Minneapolis: University of Minnesota Press, 1997.

King, Richard, and Timothy J. Craig. *Global Goes Local: Popular Culture in Asia.* Vancouver: UBC Press, 2002.

Klenner, Wolfgang, and Hisashi Watanabe. *Globalization and Regional Dynamics: East Asia and the European Union from the Japanese and the German Perspective.* New York: Springer, 2002.

Klingner, Donald, and Charles Washington. "Through the Looking Glass: The Benefits of an International and Comparative Perspective on Teaching Public Affairs." *Journal of Public Affairs Education* 6.1 (2000): 35–44.

Kohler, Martin. "From the National to the Cosmopolitan Public Sphere." In *Re-imagining Political Community Studies in Cosmopolitan Democracy,* ed. Daniele Archibugi, David Held, and Martin Kohler. Stanford, Calif.: Stanford University Press, 1999.

Kohno Kensuke, et. al. "Senso no Kioku ha Donoyoni Tsutaeraretaka (How the memory of war was broadcast on TV News)." *NHK Hoso Bunka Chosa Kenkyu Nenpo,* no. 43 (1998): 79–141.

Korean Ministry of Culture and Tourism. *White Paper on Cultural Policies* (2001). Available at www.culturelink.or.kr/policy_korea.html.

Korean Political Science Association. "The Korean Political Economy: Crisis and Response." Proceedings of the Special Conference of the Korean Political Science Association, Seoul, March 21, 1998 (in Korean).

Kral, Alexei T. *"Us" versus "Them": Cultural Nationalism in Japanese Textbooks.* The Woodrow Wilson Center, Asia Program Special Report, July 2000.

Krasner, Stephen D. *Sovereignty: Organized Hypocrisy.* Princeton, N.J.: Princeton University Press, 1999.

Kuo, Ming-fong, and Andreas Weiland. "Modern Literature in Post-War Taiwan." *Intercultural Studies* no. 1 (Spring 2003). Available at www.intercultural-studies.org/ICSI/Kuo.htm.

Kwok, Kian-Woon, and Kee-Hong Low. "Cultural Policy and the City-State: Singapore and the 'New Asian Renaissance.' " In *Global Culture: Media, Arts, Policy and Globalization,* ed. Diana Crane et al. London: Routledge, 2002, 149–168.

Landau, Martin. "On the Use of Metaphor in Political Science." *Social Research* 28 (1961): 331–353.

Lardy, Nicholas R. "Issues in China's WTO Accession, U.S.-China Security Review Commission." May 9, 2001. Available at www.brookings.edu/views/testimony/lardy/20010509. htm.

Lawson, Stephanie. *Cultural Traditions and Identity Politics: Some Implications for Democratic Governance in Asia and the Pacific.* Canberra: Australian National University, 1997.

Le, Heron, Richard B., and Sam Ock Park. *The Asian Pacific Rim and Globalization: Enterprise, Governance and Territoriality, The Organization of Industrial Space.* Aldershot, England: Avebury, 1995.

Lechner, Frank J., and John Boli, eds. *The Globalization Reader.* Malden, Mass.: Blackwell Publishers, 2000.

Lee, Su-Hoon. "The Rise of East Asia and East Asian Social Science's Quest for Self-Identity." *Journal of World-Systems Research* 6.3 (Fall/Winter 2000): 768–783.

Lee, Yong-Sung. "KOCCA Expects Cultural Content Industry to Be Leading Business." *The Korea Times,* September 19, 2003, 14.

Leopold, Joan. *Culture in Comparative and Evolutionary Perspective: E. B. Tylor and the Making of Primitive Culture.* Berlin: Dietrich Reimer Verlag, 1980.

Lewellen, Ted C. *Political Anthropology: An Introduction.* Westport, Conn.: Bergin & Garvey, 1992,

Lieven, Anatol. "The Dilemma of Sustaining an American Empire." *The Financial Times,* January 2, 2003, 13.

Lindsay, Jennifer. "A Drama of Change: Cultural Policy and the Performing Arts in Southeast Asia." In *Global Culture: Media, Arts, Policy and Globalization,* ed. Diana Crane et al. London: Routledge, 2002, 63–77.

Lipset, Seymour Martin. *The First New Nation: The United States in Historical and Comparative Perspective.* New York: Basic Books, 1963.

Loader, Brian D. *The Governance of Cyberspace.* New York: Routledge, 1997.

London School of Economics and Political Science, Centre for the Study of Global Governance and Centre for Civil Society (London School of Economics and Political Science). *Global Civil Society.* New York: Oxford University Press, 2001.

Lowe, Ian. "Governing in the Interests of Future Generations." In *Co-Creating a Public Philosophy for Future Generations,* ed. Tae-Chang Kim and Jim Dator. Twickenham, UK: Adamantine Press, 1999, 131–143.

Luke, Carmen. *Globalization and Women in Academia: North/West South/East.* Mahwah, N.J.: Lawrence Erlbaum Associates, 2001.

MacCormick, Neil. "Beyond the Sovereign State." *Modern Law Review* 56 (1993): 1–18.

Maier, Charles. "An American Empire?" *Harvard Magazine* 105, no. 2 (November/December 2002), 28–31. Available at www.harvard-magazine.com.

Manning, Nick. "The Legacy of the New Public Management in Developing Countries." *International Review of Administrative Sciences* 67 (2001): 297–312.

Margolis, Michael, and David Resnick. *Politics as Usual: The Cyberspace "Revolution."* Thousand Oaks, Calif.: Sage Publications, 2000.

Marien, Michael, ed. *Globalization Guide: A Short Review of Recent Literature on Perspectives, Problems, and Policies.* Bethesda, Md.: World Future Society, 2001.

Markoff, John. "Tiniest Circuits Hold Prospect of Explosive Computer Speeds." *New York Times,* July 16, 1999, A1.

Marquand, David. *Decline of the Public.* Cambridge: Polity Press, 2004.

Martin, H., and H. Schumann. *Die Globalisierungsfall.* Hamburg: Rowohlt Verag GmbH, 1997.

Martin, Peter. "The Moral Case for Globalization." In *The Globalization Reader,* ed. F. Lechner and J. Boli. Malden, Mass.: Blackwell Publishers, 2000, 12–14.

Masini, Eleanor B. "A Vision of Futures Studies." *Futures* 34 (2002): 249–261.

———. *Visions of Desirable Societies*. Oxford: Pergamon Press, 1983.

———. *Women as Builders of Alternative Futures*. Trier, Germany: Centre for European Studies, Trier University, 1993.

Mason, P. H. P., and J. G. Caiger. *A History of Japan*. Boston: Tuttle Publishing, 1997.

Massey, Andrew, ed. *Globalization and the Marketization of Government Services*. New York: St. Martin's Press, 1997.

Massey, Doreen. *Space, Place and Gender*. Minneapolis: University of Minnesota Press, 1994.

McAlister, J. T., Jr. *Southeast Asia: The Politics of National Integration*. New York: Random House, 1973.

McBride, Stephen, and John Richard Wiseman. *Globalization and Its Discontents*. New York: St. Martin's Press, 2000.

McDonald, Forrest. *The American Presidency: An Intellectual History*. Lawrence: University of Kansas Press, 1984.

McGray, Douglas. "Japan's Gross National Cool." *Foreign Policy* (May/June 2003): 45–54.

McKibben, Bill. *Enough: Staying Human in an Engineered Age*. New York: Times Books, 2003.

McLuhan, Marshall. *The Gutenberg Galaxy: The Making of Typographic Man*. Toronto: University of Toronto Press, 1962.

McLuhan, Marshall, and Quintin Fiore. *The Medium is the Massage: An Inventory of Effects*. Reprint. Corte Madera, Calif.: Gingko Press, 2001.

McMillan, John, and Christopher Woodruff. "Private Order under Dysfunctional Public Order." *Michigan Law Review* 96 (2000): 2421–2459.

Melman, Seymour. *The Permanent War Economy: American Capitalism in Decline*. New York: Simon & Schuster, 1985.

Meyerson, Michael. *Political Numeracy: Mathematical Perspectives on Our Chaotic Constitution*. New York: W. W. Norton, 2002.

Michalski, Wolfgang, ed. *Governance in the 21st Century*. Paris: OECD, 2001.

Micklethwait, John, and Adrian Wooldridge. *A Future Perfect: The Challenge and Hidden Promise of Globalization*. New York: Crown Business, 2000.

Midgal, Joel S., Atul Kohli, and Vivienne Shue. *State Power and Social Forces: Domination and Transformation in the Third World*. Cambridge: Cambridge University Press, 1994.

Miles, Edward, et al. *Environmental Regime Effectiveness: Confronting Theory with Evidence*. Cambridge, Mass.: MIT Press, 2002.

Milius, S. "Unfair Trade: Monkeys Demand Equitable Exchanges." In *Science News* 164, no. 12 (September 20, 2003), 12.

Milkis, Sidney M., and Michael Nelson. *The American Presidency: Origins and Development, 1776–1998*. 3d. ed. Washington, DC: Congressional Quarterly Press, 1999.

Ministry of Defense. *The White Paper 2002*. Phnom Penh: MOD, 2002.

Ministry of Government Affairs and Home Affairs (Republic of Korea). *Annual Report, 1993–2001*. Seoul, 2002.

Ministry of Planning and Budget (Republic of Korea). *Annual Report, 2001*. Seoul, 2002.

Mische, Patricia. "Ecological Security and the Need to Reconceptualize Sovereignty." *Alternatives* 14 (1989): 389–427.

Mittelman, James H., ed. *Globalization: Critical Reflection.* Boulder, Colo.: Lynne Rienner, 1996.

———. *The Globalization Syndrome: Transformation and Resistance.* Princeton, N.J.: Princeton University Press, 2000.

Miyazawa, Setsuo. "The Politics of Judicial Reform in Japan: The Rule of Law at Last?" *Asia Pacific Law Journal* 2.2 (Spring 2001): 88–121. Available at www.hawaii.edu/aplpj.

Moffett, Samuel H. *A History of Christianity in Asia.* Maryknoll, N.Y.: Orbis Books, 1998.

Moon, Myung-Jae, and Patricia Ingraham. "Shaping Administrative Reform and Governance: An Examination of the Political Nexus Triads in Three Asian Countries." *Governance: An International Journal of Policy and Administration* 11.1 (January 1998): 77–100.

Morgan, Garth. *Images of Organization.* 2d ed. Thousands Oaks, Calif.: Sage Publications, 1997.

Morrison, Charles Edward, Hadi Soesastro, and Nihon Kokusai Kyoryu Senta. *Domestic Adjustments to Globalization.* Tokyo: Japan Center for International Exchange, 1998.

Morris-Suzuki, Tessa. "Guro-baruna Kioku, Nashonaru-na Kijutsu" (Global memory and national description). *Shiso* (August 1998): 35–56. .

Mowshowitz, Abbe. *Virtual Organizations: Toward a Theory of Societal Transformation Stimulated by Information Technology.* Westport Conn.: Quorum Books, 2002.

Muchlinski, Peter. "Globalisation and Legal Research." *The International Lawyer 37* (2003): 221–242.

Munck, Ronaldo, and Barry K. Gills, eds. "Globalization and Democracy." *Annals of the American Academy of Political and Social Science* 581 (2002).

Myerson, Harold. "Democrats Campaign Online." *Honolulu Advertiser,* June 19, 2002, A10.

Nakane, Chie, and Shinzaburo Oishi, eds. *Tokugawa Japan: The Social and Economic Antecedents of Modern Japan.* Tokyo: University of Tokyo Press, 1990.

National Geographic Society, *Millennium in Maps* (Washington, DC: NGS, 1999).

"The National Security Strategy of the United States of America." September 17, 2002. Available at www.whitehouse.gov/nsc/nss.pdf.

Neary, Ian. "Serving the Japanese Prime Minister." In *Administering the Summit: Administration of the Core Executive in Developed Countries,* ed. Guy Peters et al. New York: St. Martin's Press, 2000, 196–222.

Nederveen Pieterse, Jan. *Global Futures: Shaping Globalization.* New York: St. Martin's Press, 2000.

Neisser, Ulric, ed. *The Rising Curve: Long-Term Gains in IQ and Related Measures.* Washington, DC: American Psychological Association, 1998.

Nelson, Michael, ed. *Guide to the Presidency.* Vol. 2, 2d ed. Washington, DC: Congressional Quarterly Press, 1995.

Nihon Boeki Shinkokai. *The Merits and Demerits of Globalization and the Future of Asia.* Tokyo: Japan External Trade Organization (JETRO), 1999.

Nihon Heiwa Gakkai, ed. *Heiwa Kenkyu* (Tokushu: 20 Seiki no Senso to Heiwa) Peace Studies Association of Japan, Peace Studies no. 25 (Special Issue: War and Peace in the 20th Century). November 2000.

Nishibe Susumu, ed. *Atarashii komin kyokasho* (New textbook on political economy). Tokyo: Fusosha, 2001.

Nishio Kanji, ed. *Atarashii Rekishi Kyokasho* (New history textbook). Tokyo: Fusosha, 2001.

Noguchi Yukio. *1940-nen Taisei: Saraba "Senji Keizai."* Tokyo: Toyo Keizai Shinposha, 1995.

Nolan, Brendan, ed. *Public Sector Reform: An International Perspective.* Houndsmill, UK: Palgrave Publishers, 2001.

Norris, Michael. *Reinventing the Administrative State.* New York: University Press of America, 2000.

Nosco, Peter. "Confucian Perspectives on Civil Society and Government." In *Civil Society and Government,* ed. Nancy L. Rosenblum and Robert C. Post. Princeton, N.J.: Princeton University Press, 2002, 334–359.

"Now You Can Have 5,999,999,999 Friends." *New York Times,* September 19, 1999, section 4, 4.

Nussbaum, Bruce. "Beyond the War: How Bush is Destroying Globalization." *Business Week,* March 24, 2003, 32–36.

Nye, Joseph, Jr., and John D. Donahue. *Governance in a Globalizing World.* Washington, DC: Brookings Institution Press, 2000.

O'Brien, Robert, et al. *Contesting Global Governance: Multilateral Economic Institutions and Global Social Movements.* Cambridge, UK: Cambridge University Press, 2000.

O'Connell, Brian. *Civil Society: The Underpinnings of American Democracy.* Hanover, N.H.: Tufts University Press, 1999.

Office of the Press Secretary. "Remarks by President Clinton at University of Chicago Convocation Ceremonies." Available at www. whitehouse.gov/WH/new/html/19990612.html (June 12, 1999), 1–2.

Ohnuki-Tierney, Emiko. *Kamikaze, Cherry Blossoms, and Nationalisms: The Militarization of Aesthetics in Japanese History.* Chicago: University of Chicago Press, 2002.

Olds, Kris, et al. *Globalisation and the Asia-Pacific: Contested Territories.* London: Routledge, 1999.

Olson, David R., and Nancy Torrance, eds. *The Making of Literate Societies.* Oxford: Blackwell Publishers, 2001.

O'Meara, Patrick, Howard D. Mehlinger, and Matthew Krain. *Globalization and the Challenges of a New Century: A Reader.* Bloomington: Indiana University Press, 2000.

Ong, Walter J. *Orality and Literacy: The Technologizing of the Word.* London: Routledge, 1982.

Organization for Economic Cooperation and Development (OECD). *Governance in the 21st Century.* Paris: OECD, 2001.

Osbourne, David, and Peter Plastrik. *Banishing Bureaucracy*. New York: Penguin Books, 1998.

———. *The Reinventor's Fieldbook: Tools for Transforming Your Government*. San Francisco: Jossey-Bass, 2000.

Osborne, Milton. *Southeast Asia: An Introductory History*. St. Leonards, NSW: Allen & Unwin, 2000.

Ostrom, Elinor. "Collective Action and the Evolution of Social Norms." *Journal of Economic Perspectives* (Summer 2000): 137–158.

Palan, Ronen. "Recasting Political Authority: Globalization and the State." In *Globalization and Its Critics: Perspectives from Political Economy*, ed. Randall D. Germain. London: Macmillian, 2000, 139–163.

Park, S. "Labor Market Policy and the Social Safety Net in Korea: One Year after 1997 Crisis." *Korean Policy Studies Review* 9.2 (2000): 291–318.

Park, Sung-Jo, and Arne Holzhausen. *Can Japan Globalize? Studies on Japan's Changing Political Economy and the Process of Globalization in Honour of Sung-Jo Park*. Heidelberg: Physica-Verlag, 2001.

Peng, Shin-yi. "The WTO Legalistic Approach and East Asia: From the Legal Culture Perspective. *Asian-Pacific Law and Policy Journal* (2000): 131–135.

Perry, William. *Forms of Intellectual and Ethical Development in the College Years: A Scheme*. New York: Holt, Rinehart and Winston, 1970.

Peters, B. Guy. *The Future of Governing*. 2nd ed. Lawrence: University Press of Kansas, 2001.

———. *Governing*. 2d ed. Lawrence: University of Kansas Press, 2001.

Peters, B. Guy, and Jon Pierre. *Politicians, Bureaucrats and Administrative Reform, Routledge/Ecpr Studies in European Political Science*. Vol. 22. London: Routledge, 2001.

Peters, B. Guy, and Donald J. Savoie, eds. *Governance in the Twenty-first Century: Revitalizing the Public Service*. Montreal: McGill-Queen's University Press, 2000.

Piaget, Jean. *The Origins of Intelligence in Children*. New York: International University Press, 1952.

Pierre, Jon. *Debating Governance*. New York: Oxford University Press, 2000.

Pierre, Jon, and B. Guy Peters. *Governance, Politics and the State*. New York: St. Martin's Press, 2000.

Pieters, Jan Nederveen. *Global Futures: Shaping Globalization*. London: Zed Books, 2000.

Phillips, Kevin. *The Politics of Rich and Poor: Wealth and the American Electorate in the Reagan Aftermath*. New York: HarperPerennial, 1991.

———. *Wealth and Democracy: A Political History of the American Rich*. New York: Broadway Books, 2002.

Platt, John. "Social Traps." *American Psychologist* 28 (1973): 642–651.

———. *The Step to Man*. New York: John Wiley, 1966.

Pollard, Vincent Kelly, and Bruce Tonn. "Revisiting the 'Court of Generations' Amendment." *Futures* 30.4 (May 1998): 345–352.

Prakash, Aseem, and Jeffrey A. Hart. *Globalization and Governance*. New York: Routledge, 1999.

————, eds. *Responding to Globalization*. London: Routledge, 2000.

Pratt, Richard. "Intellectual Structures, Committed Openness, and Future Public Organizations." Presented at the Public Administration Theory Conference, Seattle, Washington, March 1995.

"Premier Urges Cultural Development." *People's Daily,* March 5, 2004. Available at http://english.people.com.cn/200403/05/eng 20040305_136608.shtml.

Prins, J. E. J., ed. *Designing E-Government: On the Crossroads of Technological Innovation and Institutional Change*. The Hague: Kluwer Law International, 2001.

Putnam, Robert D. *Bowling Alone: The Collapse and Revival of American Community*. New York: Simon & Schuster, 2000.

Quah, J. "Corruption in Asian Countries: Can it be Minimized?" *Public Administration Review* 59.6 (1999): 483–494.

Rasanen, Jiri. "The Platform of Aanivalta (The Finnish Citizens' Power Movement)." Unpublished. Contact: <jiri.rasanen@nic.fi>.

Rawls, John. *Justice as Fairness: A Restatement*. Cambridge, Mass.: Harvard University Press, 2001.

————. *A Theory of Justice*. Cambridge, Mass.: Harvard University Press, 1971

Rees, Martin. *Our Final Hour: A Scientist's Warning: How Terror, Error, and Environmental Disaster Threaten Humankind's Future in this Century, On Earth and Beyond*. New York: Basic Books, 2003.

Relyea, Harold C. *Government at the Dawn of the 21ˢᵗ Century*. Huntington, N.Y.: Novinka Books, 2001.

Rhodes, R. A. W. "Governance and Public Administration." In *Debating Governance*, ed. Jon Pierre. Oxford: Oxford University Press, 2000, 54–90.

Riggs, Fred W. "Global Forces and the Discipline of Public Administration." In *Public Administration in the Global Village*, ed. Garcia Zamor, Jean Claude, and Renu Khator. Westport, Conn.: Praeger, 1994, 17–44.

————. "Presidentialism: A Problematic Regime Type." In *Parliamentary versus Presidential Government*, ed. Arend Lijphart. Oxford: Oxford University Press, 1992, 217–222.

Robertson, Roland. *Globalization: Social Theory and Global Culture*. London: Sage, 1992.

Robinson, James. "Newtonianism and the Constitution." *Midwest Journal of Political Science* 1.1 (1957): 252–256.

Robinson, Kim Stanley. *Red Mars*. New York: Bantam Books, 1993.

Rockman, Bert. "Administering the Summit in the United States." In *Administering the Summit: Administration of the Core Executive in Developed Countries*, ed. Guy Peters et al. New York: St. Martin's Press, 2000, 245–262.

Rodrik, Dani. *Has Globalization Gone Too Far?* Washington, DC: Institute for International Economics, 1997.

————. "Trading in Illusions." *Foreign Policy* (March/April 2001), 55–62.

"Roh Vows to Build Korea into Cultural Power." Available at www.kois.go.kr/menu/government/newscontent.asp?Number=20030901008.

Rosemont, Henry, Jr. "Commentary and Addenda on Nosco's 'Confucian Perspectives on Civil Society and Government.' " In *Civil Society and Government*, ed. Nancy L. Rosenblum and Robert C. Post. Princeton, N.J.: Princeton University Press, 2002, 360–369.

Rosenau, James N. *Along the Domestic-Foreign Frontier: Exploring Governance in a Turbulent World*. Cambridge: Cambridge University Press, 1997.

———. *Distant Proximities: Dynamics beyond Globalization*. Princeton, N.J.: Princeton University Press, 2003.

———. "Letter from James N. Rosenau." *Fairglobe-1* (2001). Available at www.fairglobe .hawaii.edu.

———. *Turbulence in World Politics: A Theory of Change and Continuity*. Princeton, N.J.: Princeton University Press, 1990.

Rosenau, James N., and W. Michael Fagen. "Increasingly Skillful Citizens: A New Dynamism in World Politics?" *International Studies Quarterly* 41 (December 1997): 655–686.

Rosenblum, Nancy L., and Robert C. Post, eds. *Civil Society and Government*. Princeton, N.J.: Princeton University Press, 2002.

Ross, J. S. Robert, and C. Kent Trachte. *Global Capitalism: The New Leviathan*. Albany: State University of New York Press, 1990.

Rowley, Chris, and John Benson. *Globalization and Labour in the Asia Pacific Region*. Portland, Oreg.: Frank Cass, 2000.

Royal Government of Cambodia. *SEILA Program Document 2001–2005*. Phnom Penh: December 2000.

Rozman, Gilbert, ed. *The East Asian Region: Confucian Heritage and Its Modern Adaptation*. Princeton, N.J.: Princeton University Press, 1991.

Ryan, M. J., ed. *The Fabric of the Future: Women Visionaries of Today Illuminate the Path to Tomorrow*. Berkeley, Calif.: Conari Press, 1998.

Sachs, J., and A. Warner. "Why Competitiveness Counts." In *The Global Competitiveness Report 1996*. Geneva: WEF, 1996, 8–13.

Sahtouris, E. *EarthDance: Living Systems in Evolution*. San Jose, Calif.: iUniverse.com, Inc., 2000.

Salamon, Lester, ed. *The Tools of Government: A Guide to the New Governance*. Oxford: Oxford University Press, 2002.

Salskov-Iverson, Dorte, Hans Hansen, and Sven Bislev. "Governmentality, Globalization, and Local Practice: Transformation of a Hegemonic Discourse." *Alternatives: Social Transformation and Humane Governance* 25.2 (April–June 2000): 183–222. As found in EBSCOhost.html.

Sargisson, Lucy. *Contemporary Feminist Utopianism*. London: Routledge, 1996.

Sassen, Saskia. *Globalization and Its Discontents*. New York: The New Press, 1999.

Savitch, H. V. "Global Challenge and Institutional Capacity." *Administration and Society* 30.3 (July 1998): 248–263.

Savoie, Donald J., and Canadian Centre for Management Development. *Globalization and Governance*. Ottawa: Canadian Centre for Management Development, 1993.

Schaede, Ulrike, and William W. Grimes. *Japan's Managed Globalization: Adapting to the Twenty-First Century*. Armonk, N.Y.: M. E. Sharpe, 2003.

Schauer, Frederick. "The Politics and Incentives of Legal Transplantation." in *Governance in a Globalizing World,* ed. Joseph Nye, Jr., and John D. Donahue. Washington, DC: Brookings Institution Press, 2000, 253–268.

Schement, Jorge Reina. "Imagining Fairness: Equality and Equity of Access in Search of Democracy." May 2001. Available at www.cisp.org/imp/may_2001/05_01schement .htm.

Schmid, Andre. *Korea Between Empires: 1895–1919.* New York: Columbia University Press, 2002.

Scholte, Jan Aart. *Globalization: A Critical Introduction.* New York: St. Martin's Press, 2000.

Schubert, Glendon. "The Evolution of Political Science Paradigms of Physics, Biology, and Politics." *Politics and the Life Sciences* 1 (1983): 97–110.

Schwartz, Benjamin. *Chinese Communism and the Rise of Mao.* Cambridge, Mass.: Harvard University Press, 1951.

Scott, Alan. *The Limits of Globalization: Cases and Arguments, International Library of Sociology.* New York: Routledge, 1997.

Sen, G., and C. Grown. *Development, Crises, and Alternative Visions: Third World Women's Perspectives.* New York: Monthly Review Press, 1997.

Sesay, Amadu, and James B. Lewis. *Korea and Globalization: Politics, Economics and Culture.* New York: Routledge, 2002.

Shapiro, Ian, and Stephen Macedo, eds. *Designing Democratic Institutions.* New York: New York University Press, 2000.

Shapiro, Michael J. *Language and Political Understanding: The Politics of Discursive Practices.* New Haven, Conn.: Yale University Press, 1981.

———. *Reading the Postmodern Polity: Political Theory as Textual Practice.* Minneapolis: University of Minnesota Press, 1992.

Shaw, Martin. *Theory of the Global State: Globality as an Unfinished Revolution.* Cambridge: Cambridge University Press, 2000.

Shawcross, William. *Cambodia's New Deal.* Washington, DC: Carnegie Endowment for International Peace, 1994.

Shields, John, and B. Mitchell Evans. *Shrinking the State: Globalization and Public Administration "Reform."* Halifax, Nova Scotia: Fernwood, 1998.

Shutt, Harry. *A New Democracy: Alternatives to a Bankrupt World Order.* New York: Zed Books, 2001.

Silberman, Bernard S. *Cages of Reason: The Rise of the Rational State in France, Japan, the United States, and Great Britain.* Chicago: University of Chicago Press, 1993.

Simmons, P. I., and Chantal de Jonge Oudraat, eds. *Managing Global Issues: Lessons Learned.* Washington, DC: Carnegie Endowment for International Peace, 2001.

"Sins of the Secular Missionaries." *The Economist,* January 29, 2000, 25–28.

Sisci, Francesco. "The American Empire." *Asia Times* (in 3 parts), October 16–18, 2002.

Slaton, Christa. "Quantum Theory and Political Theory." In *Quantum Politics,* ed. Theodore Becker. Westport, Conn.: Praeger, 1991, 41–63.

———. *Televote: Expanding Citizen Participation in the Quantum Age.* Westport, Conn.: Praeger, 1992.

"Slowdown of US Economy and Its Negative Impact on China." *Hong Kong Commercial Daily,* May 16, 2001, 12.

Smith, Gordon, Moisas Naim, and International Development Research Centre (Canada). *Altered States: Globalization, Sovereignty, and Governance.* Ottawa: International Development Research Centre, 2000.

Sohn, Pow-key, Kim Chol-choon, and Hong Yi-sup. *The History of Korea.* Seoul: Korean National Commission for UNESCO, 1984.

Spicer, Michael. *Public Administration and the State.* Tuscaloosa: The University of Alabama Press, 2001.

Staff Report of the Select Committee on Committees, House of Representatives. *Committee Reform Amendments of 1974: Explanation of H. Res 988 as Adopted by the House of Representatives, October 8, 1974.* 93rd Cong., 2d sess., H41-730-O, 56.

Stevenson, Nick. "Globalization and Cultural Political Economy." In *Globalization and Its Critics: Perspectives from Political Economy,* ed. Randall D. Germain. London: Macmillian, 2000, 91–113.

Stevenson, Richard. "Weakening Dollar Mirrors Economy." *Honolulu Star-Bulletin,* June 21, 2002, C5.

Stiglitz, Joseph. *Globalization and Its Discontents.* New York: W. W. Norton, 2002.

Stillman, Richard. "American vs. European Public Administration: Does Public Administration Make the Modern State, or Does the State Make Public Administration." *Public Administration Review* 57.4 (July/August 1997): 332–338.

Storing, Herbert. *What the Anti-Federalists Were For.* Chicago: University of Chicago Press, 1981.

Strange, Susan. *The Retreat of the States: The Diffusion of Power in the World Economy.* Cambridge: Cambridge University Press, 1996.

Stromquist, N., and K. Monkman. *Education: Integration and Contestation Across Cultures.* Lanham, Md.: Rowman & Littlefield Publishers, Inc., 2000.

Stubbs, Richard, and Geoffrey Underhill, eds. *Political Economy and the Changing Global Order.* Oxford: Oxford University Press, 2000.

Studer, Raymond. "Human Systems Design and the Management of Change." *General Systems* 16 (1971): 131–143.

Stychin, Carl. "Relatively Universal: Globalisation, Rights Discourse and the Evolution of Australian Sexual and National Identity." *Legal Studies* 18 (1998): 265–292.

Sum, Ngai-Ling. "Globalization and Its 'Other(s)': Three 'New kinds of Orientalism' and the Political Economy of Trans-border Identity." In *Demystifying Globalization,* ed. Colin Hay and David Marsh. London: Macmillan Press, 2000, 105–126.

Sunstein, Cass. *Designing Democracy: What Constitutions Do.* Oxford: Oxford University Press, 2001.

———. *Republic.com.* Princeton, N.J.: Princeton University Press, 2001.

Supreme Court (of the Philippines). *Reports Annotated.* Vol. 224, July 30, 1993, 802f.

Suranovic, Steven. "International Trade Fairness." 2001. Available at www.internationalecon.com/fairtrade/index.html.

Suzuki Yuko. *Chosenjin Jugun Ianfu* (Korean comfort women). Tokyo: Iwanami Shoten, 1991.

Tamney, Joseph B., and Linda Hsueh-Ling Chiang. *Modernization, Globalization, and Confucianism in Chinese Societies, Religion in the Age of Transformation.* Westport, Conn.: Praeger, 2002.

Tan, Poh-Ling. *Asian Legal Systems: Law Society and Pluralism in East Asia.* Sydney: Butterworths, 1997.

Tardif, Jean. "The Hidden Dimensions of Globalization: What is at Stake Geoculturally." ATTAC's International Portal, May 29, 2002. Available at http://attac.org/indexen/index.html.

Taylor, Peter J. "Izations of the World: Americanization, Modernization, and Globalization." In *Demystifying Globalization,* ed. Colin Hay and David Marsh. London: Macmillan Press, 2000, 49–70.

Taylor, Timothy Dean. *Global Pop: World Music, World Markets.* New York: Routledge, 1997.

Tharoor, Shashi. "The Future of Civil Conflict." *World Policy Journal* 16 (Spring 1999): 1–12.

Therborn, Goran. "Dimensions of Globalization and the Dynamics of (In)Equalties." In *The Ends of Globalization: Bringing Society Back In,* ed. Don Kalb et al. Oxford: Rowman & Littlefield, 2000, 33–48.

Thorpe, Richard, and Stephen E. Little. *Global Change: The Impact of Asia in the 21st Century.* New York: Palgrave, 2001.

Thorsby, D. *Economics and Culture.* Cambridge: Cambridge University Press, 2001.

Thrift, Nigel. "State Sovereignty, Globalization and the Rise of Soft Capitalism." In *Demystifying Globalization,* ed. Colin Hay and David Marsh. London: Macmillan Press, 2000, 71–102.

Toby, Ronald P. *State and Diplomacy in Early Modern Japan: Asia in the Development of the Tokugawa Bakufu.* Stanford, Calif.: Stanford University Press, 1991.

Tomlinson, John. *Globalization and Culture.* Chicago: University of Chicago Press, 2000.

Tomooka, Kuniyuki, Sachiko Kanno, and Mari Kobayashi. "Building National Prestige: Japanese Cultural Policy and the Influence of Western Institution." In *Global Culture: Media, Arts, Policy and Globalization,* ed. Diana Crane et al. London: Routledge, 2002, 49–62.

Tonn, Bruce. "The Court of Generations: A Proposed Amendment to the US Constitution." *Futures* 23.5 (June 1991): 482–498.

Tonn, Bruce, and David Feldman. "Non-Spatial Government." *Futures* 27.1 (January/February 1995): 11–36.

Toonen, Theo A. J., et al. *Civil Service Systems in Comparative Perspectives.* Bloomington: Indiana University Press, 1996.

———. "The Comparative Dimension of Administrative Reform." In *Politicians, Bureaucrats and Administrative Reform,* ed. B. Guy Peters and Jon Pierre. London: Routledge, 2001, 183–201.

Tribe, Laurence H. "The Curvature of Constitutional Space: What Lawyers can Learn from Modern Physics." In *Quantum Politics: Applying Quantum Theory to Political Phenomena,* ed. Theodore Becker. Westport, Conn.: Praeger, 1991, 169–200. (Originally published in *Harvard Law Review* 103.1 [1989]: 1–56.)

Tu, Wei-ming, ed. *Confucian Traditions in East Asian Modernity: Moral Education and Economic Culture in Japan and the Four Mini-Dragons.* Cambridge, Mass.: Harvard University Press, 1996.

Tugwell, Rexford. *A Model Constitution for a United Republics of America.* Santa Barbara, Calif.: Center for the Study of Democratic Institutions, 1970.

Tully, James. "The Unfreedom of the Moderns in Comparison to Their Ideals of Constitutional Democracy." *Modern Law Review* 65 (2002): 204–229.

Twining, Charles. "The Economy." In *Cambodia 1975–78,* ed. Karl Jackson. Princeton, N.J.: Princeton University Press, 1989, 109–150.

Twining, William. *Globalization and Legal Theory.* London: Butterworths, 2000.

United Nations. *1999 World Survey on the Role of Women in Development: Globalization, Gender and Work.* New York: United Nations, 1999.

United Nations Development Fund for Women (UNIFEM). *Progress of the World's Women 2000.* New York: UNIFEM, 2000.

United Nations Development Program (UNDP). "A Breakthrough in Cambodian Election Broadcasting." *Equity News* (Cambodia: August 2003): 1–24.

United Nations Educational, Scientific, and Cultural Organization (UNESCO). *Culture, Trade and Globalization: Questions and Answers.* New York: UNESCO Publishing, 2000.

USA PATRIOT Act. "Uniting and Strengthening America by Providing Appropriate Tools Required to Intercept and Obstruct Terrorism Act." (Oct. 25, 2001) HR 3162 RDS 107th CONGRESS 1st Session "AN ACT To deter and punish terrorist acts in the United States and around the world, to enhance law enforcement investigatory tools, and for other purposes." Available at www.eff.org/Privacy/Surveillance/ Terrorism_militias/ 20011025_hr3162_usa_patriot_bill.html.

Van Hoecke, Mark, and Mark Warrington. "Legal Cultures, Legal Paradigms and Legal Doctrine: Towards a New Model of Comparative Law." *International Comparative Law Quarterly* 47 (1998): 495–536.

Varian, Hal R. "Fairness." In *The New Palgrave, A Dictionary of Economics and Law,* ed. John Eatwell, Murray Milgate, and Peter Newman. New York: The Stockton Press, 1987, 275–276.

Vickery, Michael. *Cambodia, Cambodia: 1975–1982.* Chiangmai: Silkworm Books, 1999.

Vogel, Ezra F. *The Four Little Dragons: The Spread of Industrialization in East Asia.* Cambridge, Mass.: Harvard University Press, 1992.

———. *Japan as Number One: Lessons for America.* Cambridge, Mass.: Harvard University Press, 1979.

Walsham, Geoffrey. *Making a World of Difference: IT in a Global Context.* New York: J. Wiley, 2001.

Walter, Benjamin. "The Work of Art in the Age of Mechanical Reproduction." In *Illuminations,* ed. (with intro) Hannah Arendt, trans. Harry Zohn. New York: Schocken Books, 1968.

Waskow, Arthur. *Running Riot: A Journey through the Official Disasters and Creative Disorder in American Society.* New York: Herder and Herder, 1970.

Weiss, Linda. *The Myth of the Powerless State.* Ithaca, N.Y.: Cornell University Press, 1998.

Welch, Eric, and Wilson Wong. "Public Administration in a Global Context: Bridging the Gaps of Theory and Practice between Western and Non-Western Nations." *Public Administration Review* 58.1 (January/February 1998): 40–50.

Westney, D. Eleanor. *Imitation and Innovation: The Transfer of Western Organizational Patterns to Meiji Japan.* Cambridge, Mass.: Harvard University Press, 1987.

"What Do We Understand by 'Cultural Industries'?" In *Culture, Trade and Globalization: Questions and Answers.* New York: UNESCO Publishing, 2000, 11–12.

"What is the Market Structure of Cultural Industries?" In *Culture, Trade and Globalization: Questions and Answers.* New York: UNESCO Publishing, 2000, 19–22.

Wheeler, Harvey. "Constitutionalism." In *Governmental Institutions and Processes: Handbook of Political Science.* Vol. 5, ed. Fred Greenstein and Nelson Polsby. Reading, Mass.: Addison-Wesley Publishing Company, 1975, 1–91.

Wilhelm, Anthony. *Democracy in the Digital Age.* New York: Routledge, 2000.

Willkie, Wendell L. *One World.* New York: Pocket Books, 1943.

Wilson, D. S. "Human Groups as Units of Selection." *Science* (June 20, 1997), 276–277.

Wilson, James Q. *Bureaucracy.* New York: Free Press, 1989.

Wincott, Daniel. "Globalization and European Integration." In *Demystifying Globalization,* ed. Colin Hay and David Marsh. London: Macmillan Press, 2000, 168–190.

Wiseman, John. "Alternatives to Oppressive Globalization." In *Globalization and Its Discontents,* ed. Stephen McBride and John Wiseman. New York: St. Martin's Press, 2000, 214–226.

Wolf, Fred Alan. *Parallel Universes: The Search for Other Worlds.* New York: Simon and Schuster, 1988.

Wolf, Martin. "Will the Nation-State Survive Globalization?" *Foreign Affairs* 80 (January/February 2001): 1816–1817.

Wolferen, Karel Van. *The Enigma of Japanese Power: People and Politics in a Stateless Nation.* Rutland, Vt.: Charles E. Tuttle Co., 1993.

Wood, Gordon S. *The Creation of the American Republic, 1776–1787.* New York: W. W. Norton, 1969.

World Bank. *World Development Report: The State in a Changing World.* Oxford: Oxford University Press, 1997.

World Economic Forum. *The Global Competitiveness Report 1996.* Geneva, Switz.: WEF, 2001.

Xiaohua, Ma. "Memory and the Lost Found Relationship between Black Americans and Japan." Paper presented to the Conference on Memory in US-Japan Relations, Honolulu, Hawai'i, March 25–26, 2001.

Yamamoto, Tadashi, Kim Gould Ashizawa, and Nihon Kokusai Kyoryu Senta. *Governance and Civil Society in a Global Age.* Tokyo: Japan Center for International Exchange, 2001.

Yamamoto, Tadashi, and Nihon Kokusai Kyoryu Senta. *Deciding the Public Good: Governance and Civil Society in Japan.* Tokyo: Japan Center for International Exchange, 1999.

Yamamoto, Yoshinobu. *Globalism, Regionalism and Nationalism: Asia in Search of Its Role in the Twenty-First Century.* Oxford: Blackwell, 1999.

Yamazumi Masami. *Gakushu Shido Yoryo to Kyokasho* (Course of study and textbooks). Tokyo: Iwanami Shoten, 1989.

———. *Kyokasho Mondai toha Nanika* (What is the problem of textbooks?). Tokyo: Iwanami Shoten, 1983.

Yan, Yunxiang. "Managed Globalization." In *Many Globalizations: Cultural Diversity in the Contemporary World,* ed. Peter L. Berger and Samuel P. Huntington. Oxford: Oxford University Press, 2002.

Yen, Duen His. "Fairness." Available at www.noogenesis.com/malama/ fairness.html.

Yergin, Daniel, and Joseph Stanislaw. *The Commanding Heights: The Battle for the World Economy.* New York: Simon and Schuster, 2002.

Yokoi-Arai, Mamiko. "Regional Financial Institutionalization of the Creation of the Zone of the Law: The Context of Financial Stability/Regulation in East Asia." *The International Lawyer* 35 (2001): 1627–1658.

Yoshida Nobuyuki. *Seijukusuru Edo: Nihon no Rekishi.* Vol. 17. Tokyo: Kodansha, 2002.

Yui Daizaburo. *Nichibei Senso Kan no Sokoku—Masatsu no Shinso Shinri* (View of war in Japan and the US: Psychology of U.S.-Japan frictions). Tokyo: Iwanami Shoten, 1995.

Contributors

Doug Allen is former deputy minister of the province of British Columbia and co-founder of Sage Management Consulting Victoria, British Columbia, Canada.

Walt T. Anderson is the president of the World Academy of Art and Science, United States.

Ron Brown is a professor of law and director of the Center for Chinese Studies at the University of Hawaiʻi, Mānoa.

Jim Dator is a professor of political science and director of the Hawaiʻi Research Center for Futures Studies at the University of Hawaiʻi, Mānoa.

Jingping Ding is a senior manager of Andersen Consulting (China), Ltd.

Christopher Grandy is an associate professor of the Public Administration Program at the University of Hawaiʻi, Mānoa.

Sohail Inayatullah is a professor at the University of the Sunshine Coast, visiting professor at Tamkang University, Taiwan, and visiting academic at Queensland University of Technology, Brisbane, Australia.

Yong-duck Jung is a professor of the Graduate School of Public Administration at Seoul National University, Seoul, Korea.

Martin Khor is director of the Third World Network, Penang, Malaysia.

Yoshiko Kojo is a professor of international relations in the Department of Advanced Social and International Studies, Tokyo University.

Le Van Anh is vice-governor of Hue/Thua Thien Province, Vietnam.

Ivana Milojevic is a Ph.D. candidate in the Graduate School of Education at the University of Queensland, Australia.

Ryo Oshiba is professor of international relations in the Department of Law at Hitotsubashi University, Tokyo, Japan.

Edgar A. Porter is interim dean of the School of Hawaiian, Asian and Pacific Studies at the University of Hawai'i, Mānoa.

Dick Pratt is a professor and director of the Public Administration Program at the University of Hawai'i, Mānoa.

Fred Riggs is professor emeritus of political science at the University of Hawai'i, Mānoa.

James Rosenau is a professor of international affairs at George Washington University, Washington, DC.

Yongseok Seo is a Ph.D. candidate in the Department of Political Science at the University of Hawai'i, Mānoa.

Chanto Sisowath is assistant director of the Cambodian Institute for Cooperation and Peace, Phnom Penh, Cambodia.

Shunichi Takekawa is a Ph.D. candidate in the Department of Political Science at the University of Hawai'i, Mānoa.

Index

Production Notes for Dator, Pratt, and Seo/*Fairness, Globalization, and Public Institutions*

Cover design by Santos Barbasa Jr.

Text design by University of Hawai'i Press Production Staff in Minion with display in Olive Antique.

Composition by BW&A Books, Inc.

Printing and binding by The Maple-Vail Book Manufacturing Group.

Printed on 60 lb. Sebago Eggshell, 420 ppi